THE CAMBRIDGE COMPANION TO JANE AUSTEN
SECOND EDITION

Jane Austen's stock in the popular marketplace has never been higher, while academic studies continue to uncover new aspects of her engagement with her world.

This fully updated edition of the acclaimed *Cambridge Companion* offers clear, accessible coverage of the intricacies of Austen's works in their historical context, with biographical information and suggestions for further reading. Major scholars address Austen's six novels, the letters and other works, in terms accessible to students and the many general readers as well as to academics. With seven new chapters, the *Companion* now covers topics that have become central to recent Austen studies: for example, gender, sociability, economics and the increasing number of screen adaptations of the novels.

Edward Copeland is Emeritus Professor of English at Pomona College, Claremont, California. His publications include *Women Writing about Money: Women's Fiction in England, 1790–1820* (Cambridge University Press, 1995) and his edition of *Sense and Sensibility* (2006) in *The Cambridge Edition of the Works of Jane Austen*.

Juliet McMaster is Emeritus Distinguished University Professor of English at the University of Alberta, Canada. She is editor, with Christine Alexander, of *The Child Writer from Austen to Woolf* (Cambridge University Press, 2005).

THE CAMBRIDGE
COMPANION TO
JANE AUSTEN

Second edition

EDITED BY
EDWARD COPELAND
Pomona College

AND

JULIET McMASTER
University of Alberta

CAMBRIDGE UNIVERSITY PRESS

Cambridge, New York, Melbourne, Madrid, Cape Town, Singapore,
São Paulo, Delhi, Dubai, Tokyo, Mexico City

Cambridge University Press
The Edinburgh Building, Cambridge CB2 8RU, UK

Published in the United States of America by Cambridge University Press, New York

www.cambridge.org
Information on this title: www.cambridge.org/9780521746502

First published 1997
Second edition 2011

Printed in the United Kingdom at the University Press, Cambridge

A catalogue record for this publication is available from the British Library

Library of Congress Cataloguing in Publication data
The Cambridge companion to Jane Austen / edited by Edward Copeland
and Juliet McMaster. – 2nd ed.
p. cm. – (Cambridge companions to literature)
Includes bibliographical references and index.
ISBN 978-0-521-76308-0 – ISBN 978-0-521-74650-2 (pbk.)
1. Austen, Jane, 1775–1817 – Criticism and interpretation. 2. Women and literature –
England – History – 19th century. 3. Love stories, English – History and criticism.
I. Copeland, Edward. II. McMaster, Juliet.
PR4036.C3 2011
823'.7–dc22
2010033971

ISBN 978-0-521-76308-0 Hardback
ISBN 978-0-521-74650-2 Paperback

CONTENTS

Notes on contributors   *page* vii

Preface   xi
EDWARD COPELAND AND JULIET McMASTER

Acknowledgements   xiii

Texts and abbreviations   xiv

Chronology of Jane Austen's life   xv
DEIRDRE LE FAYE

1   The professional woman writer   1
     JAN FERGUS

2   *Northanger Abbey* and *Sense and Sensibility*   21
     THOMAS KEYMER

3   *Pride and Prejudice* and *Mansfield Park*   39
     JOCELYN HARRIS

4   *Emma* and *Persuasion*   55
     PENNY G

5   The early short fiction   72
     MARGARET ANNE DOODY

6   'Lady Susan', 'The Watsons' and 'Sanditon'   87
     JANET TODD

CONTENTS

7   The letters   97
    CAROL HOULIHAN FLYNN

8   Class   111
    JULIET McMASTER

9   Money   127
    EDWARD COPELAND

10 Making a living   144
    DAVID SELWYN

11 Gender   159
    E. J. CLERY

12 Sociability   176
    GILLIAN RUSSELL

13 Jane Austen and literary traditions   192
    ISOBEL GRUNDY

14 Jane Austen on screen   215
    KATHRYN SUTHERLAND

15 Austen cults and cultures   232
    CLAUDIA L. JOHNSON

16 Further reading   248
    BRUCE STOVEL AND MARY M. CHAN

    Index   267

NOTES ON CONTRIBUTORS

MARY M. CHAN is completing her Ph.D. at the University of Alberta, where she is writing her dissertation on domestic interiors in the eighteenth-century novel. Her articles on physical height in Austen's fiction and on Austen film adaptations have appeared in the print and on-line editions of *Persuasions*, the journal of the Jane Austen Society of North America.

E. J. CLERY is Professor of Eighteenth-Century Literature at the University of Southampton. She is the author of *The Rise of Supernatural Fiction, 1762–1800* (1995), *Women's Gothic from Clara Reeve to Mary Shelley* (2000) and *The Feminization Debate in Eighteenth-Century England: Literature, Commerce and Luxury* (2004).

EDWARD COPELAND, Emeritus Professor of English at Pomona College (Claremont, California) is the editor of the Cambridge University Press edition of *Sense and Sensibility* (2006) and the author of a study of Austen and contemporary novelists, *Women Writing about Fiction: Women's Fiction in England, 1790–1820* (1995). He co-edited with Carol Houlihan Flynn *Clarissa and Her Readers: New Essays for the Clarissa Project* (1999) and, with Andrea Hibbard, the Pickering & Chatto edition (2005) of Catherine Gore's novel of fashionable life, *Cecil: or, the Adventures of a Coxcomb* (1841).

MARGARET ANNE DOODY is John and Barbara Glynn Family Professor of Literature at the University of Notre Dame (Indiana), where she has served as a founder and first Director of the Ph.D. in Literature Program. In 2007 she received an NEH grant for work on a project on Pico, Paracelsus, Jakob Boehme and the Enlightenment. She is the editor (with Douglas Murray) of Jane Austen's early works in *Catharine and Other Writings*. The author of a number of critical and biographical books, including *Frances Burney: The Life in the Works* (1988), *The True Story of the Novel* (1996) and *Tropic of Venice* (2006), Margaret Doody is also the author of six published novels, *The Alchemists* (1980) and five books in the 'Aristotle Detective series', most recently *Mysteries of Eleusis* (2005). The mystery stories have been translated into Italian, French, Portuguese, Spanish, Greek, Polish and Russian.

JAN FERGUS has retired as Professor of English at Lehigh University and resides in Montreal, Canada. In addition to many articles on Jane Austen and on the eighteenth-century reading public, she has published two book-length Austen studies: *Jane Austen and the Didactic Novel* (1983) and *Jane Austen: A Literary Life* (1991), as well as *Provincial Readers of Eighteenth-Century Fiction* (2006).

CAROL HOULIHAN FLYNN is Professor of English at Tufts University, and the author of *Samuel Richardson: Man of Letters* (1982), *Washed in the Blood* (a novel, 1983) and *The Body in Swift and Defoe* (1990), and is co-editor with Edward Copeland of *Clarissa and Her Readers: New Essays for the Clarissa Project* (1999). She has also published many essays, on Smollett, Sterne, Cleland and Fielding, and about London life and culture. She has just written a novel, *The Burnt Hills*, set in Berkeley, 1969–70, and is finishing her monograph, *Learning London: Becoming the Urban Subject*.

PENNY GAY, Honorary Professor of English and Drama at the University of Sydney, is the author of *Jane Austen and the Theatre* (2002), *As She Likes It: Shakespeare's Unruly Women* (1994) and *The Cambridge Introduction to Shakespeare's Comedies* (2008). She has published numerous essays on Austen's novels and on the film adaptations, and is currently working on a study of the roles written for women performers in the drama of the eighteenth century.

ISOBEL GRUNDY is Professor Emeritus at the University of Alberta. Her publications include *Samuel Johnson and the Scale of Greatness* (Georgia, 1986); with Virginia Blain and Patricia Clements, *The Feminist Companion to Literature in English* (Yale, 1990); *Lady Mary Wortley Montagu: Comet of the Enlightenment* (Clarendon, 1999); and with Susan Brown and Patricia Clements, *Orlando: Women's Writing in the British Isles from the Beginnings to the Present* (Cambridge University Press On-line, 2006–).

JOCELYN HARRIS, Emeritus Professor of English at the University of Otago, New Zealand, edited Jane Austen's favourite novel *Sir Charles Grandison* (1972) and published *Jane Austen's Art of Memory* (1989, repr. 2003). Her most recent book, *A Revolution Almost beyond Expression: Jane Austen's 'Persuasion'* (2007), explores the literary, social and political contexts of Austen's last novel.

CLAUDIA L. JOHNSON is Murray Professor of English and Department Chair at Princeton University. Her publications include *Jane Austen: Women, Politics, and the Novel* (1988), *Equivocal Beings* (1995), and with Clara Tuite, *A Companion to Jane Austen* (2009). She has prepared editions of Austen's novels for Norton and Oxford World's Classics and has just finished a manuscript about the history of Austen's reputation entitled *Jane Austen's Cults and Cultures* (forthcoming from the University of Chicago Press, 2011).

THOMAS KEYMER is Chancellor Jackman Professor of English at the University of Toronto and General Editor of *Review of English Studies*. He has published widely on Restoration, eighteenth-century and Romantic-period literature, most recently as editor of *The Cambridge Companion to Laurence Sterne* (2009) and the Oxford World's Classics edition of Johnson's *Rasselas* (2009).

DEIRDRE LE FAYE is the author of *Jane Austen: A Family Record* (1989, 2004), the definitive factual biography, editor of the new edition of *Jane Austen's Letters* and of the Cambridge University Press edition of *Northanger Abbey* (with Barbara Benedict, 2006). She has also published *The Jane Austen Cookbook* (with Maggie Black, 1995), *Writers' Lives: Jane Austen* (1998), *Jane Austen's 'Outlandish Cousin', the Life and Letters of Eliza de Feuillide* (2002), *Jane Austen, the World of Her Novels* (2002), *So You Think You Know Jane Austen?* (with John Sutherland, 2005), *A Chronology of Jane Austen and her Family 1600–2000* (2006) and numerous articles on Austenian subjects in *Notes and Queries*, *Review of English Studies* and *The Book Collector*.

JULIET MCMASTER is Distinguished University Professor Emeritus at the University of Alberta, and founder of the Juvenilia Press. Besides her books on Thackeray, Trollope, Dickens and the eighteenth-century novel, she is the author of *Jane Austen on Love* (1978) and *Jane Austen the Novelist* (1995), and the co-editor with Bruce Stovel of *Jane Austen's Business* (1996), with Christine Alexander of *The Child Writer from Austen to Woolf* (2004) and with Edward Copeland of the present book. She is currently writing a biography of the Victorian painter James Clarke Hook.

GILLIAN RUSSELL is Professor of English at the Australian National University, Canberra. She is author of, most recently, *Women, Sociability and Theatre in Georgian England* (2007) and in 2002 edited, with Clara Tuite, *Romantic Sociability: Social Networks and Literary Culture in Britain, 1770–1840*. She is currently working on a project on ephemeral print culture, the novel and sociability in the long eighteenth century.

DAVID SELWYN is the author of *Jane Austen and Leisure* (1995) and the editor of *Jane Austen: Collected Poems and Verse of the Austen Family* (1996), *The Complete Poems of James Austen* (2003), *Fugitive Pieces: The Poems of James Edward Austen Leigh* (2006) and, with Maggie Lane, *Jane Austen: A Celebration* (2000). He has recently published *Jane Austen and Children* (2010). He is Chairman of the Jane Austen Society.

BRUCE STOVEL was Emeritus Professor of English at the University of Alberta, but died suddenly in 2007. Co-editor with Juliet McMaster of *Jane Austen's Business* (1996) and co-editor with Lynn Weinlos Gregg of *The Talk in Jane Austen* (2007), he published many essays and reviews on Austen, Richardson, Fielding, Swift, Sterne, Charlotte Lennox, Frances Burney, Scott, Evelyn Waugh, Kingsley Amis, Brian Moore and Margaret Laurence. A commemorative volume in his honour,

Jane Austen Sings the Blues, was published by the University of Alberta Press in 2009, and a collection of his essays is under way.

KATHRYN SUTHERLAND is Professor of Bibliography and Textual Criticism at the University of Oxford. She is author of *Jane Austen's Textual Lives: From Aeschylus to Bollywood* (2005) and co-author (with Marilyn Deegan) of *Transferred Illusions: Digital Technology and the Forms of Print* (2009). She is currently preparing a digital and print edition of Jane Austen's fiction manuscripts.

JANET TODD is President of Lucy Cavendish College, University of Cambridge. The author of many books on women's writing, she has most recently authored three biographies: *Mary Wollstonecraft: A Revolutionary Life* (2000); *Daughters of Ireland: The Rebellious Kingsborough Sisters and the Making of a Modern Nation* (2004); and *Death and the Maidens: Fanny Wollstonecraft and the Shelley Circle* (2007). She is the general editor of the *Cambridge Edition of the Works of Jane Austen*, 9 vols. (2009) and the editor of *Jane Austen in Context* (2005) and the *Cambridge Introduction to Jane Austen* (2006).

PREFACE

A general condition faced by books written for Jane Austen readers is simply stated: which Jane Austen readers? The first edition of the *Cambridge Companion to Jane Austen* attempted to address diverse readerships in 1997, and the aim of this new edition remains the same, though with the new interests of the twenty-first century included. Those people who gather to talk about Jane Austen, for example, still divide loosely into two friendly groups seeking mutual conversation, but often sailing past one another – energetic non-academics with avid feelings for Austen and limited tolerance for bookish harangues, and academics also with great love for Austen, but certainly bookish and with perhaps less enthusiasm of the Janeite kind. Generational divisions continue as well – older readers jealously protective of the Austen they have known and loved for decades, and younger readers equally enthusiastic for an Austen they regard as responding to twenty-first-century issues. Meanwhile, first-time readers arrive at the novels with diverse motives for appreciation: 'I'm reading Jane Austen for graduate school', 'I read Jane Austen because I want to understand my mother' and now the most challenging new set of readers, 'I read Jane Austen because I loved her latest movie'.

The editors, with the advice of readers for Cambridge University Press, have made changes and additions to the 1997 edition with the refreshed conviction that a contextual examination of Austen's works remains a useful approach. Students who first encounter her works and even old hands who read her novels annually all sense that Austen's culture recedes at unsettling speed. Younger readers, for example, can find themselves puzzled by the insistent economics of Austen's novels or by her subtle class distinctions. They are startled to find that Austen's works possess political resonance. That old Janeite enthusiasm, 'How do they make whip't syllabub?', has altered almost universally to '*Why* do they make whip't syllabub?' Hence a chapter entitled 'Sociability' by Gillian Russell joins the collection. A chapter entitled 'Gender' by Emma Clery and one entitled 'Making a Living' by David

Selwyn supplement the offerings, as well as a new chapter by Kathryn Sutherland that addresses that very pressing field of interest, 'Jane Austen on Screen'. Also, this edition of the *Companion* is able to take advantage of recent scholarship in the now-complete Cambridge Edition of the Works, used here for citation.

The essays that discuss Austen's published novels divide the six novels into three pairs by dates of composition, again with the goal of enriching the contexts of her works. Austen scholars Tom Keymer, Jocelyn Harris and Penny Gay share the wealth. Austen's writing not designed for publication receives separate treatment. Margaret Anne Doody's chapter on the short fiction presents a provocative glimpse of the kind of writer Austen might have become if not for her accommodation to regency culture; Janet Todd contributes a new chapter entitled '"Lady Susan", "The Watsons" and "Sanditon"' and Carol Houlihan Flynn examines Austen's correspondence both as literary production and as a register of Austen's marginalized position as a woman writer.

Deirdre Le Faye, Austen's biographer and the editor of her letters, provides readers with a chronology that maps the author's life by significant personal dates and dates of historical note. Jan Fergus presents Jane Austen's professional accomplishment in the context of the contemporary publishing industry. Juliet McMaster examines class and class consciousness in the novels; Edward Copeland presents a guide to money, income and material culture; Claudia Johnson examines the 'cults and cultures' that have grown to surround Jane Austen; and Isobel Grundy, in a far-reaching chapter, demonstrates the multiple literary sources, influences and light allusions that inform Austen's writing in her letters and fiction. The late Bruce Stovel's chapter entitled 'Further Reading' has been updated by Mary Chan.

Jane Austen's stock in the popular marketplace has never been higher, for good or ill. The *Cambridge Companion to Jane Austen* can't hope to capture all aspects of this Austen boom. This collection of essays, however, seeks rather to recover and illuminate elements of *her* culture so that her novels may speak more lucidly to our own.

ACKNOWLEDGEMENTS

The *Cambridge Companion to Jane Austen* draws on the talents of a number of outstanding scholars, and the first debt we would like to acknowledge is that to our contributors, for their patience under our editorial onslaughts as well as for their scholarly expertise. We are grateful too for the generous and skilled assistance of Meg Mathies in editing, compiling and generally bringing the essays into order. A version of Margaret Anne Doody's chapter on the short fiction appeared in *Persuasions*, the annual journal of the Jane Austen Society of North America (16, 1994) and Deirdre Le Faye's 'Chronology' of Jane Austen's life appears in longer form in *Jane Austen: A Family Record* (London: British Library, 1989, 2004). We are grateful to the publishers for permission to reprint. Thanks are also due to John Murray, for permission granted to Jan Fergus to quote from the Murray Archives in her chapter 'The Professional Woman Writer'.

TEXTS AND ABBREVIATIONS

References to Jane Austen's works are to these editions:

The *Cambridge Edition of the Works of Jane Austen*, 9 vols., general editor Janet Todd (Cambridge University Press, 2009). Citations are given as follows: (*novel* volume: chapter: page in Cambridge University Press edition).

Jane Austen's Letters, collected and edited by Deirdre Le Faye (Oxford University Press, 1995).

Abbreviations

E	*Emma*
J	*Juvenilia*
L	*Jane Austen's Letters*
LM	*Later Manuscripts*
'LS'	'Lady Susan'
MP	*Mansfield Park*
NA	*Northanger Abbey*
P	*Persuasion*
PP	*Pride and Prejudice*
'S'	'Sanditon'
SS	*Sense and Sensibility*
'W'	'The Watsons'

DEIRDRE LE FAYE

CHRONOLOGY OF JANE AUSTEN'S LIFE

1764	26 April	Marriage of Revd George Austen and Cassandra Leigh; they live at Deane in Hampshire.
	9 October	Marriage of James Leigh-Perrot (Mrs Austen's brother) and Jane Cholmeley; they live at Scarlets in Berkshire and also in Bath.
1765	13 February	James Austen born at Deane.
	Summer	Mr and Mrs Hancock (Mr Austen's sister) and their daughter Eliza return from India; they live in London.
1766	26 August	George Austen the younger born at Deane.
1767	7 October	Edward Austen born at Deane.
1768	July/August	Austen family move to Steventon, Hampshire.
	?Autumn	Mr Hancock returns alone to India.
	29 December	Marriage of Jane Leigh (Mrs Austen's sister) and Revd Dr Edward Cooper.
1770	1 July	Edward Cooper the younger born in London.
1771	8 June	Henry Thomas Austen (hereafter 'HTA') born at Steventon.
	27 June	Jane Cooper born at Southcote, near Reading.
	?Autumn	Cooper family move to Bath, 12 Royal Crescent.
1773	9 January	Cassandra Elizabeth Austen (hereafter 'CEA') born at Steventon.
	23 March	Mr Austen becomes Rector of Deane as well as Steventon. Pupils live at Steventon from now until 1796.
1774	23 April	Francis William Austen (hereafter 'FWA') born at Steventon.
1775	5 November	Mr Hancock dies in Calcutta.
	16 December	Jane Austen (hereafter 'JA') born at Steventon.

1777	Winter	Mrs Hancock and Eliza go to the Continent.
1779	23 June	Charles John Austen (hereafter 'CJA') born at Steventon.
	3 July	James Austen matriculates at St John's College, Oxford.
	Summer	Mr and Mrs Thomas Knight II of Godmersham (cousins of Mr Austen) visit Steventon.
?1780		The Coopers move to 14 Bennett Street, Bath.
1781	Winter	Marriage of Eliza Hancock to Jean François Capot de Feuillide, in France (hereafter 'EdeF').
1782	Summer	First mention of JA in family tradition.
	December	First amateur theatrical production at Steventon – *Matilda*, by Thomas Francklin.
1783		Edward Austen (hereafter 'EAK') adopted by Mr and Mrs Thomas Knight II.
	Spring	JA, CEA and Jane Cooper go to Mrs Cawley in Oxford for tuition.
	3 May	Revd I. P. G. Lefroy instituted to Ashe.
	Summer	Mrs Cawley moves to Southampton and the girls fall ill.
	25 October	Mrs Cooper dies in Bath.
1784	July	*The Rivals*, by Richard Brinsley Sheridan, performed at Steventon.
	July	Dr Cooper moves to Sonning.
1785	Spring	JA and CEA go to the Abbey House School, Reading.
1786		EAK abroad on Grand Tour from 1786–90.
	April	FWA enters Royal Naval Academy, Portsmouth.
	25 June	EdeF's son Hastings born in France.
	July	Mrs Hancock, EdeF and baby arrive in London.
	November	James Austen goes to the Continent.
	December	JA and CEA have now left school.
1787		JA starts writing her *Juvenilia*.
	Autumn	James Austen returns from the Continent.
	December	*The Wonder*, by Susanna Centlivre, performed at Steventon.

1788	*January*	*The Chances*, adapted by David Garrick from Beaumont and Fletcher's seventeenth-century play, performed at Steventon.
	March	*Tom Thumb*, by Henry Fielding, performed at Steventon. A 'private theatrical exhibition' also performed at Steventon some time later this year.
	1 July	HTA matriculates at St John's College, Oxford.
	Summer	Mr and Mrs Austen take JA and CEA to Kent and London.
	September	The Hancock family return to France.
	23 December	FWA sails to East Indies.
	Winter	*The Sultan*, a two-act farce by Isaac Bickerstaffe and *High Life Below Stairs*, a two-act farce by James Townley [purportedly by Garrick], performed at Steventon.
1789	*31 January*	First issue of *The Loiterer* appears – written largely by James Austen and HTA, and published weekly in Oxford until March 1790.
	Spring	Lloyd family rent Deane parsonage.
	7 July	The Hancock family arrive in London.
	14 July	The storming of the Bastille.
1790	*April*	James Austen takes up residence as curate of Overton.
	Autumn	EAK returns to England from Grand Tour.
1791	*21 June*	Death of Mr Francis Austen of Sevenoaks (Mr Austen's uncle).
	July	CJA enters Royal Naval Academy, Portsmouth.
	15 September	James Austen becomes vicar of Sherborne St John.
	27 December	Marriage of EAK and Elizabeth Bridges, in Kent; they live at Rowling.
1792	*January*	The Lloyds leave Deane for Ibthorpe.
	26 February	Death of Mrs Hancock, in London.

	27 March	Marriage of James Austen and Anne Mathew, at Laverstoke; they presently take up residence at Deane parsonage.
	27 August	Death of Dr Cooper, at Sonning.
	October	JA and CEA visit the Lloyds at Ibthorpe.
	11 December	Marriage of Jane Cooper and Capt Thomas Williams, RN, at Steventon.
	?Winter	CEA engaged to Revd Tom Fowle.
1793	*21 January*	Louis XVI of France guillotined.
	23 January	EAK's first child, Fanny, born at Rowling.
	1 February	Republican France declares war on Great Britain and Holland.
	14 March	Marriage of Edward Cooper and Caroline Powys; they live at Harpsden until 1799.
	8 April	HTA becomes Lieutenant in the Oxfordshire Militia.
	15 April	James Austen's first child, Anna, born at Deane.
	3 June	JA writes the last item of her *Juvenilia*, 'Ode to Pity'.
	Winter	FWA returns home from Far East.
	December	JA and CEA visit Butler-Harrison cousins in Southampton.
1794	*22 February*	M de Feuillide guillotined in Paris.
	Midsummer	JA and CEA visit the Leighs at Adlestrop.
	?August	JA and CEA visit EAK and Elizabeth at Rowling.
	September	CJA leaves the RN Academy and goes to sea.
	23 October	Death of Mr Thomas Knight II.
	?Autumn	JA probably writes the novella 'Lady Susan' this year.
1795		JA probably writes *Elinor and Marianne* this year.
	3 May	Death of Anne Mathew at Deane; infant Anna is sent to live at Steventon.
	Autumn	Revd Tom Fowle joins Lord Craven as his private chaplain for the West Indian campaign.
	December 1795/ January 1796	JA's flirtation with Tom Lefroy on his visit to Ashe Rectory.

1796	*January*	Tom Lefroy leaves Ashe for London.
		Revd Tom Fowle sails for West Indies.
	April	JA and CEA visit the Coopers at Harpsden.
	?Summer	James Austen courting EdeF.
	June	Capt Thomas Williams knighted for his successful naval service.
	August	EAK and FWA take JA to Rowling via London; she returns to Steventon late September/early October.
	October	JA starts writing *First Impressions*.
	end November	James Austen engaged to Mary Lloyd.
1797	*17 January*	Marriage of James Austen and Mary Lloyd at Hurstbourne Tarrant; Anna returns to live at Deane.
	February	Revd Tom Fowle dies of fever at San Domingo and buried at sea.
	August	JA finishes *First Impressions*.
	1 November	Mr Austen offers *First Impressions* to publisher Cadell; rejected sight unseen.
	November	JA starts converting *Elinor and Marianne* into *Sense and Sensibility*.
		Mrs Austen, JA and CEA visit the Leigh-Perrots in Bath, at Paragon Buildings.
		EAK and family move from Rowling to Godmersham.
	Winter	Revd Samuel Blackall visits Ashe; offers mild courtship to JA.
	December 31	Marriage of HTA and EdeF, in London.
1798	*6 April*	Death of Mr William-Hampson Walter (Mr Austen's elder half-brother), in Kent.
	August	Mr and Mrs Austen, with JA and CEA, visit Godmersham.
	9 August	Lady Williams (Jane Cooper) killed in road accident.
	24 October	JA and her parents leave Godmersham for Steventon.
	Autumn	JA probably starts writing *Susan* (*Northanger Abbey*). Mrs Austen ill until end November.
	17 November	James Austen's son James Edward born at Deane.

1799	*February*	JA possibly visits the Lloyds at Ibthorpe.
	March	CEA returns to Steventon from Godmersham.
	17 May	Mrs Austen and JA arrive in Bath, with EAK and Elizabeth, and stay at 13 Queen Square.
	end June	They return home.
		JA probably finishes *Susan* (*Northanger Abbey*) about now.
	late summer	The Austens pay round of visits to the Leighs at Adlestrop, the Coopers at Harpsden, and the Cookes at Great Bookham.
	14 August	Mrs Leigh-Perrot charged with theft and committed to Ilchester Gaol.
	October	The Coopers move to Hamstall Ridware, Staffordshire.
1800	*29 March*	Mrs Leigh-Perrot tried at Taunton and acquitted. Probably visits Steventon afterwards.
	October	EAK visits Steventon and takes CEA back to Godmersham with him via Chawton and London.
	end November	JA visits the Lloyds at Ibthorpe; returns home mid-December.
	December	Mr Austen decides to retire and move to Bath.
1801	*24 January*	HTA resigns commission in Oxfordshire Militia and sets up as banker and army agent in London, living at 24 Upper Berkeley Street and with office at Cleveland Court, St James'.
	end January	JA visits the Bigg-Wither family at Manydown.
	February	CEA returns to Steventon from Godmersham via London.
	May	The Austen family leave Steventon; Mrs Austen and JA travel to Bath via Ibthorpe, and stay with the Leigh-Perrots.
		James Austen and his family move into Steventon rectory.
	end May	The Austens lease 4 Sydney Place, Bath, and then go on West Country holiday; probably visit Sidmouth and Colyton.

		JA's traditional West Country romance presumably occurs between now and the autumn of 1804.
	September	The Austens visit Steventon and Ashe.
	5 October	They return to Bath.
	9 October	Hastings de Feuillide dies, in London.
1802	*Spring*	Mrs Powys visits the Austens in Bath.
	25 March	Peace of Amiens commences, concluding the war with France.
	April	James and Mary, with Anna, visit the Austens in Bath.
	Summer	CJA joins the Austens for holidays; visit Dawlish and probably Teignmouth, also Tenby and Barmouth in Wales. HTA and EdeF visit France.
	1 September	JA and CEA arrive at Steventon.
	3 September	CJA takes JA and CEA to Godmersham.
	28 October	CJA brings his sisters back to Steventon.
	25 November	JA and CEA visit Manydown.
	2 December	Harris Bigg-Wither proposes to JA, and she accepts him.
	3 December	JA rejects the proposal; she and CEA return to Steventon and set off at once for Bath.
	Winter	JA revises *Susan* (*Northanger Abbey*).
1803	*February*	Mrs Powys visits the Austens in Bath.
	Spring	JA sells *Susan* (*Northanger Abbey*) to Crosby, of London. HTA returns from France.
	18 May	Napoleon breaks the Peace of Amiens and hostilities recommence; EdeF nearly trapped in France.
	Summer	JA possibly visits Charmouth, Up Lyme and Pinny.
	July	FWA stationed in Ramsgate.
	September/October	Mr and Mrs Austen, probably accompanied by JA and CEA, stay at Godmersham.
	October	JA and CEA visit Ashe.
	24 October	They return to Bath.
	November	The Austens visit Lyme Regis.

1804		JA probably writes 'The Watsons' this year.
	January	Mrs Powys visits the Austens in Bath.
	Spring	Mrs Austen seriously ill.
		HTA moves house to 16 Michael's Place, Brompton, and moves office to Albany, Piccadilly.
	Summer	The Austens, with HTA and EdeF, visit Lyme Regis.
	25 October	The Austens return to Bath and move to 3 Green Park Buildings East.
	16 December	Madam Lefroy of Ashe killed in a riding accident.
1805	*21 January*	Death of Mr Austen at 3 Green Park Buildings East.
	25 March	Mrs Austen and her daughters move to 25 Gay Street, Bath.
	16 April	Mrs Lloyd dies at Ibthorpe, and thereafter Martha Lloyd joins forces with Mrs Austen, JA and CEA.
	June	Mrs Austen, JA and CEA travel to Godmersham via Steventon, taking Anna with them.
	18 June	James Austen's younger daughter, Caroline, born at Steventon.
	Summer	Possible courtship of JA by Edward Bridges.
	17 September	JA and CEA go to Worthing, and stay there with Mrs Austen and Martha Lloyd until at least early November.
	21 October	Battle of Trafalgar – FWA unable to participate.
1806	*January*	Mrs Austen and her daughters visit Steventon.
	29 January	Mrs Austen returns to Bath and takes lodgings in Trim Street.
	February	JA and CEA visit Manydown, returning to Bath via Steventon mid-March.
	2 July	Mrs Austen and her daughters finally leave Bath, and go via Clifton to Adlestrop.
	24 July	Marriage of FWA to Mary Gibson, at Ramsgate.

	5 August	Adlestrop family go to Stoneleigh Abbey.
	14 August	Mrs Austen and her daughters go from Stoneleigh to visit the Coopers at Hamstall Ridware and stay about five weeks.
	October	The Austens call at Steventon, and with FWA and Mary Gibson take lodgings at Southampton.
	Winter	CEA visits Godmersham.
1807		HTA moves office from Albany to 10 Henrietta Street, Covent Garden.
	March	The Austens move into house in Castle Square, Southampton.
	April	HTA brings CEA back to Southampton from Godmersham via London.
	19 May	Marriage of CJA to Fanny Palmer, in Bermuda.
	August	The Coopers visit Southampton.
	September	EAK arranges family gathering at Chawton Great House, followed by further family gathering in Southampton.
1808	*January/ March*	JA and CEA staying at Steventon, Manydown, and with the Fowles at Kintbury.
	15 May	HTA and JA at Steventon en route for London.
	14 June	JA goes to Godmersham with James and Mary.
	8 July	JA returns to Southampton.
	28 September	CEA goes to Godmersham.
	10 October	Death of Elizabeth Austen (Knight) at Godmersham.
1809	*February*	CEA returns to Southampton.
	5 April	JA attempts to secure the publication of *Susan* (*Northanger Abbey*).
	15 May	Mrs Austen and her daughters arrive at Godmersham.
	June	HTA and EdeF move house to 64 Sloane Street, London.
	7 July	Mrs Austen and her daughters, and Martha Lloyd, move into Chawton Cottage.
	August	JA regains interest in composition.
	October	EAK and Fanny visit Chawton.

1810	July/August	JA and CEA visit Manydown and Steventon.
	November	EAK and Fanny visit Chawton.
	Winter	Sense and Sensibility accepted for publication by Thomas Egerton.
		The Leigh-Perrots buy 49 Great Pulteney Street, Bath.
1811	February	JA planning Mansfield Park.
	March	JA staying with HTA in London and correcting proofs of Sense and Sensibility; CEA at Godmersham.
	May	JA returns to Chawton via Streatham.
	August	CJA and family return to England.
	30 October	Sense and Sensibility published.
	November	JA visits Steventon.
	?Winter	JA starts revising First Impressions into Pride and Prejudice.
1812	April	EAK and Fanny visit Chawton.
	9–25 June	Mrs Austen and JA visit Steventon – the last time Mrs Austen does so; CEA goes to Godmersham.
	17 June	America declares war on Great Britain.
	14 October	Death of Mrs Thomas Knight II; EAK now officially takes surname of Knight.
	Autumn	JA sells copyright of Pride and Prejudice to Egerton for £110.
1813	28 January	Pride and Prejudice published; JA half-way through Mansfield Park.
	21 April	EAK and family come to Chawton Great House and stay for four months.
	22 April	JA goes to London to attend EdeF.
	25 April	Death of EdeF.
	1 May	JA returns to Chawton.
	19 May	HTA takes JA to London again, for a fortnight.
	June	HTA moves house to 10 Henrietta Street.
	?July	JA finishes Mansfield Park.
	17 August	Anna Austen engaged to Ben Lefroy.
	September	EAK and JA travel via London to Godmersham; her last visit there.

	13 November	EAK takes JA back to Chawton via London; *Mansfield Park* probably accepted for publication by Egerton at this time.
1814	*21 January*	JA commences *Emma*.
	1 March	HTA takes JA to London.
	April	JA returns to Chawton via Streatham. EAK and family stay at Chawton Great House for two months.
	5 April	Napoleon abdicates and is exiled to Elba.
	9 May	*Mansfield Park* published.
	Midsummer	JA visits the Cookes at Great Bookham. HTA moves house to 23 Hans Place, London.
	August	JA visits HTA in London. FWA and family move into Chawton Great House and stay there for about two years.
	3 September	HTA takes JA home to Chawton.
	6 September	CJA's wife Fanny dies after childbirth.
	Autumn	Hinton/Baverstock lawsuit against EAK commences.
	8 November	Marriage of Anna Austen and Ben Lefroy at Steventon; they go to live in Hendon, north of London.
	25 November	JA visits HTA in London.
	5 December	HTA takes JA home to Chawton.
	24 December	Treaty of Ghent officially ends war with America.
	26 December	JA and CEA stay with Mrs Heathcote and Miss Bigg in Winchester.
1815	*2–16 January*	JA and CEA stay at Steventon, also visiting Ashe and Laverstoke.
	March	Napoleon escapes and resumes power in France; hostilities recommence.
	29 March	*Emma* finished.
	?March or April	JA and CEA probably visit HTA in London.
	18 June	Battle of Waterloo finally ends war with France.
	July	Mary Lloyd and Caroline stay at Chawton.
	8 August	JA starts *Persuasion*.

	August	Anna and Ben Lefroy move to Wyards, near Chawton.
		JA possibly goes to London to negotiate publication of *Emma*, returning early in September.
	4 October	HTA takes JA to London; he falls ill, and she stays longer than anticipated.
	13 November	JA visits Carlton House; receives invitation to dedicate a future work to the Prince Regent.
	16 December	JA returns to Chawton.
	end December	*Emma* published by John Murray, dedicated to the Prince Regent.
1816	*Spring*	JA begins to feel unwell.
		HTA buys back MS of *Susan* (*Northanger Abbey*), which JA revises and intends to offer again for publication.
	15 March	HTA's bank fails; he leaves London.
	May	EAK and Fanny stay at Chawton for three weeks.
	22 May	JA and CEA go to Cheltenham via Steventon.
	15 June	They return to Chawton via Kintbury.
	Midsummer	FWA and family move from Chawton Great House to Alton.
	18 July	First draft of *Persuasion* finished.
	6 August	*Persuasion* finally completed.
	September	CEA and Mary Lloyd go to Cheltenham.
	December	HTA ordained, becomes curate of Chawton.
1817		FWA and family living in Alton this year.
	27 January	JA starts 'Sanditon'.
	18 March	Ceases work on this MS.
	28 March	Death of Mr Leigh-Perrot, at Scarlets.
	27 April	JA makes her will.
	24 May	CEA takes JA to Winchester for medical attention; they lodge at 8 College Street.
	18 July	JA dies in early morning.
	24 July	Buried in Winchester Cathedral.
	?Autumn	HTA arranges publication of *Northanger Abbey* and *Persuasion*.
	end December	*Northanger Abbey* and *Persuasion* published together, by Murray, with a 'Biographical Notice' added by HTA.

I

JAN FERGUS

The professional woman writer[1]

You will be glad to hear that every Copy of S[ense] & S[ensibility] is sold &
that it has brought me £140 – besides the Copyright, if that sh^d ever be of
any value. – I have now therefore written myself into £250. – which only
makes me long for more.

These words of Jane Austen to her brother Frank, written on 3 July 1813
(*L* 217) after she had published two novels, are those of a professional author
who is acutely conscious of her sales (as well as the possible future value of her
copyright) and eager to increase her profits. Austen's professionalism here
exists in startling contrast to her brother Henry's earliest biographical
accounts of her, accounts that helped to create the longstanding myth of
Austen as a genteel amateur, the spinster lady author who sketched her novels
in moments of leisure. Henry wrote in his first 'Biographical Notice' (printed
with *Northanger Abbey* and *Persuasion* in 1818):

> Neither the hope of fame nor profit mixed with her early motives ... She could
> scarcely believe what she termed her great good fortune when 'Sense and
> Sensibility' produced a clear profit of about £150. Few so gifted were so truly
> unpretending. She regarded the above sum as a prodigious recompense for that
> which had cost her nothing ... [S]o much did she shrink from notoriety, that no
> accumulation of fame would have induced her, had she lived, to affix her name
> to any productions of her pen ... in public she turned away from any allusion to
> the character of an authoress. (*P* 329–30)

Henry's wish to project an image of a ladylike, unmercenary, unprofessional,
private, delicate and domestic author led him to repeat these statements fifteen
years later, in the expanded 'Memoirs of Miss Austen' that were printed with
Richard Bentley's edition of *Sense and Sensibility*. He then added an anecdote
omitted earlier, that Austen refused to meet the writer Germaine de Staël, so as to
emphasize Austen's ladylike disdain for publicity.[2] This distaste did not make her
less professional, however. During probably the same visit to London (September
1814) in which she avoided Madame de Staël, she kept a careful eye to business:
she was 'in some hope', she wrote, 'of getting Egerton's account [for *Mansfield
Park*] before I go away – so we will enjoy ourselves as long as we can' (*L* 274).

The image that Henry Austen creates – at odds with the evidence that both
Austen's letters and her publishing decisions offer of her professionalism – is

precisely the one that so annoyed Henry James, according to Brian Southam: 'the myth of the inspired amateur, the homely spinster who put down her knitting needles to take up her pen'.[3] That myth, and others like it, have prevented subsequent readers from understanding that, for Austen, being a professional writer was, apart from her family, more important to her than anything else in her life.

Austen wrote when opportunities for women to publish had never been greater, and from her childhood her aim was to see her works in print. She collected her juvenilia in volumes made to resemble published books as closely as possible. She wrote three novels before she was 25, although she did not manage to publish them until much later. Her literary career depended to some extent upon the other women novelists of her time, who created and sustained a market for domestic fiction by women, and whose attitudes towards writing, like Austen's own, became increasingly professional. Many of Austen's contemporaries, including Ann Radcliffe, Frances Burney, Charlotte Smith, Elizabeth Inchbald, Maria Edgeworth and Amelia Opie, among others, received much greater fame and fortune as novelists in their own time than Austen did. But these novelists are only the most visible of a large mass of women who rushed into print at the end of the eighteenth century. The number of women writers increased dramatically throughout the century, as Judith Phillips Stanton's research has shown, but exploded at the end, rising by 'around 50 percent *every decade* starting in the 1760s'.[4]

The cultural context: obstacles to authorship

This publishing explosion occurred despite the presence of many social obstacles to women's writing. Publishing her own writing could threaten a woman's reputation as well as her social position. For any woman, the fame of authorship could become infamy, and novels were particularly reprehensible, as their famous defence in *Northanger Abbey* indicates (*NA* 1:5:30–1). Proper women, as Henry Austen makes clear, were modest, retiring, essentially domestic and private. Authorship of any kind entailed publicity, thrusting oneself before the public eye – thus loss of femininity. These prejudices led many women besides Austen to publish their first novels anonymously, among them Sarah Fielding, Frances Burney and Ann Radcliffe; they affixed their names to their works only when their excellent reputations as novelists were established. And writing for profit – professional writing – could be even more disreputable than writing for fame; Henry Austen, in the first passage quoted from him, takes care to assert that at first Austen hoped for neither fame nor profit.

Before Austen's birth in 1775, literature had become firmly fixed in the marketplace, to the dismay of many. Alvin Kernan has succinctly summarized the change: 'An older system of polite or courtly letters – primarily oral, aristocratic, amateur, authoritarian, court-centered – was swept away at this time and gradually replaced by a new print-based, market-centered, democratic literary system.'[5] The public replaced the patron as a source of income. But the older aristocratic attitudes that saw print and payment as vulgar were surprisingly persistent among elite women and some men. Most male writers, however, were happy to be paid for their writing, and once they established themselves in this new literary marketplace, as reviewers, essayists, and so forth, with few exceptions they tended to discourage competition from women writers. They transferred (with renewed energy) much of the old aristocratic disdain for all print to hack writers – the male denizens of Grub Street – and to women who wrote. Women were attacked for having the temerity to write without having the necessary learning and taste. Only desperate financial need, preferably to support aged parents, a sick husband or destitute children, could (according to literary men) excuse a woman's exposing herself in print to obtain money. Accordingly, women's prefaces often apologize for writing by alluding to distresses of this sort, causing reviewers frequently to condescend kindly to their work, though increasingly they bemoaned the number and grammar of 'female scribblers'.

A woman might also face legal obstacles to authorship if she were married. Married women had no legal existence. They could not own property or sign contracts. Although Charlotte Smith began to publish in order to support herself and her children after her feckless husband was imprisoned for debt, a contract for her novel *Desmond* (1792) survives signed not by her but by Benjamin Smith, who was at the time residing in Scotland under an alias.[6] The publishing records for Ann Radcliffe's *The Romance of the Forest* (1791) list William Radcliffe, her husband, as the work's author; he apparently received £40 for the second edition (1792).[7] Comparable restrictions survived in France within living memory: 'it was not until 1965 that married women were legally permitted to publish a work or to engage in any profession without the consent of their husbands'.[8] Unmarried women in the eighteenth century did not face these restrictions, but they generally lived under their fathers' authority, and fathers (like Frances Burney's) might tend to disapprove of their daughters risking their modesty, their reputations and possibly their marriageability by publishing. By contrast, Austen's father tried to help her publish *First Impressions*, the early version of *Pride and Prejudice*, writing to a possible publisher himself.

The process of publishing

The obstacles to women's writing make their success in publishing novels all the more remarkable. Admittedly, it was much easier then for authors to have novels published, nationally distributed and reviewed in the major review journals than it is now. When Austen gave advice to her niece Anna Austen on a novel in progress, she assumed that the novel would be not only finished but published. Although today few would be likely to encourage young unpublished writers to expect to see their novels in print, Austen did not hesitate. In her own circle of family and friends, in fact, Austen knew several published authors, many of them women, including her much older friend Anne Lefroy, whose 1804 obituary mentions that she had published poetry when quite young.[9] Austen's mother's first cousin Cassandra Cooke produced *Battleridge: An Historical Tale, Founded on Facts* (2 vols., 1799). Other slightly more distant Leigh cousins published during Austen's childhood: James Henry Leigh's poem *The New Rosciad* appeared in 1785, and Cassandra, Lady Hawke's novel *Julia de Gramont* came out in 1788. In the next year, Austen's brothers James and Henry, along with other friends, began publishing their weekly periodical essays, *The Loiterer*; the collected essays were brought out in 1790. All these books were reviewed in major review journals.[10]

This family access to print must have encouraged the youthful Austen, and helps to account for the way that her advice to her niece takes printing for granted, reflecting the greater availability of publication in her lifetime. All writers, known or unknown, who wished to obtain payment for a novel had four options for publishing: (a) by subscription; (b) by profit-sharing; (c) by selling copyright; and (d) on 'commission', a system whereby the author was responsible for paying all the expenses of publication while the publisher distributed the copies and took a commission on all sold. Austen most frequently employed this last form, also known as publishing for oneself. The closest equivalent we have to this method is to employ a 'vanity press' – that is, to pay for printing one's own works – or to self-publish on the Internet. Such 'published' works are neither reviewed by the media nor sold in shops. By contrast, in Austen's lifetime a book published on commission was perfectly respectable, as likely as any other book to be reviewed and sold.

Publication by subscription

Subscription was declining somewhat, for it was a cumbersome and demeaning business, and not always remunerative. Subscribers paid for a projected book, preferably in advance. A list of their names would be printed in the work when it appeared. An author solicited subscribers (usually by publishing proposals), kept records and collected money – or asked friends to do so, rather a heavy tax on friendship because subscribers generally were reluctant to part with cash. Admittedly, Frances Burney made £1,000 – a tremendous sum – by selling subscriptions to *Camilla, or a Picture of Youth* (1796); 'Miss J. Austen, Steventon' is listed as a subscriber in the first volume. Burney also received £1,000 in copyright money for *Camilla*.[11] But her success in combining these two forms of publication was possible only because her reputation was pre-eminent. The Hookham records show how unlikely such rewards were for other women. A Mrs Clutterbuck attempted to get subscribers through Hookham and Carpenter for a projected 'Beauties of St. Pierre' in June and July, 1798; she got five and had Hookham return the money (G/127).

Publication by profit-sharing

Profit-sharing became frequent only in the early nineteenth century. Publishers who chose this form of publication paid for printing and advertising, repaid themselves as the books were sold, and shared any profit realized over and above the costs. If the sale did not cover expenses, the firm absorbed the loss. Publishers generally offered profit-sharing to untried authors whose market they could not predict. In some cases, sharing profits could be more remunerative than publishing for oneself or selling copyright. If Austen had published all the editions of her works that appeared during her lifetime by profit-sharing, she would have made more money than she actually did.[12] Obviously, an author who published for himself took all the profits, not just half, but in practice this meant only about 50 per cent more money.

Sale of copyright

To most eighteenth-century British authors eager to dispose of their property, sale of limited copyright for a fee was by far the most prestigious and desirable option available, if they could find a purchaser. The fee offered a clear sum of money, generally payable within a year of publication, and it removed the writer comfortably and decorously from the marketplace as none of the other options did, for the publisher was obliged to pay the sum agreed upon, however poorly the work sold. If sales were good and further editions were printed, a publisher who had purchased copyright might send the author an additional payment. Established authors, unwilling to leave themselves at the mercy of publishers' generosity, might contract for additional payments once a specified number of copies or editions were printed or sold, as Radcliffe had probably done when she sold the copyright of *The Romance of the Forest* for an unnamed sum to Hookham and Carpenter.

Publishing on commission

Austen's most frequent mode of publication was at her own risk, or 'on commission' as it was called. The author was ultimately responsible for the cost of paper, printing and advertising; the publisher kept accounts, distributed the books to the trade and charged a 10 per cent commission on each copy sold – a kind of royalty in reverse. If not enough copies were sold to cover costs, the author had to make up the difference. Austen herself assumed that this method required an initial outlay of capital: she wrote to her sister on the appearance of the second edition of *Sense and Sensibility* that 'I suppose in the meantime I shall owe dear Henry a great deal of Money for Printing &c' (*L* 250). But surviving publishers' records indicate that as a rule the publisher seems to have paid for production of a book, charging the expenses off against receipts some months later, after the work had sold. Even Hookham and Carpenter, fashionable booksellers but a relatively small publishing firm, operated this way. When Miss Mary Barker published 750 copies of her three-volume novel *A Welsh Story* in June 1798, Hookham carried the cost of about £61 for paper, not quite £50 for composing, printing and correcting, and £6 for advertising. Less than half the copies were disposed of by the end of September, so that the author owed the firm over £48 (G/138). This mode of publication could be more remunerative to an author than selling copyright, but clearly the risks were great – to publishers also, if they financed the outlay. Hookham and Carpenter may never have recovered the money owed to them by Mary Barker. Her debt of £48 includes the commission gained on selling 180 copies, only about £5. If the work had sold out, their total profit on commission would have been less than £25 – a small sum for which to risk nearly £120.

Money and the market

Probably the major reason for the explosion of women into print towards the end of the eighteenth century was their need for money. Publishing was one of the few means by which a woman of the middling or upper classes could earn cash. Laetitia-Matilda Hawkins' account of her first venture into print makes this motive clear: 'Some few years previous to this time [Samuel Johnson's death in 1784], being in want of a sum of money for a whim of girlish patronage, and having no *honest* means of raising it, I wrote a downright novel.'[13] Hawkins sold her novel to Thomas Hookham,[14] probably for no more than £10 or £20 – sufficient for 'a whim of girlish patronage' but not for full support. With few exceptions, as Edward Copeland's research has shown,[15] women could not live on their earnings from publishing novels alone; these funds had to supplement other sources of income.

One reason for most women's very limited income from publishing was that the novel-reading public at this time was small and, through the 1790s, audiences at least in the provinces were predominantly male – a problem for women writers, since male purchasers preferred male-authored novels while female buyers preferred female-authored ones.[16] Through the 1790s, novels by unknown writers would be published in editions of just 750, 500 or (later) 1,000 copies, while proven novelists might sell 2,000 or 3,000 in one or more editions. Walter Scott's novels, beginning with the publication of *Waverley* in 1814, were the first to be regularly published in much larger numbers.[17] The largest known edition for an Austen novel was 2,000, for *Emma* (1816), and it failed to sell out. The limited market for novels was partly dictated by their cost. All Austen's novels were printed on hand presses similar in principle to those used by Gutenberg three hundred years earlier. These techniques and especially the great expense of handmade paper kept the price of books high,[18] making small editions more economical than large ones unless a strong and steady demand were assured. It was much cheaper to print a small edition of 750 copies and to recompose and reprint if it sold out than to risk a large edition of 2,000 or 3,000 that might ultimately be sold as waste paper. The paper for even a small edition, like the 750 copies of Mary Barker's *Welsh Story*, absorbed more than half the costs.

Barker's book, unlike those of Austen's brothers and cousins, does not seem to have been reviewed.[19] Reviews were thought then as now to increase sales, though they may have had less influence upon purchases by individuals than upon purchases made by book clubs and book societies, which frequently subscribed to review journals.[20] On the whole, Austen received few reviews – during her lifetime, two for *Sense and Sensibility*, three for *Pride and Prejudice*, none for *Mansfield Park* and ten for *Emma* (although two of these were written in German). Most were short and reasonably favourable. The longest, on *Emma*, was written by Walter Scott at her publisher John Murray's urging: 'Have you any fancy to dash off an article on "Emma"? It wants incident and romance, does it not? None of the author's other novels have been noticed [by Murray's own periodical, the *Quarterly Review*], and surely "Pride and Prejudice" merits high commendation.'[21] Murray sent Austen a copy of the review, and her response survives – a surprising one: 'I return you the Quarterly Reveiw with many Thanks. The Authoress of *Emma* has no reason I think to complain of her treatment in it – except in the total omission of Mansfield Park. – I cannot but be sorry that so clever a Man as the Reveiwer of *Emma*, should consider it as unworthy of being noticed' (*L* 313). Austen's response is professional. She regrets Scott's failure to mention *Mansfield Park*, no doubt because the novel had never been reviewed and, more important, because she may have known that sales of the second edition had already stalled by the time she wrote.

Austen's publishing career

When Austen arrived in her final home at Chawton on 7 July 1809, she was 34 and unpublished, a condition that she was determined to alter. Her earlier attempts to publish *First Impressions* and *Susan*, versions of *Pride and Prejudice* and *Northanger Abbey*, had failed. Cadell and Davies, respectable publishers, had refused George Austen's offer on 1 November 1797 of the manuscript of *First Impressions*. Austen had sold the manuscript of *Susan* to the London publisher B. Crosby and Company and had received £10 for it by 'the Spring of the year 1803', according to her angry letter to the firm on 5 April 1809 (*L* 174). She adopted the pseudonym 'Mrs Ashton Dennis' for this enquiry to Crosby about the delay in publishing *Susan*; this name allowed her to sign herself 'MAD.' Her letter makes clear her determination to publish.

Sense and Sensibility

At this point, Austen had three completed manuscripts available to her: *Susan* (although to publish it, she would have to return Crosby's £10), *First Impressions* and *Sense and Sensibility*. She chose shrewdly to work on *Sense and Sensibility*. Its emphasis upon the importance as well as the costs of self-command made it her most orthodox novel both aesthetically and morally. *Susan* or *Northanger Abbey* constituted a bold experiment in burlesque over which Crosby had clearly vacillated, thinking it a profitable speculation at first, and then a poor risk. The manuscript version of *Pride and Prejudice* contained an extremely unorthodox heroine, and Austen may have feared either similar vacillation from another publisher, if she succeeded in selling the copyright, or a more ambivalent reception from reviewers and the reading public than *Sense and Sensibility* was likely to obtain. Mary Russell Mitford wrote to a friend in December 1814, for instance, deploring 'the entire want of taste which could produce so pert, so worldly a heroine as the beloved of such a man as Darcy'.[22] Austen may have approached the publisher Thomas Egerton early in 1811 through Henry. Egerton had sold James' and Henry's *The Loiterer* in his Whitehall shop more than twenty years earlier and may have liked the novel well enough to feel that he would gain prestige by being associated with it. Perhaps more important, he must have felt that he could trust Henry Austen, at this time a banker, to settle the bill for costs.

Once Egerton had agreed to publish the novel on commission, he sent it to the printer Charles Roworth, perhaps in February or March 1811. Roworth took his time: Austen wrote near the end of April that 'M^{rs} K[night] regrets in the most flattering manner that she must wait *till* May [for *Sense and Sensibility*], but I have scarcely a hope of its being out in June. – Henry does not neglect it; he *has* hurried the Printer ' (L 182). The delay was much worse than Austen anticipated; the novel was not advertised until the end of October. She experienced some delay from printers on *every* novel that she published for herself, though none was as lengthy as this. By contrast, Egerton was later able to issue *Pride and Prejudice* within a few months of purchasing it, doubtless because his own profit was at stake. He would earn less than £36 by publishing *Sense and Sensibility* on commission in an edition of 750 copies, by my calculations, whereas Austen herself made £140, as she wrote to her brother Frank (217). It was not worth Egerton's while to hurry the printers.

Although he stood to gain little by agreeing to publish *Sense and Sensibility* on commission, Egerton ran no risk; only the author did. Austen was, according to her brother Henry's 'Biographical Notice', 'so persuaded ... that its sale would not repay the expense of publication, that she actually made a reserve from her very moderate income to meet the expected loss' (P 329). At this time, the expenses of publishing 750 copies of the novel would come to about £155, and advertisements would ordinarily take another £24 or so.[23] The novel retailed at 15s., but the books were accounted for to the author at the trade price of 9s. 6d. If every copy were sold, receipts at the trade price would be over £356, leaving a maximum profit of about £140 after deducting expenses of £179 and Egerton's 10 per cent commission on the sales.

Austen was risking, then, about £180 on the chance of earning £140. In fact, however, her risk was substantially less. The buyer's market for novels was small, but sales to circulating libraries were fairly certain. A novel normally would have to sell between one-half and two-thirds of an edition to become profitable. For example, within five months of being issued in February 1810, Maria Benson's *The Wife. A Novel* had sold 275 of the 500 copies printed, and in two more years another 49, realizing £7.6.4 to split with Longman, who had agreed to share profits with the author.[24] If only 275 copies of *Sense and Sensibility* had sold, Austen would have had £130, less Egerton's 10 per cent, to offset her expenses of £179; that is, she would have owed about £62. If the other 475 copies had been remaindered at the same price that Benson's novel was in 1813 (1s. 6d. each), Austen would have received another £32 or so. At worst, then, her loss was unlikely to be more than £30. Although she probably was unable to 'reserve' such a sum from her own 'moderate income' (her dress allowance had been £21 a year (L 31, 32)), she could perhaps set aside about half. And every additional copy of her novel that was sold at the full trade price of 9s. 6d. would reduce this possible debt. She would break even once 419 copies were bought, even allowing for Egerton's commission. Had Austen known earlier that even at worst her losses were likely to be manageable, she might have published sooner – perhaps when she inherited £50 in 1807. Fortunately, by 1811 Austen was prepared to invest money in herself, in her own authorship.

Pride and Prejudice

Egerton had almost certainly accepted *Sense and Sensibility* by February 1811. This acceptance evidently made Austen optimistic enough about the possibilities of publication to begin her most ambitious novel to date, *Mansfield Park*. According to Cassandra's memorandum, this novel was begun 'somewhere about Feb[y] 1811 – Finished soon after June 1813'.[25] No other novel took Austen so long to write. Probably part of the time was spent revising *First Impressions* into *Pride and Prejudice*. She perhaps began this revision when she discovered that *Sense and Sensibility* had sold well enough to break even; this point was quite likely to be reached within six months of issue, in May 1812. By the following November, Austen had completed her revisions to *Pride and Prejudice*, made a fair copy, and sold the manuscript to Egerton for £110, as she wrote to Martha Lloyd: 'Its' being sold will I hope be a great saving of Trouble to Henry, & therefore must be welcome to me. – The Money is to be paid at the end of the twelvemonth.' Austen had been disappointed by Egerton's offer: 'I would rather have had £150, but we could not both be pleased, & I am not at all surprised that he should not chuse to hazard so much' (L 197). The offer was rather niggardly. By my calculations, Egerton made a profit of more than £450 on just the first two editions. Austen's unfortunate decision to part with the copyright of *Pride and Prejudice* was made, however, before she could predict that the first edition of *Sense and Sensibility* would sell out and bring her £140.

• Issued at the end of January 1813, *Pride and Prejudice* was Austen's most popular novel, both with the public and with her family and friends. By the spring of 1813, three favourable reviews had appeared (compared to two for *Sense and Sensibility*). Before May 1813, *Pride and Prejudice* had become the
• 'fashionable novel', according to Anne Isabella Milbanke, who was to marry Lord Byron.[26] Its popularity eventually meant the end of Austen's anonymity. By the following September, her authorship was pretty well known, as she wrote to her brother Frank: 'the truth is that the Secret has spread so far as to be scarcely the Shadow of a secret now – & that I beleive whenever the

3^{d} appears, I shall not even attempt to tell Lies about it. – I shall rather try to make all the Money than all the Mystery I can of it. – People shall pay for their Knowledge if I can make them' (*L* 231). Although Austen joked about both, money was important to her, and anonymity had been so essential that she had had Cassandra write to Godmersham in September 1811, 'to beg we would not mention that Aunt Jane Austen wrote "Sense & Sensibility"'.[27]

Because she had sold the copyright, Austen did not profit from her most popular novel as she should have done. Egerton probably issued a first edition of 1,000 copies of *Pride and Prejudice* and, in the following October, a second edition of perhaps 750, both of which were sold at 18s., three shillings more than *Sense and Sensibility*. Had Austen published such editions for herself, she would have made about £475, allowing for Egerton's commission of approximately £100, when they sold out – supposing that Egerton had brought them out as economically for her as he did for himself. Certainly he produced *Pride and Prejudice* more cheaply, using cheaper paper and less of it, even though the novel was longer than *Sense and Sensibility*.[28] And furthermore, he seems to have been guilty of overcharging for *Pride and Prejudice*, which cost three shillings more than *Sense and Sensibility*. The latter had in fact been slightly underpriced: Longman charged 16s. 6d. for a shorter three-volume novel like Benson's *The Wife* early in 1810, and retained that price for *She Thinks for Herself*, which appeared almost exactly when *Pride and Prejudice* did and was of comparable length. Austen seems to have been professionally alert to Egerton's manoeuvrings, for she wrote shrewdly to Cassandra on 29 January 1813: 'The Advertisement is in our paper to day for the first time; – 18^{s} – He shall ask £1 – 1 – for my two next, & £1 – 8 – for my stupidest of all' (*L* 201). For Austen, 'shall' in the second or third person is always emphatic: it 'commands or threatens', to use an eighteenth-century grammarian's formula.[29] By naming sums in excess of one pound – not yet appropriate for a three-volume novel – she jokingly suggests that she will imitate Egerton's sharp business practices. More seriously, she implies that she will not permit him to undercharge again when her own profit is at stake – and she did not. *Mansfield Park* retailed at 18s.

The success of *Pride and Prejudice* certainly increased the demand for *Sense and Sensibility*, sold out by 3 July 1813, according to a letter written on that date to Frank (*L* 217). It had taken about twenty months to clear the edition. Austen wrote as a postscript to Frank on 25 September 1813, that 'There is to be a 2^{d} Edition of S. & S. Egerton advises it' (232), and the second editions of both *Sense and Sensibility* and *Pride and Prejudice* were advertised together on 29 October. On the whole, Egerton's advice to Austen was sound. She never lost money by publishing with him, although she had to wait until 1816 before receiving profits on the second edition of *Sense and Sensibility*.[30]

Mansfield Park

In her dealings with Egerton, Austen seems to have learned quickly that his interests were very different from hers. Her wry remark on the price that he charged for *Pride and Prejudice* shows her awareness that he was likely to profit from the novel more than she had – and more than she had profited from publishing *Sense and Sensibility* for herself. After the success of *Pride and Prejudice*, Egerton certainly offered to purchase the copyright of Austen's next novel, but she did not accept his offer. It was no doubt rather low – perhaps £150. She evidently had learned to prefer her own judgement of the value of her work to Egerton's, and she was prepared to risk an unfavourable response from the reading public. In other words, as Austen wrote to her brother, she had 'written myself into £250' (*L* 217); she chose to invest that money in underwriting her own work – wisely. She probably offered *Mansfield Park* to Egerton in January 1814. On 21 March, Austen expected a delay of at least a month before publication: 'Perhaps before the end of April, *Mansfield Park* by the author of S & S. – P. & P. may be in the World. – Keep the *name* to yourself. I sh^d not like to have it known beforehand' (262).[31]

Egerton seems to have produced *Mansfield Park* quite cheaply, perhaps at Austen's request. The paper is thinner (thus less expensive) than the thin paper used for *Pride and Prejudice*, and because each page contains twenty-five lines, not twenty-three as in the earlier novels, further savings on paper were achieved. R. W. Chapman has conjectured that Egerton printed only 1,250 copies; later, Henry Austen reminded John Murray that he himself had 'expressed astonishment that so small an edition of such a work should have been sent into the world'.[32] This edition sold out in only six months, more quickly than that of *Pride and Prejudice*, which had taken eight or nine months to clear despite being almost certainly smaller. Using Chapman's estimate of 1,250 copies, we must assume that Egerton produced *Mansfield Park* extremely cheaply indeed, based on what we know of Austen's earnings. Her profit exceeded £310, more than she received during her lifetime for any novel.[33]

Emma

Austen composed *Emma* in only fourteen months, from 21 January 1814 to 29 March 1815; she was clearly at the height of her genius. During this time, she also saw *Mansfield Park* through the press, made three visits to Henry in London, and three more to other friends. She wrote on 18 November 1814 that the first edition of *Mansfield Park* was sold out, and that her brother wanted her to come to London, 'to settle about a 2^d Edit: – but as I could not very conveniently leave home now, I have written him my Will & pleasure, & unless he still urges it, shall not go. – I am very greedy & want to make the most of it' (L 281). She did go, for on 30 November 1814, she wrote: 'it is not settled yet whether I *do* hazard a 2^d Edition. We are to see Egerton today, when it will probably be determined. – People are more ready to borrow & praise, than to buy … but tho' I like praise as well as anybody, I like what Edward calls *Pewter* too' (287). Egerton must already have advised against a second edition. He may have pointed to a falling-off in demand for the first edition before it sold out. Austen had hoped in July, 1813, that *Mansfield Park* 'on the credit of P. & P. will sell well, tho' not half so entertaining' (217). Although in fact *Mansfield Park* sold out faster than *Pride and Prejudice*, perhaps word of mouth reduced later demand. The second edition was finally issued more than a year later on 19 February 1816, by John Murray, who brought out *Emma* at the end of 1815.

Unfortunately, Egerton's advice turned out to be good. Murray's second edition of *Mansfield Park* lost money. In addition, Murray produced Austen's books more expensively during her lifetime than Egerton had, which reduced her possible profit. Nonetheless, her decision to approach Murray was not, on the face of it, a bad one. Murray's imprint carried much more prestige than Egerton's. By the time Austen submitted *Emma* to him in August or September 1815, he was Lord Byron's publisher and had co-published many of Walter Scott's works, including *Waverley* (1814). Furthermore, Murray was reputedly very open-handed to authors, offering large copyright fees. Accordingly, once Murray received a favourable opinion of *Emma* from his editor William Gifford, who wrote that 'Of "Emma", I have nothing but good to say', Austen might well have expected a generous fee for the copyright.[34] Instead, on 15 October 1815, Murray offered the sum of £450 altogether for the copyrights of *Emma*, *Mansfield Park* and *Sense and Sensibility*. Austen commented, accurately enough, 'It will end in my publishing for myself I daresay' (L 291). Despite illness, Henry dictated early in November an exasperated reply to Murray: 'The terms you offer are so very inferior to what we had expected, that I am apprehensive of having made some great error in my arithmetical calculation.' He went on to point out that his sister had made more than £450 by one small edition of *Sense and Sensibility* and a moderate one of *Mansfield Park*.[35] Henry's illness worsened, and Austen conducted most of the remaining negotiations for herself. In a letter of 3 November, she requested a meeting with Murray, at which time he must have agreed to publish *Emma* on commission, and on 23 November she was already 'vexed' by printers' delays (297). Murray responded civilly, promising 'no farther cause for dissatisfaction … In short, I am soothed & complimented into tolerable comfort' (298).

Hindsight indicates that Murray's offer of £450 for the three copyrights was fair if not generous. Austen would have done well to accept it. First, she would have received that sum within a year. Instead, because losses on the second edition of *Mansfield Park* were set against the profits of *Emma*, Austen received during her lifetime only £38.18.0 profit on her greatest work.[36] Ultimately, her heirs received a total of about £385 more from the sole edition of *Emma*, from the second of *Mansfield Park* (both of which were remaindered in 1821), and from the sale in 1832 of the copyrights of the three novels for £42 each.[37] In short, Murray's estimate in 1815 of the market value of her copyrights was if anything exaggerated. Nonetheless, Murray treated Austen rather less generously than other writers. He frequently gave such large payments to his authors that he lost money by their works. For instance, he offered Helen Maria Williams 50 guineas in 1816 for her pamphlet, *Letters on Protestants*; the work sold out, but Murray still realized a loss of £18.2.6.[38] Austen's refusal to accept Murray's £450 suggests how highly she valued *Emma* and how willing she was to risk a different valuation from the public. Her recent profit on *Mansfield Park* may have encouraged her to insist that Murray publish the fairly large edition of 2,000 copies of *Emma*. Unfortunately, *Emma* was not as popular as her earlier works: in the first nine months it had sold only 1,248 copies. After four years, the total was 1,437, and the rest were remaindered.

Ironically enough, at about the same time that Austen was refusing Murray's money and insisting on publishing for herself, she was exposed to her only experience of 'patronage' – the support of polite letters by wealthy patrons. When *Emma* was in the press, the Prince Regent – who admired the novels – apparently learned of Austen's presence in London and sent his librarian to visit her. This officious and obtuse character, James Stanier Clarke, invited Austen to visit him at Carlton House and during the course of the visit imparted, in her words, 'the Information of my being at liberty to dedicate any future work to HRH the P.R. without the necessity of any Solicitation on my part' (*L* 296). On 15 November 1815, just over a month before *Emma* was issued, Austen wished to know 'whether it is incumbent on me to shew my sense of the Honour, by inscribing the Work now in the Press, to H.R.H. – I sh^d be equally concerned to appear either presumptuous or Ungrateful' (296). The word 'incumbent' suggests her annoyance. She or perhaps Henry subsequently wrote the briefest possible dedication to be prefixed to *Emma*, and she was obliged to send an expensively bound copy to the Regent; he took no notice of it or the dedication and certainly sent no money. Austen's last letter to Clarke contains her very professional reply to his suggestion that she write 'an Historical Romance, founded on the House of Saxe Cobourg', which she acknowledged 'might be much more to the purpose of Profit or Popularity than such pictures of domestic Life in Country Villages as I deal in'. She concluded, however, 'No – I must keep to my own style & go on in my own Way; And though I may never succeed again in that, I am convinced that I should totally fail in any other' (312).

Persuasion and *Northanger Abbey*

When Austen wrote this letter to Clarke on 1 April 1816, she had been writing *Persuasion* for nearly eight months, and the phrase 'though I may never succeed again' – though properly modest – may hint at a fear that this novel might fail to earn money, as her second edition of *Mansfield Park* was failing. At this time, 'Profit or Popularity' was of even more concern to her as a writer than it had been. Her family had suffered financial reverses. Her brother Henry's bank had failed on 15 March 1816; he took orders and became a curate in the Chawton neighbourhood. Austen herself had lost £13.7.0 of profit on *Mansfield Park* that had remained in her account with Henry, but fortunately the remainder of her earnings had already been invested in the 'Navy Fives'. Other members of her family were much more seriously affected. Her brother Edward lost £20,000, her uncle James Leigh-Perrot £10,000, her brothers James and Frank several hundreds each. As a result, neither Frank nor Henry could afford any longer to contribute to their mother's income.[39] These losses and threats may have kept Austen from any immediate attempt to publish *Northanger Abbey*, which Henry had probably reclaimed from the London publisher Crosby, returning his £10, fairly soon after the publication of *Emma*.[40] In any case, the strain of so many family reverses helped to undermine Austen's own health. Symptoms resembling those of Addison's disease, perhaps the condition that killed her, showed themselves early in 1816.[41]

When *Persuasion* was finally completed on 6 August 1816, almost precisely a year after it was begun on 8 August 1815, Austen put it aside for longer than any other novel, probably because of the family's financial troubles. In February 1817, she received the first small profits on *Emma*. At this point, she had two completed but unpublished novels on her hands. Possibly she had expected that she could use earnings on *Emma* to underwrite the publication of *Northanger Abbey* or *Persuasion*, or both. Her meagre profit of about £39 may have caused her to write to her niece Fanny Knight on 13 March 1817: 'I have a something ready for Publication, which may perhaps appear about a twelvemonth hence' (*L* 333). Austen perhaps hoped that next year's profits would permit the publication of *Persuasion*. Since the failure of Henry's bank, she had been allowing her half-yearly dividends of £15 on the £600 in the 'Navy Fives' to accumulate in a new account at Hoare's bank; they amounted to £45 by the time she died.[42] She may have planned to draw upon these also, if necessary, to publish *Persuasion* and perhaps *Northanger Abbey* as well. In the same letter, she told Fanny that 'Miss Catherine is put upon the Shelve for the present, and I do not know that she will ever come out' (333). The phrase 'upon the shelf' is appropriately mercantile, whether applied to an unsuccessful debutante unable to come out into the market or to an unsaleable commodity like a book. Austen's mind and language seem to have been particularly attuned to the market after the disappointing failure to earn money from *Emma*.

Nonetheless, Austen did not permit herself to be discouraged from further publication by illness, by having two unpublished manuscripts by her, by the failure of her second edition of *Mansfield Park* or by the relative unpopularity of *Emma*. She was forced to postpone publication, but it remained her goal, as is evident in her decision to begin a new novel, 'Sanditon', on 27 January 1817. She wrote twelve chapters before stopping on 18 March 1817, when presumably her health failed. She died four months later.

Although anxiety about money and ill health had prevented Austen from publishing *Persuasion* before her death, her sister Cassandra was evidently determined to see her sister's last works in print. She had Austen's will proved on 10 September 1817. After paying burial expenses of £92, £100 in legacies, more than £22 in probate costs and £25 in debts, Cassandra owed duty on an estate of £561.2.0.[43] Once the estate was settled, Cassandra arranged to publish the two remaining novels with Murray; as a result, she had no duty to pay on those receipts. Possibly the family's financial problems lay behind the apparent insistence that Murray produce *Northanger Abbey* and *Persuasion* as cheaply as possible: only 1,750 copies were printed on very inexpensive paper. They appeared at the end of December 1817, and 1,409 copies sold within a year. This four-volume dual publication on commission earned £518.6.5, more than any earlier Austen novel, even though the last 283 copies had to be remaindered at 3s. 1d. each – a far cry from the £1.4.0 retail price.[44] Overall, Cassandra collected £784.11.0 from Murray on this edition and on the final sales of *Emma* and *Mansfield Park*.[45] The sale of the
• five remaining copyrights to Richard Bentley in 1832 for £210 brought Austen's overall literary earnings to at least £1,625, most of which was received after her death. During her life she received something over £631, perhaps as much as £668 and loose change.[46] She earned, despite her increasing professionalism, rather less than has usually been thought, much less than contemporaries like Maria Edgeworth (£11,062.8.10) or Frances Burney (£4,280).[47]

This £630 or so that Austen 'wrote herself into', to use her own phrase, was not very substantial by any contemporary standard. As Edward Copeland points out elsewhere in this volume, lump sums of money were always translated into yearly incomes. Invested in the Navy Fives, part of Austen's earnings brought her £30 a year, not much more than her dress allowance of £20 a year during her father's lifetime and much less than the income of anyone else in her family.[48] This sum would not afford genteel maintenance to a single woman, even though women alone were certainly supposed to require very little: as Fanny Dashwood puts it, her mother- and sisters-in-law 'will live so cheap' (SS 1:2:14).

If we depart from Austen's practice, however, and calculate her earnings of just over £630 between 1811 and 1817 as a yearly income of £90, we cannot conclude that she wrote herself into even temporary wealth. Novelists like Amelia Opie and Mary Darby Robinson, who did not invest their earnings but applied them to daily expenses, found that even when they made as much as £150 to £200 a year for several years, those sums did not keep them out of debt despite other sources of income.[49] By contrast, Austen not only invested most of her earnings but allowed the dividends to accumulate in her account at Hoare's bank.[50] When she wrote to her niece Fanny Knight on 13 March 1817 that 'I have a something ready for Publication, which may perhaps appear a twelvemonth hence' (L 333), she had learned a month earlier that her profits on Emma were small because the second edition of Mansfield Park had sold so poorly. Her dividends amounted to £30 by January 1817; in a year, they would come to £60. I imagine that, after the family catastrophe of Henry's bankruptcy a year before, and the weak sale of Mansfield Park, Austen was waiting to publish Persuasion (and perhaps Northanger Abbey) until she could underwrite the publication herself. We see here, I believe, and in her continuing until 18 March, despite failing health, to write her new novel 'Sanditon', perhaps the most poignant evidences of Austen's professionalism.

NOTES

1. The arguments in this chapter summarize and expand those presented earlier in *Jane Austen: A Literary Life* (London: Macmillan, 1991).
2. [Henry Austen,] 'Memoir of Miss Austen', in Jane Austen, *Sense and Sensibility* (London: Richard Bentley, 1833), p. ix.
3. B. C. Southam, ed., 'Introduction', *Jane Austen: The Critical Heritage* (London: Routledge & Kegan Paul, 1968), p. 32.
4. 'Profile of Women Writing in English from 1660 to 1800', *Eighteenth-Century Women and the Arts*, ed. Frederick M. Keener and Susan E. Lorsch (New York: Greenwood Press, 1988), p. 248.
5. Alvin Kernan, *Printing Technology, Letters and Samuel Johnson* (Princeton University Press, 1987), p. 4.

6. Judith Phillips Stanton, 'Charlotte Smith's "Literary Business": Income, Patronage, and Indigence', in Paul J. Korshin, ed., *The Age of Johnson*, vol. 1 (New York: AMS Press, 1987), pp. 376–7.

7. Hookham and Carpenter published *The Romance of the Forest*. Their records are located in the Public Record Office, C104/75/1–3. They comprise three ledgers, the first labelled F (= 1), the second G (= 2) and the third Petty Ledger F (=3). This information comes from the Petty Ledger, p. 191, where the name is spelled 'Mr Ratcliff'. All subsequent references to the ledgers will be indicated in the text by the alphabetical abbreviation of the ledger followed by page number.

8. Carla Hesse, 'Reading Signatures: Female Authorship and Revolutionary Law in France, 1750–1850', *Eighteenth-Century Studies*, 22(3) (1989), 486.

9. *Gentleman's Magazine*, vol. 84, part ii (Dec. 1804), 1178.

10. See Antonia Forster, *Index to Book Reviews in England, 1775–1800* (London: British Library, 1997).

11. Frances Burney, *Camilla*, ed. Edward A. and Lillian D. Bloom (Oxford University Press, 1982), pp. xix–xx.

12. Jan Fergus and Janice Farrar Thaddeus, 'Women, Publishers, and Money, 1790–1820', *Studies in Eighteenth-Century Culture*, 17 (1987), 198 and n. 38, 206–7.

13. Laetitia-Matilda Hawkins, *Memoirs, Anecdotes, Facts, and Opinions*, 2 vols. (London: Longman, Hurst, *et al.*, 1824), vol. 1, p. 156.

14. Jan Fergus, 'Laetitia-Matilda Hawkins's Anonymous Novels Identified', *Notes and Queries*, New Series, 54 (2007), 152–6.

15. Edward Copeland, *Women Writing about Money: Women's Fiction in England, 1790–1820* (Cambridge University Press, 1995), ch. 7. See also calculations of various levels of income, pp. 24–33.

16. Jan Fergus, *Provincial Readers in Eighteenth-Century England* (Oxford University Press, 2006), p. 82.

17. William St Clair, *The Reading Nation in the Romantic Period* (Cambridge University Press, 2004), pp. 221–2.

18. When Austen sold the copyright of *Susan* for £10 in 1803, novels cost about 3s. 6d. per volume; by 1813, they had doubled: Egerton charged 6s. per volume for *Pride and Prejudice*.

19. See James Raven and Antonia Forster, *The English Novel 1770–1829: A Bibliographical Survey of Prose Fiction Published in the British Isles*, vol. 1 (Oxford University Press, 2000).

20. Fergus, *Provincial Readers*, pp. 52–9.

21. Samuel Smiles, *A Publisher and His Friends: Memoir and Correspondence of the Late John Murray*, 2 vols. (London: John Murray, 1891), vol. 1, p. 228.

22. Mary Russell Mitford, *The Life of Mary Russell Mitford*, ed. A. G. L'Estrange and William Harness, 3 vols. (London: Richard Bentley, 1870), vol. 1, p. 300.

23. I have arrived at these figures by examining the Archives of the House of Longman, microfilmed by Chadwyck-Healey (Cambridge, England), hereafter cited as Longman; I have used Longman's costs for books of comparable length produced at the same time as Austen's to calculate the probable sizes and costs of editions she published with Egerton (whose records do not survive). Because my conclusions about Austen's editions and profits differ significantly from other accounts, I have documented my calculations in detail in the notes to ch. 5 of *Jane*

Austen: A Literary Life; those interested may refer to those notes. The Longman records usefully supplement those of Austen's later publisher John Murray. For very different estimates of Austen's editions and profits, see (among others) Jane Aiken Hodge, 'Jane Austen and her Publishers', in John Halperin, ed., *Jane Austen: Bicentenary Essays* (Cambridge University Press, 1975), pp. 75–85.

24. Longman reel 1, 1/2/156.
25. R. W. Chapman (ed.), *The Novels of Jane Austen*, vol. 6: *Minor Works* (Oxford University Press, 1954), plate facing p. 242.
26. Quoted by David Gilson, *A Bibliography of Jane Austen* (Oxford: Clarendon Press, 1982), p. 25.
27. Quoted by Deirdre Le Faye, *Jane Austen: A Family Record*, 2nd edn (Cambridge University Press, 2004), p. 188.
28. These estimations are based upon Gilson's bibliographical analysis of the novel: despite being somewhat longer than *SS*, *PP* was printed in fewer sheets, 36.5 instead of 38, using slightly smaller type in the second and third volumes. With his own profits at stake, Egerton shaved costs.
29. Robert Lowth, *A Short Introduction to English Grammar* (1762), p. 58, quoted by K. C. Phillipps, *Jane Austen's English* (London: André Deutsch, 1970), p. 125.
30. See Austen's note of 'Profits of my Novels', reproduced in facsimile in *Plan of a Novel* (Oxford: Clarendon Press, 1926); hereafter cited as 'Note on profits'.
31. Sidney Ives, *The Trial of Mrs. Leigh Perrot* (Boston, MA: Stinehour Press, 1980), p. iii; Deirdre Le Faye conjectures that this fragment was written to Frank Austen, *Family Record*, p. 210.
32. Bodleian MS Autog d 11/244^r; printed in William and Richard Arthur Austen-Leigh, *Jane Austen: Her Life and Letters. A Family Record*, 2nd edn (London: 1913; reissued New York: Russell and Russell, 1965), p. 311.
33. Austen must have made over £310 from *MP*, according to the letter from Henry to John Murray cited later in the text, for Henry asserts that she received from her small edition of *SS* (£140) and a moderate one of *MP* more than the £450 Murray had offered for the copyrights of *SS*, *MP* and *E*. She also invested the bulk of profits from her novels in £600 worth of 'Navy Fives', according to her own 'Note on profits'. Scholars have assumed that this £600 represents clear profit, but in fact 'Navy Fives' always sold at a discount during the period when Austen could have purchased them. Her investment cost her less than £600, and her profits were accordingly smaller than has been assumed. Although we cannot calculate her earnings precisely without knowing the date on which she made her purchase, we can nonetheless infer the size of the first edition of *MP* and arrive at an approximation of Austen's profits on it. Accordingly, I calculate that she earned from £310 on *MP* to a little over £347.
34. Quoted by Gilson, *A Bibliography of Jane Austen*, pp. 66–7.
35. Bodleian MS Autog d 11/224^r; W. and R. A. Austen-Leigh, *Jane Austen: Her Life and Letters. A Family Record*, p. 310.
36. See 'Note on profits'.
37. Exactly 539 copies of *E* were remaindered at 2s. apiece on 25 January 1821, 498 copies of *MP* at 2s. 6d. and 282 copies of *NA* and *P* at 3s. 1d. (Murray Archives, BB 1/228–9; BB 1/242–3; BB 2/28–9; Copies Ledger B/151). British Library Add. Mss. 46611, ff. 305, 311, 313 records the sale of Austen's copyrights to Richard Bentley. Austen and her heirs also received profits on the second edition of *Sense*

and Sensibility, which came to about £32 during her lifetime, according to her 'Note on profits', and an unknown sum afterwards; the existence of this edition no doubt helped to lower Murray's offer for the three copyrights.

38. Murray Archives, Copies Day Book (CB)/B/128.

39. Le Faye, *A Family Record*, pp. 234, 247.

40. James Edward Austen Leigh, *Memoir of Jane Austen*, ed. R. W. Chapman (1926; repr. Oxford: Clarendon Press, 1967), p. 138. The *Memoir* was originally issued in 1870.

41. For this diagnosis, see Zachary Cope, 'Jane Austen's Last Illness', reprinted in *Collected Reports of the Jane Austen Society, 1949–1965* (1967; repr. Folkestone: William Dawson and Sons, 1990), pp. 267–72.

42. Elizabeth Jenkins, 'Some Banking Accounts of the Austen Family', *Annual Report of the Jane Austen Society* (1954); repr. *Collected Reports of the Jane Austen Society, 1949–1965*, intro. Elizabeth Jenkins (1967; repr. Overton, Hampshire: Jane Austen Society, 1990), p. 59.

43. *Collected Reports, 1966–1975*, p. 39 (1967). Legacy duty came to £16.16.8; see Le Faye, *Family Record*, p. 259.

44. Murray Archives, Copies Ledger B/142,151.

45. Murray Archives, Customer Ledger D/550.

46. Austen had received during her lifetime more than £310 (and up to £347) from *MP*, £250 from *SS* and *PP*, £71.6.1 partial profits on *E* and the second edition of *SS*; Cassandra's £784.11.0 from Murray and £210 from Bentley bring the total to £1625.17.1 at least (see British Library Add. Mss. 46611, ff. 305, 311, 313). Some further payments from Egerton for the second edition of *SS* were certainly also received, and more profit on *MP* is very likely.

47. Fergus and Thaddeus, 'Women, Publishers, and Money, 1790–1820', p. 205, n. 27.

48. Her sister Cassandra had an income of £50 a year from the legacy of £1,000 left her by her fiancé Tom Fowle; her mother had by her own account £122 a year in 1820 (Richard A. Austen-Leigh, *Austen Papers, 1704–1856* (London: Spottiswoode, Ballantyne, 1942), p. 264); even her brother Henry after his bankruptcy obtained the curacy of Chawton at 52 guineas a year (Le Faye, *A Family Record*, p. 212).

49. Fergus and Thaddeus, 'Women, Publishers, and Money', *passim*.

50. *Collected Reports of the Jane Austen Society, 1949–1965*, intro. Jenkins, p. 59.

2

THOMAS KEYMER

Northanger Abbey and Sense and Sensibility

Walter Scott was reviewing *Emma* when he noted Jane Austen's resistance to the trashy sensationalism of much modern fiction – 'the ephemeral productions which supply the regular demand of watering-places and circulating libraries' – and her commitment instead to close, nuanced representation of quotidian life.[1] Yet it is in *Northanger Abbey* and *Sense and Sensibility*, respectively the first of Austen's novels to be accepted for publication and the first to be actually published, that the process Scott described is best observed. As well as showing the emergence of Austen's own distinctive manner, these novels make clear that her relationship to the extravagant themes and overwrought conventions of fashionable genre fiction involved something more complex and interesting than outright rejection. Scott was right, of course, that Austen distances herself from escapist romance, and on some counts we might compare her stance with the contrarian aesthetic of William Wordsworth, whose 1800 preface to *Lyrical Ballads* excoriates 'frantic novels' and the 'degrading thirst after outrageous stimulation' to which they catered, insisting instead that 'the human mind is capable of being excited without the application of gross and violent stimulants'.[2] In Austen too, as in Wordsworth, we find a writer of great innovative power substituting new kinds of discipline and measure in place of hyperbole and excess, convinced that rhetorically less is artistically more. Yet *Northanger Abbey* and *Sense and Sensibility* also display an exuberant immersion in, even a wry appreciation of, the nervy routines and tawdry formulas of circulating-library fiction. In their close parodic attention to the Gothic novel and the novel of sensibility in particular, they show Austen's engagement with the market-leading genres of fiction in her day – the fiction disparaged by Scott and denounced by Wordsworth – to be a matter of creative transformation, not fastidious recoil.

A long tradition in Austen criticism approaches *Northanger Abbey* and *Sense and Sensibility* (typically alongside *Pride and Prejudice*) as early novels: works by an aspiring twenty-something writer who was steeped in the fiction of her published contemporaries and yearned to join their ranks. Family memory records that *Sense and Sensibility*, though not appearing in print until 1811, was begun in 1797, drawing on a yet earlier manuscript fiction that probably dates back to 1795 and was probably epistolary in form. 'I am sure that something of the same story & characters had been written earlier & called Elinor & Marianne', writes Austen's sister Cassandra in a much-cited memorandum, to which she adds that 'North-hanger Abbey was written about the years 98 & 99'.[3] Prophecy, not memory, is the special field of Cassandras, and too much weight may have been attached to her testimony by critics wanting to reconstruct the development of Austen's art. But *Northanger Abbey* certainly existed in publishable form by spring 1803, when it was bought by the bookseller Benjamin Crosby under the title 'Susan' – a title that later became 'Catherine', probably because another author's *Susan: A Novel* was published in 1809, at which point Austen made the first of two attempts to recover publication rights from the inactive Crosby. Her enduring anger about Crosby's suppression of a work he at first seemed eager to publish (*Susan* was announced several times in 1803 as 'In the Press')[4] is evident from the 'Advertisement' she wrote on finally buying back her manuscript in 1816. 'That any bookseller should purchase what he did not think it worth while to publish seems extraordinary', Austen now declares in Johnsonian tones of controlled contempt (note the crushing parallelism of 'purchase ... publish'). Hence the regrettable belatedness, she adds, of 'parts of the work which thirteen years have made comparatively obsolete'. By the time of posthumous publication in December 1817, packaged into a four-volume set with the much more recent *Persuasion*, the thirteen years had stretched to almost fifteen.

Considerable blurring arises, however, from any attempt to divide Austen's six full-length novels into radically separate categories of 'early' and 'late': three clever, self-conscious but callow experiments of the later 1790s (three because *Pride and Prejudice*, as 'First Impressions', had been submitted and rejected for publication in 1797), followed after a largely fallow decade by the three psychologically complex, technically flawless achievements of Austen's maturity in the 1810s. Quite apart from the possible origin of elements from *Emma* or *Mansfield Park* in years-old manuscript fragments such as 'The Watsons', internal as well as external evidence makes clear that Austen's confession of belatedness did not tell the whole story about *Northanger Abbey*, or by association *Sense and Sensibility*, both of which bear significant traces of later, perhaps multi-stage, revision. It is true that certain specifications were not updated, and changing fashions in dress are a mark of this. In *Northanger Abbey*, Mrs Allen scoffs at the outmoded gown of a woman at Bath ('How old fashioned it is! Look at the back'), but by regency standards she and everyone else in the novel are no less out of style, with their very 1790s muslins and their retro high-piled hair (*NA* 1:2:14–15). Yet the same novel also bears traces of events and texts that Austen could not have known when she wrote the original version, or even when she sold it to Crosby. When Catherine emerges 'through the Pump-yard to the archway, opposite Union-passage', she comes on a thoroughfare that was not so named until 1807 (1:7:38). When Henry Tilney mocks the expression 'a very nice walk', remarking that 'now every commendation on every subject is comprised in that one word' (1:14:109), Austen seems to be reworking a joke about another voguish but vacuous usage of interest to her – the word 'sentimental' – which did not appear in print until 1804. 'Every thing clever and agreeable is comprehended in that word', as Lady Bradshaigh told the novelist Samuel Richardson in an otherwise unpublished letter of 1749, dryly adding that she had heard a friend speak of 'taking a *sentimental* walk'.[5]

The revision of *Northanger Abbey* cannot be dated with certainty, then, to 1809, 1816 or any other year or years, but it demonstrably took place, and however incomplete or unsystematic it may have been, it reminds us that this, *Sense and Sensibility*, and Austen's novels in general were incremental processes, not instant products. The definitive statement is by Kathryn Sutherland, for whom stories about Austen based on essentially discrete phases of output are falsifying. The years of publication from 1811 to 1817 were 'the culmination of some twenty to thirty years of drafting, redrafting and continued experiment ... there is no seamless division into early, middle and late writing, but instead a vital and unexpected revision of material over a considerable period.'[6]

Northanger Abbey

If the *Northanger Abbey* of 1817 is not exactly the *Susan* of 1803, and probably not the *Catherine* of 1809 or later, the most obvious difference to comment on is the title. There is no knowing that this title was chosen by Austen herself, and scholars tend to attribute it to Cassandra or her brother Henry. But it is nonetheless appropriate to the text in its posthumously published form. As in *Mansfield Park*, 'North-hanger Abbey' (to return to Cassandra's instructive spelling) emphasizes the resonances and implications of setting over character (*Emma*) or abstract theme (*Persuasion*), and at one level can be understood naturalistically. A hanger is a steep-sloped or 'hanging' wood, as at Colonel Brandon's picturesque Delaford Hanger (*SS* 3:14:425), and there was a real-life North Hanger Farm outside Southampton, where Austen resided between leaving Bath in 1806 and settling at Chawton three years later.[7] More important, as Tony Tanner notes in his landmark essay 'Anger in the Abbey', Austen's place name expresses the hidden but in the end dominant mood of the Abbey's mercurial owner.[8] It also indicates the heroine's humiliating transformation, in General Tilney's eyes, from a guest to be honoured and courted as a prize into a suspect hanger-on – a dependant or parasite, in the usage of the day – to be peremptorily expelled.

Above all, the published title establishes from the outset, long before Catherine leaves Bath for Northanger, the prevailing intertextual range of Austen's work: a range dominated by the Gothic novel, a well-established but still immensely popular genre that had been inaugurated by romances such as Horace Walpole's *The Castle of Otranto* (1764) and was still going strong when Thomas Love Peacock wrote his satirical *Nightmare Abbey* in 1818. A literature of terror that included in its gory repertoire sensational stories of abduction and atrocity, spine-tingling occult or supernatural effects, and a hyperbolic rhetoric of sublime description, the Gothic novel was diversifying rapidly by the 1790s, and recent scholarship has emphasized the heterogeneity of the mode. For Terry Castle, the 1790s were 'the break-out decade of Gothic experimentation'; James Watt describes Gothic throughout the Romantic period as a set of competing assumptions and conventions, not a stable or cohesive whole.[9] That said, certain basic tropes were widely shared, and Gothic fiction was characterized in general by temporally or geographically remote settings – often medieval, often Mediterranean – in which enlightened modern constraints on plot and action – manners and morals, customs and laws – were conveniently in abeyance. By locating climactic plot events in the winding labyrinths and gloomy recesses of ancient monasteries or ruined castles, it cultivated an atmosphere headily laden with enthralling psychosexual connotation.

Settings of this kind were almost mandatory in the years before Austen drafted the novel, and in 1796 the *Critical Review* complained about the formulaic monotony of the genre while exempting its foremost exponent: 'Since Mrs Radcliffe's justly admired and successful romances, the press has teemed with stories of haunted castles and visionary terrors; the incidents of which are so little diversified, that criticism is at a loss to vary its remarks.'[10] Abbeys held special allure, with the opportunities they offered for tales of perverted religiosity and inquisitorial torment. Publications from these years include *Roach Abbey* (1794), *The Abbey of St Asaph* (1795), *The Abbey of Clugny* (1796), *Munster Abbey* (1797) and *Grasville Abbey* (1798); Barbara Benedict and Deirdre Le Faye calculate that 'between 1784 and 1818 no fewer than thirty-two novels had been published containing "Abbey" in the title' (*NA* xxx). Austen neatly evokes the representational clichés common to these works to indicate her heroine's fervid anticipation of Northanger. First

Catherine imagines Northanger 'standing low in a valley, sheltered from the north and east by rising woods of oak' (2:2:144), her expectation recalling now-forgotten novels like the anonymous *Waldeck Abbey* (1795), which places the forbidding Waldeck 'on the declivity of a hill ... sheltered on the back by towering woods and groves'.[11] She then makes the elementary error of approaching Northanger before nightfall, but is confident of sublime experience even so: 'every bend in the road was expected with solemn awe to afford a glimpse of its massy walls of grey stone, rising amidst a grove of ancient oaks, with the last beams of the sun playing in beautiful splendour on its high Gothic windows' (2:5:164). Now her mind's eye reflects blood-curdlers such as Regina Maria Roche's *The Children of the Abbey* (1796), where the heroine traverses oakwoods 'scattered over with relics of druidical antiquity', and then admires from 'the massy door' of the abbey 'the dark and stupendous edifice, whose gloom was now heightened by the shadows of evening, with venerable awe'.[12]

Here and elsewhere, Austen points in the direction of sublime overkill but holds back from full-throttle parody, and in the chapters to follow her comedy works through studiously bathetic descriptions of the mundane actualities of Northanger – the elegant, light-filled rooms, the consumer durables and modern comforts – that frustrate Catherine's novel-fuelled desires. Clearly Northanger is not quite the teardown that readers would have known from famous estates such as Wanstead Abbey in Essex, where the original structure had been entirely replaced in the eighteenth century by Richard Tylney, later Earl Tylney, only for the new building to be sold and demolished following the 1812 marriage of Catherine Tylney-Long, reputedly the richest heiress in England at the time, to a profligate gambler.[13] For the future Catherine Tilney of Austen's text, genuine traces of architectural Gothic remain to be seen, like the pointed arches atop the General's bright replacement windows. But her impression above all is of disappointing rational modernity: swept gravel, even casements, pretty china.

At the same time, much of the pleasure of *Northanger Abbey* for readers used to bingeing on disposable fiction must have arisen from the incongruous reiterations of Gothic tags – 'motionless with horror' (2:6:174); 'her blood was chilled' (2:6:175) – that Austen works in throughout the text. It may have been in part for this reason that Austen was so concerned about the novel's best-before date, though some of her best Gothic flourishes – 'Darkness impenetrable and immoveable filled the room' (2:6:174) – are timeless enough to sound like Milton and Mary Shelley at once. Asked by Catherine if Northanger is 'a fine old place, just like what one reads about', Henry replies that they will not need to penetrate 'a hall dimly lighted by the expiring embers of a wood fire' (2:5:161); they will not encounter, in other words, the hackneyed thrills and off-the-peg shivers of Richard Warner's *Netley Abbey* (1795), in which the hero, summoned 'by screams of female distress' into a gloomy refectory, finds the villainous abbot creepily illuminated, as convention required, 'by the expiring embers of a large fire'.[14]

Austen is not playing here, of course, on particular novels, but rather on their idiom in general. The exception is Ann Radcliffe's *The Mysteries of Udolpho* (1794), a point of reference throughout *Northanger Abbey*, and a work that provides Catherine with 'the luxury of a raised, restless, and frightened imagination' (1:7:46) when she devours it on the recommendation of Isabella Thorpe. Even sophisticated Henry has read *Udolpho*, with, he jokes, his 'hair standing on end the whole time' (1:14:108). Creatively and commercially a peak of the genre (Radcliffe received £500 for the manuscript, fifty times more than Crosby paid Austen), *Udolpho* was celebrated especially for the character of Montoni, a brooding sixteenth-century brigand who starves his wife to death in a haunted castle and immures the orphaned heroine there to gain control of her inheritance. It is this novel that dominates Catherine's consciousness in Bath and sets up her exotic fantasies about Northanger, beguiling her mind from the commonplace realities of civilized life in ways that lead to her humiliation.

Yet Austen quietly distinguishes between Radcliffe and her imitators when Catherine at last breaks loose from 'the visions of romance' (2:10:204), and her satirical target is not so much *Udolpho* as the torrent of clumsy replicas that followed in its wake – replicas such as the seven novels 'of the same kind' that Isabella lines up for Catherine to read next, all of which, even the too-good-to-be-true *Horrid Mysteries*, were actual publications of the 1790s (1:6:33). Austen's satire ranges in general over the undistinguished hinterland of bone-chillers that imitated and debased Radcliffe's example, and it also extends – in a work finely attuned to the inanities of genteel slang – to the serious moral fiction that was sometimes held up as a salutary alternative to Gothic. 'Horrid' is for Isabella a term of approval, expressing her frivolous relish for sensation and fright, but a diminished colloquial sense is in play ('horrid' as merely disagreeable to one's taste) when she speaks of Richardson's sprawling novel of manners *Sir Charles Grandison* (1753–4), the favourite reading of Catherine's mother, as an 'amazing horrid book' (1:6:35). On the face of it, Isabella's dislike of Richardson's massive, glacially paced work is an implicit recommendation, and we know from other sources that Austen admired much about *Grandison*. Yet there is also a laugh here at the expense of Richardson's now somewhat dated achievement, an antique, lumbering dinosaur in the smart world of new novels, and one lacking the stylish economy that Austen herself practised and prized. Mrs Morland, with her habit of ignoring the latest books and regularly rereading *Grandison*, sounds like the elderly lady once described by Walter Scott, who liked

Grandison to be read to her above anything else '"because," said she, "should I drop asleep in course of the reading, I am sure, when I awake, I shall have lost none of the story"'.[15]

Austen's witty self-consciousness about the genres of fiction and the techniques of narrative is such, indeed, that little in the history and present state of novel production escapes her satire. Conspicuously, this is the work of a writer whose confidence in her entitlement to publish flows from a knowing immersion in all the varieties of modern fiction, and from a sharp sense of the weaknesses or absurdities of each. It is the work of a writer, moreover, whose excluded position when drafting the novel (following the *First Impressions* disappointment) is rhetorically offset by tones of assured and amused condescension. Even before the satire on Gothic begins, Austen mocks the hackneyed plot devices of other traditions – novels of sensibility, novels about adventurous foundlings, novels of virtue in distress – to which Catherine's placid existence has failed to conform. She also mocks the creaking technical resources of much mainstream fiction since Richardson and Fielding, including the increasingly tired enabling conventions of epistolary and diary fiction (1:3:19–20) and the structural havoc created by interpolated background tales (1:4:27). A wry prediction that Mrs Allen will finally 'reduce poor Catherine to all the desperate wretchedness of which a last volume is capable ... whether by intercepting her letters, ruining her character, or turning her out of doors' (1:2:12) resumes the satire on novels of female persecution – though with some proleptic irony in this case, since being turned out of doors in disgrace is just what Catherine has in store.

Moves of this kind continue throughout *Northanger Abbey*, up to and including Austen's final disavowal – in her teasing inability to decide whether her text works 'to recommend parental tyranny, or reward filial disobedience' (2:16:261) – of didactic domestic fiction. With playful Sternean recognition of the materiality of books, she mocks the wish-fulfilling artifices of the courtship novel, acknowledging that readers 'will see in the tell-tale compression of the pages before them, that we are all hastening together to perfect felicity' (2:16:259). Again the register is pitch perfect, and seasoned novel-readers might have remembered the 'prospects of the most perfect felicity' that open up towards the end of the anonymous *Emilia Belville* (1768), or the happy lovers of Charlotte Smith's *Celestina* (1791), fixed 'in such perfect felicity as is seldom enjoyed'. It is not impossible that Austen stole the underlying joke – a Jane West novel of 1796 censures behaviour 'very opposite to the perfect excellence and perfect felicity which exists in the land of Hymen; as described in the

Utopian geography of many modern novelists' – but she punctures the fictional cliché far more deftly.[16]

Yet Austen is not quite alone in her posture of knowing superiority. Elsewhere her writing betrays real anxieties about options closed off by the achievements of existing novelists, and Frances Burney's *Camilla* (1796) is singled out for praise when the narrative touches on, then rapidly leaves, a subject 'already set forth by the capital pen of a sister author' (1:14:112). Burney is also to the fore in Austen's famous promotion of her fiction (with a novel of 1801 by Maria Edgeworth; this whole passage may be a late addition) as work 'in which the greatest powers of the mind are displayed, in which the most thorough knowledge of human nature, the happiest delineation of its varieties ... are conveyed to the world' (1:5:31). Here Austen associates herself with a tradition of sophisticated social and moral satire that reaches back through Burney to mid-century women writers in Richardson's circle such as Jane Collier, Sarah Fielding and Charlotte Lennox. Sometimes cited as an inspiration behind *Northanger Abbey* is Lennox's *The Female Quixote* (1752), in which a romance-obsessed heroine embarrassingly expects modern life to conform to magical chivalric norms, and is cured at last by an alternative course of reading with Richardsonian realism at its centre. Even in the opening sentence of *Northanger Abbey*, on Catherine's unlikely credentials as 'an heroine' (1:1:5), the gratuitously fussy indefinite article calls to mind Lennox's running (indeed somewhat overplayed) joke about the stereotypes of romance. 'One never has the Idea of an Heroine older than Eighteen', declares Lennox's Arabella, and a later chapter adumbrates 'The necessary Qualities of an Hero and Heroine'.[17] That said, Austen seems not to have worried that she was merely recycling, with application to more recent fashions in fiction, the patterns of Lennox's satire. When another updating of Lennox, Eaton Stannard Barrett's *The Heroine, or Adventures of a Fair Romance Reader*, was published in 1813, Austen could enjoy it as 'a delightful burlesque, particularly on the Radcliffe style' (*L* 256), without any apparent regret that its appearance might jeopardize the still unpublished *Northanger Abbey*.

Perhaps this is because Austen had something subtler in view than Lennox or Barrett. A superficial account of *Northanger Abbey* would see it as the same kind of satire on fiction and delusion, and as a novel of female education in which a naive, novel-fired heroine loses her grasp on reality, confuses a modern gentleman with a Gothic villain, and is instructed out of her errors by a wise suitor. Part of the cleverness of Austen's second volume lies in the mixed messages sent out about General Tilney, but at one level he seems genial enough, not so much the Montoni of Catherine's imaginings as an inoffensive Uncle Toby: a retired veteran whose 'hobby-horse' is growing fruit, and who takes the trouble to procure 'every modern invention to facilitate the labour of the cooks' (*NA* 2:7:182, 2:8:189). By imagining him instead as the murderer of his wife, Catherine has entertained 'grossly injurious suspicions' inspired by her reading. But finally her mind is brought back from 'the alarms of romance' to encounter and recognize, free of distraction from bad literature, the sober and salutary 'anxieties of common life' (2:10:206).

Yet Austen uses Gothic fiction more ingeniously than this, and although she enjoys sending up its more outré mannerisms, it is worth taking more seriously than critics sometimes do her refusal to denigrate it explicitly. Not only does she praise the serious literary novels of Burney and Edgeworth; she will not turn 'contemptuous censure' on pulp fiction and will not echo reviewers who drone on (like Sir Edward Denham in 'Sanditon') about 'the trash with which the press now groans' (1:5:30). To take Gothic novels literally as a guide to modern life may be absurd, but that does not mean that such novels are absurd in themselves, and it may well be that they also have, when approached more intelligently as metaphors of evil, real explanatory power. For the polite world of a modern spa still has its perils and pains, and through clever deployment of Gothic hyperbole in her opening volume – Catherine repeatedly suffers 'dread', 'mortification', 'agony', 'torment' – Austen draws quiet analogies between the trials of a Radcliffe heroine and the everyday but no less absorbing tribulations of an ingénue at Bath. Catherine, after all, is manipulated and deceived by Isabella, and in effect abducted to Blaise Castle by boorish John Thorpe; she is constrained, even imprisoned, in a world of regulated proprieties (the rules of the ballroom, the conventions of the assembly), and cynically exploited by friends whose arms are linked though their hearts are at war (1:13:100). Her predicament is not literally that of a Gothic novel, yet Gothic novels can still express and reveal, as soon as one reads their 'screams of female distress' as metaphorical things, forms of persecution and entrapment that continue to operate, though in new guise, in a world of polite sociability.

In other ways the abortive trip to Blaise Castle, while in the first place indicating the phoniness of the Gothic craze, also brings with it genuinely sinister implications, and in this respect anticipates the alarming subtext of *Mansfield Park*. Antiquity and atmosphere are promised by John Thorpe, and his words arouse in Catherine thrilling fantasies of 'a long suite of lofty rooms, exhibiting the remains of magnificent furniture, though now for many years deserted' (1:11:86). Yet there was nothing authentic at all about Blaise Castle, which consisted of three modern towers encircling a large chamber. An overblown piece of cod medievalism, it had been built in 1766 as a viewpoint and party venue by Thomas Farr, a Bristol merchant whose wealth derived from sugar plantations and the slave trade. Here is another of those moments at which Austen delicately associates the fashions and luxuries satirized in her fiction – the trade in governesses in *Emma*, the opulence of Sir Thomas Bertram's estate – with the pressing offstage evil of Caribbean slavery. Even as Catherine's spine tingles at the thought of Blaise Castle, Austen evokes dungeons built on the suffering not of medieval serfs but of modern slaves. Yet Blaise might also have suggested a better future, a hoped-for end to the mass forms of abduction and imprisonment – those quintessentially Gothic perils – involved in the Atlantic slave trade. By the time Austen drafted *Northanger Abbey*, Farr had been bankrupted by the American war, and his Gothic folly had been acquired by John Scandrett Harford, a Quaker banker and leading Bristol abolitionist; by the time of publication Harford's son and heir, a close ally of Wilberforce, had made the Blaise estate a centre of the abolitionist campaign.[18]

But what of General Tilney? On the face of it, the much-quoted speech in which Henry disabuses Catherine of her suspicions supports Austen's dry observation, a page or two later, that Gothic novels are no guide to life in modern England. Henry's speech is also a masterpiece of double meaning on Austen's part, and he inadvertently implicates General Tilney even as he exonerates him on the surface. The General may not literally have confined his fevered wife in a turret, like Radcliffe's Montoni, or starved her to death. But as Henry's words make plain in spite of himself, he did commit a more muted modern version of the same crime, imprisoning his wife in a loveless marriage ('We have not all, you know, the same tenderness of disposition'), oppressing her everyday life with burdens ('I will not pretend to say that while she lived, she might not often have had much to bear'), and assailing her with irrational anger ('though his temper injured her, his judgment never did'). Perhaps there even is a meaningful sense in which he did kill his long-suffering wife, or at least give her little to live for. It is hard not to be reminded, at any rate, of her merely economic value to the General when Henry concludes, still with conspicuous awkwardness, that 'His value of her was sincere; and, if not permanently, he was truly afflicted by her death' (2:9:203). As Austen takes care to let slip in advance, the former Miss Drummond had been a wealthy heiress whose father 'gave her twenty thousand pounds, and five hundred to buy wedding-clothes' (1:9:65); happily for the General, the cash has lasted longer than his grief. It continues to fund the little luxuries of Northanger – the fruit trees, the kitchen gadgets, the costly gilding – as surely as the labour of slaves funds the pleasures of Mansfield.

In this context, other things about the General fall into place: the damp he casts on his children's spirits in Bath even as Catherine still thinks him 'so charming a man' (2:5:159); the 'violence' and 'scolding' that alternate with his smiles at the first Northanger dinner (2:6:170); the pervasive impression of suppressed malignity from which Catherine eventually concludes 'that in suspecting General Tilney of either murdering or shutting up his wife, she had scarcely sinned against his character, or magnified his cruelty' (2:15:201). More subliminal touches reinforce the sense of menace that Austen builds around the General, including the 'unquiet slumbers' that Catherine suffers at Northanger, which ominously connect her with a murder victim of Shakespeare's Richard III (2:13:234; cf. *Richard III*, III.ii.27). He is indeed a latter-day Montoni, as he goes on to prove in his brutal expulsion of Catherine from Northanger – a clever reversal of Gothic convention by Austen (since heroines are normally walled in, not thrown out) that nonetheless reveals his underlying affinity with Radcliffe's villain. Just as Montoni seeks to acquire the inheritance of *Udolpho*'s heroine, so the General seeks money and land – more land – from Austen's Catherine Morland, mistakenly assuming her to be a second Miss Drummond.[19] It is fair to say in this context that reading Radcliffe has in the most important sense not misled Catherine at all; on the contrary, Radcliffe has helped her perceive the General's nature more accurately than anyone else, including his son. Her one mistake has been to think of Gothic as literally applicable to a modern world in which there is 'security for the existence even of a wife not beloved, in the laws of the land, and the manners of the age' (2:10:205). Conspicuously, Austen leaves this list of securities for existence at that, as though to imply that while laws and manners may have changed, human malice has not, and has merely adjusted its methods to fit the times. Without the rather fragile infrastructure of modern society, with its newspapers, roads and nosy neighbours, unloved wives might still be done away with, and unsuspecting heiresses fleeced.

Sense and Sensibility

Elements of parody and metafiction are less overt in *Sense and Sensibility*, and it has been argued that Austen at last broke into the world of publication by melting into the generic background rather than by asserting her difference. For Barbara Benedict, *Sense and Sensibility* in its post-epistolary incarnation of 1811 becomes a state-of-the-art regency novel, or at least open to consumption as such. With its focus on female experience and emotion, and the struggles of young women against romantic obstacles and social conventions, it did not resist so much as repeat the popular, marketable routines of love fiction: 'episodic adventures of familiar, sympathetic heroines, designed for a rapid read'.[20] Deidre Lynch places stronger emphasis on what distinguishes Austen from, as well as links her with, standard circulating-library fare, but similarly concludes that *Sense and Sensibility* 'indulges novel readers with the pleasures of instant legibility – the pleasure of character *types*'. Lynch points out here the overlapping language of mechanized printing and formula fiction (the terms 'stereotype' and 'cliché' were both coined in Austen's day to denote new technologies of reproduction), but also sees Austen as investing the staple characters from which she begins with complex new impressions of interior life. Pitting round characters against flat, and 'reworking what her contemporaries did in juxtaposing a self-effacing heroine with her overdressed foil', *Sense and Sensibility* uses a uniquely flexible version of free indirect discourse (a technique for representing consciousness inherited from Burney and *Grandison*) to refresh and reanimate otherwise fairly familiar plot material.[21]

That said, Austen intermittently continues to flaunt her disruption of standard fictional patterns, and as in *Northanger Abbey* she does so by creating a heroine whose experience fails to conform to the literary models shaping her imagination. We hear less in *Sense and Sensibility* than in *Northanger Abbey* about what the co-heroine Marianne Dashwood reads, but even when poetry rather than fiction is specified, her reading locates us firmly in the realm of the novel of sensibility, a genre characterized by mawkish, emotionally overwrought representations of feeling, and underpinned by an ethics in which the capacity to feel displaces traditional virtues as the highest mark of moral worth. Marianne is a devotee of the poet Cowper, we soon learn (*SS* 1:3:20), and this detail not only aligns her with sentimental types like the tremulous heroine of Elizabeth Isabella Spence's *Helen Sinclair* (1799), whose favourite recreation is to stroll in the woods with her like-minded lover and 'a volume of Cowper', on reading which 'a look of intelligence spoke how much they felt'. Marianne's choice also recalls, in view of Austen's title, Cowper's valorization of feeling and sympathy over worldly reason: 'I would not enter on my list of friends / (Though graced with polish'd manners and fine sense / Yet wanting sensibility) the man / Who needlessly sets foot upon a worm.'[22]

In a manner reminiscent of Catherine Morland and Gothic, Marianne approaches her daily experience as a lived-out novel of sensibility. When Colonel Brandon mentions but then abruptly leaves a story about female ruin, Elinor senses how Marianne's imagination would have novelized it 'in the most melancholy order of disastrous love' (1:11:67); rescued by Willoughby from the rain-lashed downs, her immediate response is to find 'his person and air . . . equal to what her fancy had ever drawn for the hero of a favourite story' (1:9:51). This particular mistake is excusable enough, since for her part Austen gives much of the plot a teasing resemblance to the same genre, and a sentimental tale has even been uncovered, in the *Lady's Magazine* for 1794, in which the heroine finds love when rescued from drowning by a dashing stranger named Willoughby (*SS* 449; the heroine is a Miss Brandon). In the somewhat dispiriting final chapter of *Sense and Sensibility*, however, Marianne is disabused. In coming to love the unglamorous Colonel Brandon, she is forced to recognize that assumptions drawn from her favourite genre – the assumption, in particular, that broken-hearted lovers can never love again – do not match experience in the world. The novel closes with a distinct anticipation of the opening of *Northanger Abbey*, in which no one 'would have supposed [Catherine] born to be an heroine' (*NA* 1:1:5), except that in this case Marianne is 'born to discover the falsehood of her own opinions, and to counteract, by her conduct, her most favourite maxims' (*SS* 3:14:429). Where Catherine finds that modern life is not literally a Gothic novel, Marianne finds that it is not a novel of sensibility, in which she would strictly speaking have fallen 'a sacrifice to an irresistible passion, as once she had fondly flattered herself with expecting' (3:14:429). By the same token, adds Austen, any assumption that a repentant Willoughby will have fallen in with generic norms and 'died of a broken heart, must not be depended on' (3:14:430).

If *Sense and Sensibility* refuses to conform to the lineaments of a sentimental novel, however, in other respects it bears comparison with an alternative fictional type. By the time Austen first drafted the text, and certainly when she published it, the late eighteenth-century culture of sensibility had come under attack on various grounds and from numerous sources, ranging from the conservative Hannah More, for whom self-regarding feeling was a pernicious distraction from duty and practical action, to the radical Mary Wollstonecraft, for whom it worked to enfeeble and marginalize its mainly female devotees. Popular novels themselves exhibit this trend, and in titles such as *Excessive Sensibility* (1787), *Arulia, or The Victim of Sensibility* (1790) and *The Errors of Sensibility* (1793), the cherished virtue of exquisite feeling comes to be associated with debility, danger or deception. In the mid-1790s, didactic contrast novels such as Maria Edgeworth's *Letters of Julia and Caroline* (1795) and Jane West's *A Gossip's Story* (1796) juxtaposed the attitudes and adventures of contrasting protagonists, typically proposing one as a model of resolute virtue, the other as a warning against disabling feeling. In the classic account of Marilyn Butler, it is directly in this mould that *Sense and Sensibility* is cast, and although detecting occasional authorial impatience with the rigidity of the contrast structure, Butler argues that Austen 'conscientiously maintains the principle of a didactic comparison … The entire action is organized to represent Elinor and Marianne in terms of rival value-systems.'[23]

It is certainly easy to detect a pattern in which Marianne's extravagant demonstrations of feeling are unfavourably contrasted with Elinor's self-command and commitment to propriety. From the opening chapter of a narrative that is typically (though by no means invariably) focalized through Elinor's perspective, we witness Elinor's concern at 'the excess of her sister's sensibility' (1:1:7), and throughout the novel Austen depicts Marianne in terms of an established fictional repertoire of faintings, fits and fevers. Later episodes show Marianne adopt exactly the postures, and reiterate exactly the gestures, of countless sentimental heroines before her. Abandoned by the capricious Willoughby, she falls into 'a silent agony, too much oppressed even for tears' (2:6:203); she then composes the obligatory epistolary *cri de cœur*, 'writing as fast as a continual flow of tears would permit her' (2:7:205). Meanwhile, and in the face of comparable trials from her own rather feckless lover, Elinor exerts herself to maintain appearances of fortitude and control, exemplary in her unruffled manner, dry eyes, and measured, undemonstrative language. The most obvious characteristic they share is a helpful habit of drawing explicit contrasts between one another – 'you, because you communicate, and I, because I conceal nothing', as Marianne spells it out at one point (2:5:193) – but in other respects they seem entirely different in attitude and conduct. The difference is dramatized as well as explained, nowhere more effectively than in their different styles of appearing at dinner in the immediate wake of emotional crisis. Following Willoughby's first snub, Marianne is swollen-eyed and unable to speak, and eventually bursts into tears and leaves the room. There is a sense, moreover, in which she does so from perverse principle and not only from uncontrolled emotion, dominated as her thinking is by novelistic models of extreme sensibility: 'she was without any power, because she was without any desire of command over herself' (1:15:95), and in the night to follow 'would have thought herself very inexcusable had she been able to sleep at all' (1:16:96).

Where Marianne thinks composure a disgrace, Elinor works obsessively in the same situation at self-command, that stoical virtue which, for the great philosopher of sentimentalism Adam Smith, was a constantly needed check on the passions and feelings. Throughout the novel, 'composure of mind' is for the elder sister a hard-won but all-important achievement, 'the effect of constant and painful exertion' (3:1:299). Yet just as there is audible mockery of Marianne in Austen's account of her determination to be unable to sleep, so there seems something less than full approval, and a sense of almost inhuman self-denial, in her later account of Elinor's inscrutable, unshaken demeanour 'when she joined them at dinner only two hours after she had first suffered the extinction of all her dearest hopes' (2:1:161). At such moments, the contrast between sensibility and sense, extravagant emotionalism and strenuous self-discipline, seems clear enough – but is this a straightforward contrast between wrong and right?

As critics of Butler's position have often maintained, there are several reasons to pause before seeing *Sense and Sensibility* as an unequivocal replication, as opposed to a subtle complication, of the polarized absolutes of the contrast novel.[24] In the first place, it is by no means self-evident that the talismanic words in Austen's title, which after all are cognate terms, should be understood in binary opposition, and in figures such as Colonel Brandon – 'undoubtedly a sensible man' (3:4:329) – they coalesce into a harmonious (though also somewhat unprepossessing) amalgam of feeling and reason. Another way of reading the title would be by analogy with *Pride and Prejudice*, which explores overlapping, interweaving characteristics, not a clash of opposites. For every novel of the period in which 'sense' and 'sensibility' are antithetical terms, moreover, another recognizes their congruence. In Elizabeth Gunning's *The Orphans of Snowdon* (1797), the bereaved heroine attempts to subdue rather than indulge her sorrows, only to find that 'the victory of sense over sensibility is not easily obtained'. But in Isabella Kelly's *The Abbey of St Asaph* (1795), the heroine (named Elinor) is introduced with 'all the mild virtues beaming in her eyes, while sense and sensibility animated her charming features'; this novel later compliments another character for her ability to console the distressed with both reason and feeling: 'your sense would direct, and your sensibility sooth me'.[25] Plenty of indications in Austen's novel suggest that her interest is not only in contrasting the sense of one sister with the sensibility of the other – 'the same steady conviction and affectionate counsel on Elinor's side, the same impetuous feelings and varying opinions on Marianne's' (2:9:228) – regular and emphatic though these contrasts are. Her several ambiguous uses of the adjective 'sensible' (possessing either sense, or sensibility, or both) look calculated to confuse the issue, so that Marianne is 'sensible and clever' when credited with Elinor-like 'sense' in the opening chapter (1:1:7–8), while Elinor is later 'feelingly sensible' in Marianne's style, afflicted by 'an emotion and distress beyond any thing she had ever felt before' (1:22:153, 155). A properly flexible account of *Sense and Sensibility* would see it as a novel in which binaries break down, with Elinor learning the legitimacy of feeling and Marianne attempting self-command, to the point where the former can be praised for a 'strongly felt' emotion, and the latter for showing 'resolute composure' (3:3:321, 2:10:246).

Yet even if one accepts that *Sense and Sensibility* is a novel of antithetical characters and characteristics, it is by no means self-evident that the 'sensibility' side of the equation is entirely rejected. Like *Northanger Abbey*, turning as it does on the subjection of Miss Morland and before her Miss Drummond to mercenary wooing, *Sense and Sensibility* is a novel about exploitation, and exploitation in a variety of senses, emotional and social as well as economic. Strict patrilineal inheritance leaves Elinor and Marianne financially vulnerable, and the attrition is compounded by their brother's monstrous wife, a one-woman Goneril and Regan show – 'They will have no carriage, no horses, and hardly any servants' (1:2:14) – who tips them into genteel poverty. From this predicament their only escape is through marriage, yet here too the deck is stacked against them by custom and convention, in particular by proprieties of courtship that confine them in roles of passive expectation while conferring agency and power on their callous suitors – an effect intensified by further interference from Fanny Dashwood. In this context, Elinor's refusal to turn a hair two hours after the extinction of her hopes implies not only robotic repression but also a certain complicity, a perverse endorsement of social codes that work to restrict and oppress her. By contrast, Marianne's habit of causing stirs and making scenes, while at one level a mark of culpable self-absorption, also works to disrupt the serenity of social mechanisms that empower rank and wealth at the expense of both sisters. In this sense, histrionics are her only available means of registering protest or fighting back. At times there seems something rather knowing about her violation of the behavioural proprieties on which the whole system depends, as when she acknowledges having 'erred against every common-place notion of decorum; I have been open and sincere where I ought to have been reserved, spiritless, dull, and deceitful' (1:10:57). At others, her attacks on cold-eyed pragmatism in society are more than mere effusions of unworldly sensibility, and in the context of Austen's plots in general they sound cogent and compelling: witness her insistence that marriage should be more than 'a compact of convenience ... a commercial exchange, in which each wished to be benefited at the expense of the other' (1:8:45).

Here Marianne puts her finger on that pervasive theme in Austen which for the poet W. H. Auden a century later made James Joyce seem comparatively 'innocent as grass': her disconcerting ability, as Auden puts it in playfully *marxisant* terms, to 'Describe the amorous effects of "brass", / Reveal so frankly and with such sobriety / The economic basis of society'.[26] Marianne is more at such moments than a vehicle for satire on novels of sensibility, and she both demonstrates and articulates an element of social critique in Austen that is no less real for being partial and indirect. As Catherine Morland in her Gothic delusions gets the master of Northanger Abbey more or less right, so Marianne in her sentimental histrionics responds to the calculating world of Willoughby and Fanny Dashwood with a quite justifiable scream of female distress.

NOTES

1. Walter Scott, unsigned review of *Emma*, *Quarterly Review* (dated October 1815, published March 1816), repr. in Southam (ed.), *Jane Austen: The Critical Heritage*, p. 59.
2. *Literary Criticism of William Wordsworth*, ed. Paul M. Zall (Lincoln, NE: University of Nebraska Press, 1966), p. 21. On the excitement of the ordinary in Austen and Wordsworth, see Patricia Meyer Spacks's witty chapter on *Sense and Sensibility* and *Lyrical Ballads* in her *Boredom: The Literary History of a State of Mind* (University of Chicago Press, 1996), pp. 111–28; also Stuart M. Tave, 'Jane Austen and One of Her Contemporaries', in John Halperin (ed.), *Jane Austen: Bicentenary Essays* (Cambridge University Press, 1975), pp. 61–74.
3. See the full transcription by Kathryn Sutherland, 'Chronology of Composition and Publication', in Janet Todd (ed.), *Jane Austen in Context* (Cambridge University Press, 2005), p. 16.
4. Crosby's abortive campaign (such as it was) is documented by Anthony Mandal, *Jane Austen and the Popular Novel* (Basingstoke: Palgrave Macmillan, 2007), pp. 69–70.
5. C. J. Rawson, '"Nice" and "Sentimental": A Parallel between *Northanger Abbey* and Richardson's *Correspondence*', *Notes and Queries* 11(5) (1964), 180. For comparable evidence about stages of revision in *Sense and Sensibility*, see SS xxiii.
6. Sutherland, 'Chronology', pp. 13, 15.
7. In Totton, Hants (*An Abstract of All the Claims on the New Forest* (Salisbury, 1776), p. 153).
8. Tony Tanner, *Jane Austen* (Basingstoke: Macmillan, 1986), pp. 43–74.
9. Terry Castle, 'The Gothic Novel', in *The Cambridge History of English Literature, 1660–1780* (Cambridge University Press, 2005), p. 693; James Watt, *Contesting the Gothic: Fiction, Genre, and Cultural Conflict, 1764–1832* (Cambridge University Press, 1999).
10. Peter Garside, James Raven and Rainer Schöwerling (eds.), *The English Novel 1770–1829: A Bibliographical Survey*, 2 vols. (Oxford University Press, 2000), vol. I, p. 629, quoting the *Critical Review* (February 1796) on *Austenburn Castle* (1795).
11. *Waldeck Abbey*, 2 vols. (1795), vol. I, p. 49.
12. Regina Maria Roche, *The Children of the Abbey*, 4 vols. (1796), vol. I, pp. 287, 288.
13. W. R. Powell (ed.), *A History of the County of Essex, Volume VI* (Woodbridge: Boydell & Brewer, 1973), pp. 322–7.
14. Richard Warner, *Netley Abbey*, 2 vols. (1795), vol. I, p. 145.
15. T. C. Duncan Eaves and Ben D. Kimpel, *Samuel Richardson: A Biography* (Oxford: Clarendon Press, 1971), p. 389, quoting Scott's 'Memoir' of Richardson in *Ballantyne's Novelist's Library*, VI (1824), p. xlvi.
16. *The History of Miss Emilia Belville*, 2 vols. (1768), vol. II, p. 214; Charlotte Smith, *Celestina*, 4 vols. (1791), vol. IV, p. 349; Jane West, *A Gossip's Story*, 2 vols. (1796), vol. II, p. 96.
17. Charlotte Lennox, *The Female Quixote*, ed. Margaret Dalziel (Oxford University Press, 1970), pp. 111, 148.

18. Peter Wakelin, 'Harford family (c.1700–1866)', *ODNB*; G.C. Boase, rev. Charles Brayne, 'John Scandrett Harford (1787–1866)', *ODNB*.

19. It has recently been argued that he confuses Catherine's patrons the Allens with descendants of the quarrying magnate Ralph Allen, the wealthiest man in mid eighteenth-century Bath (Janine Barchas, 'Mapping *Northanger Abbey*', *Review of English Studies*, 60(245) (2009) 431–59).

20. Barbara M. Benedict, 'Sensibility by the Numbers: Austen's Work as Regency Popular Fiction', in Deidre Shauna Lynch (ed.), *Janeites: Austen's Disciples and Devotees* (Princeton University Press, 2000), p. 64.

21. Deidre Shauna Lynch, *The Economy of Character: Novels, Market Culture, and the Business of Inner Meaning* (University of Chicago Press, 1998), pp. 211, 232.

22. Elizabeth Isabella Spence, *Helen Sinclair*, 2 vols. (1799), vol. II, pp. 116–17; William Cowper, *The Task* (1785), book VI, lines 560–3.

23. Marilyn Butler, *Jane Austen and the War of Ideas* (Oxford: Clarendon Press, 1975), pp. 183, 184.

24. See, for example, alternative readings by Claudia L. Johnson, *Jane Austen: Women, Politics, and the Novel* (University of Chicago Press, 1988), pp. 49–72; Peter Knox-Shaw, *Jane Austen and the Enlightenment* (Cambridge University Press, 2004), pp. 129–54.

25. Elizabeth Gunning, *The Orphans of Snowdon*, 3 vols. (1797), vol. II, 49; Isabella Kelly, *The Abbey of St Asaph*, 3 vols. (1795), vol. I, p. 3; vol. III, p. 65.

26. W. H. Auden, 'Letter to Lord Byron', in *Collected Poems*, ed. Edward Mendelson, rev. edn (London: Faber, 2007), p. 84.

3

JOCELYN HARRIS

Pride and Prejudice and *Mansfield Park*

In *Pride and Prejudice*, Jane Austen draws on a battery of theatrical techniques to create her 'light & bright & sparkling' novel (*L* 203). In the more serious *Mansfield Park*, which she published next, theatricality itself becomes her subject. Elizabeth Bennet and Fanny Price could hardly be more different, but seeing that the action of *Pride and Prejudice* matches calendars for 1811–12, and *Mansfield Park* was 'begun sometime about Feby 1811 – Finished soon after June 1813', she was probably working on both manuscripts at once for a few months of 1811.[1] It looks as if Austen built the first novel on dramatic devices, then went on to examine the whole enterprise of plays and play-acting in the second. In so doing, she brings to life a controversy as old as the stage itself.

Critics blame Evangelicalism for Austen's apparent disapproval of drama in *Mansfield Park*, and yet the family put on plays, she enjoyed seeing plays performed, and she was extremely familiar with drama, players and theatre practices. Throughout her writing life, she turned plays into novels and delighted in reading her own scenes as well as other people's out aloud. She may even have attended a performance of *Lovers' Vows*, the play rehearsed at Mansfield Park.[2] These contradictions may be resolved if Austen, rather than taking any definitive stance about the stage in *Mansfield Park*, threw herself into the long-running debate about dramatic embodiment.

The crux of the matter has always been the actor's body, that powerful signifying system for controlling representation, communication and affect. It was precisely because Austen was so steeped in drama that in *Mansfield Park* she plunges confidently into the issues of the controversy: whether the actor is a hypocrite; whether he corrupts himself and his audience by becoming the character he impersonates; the value of drama in the education of boys; the battle for primacy between pulpit and stage over the representation of reality; the effect of familiarity on the cast; and the pleasure to be gained from professional performances.[3] She enquires into all these issues through what Julia Bertram calls sarcastically 'the Mansfield Theatricals' (*MP* 1:15:174), casting an analytical eye on the dramatic devices she deployed to such dazzling effect in *Pride and Prejudice*.

Pride and Prejudice

Pride and Prejudice particularly aspires to the condition of a play, being neat, compact and tightly structured, with a limited cast of characters and a continuous action. As well as being knowledgeable about plays and players, Austen was extremely familiar with Samuel Richardson's dramatic novels, drawing extensively on *Sir Charles Grandison* for *Pride and Prejudice* before transposing it into a different key for *Mansfield Park*. So close was her acquaintance with the novel that she even modelled her pretty new cap on that of its heroine, Harriet Byron (*L* 219–20). The family at Steventon also owned a copy of his *Clarissa*, which she reworked in 'Lady Susan' and *Sense and Sensibility*.[4]

Richardson, who called *Clarissa* a 'Dramatic Narrative', wove stage techniques into fiction. The rise of the novel occurred at least in part because of the vacuum in representation caused by the Licensing Act of 1737, which censored and subdued the stage. Although Richardson advocated reform, he was also a star-struck apprentice, he published plays, and he befriended players, playwrights and managers. Familiar like Austen with plays both printed and performed, he built his novels around dramatic allusions, and appropriated stage devices to recreate the affect, suspense and immediacy of theatre. His soliloquies, dialogue, distinctive idiolects, stage directions, meaningful gestures and expressions, indications of tone and pace, costume, properties, attitudes, tableaux, dramatic entrances and exits, *coups de théâtre*, ironic reversals and set pieces make his novels look like plays. So do Austen's. But she adds famously to Richardson by deploying a narrative voice so coloured by a character's thoughts that it might just as well be called an unspoken soliloquy.

In live theatre, the actors' presence reinforces the illusion by making plays audible, visible and tangible all at once. But if to Aristotle the 'reality of presentation is felt in the play as read, as well as in the play as acted',[5] readers could still unroll Richardson's dramas within the theatre of their minds. Playwrights frequently alter their texts after the first night, and Richardson's 'rehearsals' of his manuscripts to audiences of family and friends made him change his novels.[6] Austen may have done so too. Richardson calls himself an editor, and the title page of *Pride and Prejudice* reads merely, 'By the Author of "Sense and Sensibility"'. That is, he hides behind his letter-writing characters, and she appears only as an authorial or a gnomic voice. The absence of these two playwright-novelists enhances the reality effect, for showing rather than telling creates impressions of vivid life. In consequence, Clarissa was 'treated like an intimate Acquaintance by all her Readers',[7] and Elizabeth Bennet is the most beloved character in fiction.

When Austen exposes the hypocrisy of Mr Collins or the double-dealing of Mr Wickham, she recalls not just Richardson but the novelist-playwright Henry Fielding, who loved to skewer such follies. Indeed it might be said that all her heroines penetrate through appearances to truth, an epistemological endeavour dear to the Enlightenment and especially to philosophers such as John Locke. But she demonstrates in *Pride and Prejudice* just how what Penny Gay calls the 'scopic seductiveness' of dramatic devices complicates that vital task of perception.[8]

Mr Bennet, Elizabeth Bennet and Mr Darcy are all wary of theatricality in daily life. After Mr Collins, who plays by turn ardent suitor, rejected lover, uxorious husband, censorious cleric and servile toady, writes that his grateful respect for Lady Catherine, rather than religious devotion, makes him 'ever ready to *perform* those rites and ceremonies which are instituted by the Church of England' (my emphasis), Mr Bennet enquires sardonically, 'whether these pleasing attentions proceed from the impulse of the moment, or are the result of previous study?' (1:13:70, 1:14:76). Similarly, when the younger Bingley sister 'performed her part indeed without much graciousness' after her brother requires her to be civil (1:9:49), Darcy is not deceived. Miss Bingley calls Elizabeth one of those young ladies who practise the 'paltry device, a very mean art' of recommending themselves to the other sex by undervaluing their own, and Darcy replies, 'there is meanness in *all* the arts which ladies sometimes condescend to employ for captivation. Whatever bears affinity to cunning is despicable.' Miss Bingley 'was not so entirely satisfied with this reply as to continue the subject' (1:8:43–4).

Characters in *Pride and Prejudice* are eager to take on roles. Mary Bennet's display of pedantry gives less pleasure than Elizabeth's easy and unaffected piano-playing (1:6:27), Lydia Bennet plays the flirt with officers in fancy and reality (2:18:258), Mrs Bennet plays the nervous hypochondriac, and Mr Bennet assumes the Voltairian cynic until shocked out of role by Lydia's elopement, saying, 'let me once in my life feel how much I have been to blame. I am not afraid of being overpowered by the impression. It will pass away soon enough.' Rapidly resuming his philosophic composure, he comments on Mrs Bennet's elaborate grieving over Lydia, 'This is a parade ... which does one good; it gives such an elegance to misfortune!' (3:6:329–30). As he asks, 'For what do we live, but to make sport for our neighbours, and laugh at them in our turn?' Elizabeth, like her father, dearly loves a laugh (3:15:403, 1:11:62), but cynicism about what Gay calls 'the inescapable theatricality of social life'[9] can easily slide into 'useless or blameable distrust', even misanthropy (2:13:230). As she tells her sister Jane after her friend Charlotte Lucas agrees to marry Mr Collins, 'There are few people whom I really love, and still fewer of whom I think well. The more I see of the world, the more am I dissatisfied with it; and every day confirms my belief of the inconsistency of all human characters, and of the little dependence that can be placed on the appearance of either merit or sense' (2:1:153).

In spite of all her wariness, Elizabeth falls prey to theatricality: the very word 'hypocrisy' means 'acting a part', in Greek. When Wickham performs the gentleman in his person, countenance, air and walk, Jane's tender nature excuses her failure to 'question the veracity of a young man of such amiable appearance'. But Elizabeth, who knows 'exactly what to think' (1:17:95–6), believes that his 'countenance, voice, and manner, had established him at once in the possession of every virtue'. She must later blame herself for not perceiving that he is a seducer, a vengeful friend, a gamester and a fortune-hunter: 'I, who have prided myself on my discernment! – I, who valued myself on my abilities!' (2:13:228, 230). One young man, she says, 'has got all the goodness, and the other all the appearance of it' (2:17:250).

Elizabeth is deceived through the eye, through theatrical illusion. Darcy is the keener observer, for although Mr Bennet thinks him a man 'who never looks at any woman but to see a blemish, and who probably never looked at *you* in his life!' (3:15:402), Darcy first looks at Elizabeth with a critical eye (1:6:26), then continues to watch her closely. Elizabeth does not look back at him carefully enough, being often incapable of lifting up her eyes to his face until his truly faithful portrait at Pemberley allows her to fix his eyes upon herself. In the surprise encounter, their eyes 'instantly met' (3:1:277–8). She, who once saw truth in Wickham's looks, has her eyes opened to his real character; she is no longer 'blind' (1:17:96, 3:4:306, 2:13:230).

If Elizabeth accuses herself of courting prepossession and ignorance, Locke says that the reception of truth 'must come from Proofs, and Arguments, and Light arising from the Nature of Things themselves', not ignorance and error.[10] Elizabeth refused to be convinced by the 'assurances' of the Bingleys about Wickham, and even had information been in her power, never felt a wish of enquiring about his real character (1:18:108, 2:13:228). Nor should she have relied on general opinion. The multitude, as fickle as any audience in a theatre, ranges from those who endorse the 'truth universally acknowledged, that a single man in possession of a good fortune, must be in want of a wife', to the 'everybody' who condemns Darcy as the worst of men, or speaks of him as a very proud, ill-natured boy, or declares Wickham to be the wickedest young man in the world (1:1:3, 2:1:157, 2:2:162, 3:6:325). 'Every one connected with him', says Lady Catherine, will see the alliance between Elizabeth and Darcy as a disgrace, while the spiteful old ladies in Meryton express ludicrously contradictory opinions about Lydia (3:14:394, 3:8:342).

Only at the end does Elizabeth use reason aright, when her conjectures about probabilities lead her to understanding. If 'a deep, intricate character' (1:9:46) such as Darcy's requires more attention than is available within the running time of a play, letters allow prolonged consideration. After perusing Darcy's again, Elizabeth reflects, reconsiders events, determines probabilities and accepts the evidence from 'more than one witness of undoubted veracity'. The objective 'testimony' of Colonel Fitzwilliam and Mrs Reynolds is confirmed by Darcy's rescue of Lydia and his civility to the Gardiners (2:13:231, 2:12:222, 225).

Such contradictory testimonies complicate Elizabeth's struggle to find truth, just as theatre audiences have to interpret – or misinterpret – the differing views spoken by actors. As she says to Mr Darcy, 'I hear such different accounts of you as puzzle me exceedingly', and to Mr Collins, 'you puzzle me exceedingly' (1:18:105, 1:19:121). Since the heroine is the main site of perception, her attempts to see past hypocritical words and deceptive body language encourage readerly participation, assistance and investment. Words such as acting, address, adorned, affectation, appearance, art, artful, behaviour, ceremony, cunning, custom, device, disguise, display, duped, exhibition, form, formal, looks, manners, misrepresentation, mode, ostentatious, parade, play, profession, pretension and represent all signal the need to penetrate the mask, while the words arts and allurements, cunning, design, duplicity, impose, pretence, scheme, stratagem and tricks warn equally that appearances deceive.

Theatricality misleads, then, but so too can the assumption that everyone must play a part. When Charlotte advises that a 'woman had better show *more* affection than she feels', Elizabeth recoils from the idea of Jane acting by design. As she protests, 'You know it is not sound, and that you would never act in this way yourself' (1:6:24–5). But Charlotte does design successfully to catch a husband. Ironically too, where Jane's apparent lack of 'any symptom of peculiar regard' convinces Darcy that she cannot love Mr Bingley, Elizabeth's outward indifference to Darcy convinces Mr Bennet that she cannot love him (2:12:219, 3:17:417).

When Elizabeth accuses the Byronic Darcy of performing pride, of claiming to have 'no defect. He owns it himself without disguise', he replies that she wilfully misunderstands him (1:11:63). At the ball, too, when she archly sketches both Darcy and herself as unsocial and taciturn, 'unwilling to speak, unless we expect to say something that will amaze the whole room, and be handed down to posterity with all the eclat of a proverb', he queries the faithfulness of her portraiture. 'I must not decide on my own performance', replies Elizabeth. Here and elsewhere, she interrogates the performative impulse as acutely as he does himself. As Darcy says, 'We neither of us perform to strangers' (1:18:103, 2:8:197). Words such as open, candour, unaffected, unreserved and truth accumulate value throughout the novel, from Elizabeth assuring Mr Collins that she is a 'rational creature speaking the truth from her heart' to her assertion that she speaks 'nothing but the truth' about her engagement to Darcy (1:19:122, 3:17:414). Nothing is more deceitful, says Darcy, than the appearance of humility, for disguise of every sort is his abhorrence (1:10:53, 2:11:215). Even the river banks at Pemberley, his stately home, are 'neither formal, nor falsely adorned' (3:1:271).

Like her creator, however, Elizabeth attends one of the London theatres, and enjoys playing roles: she imitates conventional talking by 'rule' when dancing with Darcy and she mimics a rapturous traveller in her 'transport' over the Lakes (1:18:102, 2:4:174–5). Her ancestors, who were equally dear to Richardson, are the witty and independent heroines of Shakespearian and Restoration drama, but Austen typically modifies what she takes, for instance, from *Much Ado About Nothing.*[11] Mr Darcy, whom even Bingley finds daunting and forbidding on occasion (1:10:55), looks at first like Shakespeare's gloomy Don John, who as Beatrice says, has made of Claudio 'a villain that hath slandered, scorned, dishonoured my kinswoman ... with public accusation, uncover'd slander, unmitigated rancour' (IV.i.299–304). After Darcy persuades Bingley out of loving Jane, Elizabeth calls Darcy 'the man, who has been the means of ruining, perhaps for ever, the happiness of a most beloved sister ... exposing one to the censure of the world for caprice and instability, the other to its derision for disappointed hopes, and involving them both in misery of the acutest kind' (2:11:213).

Darcy declares himself a Benedick when his accusation, like Benedick's about Hero, that Elizabeth is unhandsome, begins the merry war with Austen's own Lady Disdain. Even after both couples cry truce to save the reputation of their kinswomen, Elizabeth like Beatrice cannot cease from teasing. When Benedick asks, 'For which of my bad parts didst thou first fall in love with me?' Beatrice replies, 'For which of my good parts did you first suffer love for me?' (V.ii.51–7). Curious as to why Darcy fell in love with her, Elizabeth enquires, 'what could set you off in the first place?' Was it her beauty, her uncivil behaviour, her impertinence? (3:18:421). Her realization that Darcy is a Benedick, not a Don John, will unite them. Clearly, then, Austen built *Pride and Prejudice* upon a considerable store of theatrical knowledge.

Mansfield Park

Dramatic devices make *Pride and Prejudice* sparkle, but in *Mansfield Park*, Jane Austen investigates their effects. Drawing again on her experience of plays, players and stage practices, she explores the controversy over the stage by means of the Mansfield theatricals, a rehearsal play with actors who cannot act.

As in *Pride and Prejudice*, Austen works up elements from actual plays in *Mansfield Park*. Both Paula Byrne and Penny Gay show just how intricately *Lovers' Vows* is involved with its characters and events. Gay also finds predecessors for Mary Crawford in two of Hannah Cowley's plays, and Byrne argues that a garden scene of seduction and intrigue in George Colman and David Garrick's *The Clandestine Marriage* (1766) anticipates the episode at Sotherton. Their Mr Sterling plans to 'improve' his country estate by cutting down fifty trees 'Smack smooth' to make a lawn, and Austen's Mr Rushworth is an equally enthusiastic feller of trees. The play's 'serpentine path' ominously anticipates the 'very serpentine course' taken by Edmund Bertram and Mary Crawford in the wilderness at Sotherton, where settings, stage directions and dialogue turn the episode into a virtual play (*MP* 1:9:110). Witty set pieces between the rakish Henry Crawford and the flirtatious Maria Bertram recall similar debates in plays, and if as Byrne says, introducing a rustic pair into urban society was a common ploy, Austen imports sophisticated Londoners into a rural setting.

As well as drawing on eighteenth-century plays, *Mansfield Park* alludes to real actors. When Mr Rushworth says of Henry Crawford, 'Nobody can call such an under-sized man handsome. He is not five foot nine. I should not wonder if he was not more than five foot eight. I think he is an ill-looking fellow'; and again, 'to see such an undersized, little, mean-looking man, set up for a fine actor, is very ridiculous in my opinion' (1:10:119, 1:18:194) he especially recalls David Garrick and Edmund Kean, both of whom were short, versatile and electrifying. But like Garrick and Kean, Henry is a very fine actor indeed. As he says, 'I could be fool enough at this moment to undertake any character that ever was written, from Shylock or Richard III. down to the singing hero of a farce in his scarlet coat and cocked hat. I feel as if I could be any thing or every thing, as if I could rant and storm, or sigh, or cut capers in any tragedy or comedy in the English language' (1:13:145).[12] In 1741, Garrick made a sensational London debut as Richard III,[13] and on 4 March 1814, Austen saw Kean play Henry's other favourite, Shylock.

For *Mansfield Park*, Austen borrows the names Yates and Crawford from two eighteenth-century actresses, Mary Anne Yates and Anne Crawford (later Mrs Barry), rival tragediennes before Sarah Siddons. Garrick found

Mrs Yates troublesome, and deliberately offended her by casting her in the comic part of Old Woman.[14] In *Mansfield Park*, when Henry asserts that Julia's 'features are not tragic features, and she walks too quick, and speaks too quick, and would not keep her countenance. She had better do the old countrywoman; the Cottager's wife', Yates protests to Tom Bertram, 'Your sister do that! It is an insult to propose it.' Perhaps recalling Garrick, he declares that Tom does not deserve the office of manager if he 'cannot appreciate the talents of your company a little better' (1:14:157–8). But like Mrs Yates, who was famed for her powerful voice,[15] Julia displays genuine tragic talent with her cry, 'My father is come! He is in the hall at this moment' (1:18:202).

By portraying Tom in his role as actor-manager, Austen reveals her grasp of contemporary theatre practice, as Byrne explains. The same is true of Fanny as prompter. Though lowly in status, prompters were actually the linchpins of rehearsals, for they heard the actors' lines, kept the play going and cut the script. As Edmund and Mary rehearse, Fanny is 'invested, indeed, with the office of judge and critic', she rehearses and prompts Mr Rushworth, she curtails 'every speech that admitted being shortened', and she chooses the colours for his dress (1:18:199, 1:15:162). Because prompters knew the play so well, they were often understudies, just as Fanny is asked to read when Dr Grant's illness prevents his wife from playing. Thus prompters occupied a curious space both within and without the play, being both the focus of the play itself and an audience who sees more clearly than the rest.[16] And so it is with Fanny.

Theatricality has always been mistrusted, with the 'real' – the undisguised, unacted and unchanging – being preferred to miming or changing.[17] 'What's Hecuba to him or he to Hecuba', asks Hamlet about the player, 'That he should weep for her?' (II.ii.552). *Mansfield Park* reflects the notion of acting as hypocrisy when Crawford delights in mimesis, but Fanny, who can only be herself, says that she 'really cannot act'. With looks and voice 'so truly feminine', she is 'no very good picture of a man' (1:15:171, 1:18:198). Edmund will tell his father that she only 'has been consistent. *Her* feelings have been steadily against it from first to last' (2:2:219). He himself objects to playing the part of Anhalt the clergyman, for he would be sorry to make the character ridiculous by bad acting. As he says, 'the man who chooses the profession itself, is, perhaps, one of the last who would wish to represent it on the stage'. Faced with the possibility of an outsider playing the role, he gives in, divided between 'his theatrical and his real part ... between love and consistency' (1:15:170, 1:17:191).

Behind this traditional mistrust lies the idea of the actor as cipher, without a habitation and a name. 'To any thing like a permanence of abode, or limitation of society, Henry Crawford had, unluckily, a great dislike'

(1:14:47), for like Wickham in *Pride and Prejudice*, who thinks first of going into the church, then the law, then the army (2:12:222–3), the consummate actor Crawford adopts by turns the roles of improver, house-renter (2:2:281–6), sailor (2:6:275–6), 'friend of the poor and oppressed!' (3:10:469) and fashionable preacher (3:3:394–5). He ends by becoming none of them. The man who is everybody is nobody, for to embrace impersonation is to forgo a stable identity. Actors like Henry exist only in their current roles, whereas Fanny values the stable continuities of memory, a faculty '*more* wonderful than the rest' (2:4:243). Shape-changing such as Crawford's and Wickham's undermines consistency and inhibits self-knowledge: as Fanny says to Henry, it is 'a pity you did not always know yourself as well as you seemed to do at that moment' (3:3:397).

Onstage, feigned emotions appear real. As Juliet McMaster points out, Richardson exploited the difference between Clarissa, whose gestures and expressions express genuine feelings, and Lovelace, who replaces involuntary responses with the learnt discourse of acting.[18] Austen exploits that same difference when Julia announces her father's arrival to Henry and Maria; 'Frederick was listening with looks of devotion to Agatha's narrative, and pressing her hand to his heart', and as Henry 'still kept his station and retained her sister's hand', Julia's 'wounded heart swelled again with injury'. To Maria, 'such a moment, a moment of such peculiar proof and importance, was worth ages of doubt and anxiety. She hailed it as an earnest of the most serious determination' (2:1:205–6). Maria believes that Crawford expresses true feelings, but real actors stay in character even through interruptions, as Henry does here.

It was said that only by an artful suspense of all feelings could Garrick produce his most astonishing effects, for he did not 'either laugh or cry ... spontaneously, involuntarily, and from the soul'.[19] Austen plays with that idea of dramatic artifice when Yates reacts to the entrance of Sir Thomas Bertram by giving 'the very best start he had ever given in the whole course of his rehearsals'. To Edmund, 'the gradual metamorphosis of the impassioned Baron Wildenhaim into the well-bred and easy Mr. Yates ... was such an exhibition, such a piece of true acting as he would not have lost upon any account' (2:1:213–14). That start, that spectacular emotional transition, makes Yates appear a very Garrick whose starts as Richard and Hamlet were called naturalistic. In fact, however, his delivery was tonal enough to be recorded in musical notation. Also, he held his starts as 'attitudes' until relieved from his post by clapping, and was said to activate a mechanical wig with 'dext'rous dash of hand or thumb' to make his hair stand on end.[20] Austen's joke is that quite by chance, Yates performs an illusion perfected by the great Garrick himself.

The theatricals in *Mansfield Park* are essentially a rehearsal play, that wildly comical genre that demonstrates how to act by showing how not to act. Here Austen draws on a tradition that harks back to Sheridan's *The Critic* (1779), Fielding's *Tragedy of Tragedies* (1731), Buckingham's *Rehearsal* (1671) and ultimately the inset plays of *Hamlet* (1599–1601) and *A Midsummer Night's Dream* (1594–6), for Shakespeare was part of this Englishwoman's constitution from her earliest years (3:3:390–1). Like these earlier authors, she replaces the outdated modes of *Lovers' Vows* with a more 'natural' style, just as she herself was writing in a subtler, more naturalistic and far less episodic style than her novelistic predecessors.

Rehearsal plays openly burlesque heroic styles, but Austen may have thought that the execrable *Lovers' Vows* contained its own spoof. The running jest of a rehearsal play is the inability of its actors to create dramatic illusions, as at Mansfield Park. Tom falls back on typecasting his inexperienced actors by appearance and status: Yates must therefore play the Baron because he is the tallest, Rushworth Count Cassel because he is a landowner, Mary Amelia because of her 'small, light, girlish, skipping figure', Edmund Anhalt because he will be a clergyman, and Fanny that 'very proper, little old woman' the Cottager's wife, because Tom thinks her a 'creepmouse' (1:14:156–9, 1:15:170–2).

Reality and role converge again if, as was thought, immoral roles like those in *Lovers' Vows* corrupt the players. As Samuel Johnson said, 'If Garrick really believed himself to be that monster, Richard the Third, he deserved to be hanged every time he played it.'[21] Like Garrick and Kean, Crawford plays evil dissimulators such as Richard III, who boasted that he could 'add colours to the chameleon, / Change shapes with Proteus for advantages, / And set the murderous Machiavel to school' (*3 Henry VI*, III.ii.191–5). Corrupted by evil roles, he deceives Julia and seduces the married Maria.

Like the seventeenth-century Puritans who closed the theatres, Fanny fears that play-acting will spread corruption. She considers *Lovers' Vows*, and especially the female roles of Agatha and Amelia, 'totally improper for home representation – the situation of one, and the language of the other, so unfit to be expressed by any woman of modesty' (1:14:161). Edmund agrees, because of Maria's engagement to Mr Rushworth. The evil effects of plays were often called contagion: as Tom says, Yates 'brought the infection from Ecclesford, and it spread as those things always spread you know, sir' (2:1:215–16). *Lovers' Vows* does indeed corrupt its audience as well as its players, for Edmund descends from his moral elevation, Mary condones her brother's behaviour, Julia elopes with Mr Yates and Maria commits adultery with Henry Crawford.

Thus Austen shows how the actor's body betrays his inward flaws of vanity, exhibitionism and hypocrisy. Amateurs especially cannot control their sensibility, for they conflate the player with the role, they lack detachment, they identify with their characters even to the loss of their own identities and they lose steadiness of self. Vulnerable to the vices of the acting trade, they are corrupted by anarchic roles. And if actors 'ghost' roles they have played before, the protean Crawford contains Richardson's Lovelace, who contains such charismatic villain-heroes as Lothario, Dorimant, Satan, Richard III and, ultimately, as Gay says, Don Juan and the medieval Vice.[22] When performed by a brilliant actor, these roles exemplify the dilemma about dramatic representation in its starkest form.

The playwright Richard Cumberland, for instance, feared that Garrick's being 'young and light and alive in every muscle and feature' made the role of Lothario in Nicholas Rowe's *Fair Penitent* dangerously attractive.[23] Richardson's biographer Anna Laetitia Barbauld said similarly that 'the gaiety and spirit of Lovelace, in the hands of Garrick, would have been too strong for the morality of the piece'. She well understood that to attract the heroine, the villain-hero must have 'wit and spirit, and courage, and generosity, and manly genteel address, and also transient gleams of feeling, and transient stings of remorse', but wished for a final scene to turn the reader with horror from the features of the gay and agreeable seducer, 'when changed into the agonizing countenance of the despairing self-accuser'.[24] Austen seems to echo Barbauld when she writes:

> we may fairly consider a man of sense like Henry Crawford, to be providing for himself no small portion of vexation and regret – vexation that must rise sometimes to self-reproach, and regret to wretchedness – in having so requited hospitality, so injured family peace, so forfeited his best, most estimable and endeared acquaintance, and so lost the woman whom he had rationally, as well as passionately loved. (3:17:542)

Thus Austen takes serious risks when she creates Crawford on the model of Richard III-Lovelace-Lothario, then endows him with Garrick's and Kean's ability to act.

The stage was thought valuable, however, for teaching schoolboys pronunciation and deportment. Even Sir Thomas encouraged his sons to 'spout' and so speak well (1:13:149). Edmund and Henry agree that 'the too common neglect of the qualification ... in the ordinary school-system for boys' results in a 'degree of ignorance and uncouthness of men, of sensible and well-informed men, when suddenly called to the necessity of reading aloud'. In church, says Edmund, distinctness and energy may have weight in recommending the most solid truths. But Crawford, who values style over substance, asserts that the eloquence of the pulpit 'is entitled to the highest praise and honour. The preacher who can touch and affect such an heterogeneous mass of hearers . . . is a man whom one could not . . . honour enough. I should like to be such a man.' His own eloquence is primarily for display, however: 'I must have a London audience. I could not preach, but to the educated; to those who were capable of estimating my composition' (3:3:392–5). Here Austen recalls debates about whether the pulpit or the stage was more persuasive.

For girls, drama was considered inappropriate. As Mary remarks of the schoolroom chairs in the East Room, they were 'not made for a theatre, I dare say; much more fitted for little girls to sit and kick their feet against when they are learning a lesson. What would your governess and your uncle say to see them used for such a purpose?' (1:18:198). When Edmund speaks of 'the *more* than intimacy – the familiarity' of the rehearsal as an evil, he expresses common anxiety about sexuality being unleashed by the theatre, because it gives players permission to express their true feelings (1:16:180). Gay cites Thomas Gisborne on acting being 'particularly injurious to the female performers', as it destroys 'diffidence by the unrestrained familiarity with persons of the other sex, which inevitably results from being joined with them in the drama',[25] and Tom reproaches himself for 'the dangerous intimacy of his unjustifiable theatre' (3:17:534). His father Sir Thomas looks like a Puritan when he burns all unbound copies of the play and restores the house to 'soberness' (2:2:223, 228).

But Austen also shows how the theatricals excite the company. If Garrick was thought to be more lively and lifelike than life itself, Henry says of the play, 'There was such an interest, such an animation, such a spirit diffused! Every body felt it. We were all alive. There was employment, hope, solicitude, bustle, for every hour of the day' (2:5:262). Even Edmund recalls the lively novelty of their evenings, saying, 'I have been feeling as if we had never lived so before' (2:3:230); even Lady Bertram says from the sofa, 'We have been all alive with acting' (2:1:211).

Scenes at Portsmouth exhibit the benefits of performance as manners. Whereas at Mansfield, thinks Fanny, 'every body had their due importance; every body's feelings were consulted. If tenderness could ever be supposed wanting, good sense and good breeding supplied its place' (3:8:453), the Prices do nothing to restrain their thumping, hallooing and squabbling until Crawford arrives and performs the gentleman. 'Wisely and kindly keeping his eyes away' from the terrified Fanny, he addresses and attends to her mother 'with the utmost politeness and propriety', and a friendliness that was making his 'manner perfect'. As a consequence, 'Mrs. Price's manners were also at their best', and Mr Price becomes a 'very different man'. Inspired by Mr Crawford, his 'manners now, though not polished, were more than passable; they were grateful, animated, manly; his expressions were those of an attached father, and a sensible man; – his loud tones did very well in the open air, and there was not a single oath to be heard. Such was his instinctive compliment to the good manners of Mr. Crawford' (3:10:464–7). Soon afterwards, the whole family is seen to advantage, dressed 'in their cleanest skins and best attire' (3:11:473), like actors putting on nobler roles along with their finer clothes.

On balance, then, Edmund is right to love plays, but only 'real acting, good hardened real acting', not the struggles of gentlemen and ladies (1:13:146). As he says of Crawford, to read Shakespeare well aloud is no everyday talent. Jane Austen, who also knew the difference, readily acknowledges the pleasures of acting by a Garrick, a Kean or a Crawford:

> in Mr. Crawford's reading there was a variety of excellence beyond what she had ever met with. The King, the Queen, Buckingham, Wolsey, Cromwell, all were given in turn; for with the happiest knack, the happiest power of jumping and guessing, he could always light, at will, on the best scene, or the best speeches of each; and whether it were dignity or pride, or tenderness or remorse, or whatever were to be expressed, he could do it with equal beauty. – It was truly dramatic. – His acting had first taught Fanny what pleasure a play might give, and his reading brought all his acting before her again. (3:3:389–91)

It is a remarkable fact that Maria Edgeworth and Frances Burney, the two women authors Austen singled out for praise in *Northanger Abbey*, both published novels containing scenes of private theatricals at much the same time as Austen's *Mansfield Park*:[26] Edgeworth's *Patronage* in December 1813, and Burney's *The Wanderer* in March 1814. Edgeworth's farcical account in *Patronage* of a performance by 'gentlemen and lady performers' rather than 'professional actors'[27] presents the same dilemma confronting Austen's characters in *Mansfield Park*, 'the raw efforts of those who have not been bred to the trade, – a set of gentlemen and ladies, who have all the disadvantages of education and decorum to struggle through' (1:13:146). Differences reveal as much about Austen's treatment of the trope as do the similarities.

Edgeworth's scenes occupy two chapters and Austen's take up five in a considerably more extended exploration. Edgeworth's summary, 'Lest we should never get to the play, we forbear to relate all the various frettings, jealousies, clashing vanities, and petty quarrels, which occurred between the actresses and their friends, during the getting up of this piece and it's [*sic*] rehearsal' sharply abbreviates the narrative, but it resembles Fanny's opinion about the Mansfield Park players as to 'the selfishness which, more or less disguised, seemed to govern them all' (1:14:154). Seeds of irreconcilable dislike are sown between friends in *Patronage*, but the more psychologically interesting and productive sin of jealousy descends on *Mansfield Park* when the Bertram sisters fall out over Henry, Fanny becomes jealous of Mary, and Rushworth, drawing on all his resources, calls Crawford undersized (*Patronage* 7:29; *MP* 1:18:194).

In chapters 7 to 10 of *The Wanderer*, Burney also introduces a private performance into a domestic setting, John Vanburgh and Colley Cibber's *The Provok'd Husband* (1728). In Burney, Miss Arbe, an outsider like Mr Yates, spurs on the play as he will do, Mrs Maple resembles Mrs Norris, and Elinor Joddrel 'threatened to carry it into execution in Farmer Gooch's barn, and to invite all the country', the very proposal objected to by Austen's Edmund (1:16:180). Like Fanny, Burney's dependent heroine Ellis refuses to be the prompter, but external pressures eventually force her to act. Seeing no alternative between 'obsequiously submitting, or immediately relinquishing her asylum', she consents to play Lady Townly in order to placate the family who shelters her.[28] The pressures on Fanny are internal and possibly more brutal. Mrs Norris says she will not urge the equally dependent Fanny, 'but I shall think her a very obstinate, ungrateful girl, if she does not do what her aunt and cousins wish her – very ungrateful indeed, considering who and what she is' (1:15:172). Finally there is the secret marriage of Burney's Ellis, which places her as 'Lady Townly' in a situation roughly parallel to Austen's Maria, whose engagement to Mr Rushworth should prevent her from acting opposite Henry the role of Agatha, former mistress of Baron Wildenhaim and an unwed mother as well.

The characters in *Patronage* and *The Wanderer* appear to know only their own parts, like hard-pressed actors in the eighteenth century, but Austen's theatrical trope unreels her novel's plot from the characters' reactions to one another. In short, what distinguishes Austen from Edgeworth and Burney in the management of their shared use of the theatre is her thoroughgoing integration of character, plot and ideas. Whereas Edgeworth and Burney frequently drop the narrative threads and resume them pages later, Austen maintains the unbroken momentum of a play.

It is a curious and inexplicable fact of literary history that the default mode for reading Jane Austen is biography. Those who want to know her better assume that the theatricals in *Mansfield Park* represent personal religious preferences instead of aesthetic, moral and intellectual enquiries. Ironically enough, it is the same mistake made by theatre-goers who equate the actor with the role. No wonder that critics disagree over Austen's opinion of the stage when what she actually dramatizes in her fiction is the ongoing controversy over the stage.

Just as the dramatic scenes of *Pride and Prejudice* invite readers, like audiences in a theatre, to judge for themselves, Austen leaves her debate over the theatricals in *Mansfield Park* dialogically open, not monologically closed. These two works, though different in tone and characterization, actually complement each other. In *Pride and Prejudice*, Jane Austen shows how theatricality masks and deceives in daily life, but in *Mansfield Park*, she interrogates more deeply the whole remarkable phenomenon of plays and play-acting.

NOTES

1. Kathryn Sutherland, *Jane Austen's Textual Lives: From Aeschylus to Bollywood* (Oxford University Press, 2005), p. 124; Cassandra Austen, in Jane Austen, *Minor Works*, ed. R. W. Chapman (Oxford University Press, 1958), opposite p. 242.
2. Penny Gay, *Jane Austen and the Theatre* (Cambridge University Press, 2002); Paula Byrne, *Jane Austen and the Theatre* (London: Hambledon, 2002).
3. Jonas Barish, *The Antitheatrical Prejudice* (Berkeley, CA: University of California Press, 1981).
4. Byrne, *Theatre*, pp. 94–8; Jocelyn Harris, *Jane Austen's Art of Memory* (Cambridge University Press, 1989, repr. 2003), pp. 56–71; chs. 3–5.
5. *Aristotle on the Art of Poetry*, trans. Ingram Bywater, ed. Gilbert Murray (Oxford: Clarendon Press, 1920), ch. 26.
6. Harris, Introduction, *Samuel Richardson's Published Commentary on 'Clarissa' 1747–65*, 3 vols. 'Prefaces, Postscripts and Related Writings' (London: Pickering & Chatto, 1998), vol. 1, pp. xxiv–lxxii.
7. Sarah Fielding, cited in Harris, 'Introduction', p. lxvii.
8. Gay, *Theatre*, p. 117.
9. Gay, *Theatre*, p. 81.
10. John Locke, *An Essay Concerning Human Understanding* [1690], ed. Peter H. Nidditch (Oxford: Clarendon Press, 1975), IV. xvii. 22.
11. Juliet McMaster, *Jane Austen on Love* (Victoria, BC: University of Victoria, 1978), pp. 48–9.
12. Judith W. Fisher, '"Don't Put Your Daughter on the Stage, Lady B": Talking about Theatre in Jane Austen's *Mansfield Park*', *Persuasions*, 22 (2000), 70–86.
13. 'David Garrick', *ODNB On-line*, 2004.
14. 'Mary Ann Yates', *ODNB On-line*, 2004.
15. Thomas Campbell, *Life of Mrs. Siddons*, 2 vols. (London: Effingham Wilson, 1834), vol. 1, p. 142.
16. Tiffany Stern, *Rehearsal From Shakespeare to Sheridan* (Oxford: Clarendon Press, 2000), pp. 94–6.
17. Barish, *Prejudice*, pp. 151–2.
18. McMaster, *Reading the Body in the Eighteenth-Century Novel* (Houndmills: Palgrave Macmillan, 2004), pp. 104–5.
19. Charles Dibdin, cited in Kalman A. Burnim, *David Garrick Director* (University of Pittsburgh Press, 1961), p. 58.
20. Stern, *Rehearsal*, pp. 257–8; Burnim, *Garrick*, p. 160.
21. Cited in Barish, *Prejudice*, p. 280.
22. Gay, *Theatre*, pp. 99, 17.

23. Cited in Allardyce Nicoll, *The Garrick Stage: Theatres and Audience in the Eighteenth Century*, ed. Sybil Rosenfeld (Athens, GA: University of Georgia Press, 1980), p. 10.
24. Anna Laetitia Barbauld, 'Life', *The Correspondence of Samuel Richardson*, ed. Barbauld, 6 vols. (London, 1804), vol. 1, pp. lxxxix, xc–xci.
25. Gay, *Theatre*, p. 103.
26. This common use of theatrical tropes by Austen, Burney and Edgeworth in 1813–14 suggests the need for richer exploration. See also Elaine Bander, '*Mansfield Park* and the 1814 Novels: *Waverley, The Wanderer, Patronage*', *Persuasions* 28 (2006), 116–25.
27. Maria Edgeworth, *Patronage*, ed. Connor Carville and Marilyn Butler, vols. 6–7 of *Novels and Selected Works of Maria Edgeworth*, 12 vols. (London: Pickering & Chatto, 1999), 7:32.
28. Frances Burney, *The Wanderer: or, Female Difficulties* [1814], ed. Margaret Anne Doody, Robert L. Mack and Peter Sabor (Oxford University Press, 1991), pp. 69, 90.

4

PENNY GAY

Emma and *Persuasion*

Pride and Prejudice and *Mansfield Park* operate in opposing aesthetic genres: the first as romantic comedy, the second as anti-romance, or moral tale. What further artistic challenges is Jane Austen setting herself in her next (and last) two novels, *Emma* and *Persuasion*? Very different in technique and form – the mature novelist never repeated herself – both novels remain concerned with young women finding their proper place and role in the world of early nineteenth-century England. But there are significant differences in the imagined 'England' they evoke, and in the way the two heroines view their world and act in it. Though each novel ends with the heroine's marriage, their narrative structures are so different as to have the reader searching for new generic descriptors.

Emma

At least two artistic challenges inform *Emma*. First, it anticipates the detective story in being a novel designed to be *re*read, with the reader each time discovering more complexities to the hidden story. Second, Austen declared that in this novel she was going to 'take a heroine whom no one but myself will much like'.[1] No longer lovable, sparkling Elizabeth or 'my Fanny', the steadfast heroine; instead, a spoilt, interfering and often deluded young woman, whose energy, good heart and desire to lead need to find their proper outlet. The novelist clearly indicates her position as ironical narrator of this young woman's story in the opening paragraph:

> Emma Woodhouse, handsome, clever and rich, with a comfortable home and happy disposition, seemed to unite some of the best blessings of existence; and had lived nearly twenty-one years in the world with very little to distress or vex her. (1:1:3)

The force of 'seemed', as the principal verb of this opening, is pointed; so too is the indication of Emma's age – she is about to attain her majority, perhaps through a process of 'distress' and vexation that she has hitherto magically avoided. How has she done so? Because 'the world', for her, is not the 'great world' of contemporary England but the little world of 'a large and populous village almost amounting to a town' in Surrey (1:1:5). Waiting for Harriet to complete a purchase at Ford's emporium:

> Emma went to the door for amusement. – Much could not be hoped from the traffic of even the busiest part of Highbury; – Mr. Perry walking hastily by, Mr. William Cox letting himself in at the office-door, Mr. Cole's carriage horses returning from exercise, or a stray letter-boy on an obstinate mule, were the liveliest objects she could presume to expect; and when her eyes fell only on the butcher with his tray, a tidy old woman travelling homewards from shop with her full basket, two curs quarrelling over a dirty bone, and a string of dawdling children round the baker's little bow-window eyeing the gingerbread, she knew she had no reason to complain, and was amused enough; quite enough still to stand at the door. A mind lively and at ease, can do with seeing nothing, and can see nothing that does not answer. (2:9:251)

Emma is apparently content with her little world – but is she really? The ironical sting is in the tail, the narrator's blandly ambiguous 'seeing nothing'. Emma rejoices in her abilities as an 'imaginist' (3:3:362), believing that she has insight that others lack. They must therefore be assisted by her *planning, promoting, encouraging, smoothing* (1:1:11), as in the case of Mr Weston's and Miss Taylor's marriage. Much of the novel's plot is driven by two further 'imaginings': Emma's attempts to match Harriet Smith to a suitor out of her class, and her creation of a salacious private narrative involving a forbidden romance between Jane Fairfax and the offstage Mr Dixon. She consequently misses the signs of a true secret romance between Jane and Frank.

In chapter 3 of volume 3, the day after the Crown ball, there occurs the episode of Harriet and the gypsies. Like virtually all the novel's events, it is narrated from Emma's point of view, or rather, by an ironical narrator who seems to be perched just behind Emma's shoulder, seeing more, and more clearly, than Emma, who is influenced by her 'imaginist's' perspective. The episode exemplifies Emma's habit of treating her world as fodder for her creative imagination: this is, of course, a novelist's habit, and Austen here offers an opportunity for reflection, three-quarters of the way through her novel, on the business of novel-writing.

From her first appearance in volume 1, Harriet is seen by Emma as 'exactly the something which her home required' (1:4:25), a sweet-natured, blonde and blue-eyed ingénue who exactly fits the model of romance heroine in the popular novels of the time. Emma is soon inventing a romance for Harriet with the handsome, smirking vicar Mr Elton. As that fails under a reality check, Emma's creative imagination turns to Jane Fairfax and the mysterious circumstances of her return to Highbury. For herself, she reserves a well-controlled flirtation with Frank Churchill, thus failing to see what even first-time readers sometimes guess, that Jane and Frank are passionately in love. But more satisfying to that 'very dear part of Emma, her fancy' (2:8:232), is the episode in which Frank rescues Harriet from harassment by a group of gypsies. Brought by the gallant Frank to Hartfield, Harriet immediately faints. Emma is thrilled:

> Such an adventure as this, – a fine young man and a lovely young woman thrown together in such a way, could hardly fail of suggesting certain ideas to the coldest heart and the steadiest brain … It was a very extraordinary thing. Nothing of the sort had ever occurred before to any young ladies in the place, within her memory; no rencontre, no alarm of the kind; – and now it had happened to the very person, and at the very hour, when the other very person was chancing to pass by to rescue her! – It certainly was very extraordinary!
> (3:3:362)

The astute reader will notice that Emma's thoughts have taken on the exclamatory register characteristic of Harriet's utterances. Emma's 'imaginings' are clearly second-rate fiction. There is a bigger and more complex story to be read, if only she could attend to it. Why was Frank walking along the Richmond road at that point? Because he had 'happened' to need to drop in on the Bateses (and Jane) before leaving Highbury. For the rest of Highbury, the story 'dwindle[s] soon into a matter of little importance' (3:3:364); that it survives only as a tale for which Emma's young nephews clamour, 'tenaciously setting her right if she varied in the slightest particular from the original recital', firmly places her fiction-making talents as trite and immature.

Emma's imaginings are part of the spectrum of social game-playing that is one of the novel's principal metaphors. In chapter 1 we are told: 'She dearly loved her father, but he was no companion for her. He could not meet her in conversation, rational or playful' (1:1:5). After dinner, Emma, weary of Mr Woodhouse's repetitive complaints, sets up the backgammon-table; 'but a visitor immediately afterwards walked in and made it unnecessary' (1:1:7). Thus arrives the novel's appropriately named hero, George Knightley, who does fulfil Emma's need for both rational and playful conversation, as the pair of them go on to demonstrate throughout the novel. Because their relationship is familiar (indeed, familial), their conversation never takes the form of courtship models, such as Mr Elton's unctuous clichés, or Frank Churchill's flirtatious double entendres. It has consequently a striking freedom and naturalness; so relaxed, indeed, that it is virtually *un*performative: it simply represents the pleasure these two clever people generally take in each other's company. When Mr Knightley does feel the need to perform a role – for example, that of the community's leader reprimanding a wayward but promising junior – he does so in private, as a friend, as with his remonstrance over Emma's insult to Miss Bates at Box Hill.

Mr Knightley is no game-player: he pointedly does not join in the game proposed by Frank at Box Hill. Mr Weston, who is not notable for his social insight, opts for a conundrum on Emma's name ('What two letters ... express perfection?' The answer, unconsciously ironical, is 'M. and A. – Em-ma' (3:7:404)). Elsewhere in the novel, in the pointless round of Highbury social life, riddles are collected and charades composed. A child's box of letters becomes a game with adult meaning as Frank tries to apologize to Jane for his 'blunder', and deliberately misleads Emma with 'Dixon' (3:5:378). Mrs Elton treats the Donwell strawberry-picking as an opportunity to dress up for a faux naif 'sort of gipsy party'. For Mr Knightley this is inappropriate: 'My idea of the simple and the natural will be to have the table spread in the dining-room. The nature and the simplicity of gentlemen and ladies, with their servants and furniture, I think is best observed by meals within doors' (3:6:385–6).

Frank Churchill is of course the greatest game-player of all, for the highest stakes. He is betting his chance of a happy and prosperous marriage not just on keeping his engagement to Jane secret, but on a risky strategy of flirting with Emma. As part of his smokescreen, he encourages Emma to believe that Jane is secretly in love with her friend's husband Mr Dixon. The long dialogue between Frank and Emma at the Coles' dinner party consists, on his part, of gleeful bluffing: he boldly suggests to Emma that the pianoforte which has mysteriously arrived at the Bateses' is 'an offering of love' (2:8:236). When he makes this a general conversational topic it produces in Jane a 'blush of consciousness' (2:8:237); to Frank this would presumably count as winning the trick. Jane's last appearance in the novel is as a trophy won by Frank: 'Did you ever see such skin? – such smoothness! Such delicacy! ... Observe the turn of her throat' (3:18:521–2). Emma admits, in this final conversation with Frank, that 'there is a little likeness between us', that she might well have had 'some amusement ... in the same situation' (3:18:522). But Emma, queen of Highbury society, has been outmanoeuvred by a more sophisticated player from the great world.

Much of Emma's naivety is due to her being 'fixed, so absolutely fixed' in Highbury (1:17:154). She rarely travels to London (because her father won't), even though her sister lives in the most 'airy' part of it – practically the country – in the recently developed area around Brunswick Square in London's north (1:12:110). Emma even finds it 'not pleasant' walking alone on the outskirts of Highbury, which makes Harriet 'a valuable addition'

(1:4:25); and she has not been to Donwell, though it is within a couple of miles, for several years. She has never been to Box Hill, only seven miles away. She has never seen the sea (1:12:108); we can read this as a metaphor for her sexual inexperience. The sea was associated with passion by the Romantic poets; and watering-places, such as Weymouth where Frank and Jane met, notoriously offered opportunities for romance.

Thus the visits to Donwell and Box Hill, the events of two successive days, carry an extraordinary weight in the novel's symbolic deployment of place, its examination of Emma's 'world' vis-à-vis the great world. Here, in the novel's third volume, Emma goes beyond the bounds of Highbury for the first time, and the two contrasting excursions represent important stages in the story of her coming of age. It is in these chapters, also, that Austen draws together the threads of a political argument that underlies the novel's domestic narrative and connects it with the novel that follows, *Persuasion*. (It is worth noting that the chronology of the novels overlaps: *Emma* is based on the calendar from the autumn of 1813 to that of 1814; *Persuasion*'s story begins in the summer of 1814.)

Mrs Elton's role in the novel parodies Emma's assumption of sovereignty over Highbury society. Her vulgarity and arrogance are greatly in evidence as she attempts to organize the summer 'exploring parties'. Labelling herself 'Lady Patroness' (a title she has appropriated from the fashionable London club Almack's, which was ruled by a committee of aristocratic ladies), she demands 'carte blanche' (3:3:385) from Mr Knightley regarding invitations to the Donwell Abbey strawberry-picking. Her use of the French term marks her as tainted with French manners, and indeed her plans to arrive on a donkey, with 'one of my little baskets hanging on my arm' (3:6:385) associate her with the doomed antics of Queen Marie Antoinette's 'milkmaid' performances at the Versailles *hameau* some thirty years earlier. Mrs Elton's silly pursuit of fashion, in another country and situation, could lead to the guillotine.

England had been at war with France for over twenty years, and the general reputation of all things French (except fashion) was low. Throughout the novel, the rather dandyish Frank Churchill is associated with French manners, which contrast with George Knightley's essential Englishness. As Mr Knightley says, perhaps somewhat self-righteously:

'No, Emma, your amiable young man can be amiable only in French, not in English. He may be very "aimable," have very good manners, and be very agreeable; but he can have no English delicacy towards the feelings of other people: nothing really amiable about him.' (1:18:160–1)

In the same conversation Mr Knightley accuses the as-yet unmet Frank of 'manoeuvring and finessing' (1:18:157), French words for slippery French habits. Frank's first name is a version of François; and his deceptively patriotic-sounding surname Churchill, recalling the great Duke of Marlborough who fought the French in the early eighteenth century, is only adoptive. At the very end of the novel, Mr Knightley is still labelling and judging his behaviour as typically French:

> 'Very bad – though it might have been worse. – Playing a most dangerous game ... Always deceived in fact by his own wishes, and regardless of little besides his own convenience ... Natural enough! – his own mind full of intrigue, that he should suspect it in others. – Mystery; Finesse – how they pervert the understanding! My Emma, does not every thing serve to prove more and more the beauty of truth and sincerity in all our dealings with each other?' (3:15:486)

And Emma, although knowing that full 'truth and sincerity' are never possible – Harriet's secret must be kept – is now inclined to judge Frank in Mr Knightley's terms: 'What has it been but a system of hypocrisy and deceit, – espionage, and treachery? – To come among us with professions of openness and simplicity; and such a league in secret to judge us all!' (3:10:435).

Emma's visit to Donwell Abbey (the Bunyanesque allegorical and religious associations of its name are significant) provides her with a revelation of a much more significant version of 'the world'. Despite the spiritual failings of much of the company there assembled, the place has extraordinary powers to refresh and renew: 'It was hot; and after walking some time over the gardens in a scattered, dispersed way, scarcely any three together, they insensibly followed one another to the delicious shade of a broad short avenue of limes' (3:6:390–1). Unfashionable in its refusal to be picturesque, Donwell offers instead a prospect of the 'favourably placed and sheltered' Abbey Mill Farm, 'with meadows in front, and the river making a close and handsome curve around it'. This is the home of the likable young farmer, Mr Knightley's tenant Robert Martin. His eventual marriage to Harriet will embody a new pastoral ideal of marriage based on companionship and a commitment to the family and community, disregarding old hierarchies of class and 'connec-tions'. Mr Knightley, local magistrate and judge of men, has a strong regard for Robert Martin, and engages cheerfully with the fluidity of Highbury society (its closeness to London in fact makes it attractive to those associated with 'trade').[2] It is this renewed, indeed optimistic, view of rural community that is comprehended in Emma's epiphanic reflection: 'It was a sweet view – sweet to the eye and the mind. English verdure, English culture, English comfort, seen under a sun bright, without being oppressive' (3:6:391).

That Frank Churchill finds the sun oppressive is just one more mark of his essential foreignness. Frank's late and ill-tempered arrival at Donwell, after having encountered and quarrelled with Jane, occurs at the very end of the

Donwell chapter, and his only conversation is with Emma, who has just assisted Jane to escape the 'horrors' of her aunt and Mrs Elton. When she hears that Frank is 'sick of England' and wishes to escape to Europe – to travel and be free of all responsibility except to pursue pleasure – Emma's calm ease and good sense demonstrate her suitability to be the future mistress of Donwell: 'These are difficulties which you must settle for yourself' (3:6:397), she says, firmly ending the conversation.

In contrast, Emma's behaviour at Box Hill the next day is out of 'bounds' (3:7:401), like Frank's. The focus here is on the failure of good community relations under the pressures of selfishness, frivolity and an indulgence in point-scoring. The same group of people (except Mrs Weston and Mr Woodhouse) gather for no reason other than to wander around: there are no strawberries to pick, no productive estate to admire. Unlike Donwell, the place fails to bring the disparate group together: 'there seemed a principle of separation, between the other parties, too strong for any fine prospects, or any cold collation, or any cheerful Mr. Weston, to remove' (3:7:399). With Mr Knightley unable to exert the leadership he displayed the previous day via the physical metaphor of his prosperous estate, the picnic becomes a mere pleasure party. It soon descends into the spiritual and emotional chaos that is evident in Frank's barely concealed insults to Jane (who indicates her repudiation of the engagement), and Emma's all too obvious insult to Miss Bates. Mr Knightley's reproach to Emma at the end of this chapter brings on 'extraordinary' tears (3:7:409), and a major shake-up of Emma's complacent self-regard.

Operating almost invariably from Emma's point of view, the novel presents Jane Fairfax as a mystery – as much to the reader as she is to Emma. Jane represents, in fact, an alternative literary mode of being to that of Emma, who is the heroine of a comedy, guaranteed by her vitality and optimism to achieve a happy ending. Comedy cannot recognize tragedy; Emma simply misunderstands, misreads and mis-'writes' Jane. The fact that Frank *performs* as a romantic comedy leading man reinforces Emma's misreading.

In this novel where the boundaries of place are so symbolic, Austen is interested in showing the limits of the comic world-view, in demonstrating that it is permeable (as Shakespeare also shows, in the sad, deluded or violent figures that haunt the edges of his comedies). Jane, mobile but without a direction of her own, is a liminal figure in the novel. She is always seen either enclosed in an oppressive room, with her aunt and grandmother, or at social occasions (for her an ordeal), or walking alone – to the post office, or in Donwell-lane, or, most tellingly, 'wandering about the meadows, at some distance from Highbury' (3:9:426) when all hope seems gone. Jane's sense of isolation and oppression occasionally expresses itself in utterances that seem extreme and indecorous in Highbury's genteel world. They share the emotional register of the tragic heroines of contemporary drama:[3] 'There are places in town, offices, where inquiry would soon produce something – Offices for the sale – not quite of human flesh – but of human intellect.' When Mrs Elton thinks she means 'a fling at the slave-trade', Austen offers through Jane an analogy that reflects on the difficult position of dependent gentlewomen: 'governess-trade, I assure you, was all that I had in view; widely different certainly as to the guilt of those who carry it on; but as to the greater misery of the victims, I do not know where it lies' (2:17:325). Frank's public acknowledgement of Jane in the novel's last chapters suggests that she is a trophy that he has cleverly won; his attitude is not far removed from that of eighteenth-century slave-buyers who bought beautiful young African women to be concubines. Jane's last utterance in the novel, to an exultant Frank – 'How you can bear such recollections, is astonishing to me! – They *will* sometimes obtrude – but how you can *court* them!' (3:18:524) – might well make us feel anxious about the future happiness of this marriage.

No such anxiety, however, need trouble the reader's contemplation of Emma and George Knightley's marriage, despite a persistent line of criticism since the mid-twentieth century accusing Emma of frigidity ('a fair but frozen maid', only concerned with her relationship with her father) or unconscious lesbianism.[4] Emma notices the 'tall, firm, upright figure' of Mr Knightley at the Crown ball (3:2:352), admires his unexpectedly excellent dancing with Harriet, and flirtatiously insists on her need to dance with him – 'if you will ask me' (3:2:358). As Austen's Henry Tilney pointed out, dancing is 'an emblem of marriage' (*NA* 1:10:74), and Austen never deviates from the perception that those who dance well together are well matched. It makes Frank's snide comment to Emma about Jane's dancing all the more distressing when, on later readings, we know how Jane is in thrall to her secret love: 'I must have asked Miss Fairfax, and her languid dancing would not have agreed with me, after your's' (2:8:248).

If Emma, for much of the novel, 'has very little intention of ever marrying at all', it is because her idea of marriage (perhaps based on her sister's) denies the woman any adult responsibility in the partnership. As she says to Harriet:

> 'I have none of the usual inducements of women to marry. Were I to fall in love, indeed, it would be a different thing! but I never have been in love; it is not my way, or my nature; and I do not think I ever shall. And, without love, I am sure I should be a fool to change such a situation as mine.' (1:10:90)

This grandstanding declaration comes early on, before Emma has met and flirted with the attractive Frank, with whom she soon determines 'she could not be very much in love' (2:13:284). But her change of mind, and heart, arrives after the events of the novel – Harriet's serial crushes, Jane's devastating secret passion – cause her finally to realize that desire is undeniable when Cupid is at work: 'It darted through her, with the speed of an arrow, that Mr. Knightley must marry no one but herself!' (3:11:444). Marriage between Emma and George Knightley will obviously benefit the community, and Emma will assume a much more responsible role as chatelaine of both Donwell and Hartfield (though she may never give up her habit of 'encouraging' likely matches in this wider sphere of power). Mr Knightley's willingness to make his home at Hartfield until the death of Mr Woodhouse signals his social flexibility. And that Mr Woodhouse's consent to the arrangement is finally brought about by a comic small-town emergency – 'Pilfering [of poultry-yards] was *housebreaking* to Mr. Woodhouse's fears' (3:19:528) – brings the novel firmly back into the optimistic world of comedy. In the last of the novel's games with punning nomenclature, the subliminal suggestion is that the poultry-house is a metonym for Mr Woodhouse: that he himself is the emotional and intellectual equivalent of a wooden shed. Emma and Mr Knightley will eventually move from the 'field of the heart' where much of the novel has been played out, to their final home of Done-well Abbey. Snobbish Mrs Elton, now thoroughly displaced as self-appointed queen of Highbury, will continue to be an irritant, but will not disturb 'the perfect happiness of the union'.

Persuasion

Shorter by the length of a volume than *Emma*, *Persuasion* operates in a very different version of 'Jane Austen's world'. As Brian Southam and Jocelyn Harris have shown,[5] in this novel Austen makes creative use of her close acquaintance with Navy culture through her family's involvement in the naval endeavours of Britain in the Napoleonic Wars. *Persuasion* is firmly anchored in the world of contemporary politics: although the action takes place during a period of peace (June 1814–February 1815), when the naval officers are on shore leave, early readers would have been aware that the novel concludes just before Napoleon's escape from Elba and the resumption of the war with France. The battle of Waterloo would end that war in June 1815.

If *Emma* is 'fixed ... absolutely fixed' in the environs of Highbury, Anne Elliot is more like Jane Fairfax, carried about from place to place in a parody of freedom that is actually dependent on her uncaring family's idea of where Anne would be most 'useful', or least in the way. In the course of the two volumes, she moves first from her home at Kellynch-hall in Somersetshire, to her sister's house at Uppercross a few miles away. The fateful excursion to Lyme, seventeen miles to the south, on the sea coast of Dorset, concludes the first volume. Volume 2 takes place almost entirely in Bath, the second most fashionable city in the country, in the north of Somerset – a place which Austen knew well, but by all accounts did not love. Anne thinks of her stay there as an 'imprisonment' (2:3:148).[6]

She does not know – as readers do, or at least hope – that she will be pursued to Bath by Austen's most romantic hero, Captain Frederick Wentworth. Clues in the first volume indicate that the novel is, generically, a romance – that is, it relies upon chance connections (preferably in different places) to reunite the heroine and hero after their first, fleeting acquaintance. It's the novelist's business to supply these connections – in this case, that the tenants of Sir Walter's country estate will be the sister and brother-in-law of Anne's former suitor, Captain Wentworth. Just as manipulative in the romance style is Louisa's fall from the Cobb at Lyme, an event that Austen deliberately ironizes in order to deflect criticism that she is writing sensational literature in the manner of popular novelists: 'By this time the report of the accident had spread among the workmen and boatmen about the Cobb, and many were collected near them, to be useful if wanted, at any rate, to enjoy the sight of a dead young lady, nay, two dead young ladies, for it proved twice as fine as the first report' (1:12:120).

Austen directs her irony at many targets in this novel. Her art was clearly heading in this direction, as the final novel-fragment 'Sanditon' indicates, with its robust satire of the contemporary fad for health resorts and the capitalist speculation associated with them. In *Persuasion*, Austen satirizes unmercifully the snobbery and shallowness of Sir Walter Elliot, who 'never took up any book but the Baronetage; there he found occupation for an idle hour, and consolation in a distressed one' (1:1:3): the proper book for such activities is, of course, the Bible. The worst of Austen's failing father figures, Sir Walter lacks affection for anyone but himself – his rooms are full of mirrors, as Admiral Croft remarks with astonishment (2:1:138). Even worse for Anne is the lack of sisterly love from either of her sisters, considering how strong that bond has been in every previous novel of Austen's: both Elizabeth and Mary are vain, silly and selfish. As the novel begins, Anne is completely alone: 'Anne, with an elegance of mind and sweetness of character, which must have placed her high with any people of real understanding, was nobody with either father or sister; her word had no weight, her convenience was always to give way – she was only Anne' (1:1:6). Anne is a Cinderella, with two uncaring sisters and a potential stepmother aptly named Mrs Clay. Sir Walter is unable to see this lady's metaphorical clay feet, though almost everyone else can see that she is only pursuing him for his social status (the widow's surname indicates that her previous marriage was far from aristocratic).

Even Anne herself, however, is at times subject to the novelist's ironical eye for self-indulgence. On the walk to Winthrop, during which Wentworth flirts with Louisa Musgrove, Anne protects herself from pain by 'repeating to herself some few of the thousand poetical descriptions extant of autumn, that season of peculiar and inexhaustible influence on the mind of taste and tenderness' (1:10:90). Here Anne sounds self-conscious and artificial in contrast to the naturalness of 'it was not possible, that when within reach of Captain Wentworth's conversation with either of the Miss Musgroves, she should not try to hear it'. One exchange between Wentworth and Louisa is particularly mortifying:

'If I loved a man, as she loves the Admiral, I would be always with him, nothing should ever separate us, and I would rather be overturned by him, than driven safely by anybody else.'
It was spoken with enthusiasm.
'Had you?' cried he, catching the same tone; 'I honour you!' (1:10:91)

We are told 'Anne could not immediately fall into a quotation again'. In Austen's fictive world, social reality, however crass, usually outweighs the solo 'musings' of sensitive souls. Anne's story in fact shows her re-entry into the social world, via utterances that are heard and attended to (unlike on this early occasion, when 'nobody heard, or at least, nobody answered her' when she attempts to enter the conversation). She increasingly takes part in conversations, even at times leading them, particularly in dialogues with her new friends in the Navy community.

One of the most notable of these occurs at Lyme with Captain Benwick, who is also a devotee of poetry. '[A] very good impulse of her nature obliged her to begin an acquaintance with him'; they are soon discussing 'poetry, the richness of the present age, and [had] gone through a brief comparison of opinion as to the first-rate poets.' Austen depicts Benwick as one who has also loved and lost, and is thus inclined to indulge in maudlin reflections aided by the current fashions in poetry:

he shewed himself so intimately acquainted with all the tenderest songs of the one poet [Scott], and all the impassioned descriptions of hopeless agony of the other [Byron]; he repeated, with such tremulous feeling, the various lines which imaged a broken heart, or a mind destroyed by wretchedness, and looked so entirely as if he meant to be understood, that she ventured to hope he did not always read only poetry, and to say, that she thought it was the misfortune of poetry to be seldom safely enjoyed by those who enjoyed it completely. (1:11:108)

This ironical commentary on the limitations of the Romantic poets of 'the present age'[7] operates through Anne, not against her; but, when she 'ventured to recommend a larger allowance of prose in his daily study', she finds herself 'amused at the idea of her coming to Lyme to preach patience and resignation to a young man whom she had never seen before; nor could she help fearing, on more serious reflection, that, like many other great moralists and preachers, she had been eloquent on a point in which her own conduct would ill bear examination' (1:11:101). Self-irony is part of Anne's necessary growth.

Having introduced the boundary-breaking explorations of contemporary Romantic poetry, Austen does not, however, simply dismiss this literature as solipsistic. Focusing on its heroine's inner life, her memories and consciousness of loss, *Persuasion* is the most poetic of Austen's novels;[8] and Austen accords with Romantic views of Nature as a powerful and potentially regenerative force. The walk to Winthrop includes a striking visual image: a 'gradual ascent through large enclosures, where the ploughs at work, and the fresh-made path spoke the farmer counteracting the sweets of poetical despondence, and meaning to have spring again' (1:10:91). This becomes a metaphor for Anne herself, who is associated throughout the novel with an image-cluster based on the indication that, physically, 'her bloom had vanished early' (1:1:6) because of her disappointment in love. By the time they are all at Lyme, however, 'She was looking remarkably well; her very regular, very pretty features, having the bloom and freshness of youth restored by the fine wind which had been blowing on her complexion, and by the animation of eye which it had also produced' (1:12:112). Nature can regenerate people in ways that Gowland's lotion, recommended by Sir Walter to counteract the signs of ageing, can only achieve through vain self-delusion. In a striking passage as the party arrives at Lyme, Austen emphasizes the charismatic power of the natural world, its potential to affect both body and spirit: 'Charmouth, with its high grounds and extensive sweeps of country, and still more, its sweet, retired bay, backed by dark cliffs, where fragments of low rock among the sands make it the happiest spot for watching the flow of the tide, for sitting in unwearied contemplation.' She concludes with positively Coleridgean admiration for 'Pinny, with its green chasms between romantic rocks' (1:12:103).

Anne's restored 'bloom' is figured also in Captain Wentworth's trusting appeal to her after Louisa's fall:

> 'You will stay, I am sure; you will stay and nurse her;' cried he, turning to her and speaking with a glow, and yet a gentleness, which seemed almost restoring the past. – She coloured deeply, and he recollected himself and moved away. (1:12:123)

The terms in which both characters are described suggest their bodily awareness of renewed attraction: Wentworth's 'glow' (a term used regularly to describe his personal warmth), Anne's blush. 'Anne hoped she had outlived the age of blushing' (1:6:52), we are told in volume 1, but in volume 2, after the events of Lyme, she blushes or colours on no fewer than seven occasions as she contemplates the possibility that Captain Wentworth is 'unshackled and free' (2:6:182). This metaphor evokes the body, and recalls those occasions in volume 1 when Anne, in confusion and delight, experiences unexpected physical contact with Wentworth: when he removes the obstreperous young nephew from her back (1:9:86–7); when he lifts her into the Crofts' carriage, and she 'felt . . . that his will and his hands had done it' (1:10:98).

Underlining this image-cluster is the novel's chronology, beginning in autumn and proceeding through the winter in Bath to the prospect of spring. The coldness associated with Anne's snobbish sister Elizabeth, as when Sir Walter and Miss Elliot's 'entrance seemed to give a general chill' (2:10:245) to the company of friends gathered at the White Hart, is offset by the continual displays of warmth and hospitality from the good-hearted elder Musgroves and the bluff, companionable Navy folk. It is the latter who, congregating in 'little knots' in the Bath streets – including Mrs Croft, 'looking as intelligent and keen as any of the officers around her' (2:6:183) – provide an image of changing social leadership: a profession that actively serves and protects the nation rather than letting the national estate run into debt, as Sir Walter has done. Anne will join this new social grouping by marrying Wentworth.[9]

Austen set herself a challenge in modernizing the Cinderella romance and making the hero a leader in a profession that requires energy, determination and luck, rather than a good family. The final artistic question was how finally to bring the lovers together, without undercutting Anne's renewed authority, hope and bloom. Austen wrote two versions of the denouement, and the cancelled chapters (2: Appendix 1:278–325) and their replacement (2:10–12:230–75) provide unique insights into her creative imagination at its peak.[10]

The first version makes Anne the passive recipient of Wentworth's renewed proposal, aided unwittingly by Admiral Croft as a sort of genie. Tactless and officious, he dragoons Wentworth into asking Anne if she is engaged to Mr Elliot, and will therefore wish to resume residency at Kellynch Hall. In the awkward conversation in the Crofts' drawing room, Anne is nearly silent as Wentworth dutifully conveys this enquiry. After she manages to stammer out a denial that there is any 'Truth in any such report', Wentworth sits by her:

> & looked, with an expression which had something more than penetration in it, something softer. – Her Countenance did not discourage. – It was a silent, but a very powerful Dialogue; – on his side, Supplication, on her's acceptance. – Still, a little nearer – and a hand taken and pressed – and 'Anne, my own dear Anne!' – bursting forth in the fullness of exquisite feeling – and all Suspense & Indecision were over. – They were re-united. (Appendix 1:318)

All the action here is on Wentworth's side, which conforms to the traditional male courtship role. Austen was soon dissatisfied with this, thinking it 'tame and flat', and undertook a radical revision.[11]

In the revised chapter 11, the action takes place in the Musgroves' Bath hotel, in a room crowded once again with many of the novel's good-hearted people. Anne listens to a conversation between Mrs Musgrove and Mrs Croft about the inadvisability of long engagements, while in another part of the room Captain Wentworth, who is writing a letter, also over-hears it, and gives 'one quick, conscious look at her' (2:11:251). What follows is an extraordinary scene in which Austen uses her knowledge of the theatre to focus attention on Anne as the heroine. Captain Harville engages her at a window – a space like a stage, but with a view out towards the world – debating with her whether men or women are more constant in love. Anne speaks with an eloquence that Harville can hardly match, as she voices the thoughts that have been the subject of her silent reflections for eight years. In doing so she echoes the arguments of contemporary feminists:[12]

> 'We certainly do not forget you, so soon as you forget us. It is, perhaps, our fate rather than our merit. We cannot help ourselves. We live at home, quiet, confined, and our feelings prey upon us. You are forced on exertion. You have always a profession, pursuits, business of some sort or other, to take you back into the world immediately, and continual occupation and change soon weaken impressions.'
>
> ... 'if you please, no reference to examples in books. Men have had every advantage of us in telling their own story. Education has been theirs in so much higher a degree; the pen has been in their hands. I will not allow books to prove any thing.' (2:11:253–5)

All this time, Wentworth is a silent audience; he even drops his pen as the force of Anne's utterances strikes him. The pen is no longer in his hands, nor, Austen implicitly claims, in those of male novelists. Wentworth picks up his pen to write an impassioned letter: 'I can listen no longer in silence. I must speak to you by such means as are within my reach. You pierce my soul. I am half agony, half hope. Tell me not that I am too late, that such precious feelings are gone for ever' (2:11:257–8); but his language seems melodramatic and second-hand. True poetic intensity is exemplified in Anne's final speech, with its interrupted rhythm, its touch of alliteration, and the dying fall of the contrasted 'existence' and 'hope' connected by the stark final verb: 'All the privilege I claim for my own sex (it is not a very enviable one, you need not covet it) is that of loving longest, when existence or when hope is gone' (2:11:256).

When Anne and Wentworth are finally able to be alone together, their reunion takes place out of doors. Even in Bath, there is an area where nature is more meaningful than elegant architecture or social spaces: 'the comparatively quiet and retired gravel walk, where the power of conversation would make the present hour a blessing indeed' (2:11:261). The reunited lovers, 'heedless of every group around them, seeing neither sauntering politicians, bustling house-keepers, flirting girls, nor nursery-maids and children', talk over the past as they 'slowly paced the gradual ascent'. Here Austen recalls the 'gradual ascent' of volume 1's walk to Winthrop, with its promise of spring again. Austen does not obtrude on the lovers at this point; just as in *Pride and Prejudice*, she leaves a further passage of reflection and explanation for a later encounter. In the revised version, Anne and Wentworth talk about whether she was right in being persuaded by Lady Russell to break off the engagement eight years earlier. 'To me', explains Anne, 'she was in the place of a parent' (2:11:267–8), and duty to one she respected (unlike her father) required her to submit – even though she would never have offered the same advice herself. Wentworth also has some rethinking to do: if he had not been 'too proud to ask again' once he had attained professional success, Anne would have been his six years earlier. Thus the issue of the moral force of 'persuasion'[13] remains unresolved, contingent on circumstances as it is in real life. Contingency, 'the dread of a future war' is 'all that could dim her sunshine', Austen writes in the final paragraph in both versions. Thus she elegantly brings together the two planes of the novel: its consciousness of contemporary political and social reality, and its deployment of romantic folk tale and the poetic imagination.

In attempting to distinguish between the artistic achievements of these two novels, we might focus on the heroines' ages: Emma 'nearly twenty-one', about to reach her majority, Anne 27 and feeling herself to be on the shelf. Love yet to be discovered, contrasted with love lost and hoping against hope to be recovered, makes *Emma* a romantic comedy and *Persuasion* something that critics have called elegiac. Yet this is to disregard the two novels' acute social commentary: Austen's observation of the ingrained habits and inexorable movements towards change of the characters making up the community of each novel's world. When Anne arrives for her visit to Uppercross, Austen writes, 'The Musgroves, like their houses, were in a state of alteration, perhaps of improvement. The father and mother were in the old English style, and the young people', full of energy and optimism, 'in the new', or 'modern' (1:5:43). To be 'English', that is, does not necessarily mean to be conservative, just as being up to date does not imply political radicalism. In each novel there is an energetic and sensible man who cheerfully fulfils his duty to develop and protect the England he lives in, eventually to be joined by the heroine as his wife. Perhaps a more telling artistic and thematic distinction is to be found in the mobility of these young women: whereas for the naturally conservative Emma to travel to the seaside will be the beginning of her life's real adventures as a married woman and mistress of Donwell, for the surprisingly progressive Anne, the sea that surrounds a beleaguered England will always be part of her consciousness as 'a sailor's wife'.

NOTES

1. Cited in Deirdre Le Faye, *Jane Austen: A Family Record* (Cambridge University Press, 2004), p. 209.
2. Richard Cronin and Dorothy McMillan, 'Introduction', *Emma* (Cambridge University Press, 2005), pp. lxvii–lxviii, lxx–lxxii. This aspect has been largely disregarded in readings that stress the novel's conservatism.
3. Penny Gay, 'Jane Fairfax and the "She-tragedies" of the Eighteenth Century', *Persuasions*, 29 (2007), 121–31.
4. Claudia L. Johnson discusses this reading of Emma's personality in Chapter 15 in this book, pp. 242–3; a longer version is in her chapter on *Emma* in *Equivocal Beings: Politics, Gender, and Sentimentality in the 1790s* (University of Chicago Press, 1995).
5. Brian Southam, *Jane Austen and the Navy* (2000, 2nd edn, rev., Greenwich: National Maritime Museum, 2005); Jocelyn Harris, *A Revolution Almost beyond Expression: Jane Austen's Persuasion* (Newark, NJ: University of Delaware Press, 2007).
6. See Harris, *A Revolution*, ch. 9 for contemporary descriptions of Bath which support Austen's dislike, and underpin her satire of the society it attracted.
7. Peter Knox-Shaw, *Jane Austen and the Enlightenment* (Cambridge University Press, 2006) and Harris, *A Revolution*, point out the specific relevance of Austen's references to these poets in their chapters on *Persuasion*.
8. William Deresiewicz, *Jane Austen and the Romantic Poets* (New York: Columbia University Press, 2004) writes illuminatingly about the intersections between *Persuasion*, Scott and Byron's poetry, and the national sense of 'bereavement' following the Napoleonic Wars, pp. 136–58. He reads the novel as 'a story of the great historical transition England was living through' (p. 153); 'England's future is Anne and Wentworth, but it is also William Walter Elliot and Mrs. Clay' (p. 157).
9. A great deal of criticism has argued for and against the idea that this progressivist view of early nineteenth-century society, in which the Navy's hierarchy of merit displaces the hereditary aristocracy, is central to the novel. See Janet Todd and Antje Blank, 'Introduction', *Persuasion* (Cambridge University Press, 2006), pp. lxxi–lxxiv. Harris develops Joseph Kestner's argument ('Revolutionizing Masculinities', *Persuasions*, 16 (1994), 147–60) that Wentworth is based to some degree on the naval hero Lord Nelson (but improves on his 'domestic virtues'), *A Revolution*, ch. 5. Southam, *Navy*, ch. 11, provides a detailed historical context for the novel's depiction of the Navy, and argues that the novel deliberately recalls the great days of the Navy, to counter its recent demoralizing losses in the American war of 1812–15.

10. See Harris' discussion of both the original and the revisions, *A Revolution*, chs. 2 and 3.

11. J. E. Austen Leigh, *A Memoir of Jane Austen*, ed. Kathryn Sutherland (Oxford University Press, 2002), p. 125.

12. Isobel Grundy has drawn attention to a similar passage by Anna Laetitia Barbauld: see '*Persuasion*, or the Triumph of Cheerfulness', in *Jane Austen's Business*, ed. Juliet McMaster and Bruce Stovel (London: Macmillan, 1996), pp. 7–8. Mary Wollstonecraft's influence on Austen's thinking about the position of women has been analysed by feminist critics since the 1970s, most notably Margaret Kirkham, *Jane Austen, Feminism and Fiction* (1983, 2nd edn, rev., London: Athlone Press, 1997), esp. ch. 6 *passim* and p. 147; and Johnson, *Equivocal Beings*, 'Afterword'.

13. As Linda Bree writes, 'Austen often plays on the varying meanings of the word, taking advantage of its potential for shifting interpretation and thus destabilizing the certainties that may seem to surround the central act of persuasion explored in the novel' ('Introduction', *Persuasion*, ed. Linda Bree (Canada: Broadview Press, 1998), p. 9).

5

MARGARET ANNE DOODY

The early short fiction

In Jane Austen's unfinished *Catharine, or the Bower*, found in the notebook *Volume the Third*, we hear silly Camilla Stanley and her mother gushing over Camilla's correspondence with her friend Augusta:

> 'You received a Letter from Augusta Barlow to day, did not you my Love? said her Mother –. She writes remarkably well I know.'
>
> 'Oh! Yes Ma'am, the most delightful Letter you ever heard of. She sends me a long account of the new Regency walking dress Lady Susan has given her, and it is so beautiful that I am quite dieing with envy for it.'
>
> 'Well, I am prodigiously happy to hear such pleasing news of my young freind; I have a high regard for Augusta, and most sincerely partake in the general Joy on the occasion. But does she say nothing else? it seemed to be a long Letter – Are they to be at Scarborough?'
>
> 'Oh! Lord, she never once mentions it, now I recollect it; and I entirely forgot to ask her when I wrote last. She says nothing indeed except about the Regency,'
>
> 'She *must* write well thought Kitty, to make a long Letter upon a Bonnet and Pelisse.' (*J* 263)

Austen's abortive novel can be heard here making fun of the epistolary mode, and of both the opposing views regarding female letter-writing. Mrs Stanley approves of female correspondence: 'I have from Camilla's infancy taught her to think the same . . . nothing forms the taste more than sensible and Elegant Letters' (262). This gush, like a pabulum concocted out of Hester Chapone's *Letters on the Improvement of the Mind* (1773), cannot quite conceal Mrs Stanley's pride in having her daughter correspond with the daughter of Lady Halifax – a name amusingly reminiscent of Lord Halifax, author of a famous treatise *Advice to a Daughter*, a conduct book inhibiting to most female activity and feeling. Mrs Percival, Catharine's aunt, takes the more traditional and sterner view, seeing 'a correspondence between Girls as productive of no good, and as the frequent origin of imprudence and Error by the effect of pernicious advice and bad Example' (262).

This mini-debate rages amusingly in this passage, as if there had been a revolution in manners. As debaters, the women manage to ignore the decorous insipidity and total triviality of the letters themselves, which reinforce a culturally desirable female vanity, empty-headedness and fashion-conscious consumerism. In Richardson's *Clarissa*, or in Eliza Fenwick's *Secresy*, authority figures are not unreasonable in imagining that a female correspondence can change someone's mind and behaviour; correspondence can corrupt or encourage, and thus bring about some revolution in manners. It is more exciting to believe that than to think that false values merely repeat themselves – as seen in Mrs Stanley's formal but hyperbolical expression – a hyperbole bought at the expense of realism. 'I . . . most sincerely partake in the general Joy on the occasion' (263) – as if Augusta had got engaged or had a baby, instead of acquiring her 'Regency walking dress'.

The phrase 'Regency walking dress' is itself my chief focus of interest. When I was preparing the edition of *Catharine and Other Writings*, I found that the manuscript of *Volume the Third* revealed that this phrase was substituted for another, but I failed to decipher exactly the expression crossed out. It could have been 'Bonnet' with an underdeveloped 'b'. It looked a little like 'Panol', or 'Parrot' – or 'Parisol'. Recently, however, with the benefit of digital-imaging technology, Jenny McAuley has discovered that the replaced word was almost certainly 'Pierrot', referring to 'a kind of sleeved, close-fitting jacket or bodice', very fashionable in the 1780s and 1790s; this term was appropriately replaced by the more up-to-the minute 'Regency walking dress'. The 'Pierrot' was excised twice, for it also appeared in the sentence 'She says nothing indeed except about the Regency.'[1]

How and when did this change come about? I cannot accept George Holbert Tucker's suggestion that it indicates *Catharine* was written as early as 1788–9, when George III's first serious attack of deranging illness brought on agitation for a Regency.[2] *Volume the Third* was begun in May 1792 and the Regency crisis of the winter of 1788–9 was over by June 1789, when George III's return to health was celebrated.

I incline, rather, to accept Deirdre Le Faye's suggestion that Jane Austen rediscovered her earlier manuscript notebooks when she, her mother and Cassandra at last came to roost in Chawton in July 1809.[3] 'Evelyn' is also added to in another hand, most likely by nephew Edward, and the last paragraph of *Catharine* is also the product of these other hands – and minds.[4] The likeliest scenario is that on digging out her old notebooks Jane Austen shared her fiction with the nephew and niece, and allowed them to join her in her old game of writing. I believe their interest, perhaps even enthusiasm, inspired her to return to writing, and thus to undertake the serious and heavy work of finally revising *Sense and Sensibility*, the first of her novels to be published, in the very year of the Regency, 1811.

Catharine, or the Bower, that unfinished fiction, was probably begun in the mid-1790s, certainly not before the date at the top of the notebook volumes – 6 May 1792; interior references to Charlotte Smith's novels accord well with the date 1792–3. The 'Regency walking dress' added to it indicates that Jane Austen turned back to this work at some point after – probably very soon after – the Regency Act was passed by Parliament on 5 February 1811. Fashion magazines were very quick to seize on the new era. The *Lady's Magazine* of 1811, along with the enticements of a running serial entitled *Sappho – An Historical Romance*, includes advertisements for, among other things, a plume of three feathers with silver and gold ornaments 'universally worn for the Regent's fête'; 'A new and elegant Pattern for Regency Borders' and a child's dress 'with the Regent hat of grey silk'. I have not yet found a 'Regency walking dress', but in picking up the comedy of such terms Austen was undoubtedly reflecting a trend of the time of 1811. Camilla's remark gains a new comedy: 'Augusta says nothing indeed except about the Regency', for Augusta is thus made to sound as if she had a political interest in current affairs, although her interest is entirely ladylike and fashionable.

In the period between 1809 and 1811 Jane Austen was working – and who can doubt *intently* working – on her own early writings. She was bringing what had been produced in the 1790s into line with current fashion. We have speculated about the 'Lost Novels' – lost to us in their old form. We know that *First Impressions* was the prototype of *Pride and Prejudice*; we believe that an *Elinor and Marianne*, perhaps epistolary, was the germ of *Sense and Sensibility*; and that *Susan*, which Jane Austen had tried to publish, and which had been once accepted (in 1803) but never brought out, was revised to make *Northanger Abbey* (published posthumously). Interestingly, 'Susan' was reclaimed from the publisher (Crosby) when the move to Chawton was an immediate prospect. Much of Jane Austen's writing career after the move to Chawton in 1809 consisted in revising or cannibalizing her own older works. But the revisions should be seen as a major matter.

In bringing her works into line with the new era – putting them into their regency walking dress, as it were – Austen underwent a sort of personal and authorial revolution. That revolution made her publishable. It is startling to realize that Jane Austen might *never* have published. During the early years of the new century she had obviously begun to feel that her style of writing was not going to be acceptable to the press and the arbiters of taste. From her mid-twenties she had started to make some effort to reach a public, but had been severely baulked by the lack of respect paid to the never-printed *Susan*. After the death of her father in 1805, Austen, now in her thirties, seems for a while to have given up writing, save for odd comic verses to friends. Removal to a real home in Chawton, and probably also the society of some young relatives interested in writing, helped to free Austen's mind and restore confidence. But it was not the same sort of confidence as that of the young woman who wrote the material in the notebook *Volumes*.

Jane Austen had to change, in short, from a 1790s writer to a 'regency' writer. The term 'regency', always loosely used (especially as an adjective), ought to refer to the period from 1811 (when the Prince of Wales, 'Prinny', was made Regent, as his father George III was unfit to govern by reason of insanity) to 1820 (when George III died and the Prince Regent became King George IV). In practice, the term in English usage has come to refer to the period from the onset of the nineteenth century to the 1820s. Jane Austen has really been recast in certain quarters as the first in line of the writers of 'regency romances' – a fact underdiscussed in academic circles. I believe the appeal of the 'regency romance' – for modern intents and purposes a genre invented by Georgette Heyer (1902–74) – lies in the combination of the traditional 'love story' with the idea of a charming and tastefully pert woman who is a *little* likely to question the status quo, but not too much. Of course, there is always the dashing lover – less likely to appear in Austen. Yet I think Jane Austen herself does bear some relation to this genre. Her kind of novel was achieved by a special mixture of eighteenth-century qualities of attitude and style combined with domestic seriousness and Romantic respect for both idealism and power. Georgette Heyer started by writing novels set in the eighteenth century (*The Black Moth*, 1921), but made her mark when she invented the story set in the Regency with *These Old Shades* (1926). Heyer, in the period from the 1920s to the 1950s, caught – and in her own way also parodied – the qualities in literature wanted by her audience. These were not at all dissimilar to some of the qualities desired by Jane Austen's public, though Heyer has the added element of a version of pastoral. Her 'regency' is a happy abode of the past, a place to escape to. So Jane Austen's temporal setting has become idyllic – though it was a present-day setting for the author.

The desire for the combination of the flippant and the serious, the nostalgic and the entertaining, can be postulated in the readership (both male and female) of both writers. Heyer, like Austen, reached a public tired by a very difficult war which had brought not only painful loss but great upheaval. Some responses to the threat of change and some modified form of patriotism had to be incorporated in women's writing if it were to succeed – yet it could not be successful if it proposed itself as too critical a commentary. Fiction had to take the fundamental shape of things seriously, and to play by the rules.

I want to propose that Jane Austen's advance to the Long Novel acceptable to her contemporaries was a process of accommodation. It was a difficult and strenuous process – she had, as it were, to reinvent herself as a regency figure. After all, the 'regency' itself is a figure for substitution. We are so devoted to the six Austen novels, it is hard for us to think of them as substitutes for anything – but they may not really have been the works Jane Austen wanted to write.

Her comments on the process reach us filtered through irony – as in the famous remark in a letter of February 1813, about the 'defects' of *Pride and Prejudice*:

> The work is rather too light & bright & sparkling; – it wants shade; – it wants to be stretched out here & there with a long Chapter – of sense if it could be had, if not of solemn specious nonsense – about something unconnected with the story; an Essay on Writing, a critique on Walter Scott, or the history of Buonaparte – or anything that would form a contrast & bring the reader with increased delight to the playfulness & Epigrammatism of the general stile. (*L* 203)

We take this simply as irony in self-praise, but there is more to it. 'Sparkle' was no longer in order – and particularly not in a woman. 'Sparkle' in general meant that old Augustan style, the taste for paradox and wit, for snip-snap antithesis – all things Jane Austen inherited. William Wordsworth, who had often praised the style of the poet Anne Finch, Countess of Winchilsea, was to say of Finch: 'her style in rhyme is often admirable, chaste, tender, and vigorous, and entirely free from sparkle, antithesis and ... over-culture'.[5] Lady Winchilsea's poetry is good because it is tender, and does *not* sparkle. Austen became increasingly aware, I think, that playfulness and epigrammatism had decided dangers. Regency readers wanted to be amused, but they liked to have a clear line drawn, the now-to-be-completely-serious line. An author like Maria Edgeworth met this demand through didacticism, and allowed herself some political leverage, though at the cost of suppressing a wit rarely allowed full emergence. Frances Burney, publishing *The Wanderer* (1814) in this new climate, got badly frozen by disapproval and some very negative reviews in reaction against her inclusive satire on England in the Revolutionary period. Burney wrote no more novels.

Jane Austen's relations to and with the 'Regency' are paradigmatically played out in the merry amusing comedy of relations between herself, the Prince Regent and the Prince Regent's librarian, James Stanier Clarke. It was he who entertained Jane Austen at the library of Carlton House in November 1815 – only a few months after Waterloo. Clarke told her that she was 'at liberty to dedicate any future Work to H[is] R[oyal] H[ighness] the P[rince] R[egent]' (*L* 296). She tried to clarify whether this request amounted to a command, and Clarke's reiteration on paper that permission had been given showed Austen clearly that she was expected to dedicate her next work to the

Prince. She was also told, flatteringly, 'The Regent has read & admired all your publications' (296). Though her opinion of the Regent himself, judging from comments in her other letters, was not high, Austen made the Prince Regent the lucky recipient of the dedication of *Emma*. The Regent undoubtedly intended to do good to Austen by getting her name more widely known; he supplied her thus with advertising that did have its effect on reviewers and readership (see Chapter 1 by Jan Fergus in this book). Had Austen lived longer, she would have reaped the full benefit of this publicity. The Prince is to be congratulated on his taste. But James Stanier Clarke did go blethering on, suggesting that Austen write the life of a clergyman, modelled on his life, glorified. It was in evading this suggestion that Austen defiantly set herself down as 'the most unlearned, & uninformed Female who ever dared to be an Authoress' (306).

Unlike James Stanier Clarke, we have the benefit of Austen's parodic 'Plan of a Novel, according to hints from various quarters', which includes many phrases lifted straight from Clarke's letters, and applied to the father of the heroine:

> At last, hunted out of civilized Society, denied the poor Shelter of the humblest Cottage, they are compelled to retreat into Kamschatka where the poor Father, quite worn down, finding his end approaching, throws himself on the Ground, & after 4 or 5 hours of tender advice & parental Admonition to his miserable Child, expires in a fine burst of Literary Enthusiasm, intermingled with Invectives against Holders of Tythes. – Heroine inconsolable for some time – but afterwards crawls back towards her former Country. (*LM* 228–9)

This is great stuff, interwoven as it is with parodic references to other fictions, as well as with hidden references to the comments on Austen's novels passed by various acquaintances. The comedy, however, expresses irritation. In this 'Plan', novel-writing itself turns into a ridiculous ordeal. Dealing with James Stanier had been something of an ordeal. As the Regent's deputy, or the Regent's regent, as well as a clergyman, he is doubly a Father, and triply a substitute father. In the company of such mock fathers you get into the cold regions of Kamschatka, the extremity of Siberia.

Jane Austen's early writings, preserved for us in the three notebook *Volumes*, are short fictional pieces. It has been customary to imagine – unconsciously to imagine – that she always aspired to write three-volume novels, and that the early writings were mere apprenticeship or practice until she could arrive at that happier capacity for sustained work. But if we think of it, this may not be true. Short fiction has its place – and sometimes it is a very high place. The short fictional piece, the 'tale', had been used to good effect by earlier women writers such as Aphra Behn and Eliza Haywood. Eliza

Haywood, however, in mid-eighteenth century had to make a turn similar to Austen's. Her kind of short story and its longer sexy cousin the 'novel', or *novella*, had to be put aside for the sake of respectable long 'history' to match the works of Fielding and Richardson. So we move from stories such as *Fantomina* to the full-length *Miss Betsy Thoughtless*. Yet it was certainly not female practitioners alone who had an allegiance to the short fiction.

Short fiction is a favourite Enlightenment mode, engaged in by Voltaire, for one notable example. It was explored by Diderot (e.g. *Ceci n'est pas un conte*) and more cautiously taken up by Marmontel in his *Contes moraux* (1789–92). Marmontel's *Contes* were appearing in France at about the time Austen began *Volume the Third*. She might have known that Horace Walpole had written his *Hieroglyphic Tales*, stories first printed in 1785 and later published by Mary Berry in Walpole's *Collected Works* (1798). Charles Burney, reviewing them, said they contained 'a great many *odd fancies*' and in their allusions were 'sarcastic, personal, and sometimes profane'.[6] Walpole in his Postscript to these *Tales* says they are 'an attempt to vary the stale and beaten class of stories and novels, which, though works of invention, are almost always devoid of imagination'. He professes himself surprised that fiction (especially current fiction) is so dull: 'that there should have been so little fancy, so little variety, and so little novelty, in writings in which the imagination is fettered by no rules' (*Oriental Tales*, ed. Mack, p. 137). His tales play with the absurd, the disproportionate, the illicit; his characters are greedy bundles of expressionistic desire:

> [the princess] had purchased ninety-two dolls, seventeen baby houses, six cartloads of sugar plums, a thousand ells of gingerbread, eight dancing dogs, a bear and a monkey, four toyshops with all their contents, and seven dozen of bibs; and aprons of the newest fashion. They were jogging on with all this cargo over mount Caucasus. (*Oriental Tales* 119)

Robert Mack points out that the tales 'reach into every conceivable area of narrative invention ... "An entire world of invention lies open for your use and enjoyment", Walpole seems to say, "why not take advantage of it?"' ('Introduction', p. xxvii). So too we might imagine Jane Austen saying – that is, the Austen of the early fiction. The characters are full of a fine excess, of energy impossible and disproportionate, of physicality unconcealed:

> My Mother rode upon our little poney and Fanny and I walked by her side or rather ran, for my Mother ... galloped all the way. You may be sure we were in a fine perspiration ... Fanny has taken a great Many Drawings of the Country, which are very beautiful, tho' perhaps not such exact resemblances as might be wished, from their being taken as she ran along. It would astonish you to see all the Shoes we wore out in our Tour ... Mama was so kind as to lend us a pair of

blue Sattin Slippers, of which we each took one and hopped home from Hereford delightfully –. ('A Tour through Wales', *J* 224)

Like Walpole's personages, Austen's are wonderfully greedy, illicit mental collectors of wealth:

> 'I shall expect a new saddle horse, a suit of fine lace, and an infinite number of the most valuable Jewels. Diamonds such as never were seen, Pearls as large as those of the Princess Badroulbadour ... and Rubies, Emeralds, Toppazes, Sapphires, Amythists, Turkey stones, Agate, Beads, Bugles & Garnets.' ('The Three Sisters', from MS version)

Much of the comedy of these early fantastic tales comes from the fantasticating capacity of the mind not only to desire, but to create wants. Narrative follows these jumps of desire. Those persons, such as parents or clergymen, who might represent law or sobriety have really only different forms of desire to offer.[7]

Austen, like Cervantes, makes us see the organization of property and propriety from a comic underside:

> Beloved by Lady Harcourt, adored by Sir George and admired by all the World, she lived in a continued course of uninterrupted Happiness, till she had attained her eighteenth year: when happening one day to be detected in stealing a bank-note of 50 £, she was turned out of doors by her inhuman Benefactors. Such a transition to one who did not possess so noble and exalted a mind as Eliza, would have been Death, but she, happy in the conscious knowledge of her own Excellence, amused herself, as she sate beneath a tree with making and singing the following Lines ... ('Henry and Eliza', *J* 38–9)

In mocking depiction of the calm way in which the abnormal can be presented as normal, the criminal as the proper, the shameful as the excellent, Austen united with Cervantes and with others who target both individual lust and social assumptions.

Her stories explore irregular unions – hardly anybody is married, or married in a regular fashion. The heroine of 'Love and Freindship' is united to her true love shortly after he has wandered into their cottage. The young pair are married by the heroine's father: 'We were immediately united by my Father, who tho' he had never taken orders had been bred to the Church' (109). Austen's early fiction is a mock-pastoral world in which eviscerated institutions, or institutionalized ideas, though sometimes honoured in gesture, are unable to contain the characters' curiosity, animation or general desire for self-gratification. The desire for self-gratification prevails everywhere – including in the heroine modelled on Jane's best friend and devoted sister. In 'The Beautifull Cassandra' the heroine goes out walking with a bonnet intended for a countess 'on her gentle Head'. 'She then proceeded to a Pastry-cooks where she devoured six ices, refused to pay for them, knocked down the Pastry Cook and walked away' (54). This is not a moral world where punishment catches up with evil doers. At the end of her libidinous excursion Cassandra can whisper to herself, 'This is a day well spent' (56).

Jane Austen shares qualities with Rabelais – as G. K. Chesteron noticed.[8] She also has some of the cool wit of an eighteenth-century writer such as Diderot or a twentieth-century one such as Borges. Yet we have wanted to see these early works as chaotic and childish, mere 'prentice-hand attempts to perform what will be done properly in the six novels. For if the shorter works are not treated as childish effusions, they begin to loom very large indeed in Austen's œuvre, pointing to the alternative Austen who might have been a different writer, who might have figured in our calendar more like Diderot or Borges. It is not enough to say she is a parodist – though that is much – or to say that she is a satirist – which is a great deal more. We have to acknowledge, I think, that she here creates in her short fiction a 'world of her own', as we say – or that such a world becomes adumbrated. The world she creates is a world of libidinous pressures only fictively constrained by conceptual structures imposed as order. English laws regarding marriage and property or the new laws of the English novel are alike revealed as pseudo-orderly and slightly crazed structures. Here, Austen's world is one where the law of the Father applies only nominally – or not even that. The law of the Father is a kind of gesture in the air.

Modes of defying the father in rebellion or *revolution*, which are likewise conventional ideas in themselves, especially between 1789 and 1800, come in for equally scornful treatment. This can be seen in Edward's stilted and conventional defiance of his father in 'Love and Freindship'. Love is refracted narcissism. Dislike of others is not only common but, as it were, decriminalized. In preposterous play with the idyll, the characters fare as they will without paying – money is everywhere, but it is always going missing, or becoming invalid. Austen proposes that libidinous desire is prior to the economic system, although constantly getting attached to it. Libidinous desire gets attached, for instance, to the feudal system of inheritance, creating a greed that cheerfully witnesses the removal of parents and siblings. Desire is officially attached to the system of monogamy. In attaching itself to any such systems, however, the libido proves itself capable of evading or transforming them – in Austen's world.

This is a very frightening philosophic production on the part of a young woman. The disconcerting elements in Austen's fiction (even in the six novels) are sometimes very palpable obstacles to our smooth approbation. But these elements in her early fiction can be redefined as lack of skill in doing the accepted thing. Doubtless Crosby, the publisher who got *Susan*, intuited that

Austen's book didn't *feel* quite right, and put his response down to a sense that the author was amateurish, that she hadn't quite got the hang of writing novels. The obstreperous qualities that work well in short fiction were not highly valued in the novel. Short fiction was not as available to writers as it had been in the mid-eighteenth century as a vehicle for new and outrageous thought. The bright wit of the eighteenth century is felt to be political, and politically dangerous. The regency is a tight time. Regency fashions may have been sexy – but they hampered women's movement in tight skirts, and left men strangulated in neckcloths.

We tend to confuse the 'regency' manners of the Prince Regent and his circle with the tone of the period in general. In English culture in general, however, raffishness was out of favour, and morality – especially as that concerned the moral behaviour of young ladies – was steadily gaining ground. As Claudia Johnson has shown,[9] the era of the Napoleonic Wars brings a backlash against cultural experiment, and particularly against experiment in the representation of women in fiction. The courtship novel *has* returned. It is softened, moralized, made safer.

Augustan wit in general is shunned. The early nineteenth century admires the serious. Byron had been serious and melancholy in *Childe Harold*. He returned in *Don Juan* to wit – with a vengeance. But Byron was already an established author, and there is an intermixture of the serious and the personal and the pathetic which saves his mock-epic from the accusation of total flippancy. One of Byron's strengths is that he (or his narrator) can give us the impression of being able to see through Culture – Culture not in the anthropological sense but in the modern urban sense, of an accumulation of knowledge about knowledge and artefacts that serves an individual's social turn and creates a unified dominant class. Jane Austen shares a doubt about the cultural – in part, such doubt is an inheritance of Enlightenment views that what is past is prologue, and that everything should be held up to question. The Romantic Age in its own way takes 'culture' very seriously. We are headed towards the world of Matthew Arnold where there is a plain distinction between 'Culture' and 'Anarchy'. To Jane Austen, culture often *is* anarchy.

> I had for many years constantly hollowed whenever she played, *Bravo*, *Bravissimo*, *Encora*, *Da Capo*, *allegretto*, *con espressioné*, and *Poco presto* with many other such outlandish words, all of them as Eloisa told me expressive of my Admiration; and so indeed I suppose they are, as I see some of them in every Page of every Music book, being the Sentiments I imagine of the Composer. ('Lesley Castle', *J* 165–6)

Such a passage moves us from the simple satire (Charlotte's stupidity in not knowing musical terms) to a complex satire on cultural knowledge and its close relation to absurdity. Our thoughtful reaction is compounded by the culturally dense meanings of the two girls' names, 'Eloisa' and 'Charlotte'. 'Eloisa' refers us to the heroine of Rousseau's novel *Julie, ou la nouvelle Héloïse* (1761). Julie, the 'New Eloisa', is an emotionally complicated and doomed young woman who has sex before marriage and will meet a tragic fate. By contrast, 'Charlotte', the virtuous and practical beloved of the emotionally overwrought Werther in Goethe's *The Sorrows of Young Werther* (1774), involves herself in no illicit sex, and leaves the suffering to others. The names of Austen's characters in 'Lesley Castle' are thus complicated for any reader who has knowledge (guilty knowledge) of two famous but controversial novels about sex and suffering. To know such works is itself a cultural achievement, if one not without risk for women. Through such works women have access to philosophical ideas. Here, however, the reader's vision is beclouded by an excess of association. Reading Austen's 'Lesley Castle' one is apt to run into a new reading of Rousseau's 'Eloisa' as too limp and die-away, as well as into a parody of the bread-and-butter 'Charlotte' of *Werther*, who becomes that fiendish cook with a one-track mind, Charlotte Luttrell. Austen turns the culture into anarchy.

But the Novel itself – what of that? In England, in particular, the Novel had undergone many trials. The Renaissance and the seventeenth century had seen a great festival of fiction-reading, much amplified by new editions and translations of older novels from antiquity, such as the works of Helidorus, and from the Middle Ages, such as Boccaccio. The rage for fiction-reading gave rise to a certain nervousness. Sixteenth-century scholars and divines had begun to take a dim view of prose fiction. Yet, on the whole, it survived and prospered until that universal European post-war period of the later seventeenth century. After the abortive French revolution of the 1640s known as the 'Fronde', after the English Civil War and the Thirty Years War, European governments reformed themselves, more or less awkwardly, either into a more absolute monarchic form to achieve the status of nation state (such as France, and later Germany and Austria), or into a more republican form, allowing rule of an oligarchy. To both kinds of new politically adjusted power the tradition of prose fiction bore special dangers. The novel is critical of what is. It gives the younger generation a chance. Reading it can make women and boys think themselves too important. In France, the novel is represented as bourgeois – a brilliant stroke initiated by Boileau. In the plutocracies (England, Holland) the Novel under the label 'Romance' was attacked as too royalist, old-fashioned and feudal. Prose fiction continued to be in a period of great experiment in the early eighteenth century, but the mid century saw more determined efforts to police it, not the least of these being novel reviewing. Whole tracts of the older fiction (and in Britain, practically all foreign fiction) were labelled off-limits – a process of banning recorded in that ambiguous and clever novel that Jane Austen knew very well, Charlotte Lennox's *The Female Quixote*, in 1752. As Lennox shows us in that book, the Novel can be allowed to continue to exist – even the novel about a woman by a woman – but only if the terms are agreed to. Nothing outlandish or dangerous must be shown. The novel is to exhibit the taming of a girl as she dwindles into a wife – the story of a girl learning her place. This is the story that Rousseau adapts in creating Sophie in his *Emile* (1762).

The novel, then, is tamed. 'Realism' is the name that we give to an ideology of tameness and tightening applied to the novel. The novel in England – which defines itself as History or ultimately Novel as against *Romance* – is especially domesticated. The history of its domestication in relation to women has been traced by many other writers, including Vineta Colby, Sandra Gilbert and Susan Gubar, and Nancy Armstrong.[10] I see the point of this domestication in another sense. The new novel is *domestic* in that it deals with home, and with England. Foreigners don't count. If you meet a Muslim in a work of fiction, then it isn't a proper novel, but Romance. All sensation (this in an era of colonization, wars, battle, murder and sudden death) is the baggage of the bad old 'Romance'. The Novel is to be allowed to exist, and to be read by women and the young, on condition that it always knows its own place in the Culture, which is a low place. It is 'only a novel!' (*NA* 1:5:31). This is a quiet, subservient, inferior form. Its best use and sole justification is that it can inform the young (especially women) of well-known truths, and teach them their place in the universe. Realism is valued because it resists thought experiment. And if a woman writes only of what she strictly and severely knows, then her fictional world – unlike that of, say, the seventeenth-century French novelist Madeleine de Scudéry – will be constricted indeed.

The courtship plot of the regular novel is always sneered at (women, bless their silly little hearts, like to read love stories). But courtship is of the essence, particularly if it ends in a synthesizing middle-class marriage. Jane Austen's early works cannot be called courtship novels, though they show an exact knowledge of the formulas. In her six full novels, she had to adapt the courtship plot in good seriousness (or with some degree of seriousness). That she was not quite successful in her regency disguise, perhaps, can be felt in the weight of Scott's complaint, in his cumulative review of *Emma*, that Austen does not pay enough attention to love. It may be because of that review that Austen discusses love, and male and female views of it, as thoroughly as she does in *Persuasion*.

Certainly, the novel as it was being shaped – the domestic novel, safe for women to write – and read – was not the appropriate home of social criticism or free aesthetic play – still less of moral questioning. Young people – especially but not only women – were to be instructed in their moral duties. So heavy did the weight of the real regency formulations lie on the novel, one may feel, that the novel became flattened under the burden and passed out. How else can we explain the paucity of novels in the period between Jane Austen's death and Queen Victoria's ascent to the throne? The 1840s were to inaugurate a new era in fiction, but the preceding decades from a novel-lover's point of view are fairly dismal. There are few new writers in the 1820s and 1830s. Scott dominates the field, and he had developed in the historical novel a route out of the impasse offered by the domestic fiction. Maria Edgeworth did not die when Jane Austen did – she lived until 1849. But had she died in 1817 we should have lost but one important work by Edgeworth – the novel *Helen* (1834). Another novel, *Taken for Granted*, finished in 1838, was (interestingly) destroyed by its author. Frances Burney, the novelist, was apparently silenced by the reviews of *The Wanderer*. The author published a three-volume biography of her father in 1832, but wrote no more novels. Peacock's early spurt of novel-writing ceases with *Nightmare Abbey* (1818). There is one novel in the 1830s (*Crotchet Castle*, 1831); Peacock waited until the High Victorian Age to produce *Gryll Grange* (1860). Looking at such a record, one begins to think better of Catherine Gore, with her satiric 'silver fork' novels in the 1830s – but even Mrs Gore turned to songwriting and drama as more profitable.

The challenge that Jane Austen offered to other writers of fiction was not then to be taken up, and by the time it was truly taken up she was burdened with a certain imposed quaintness never quite totally shaken off. She could also be smothered in Aunt Jane-ism.

The challenge that Austen offered contemporary fiction arose from the challenge she herself faced – how to sustain some of her own deeper interests while submitting to the restrictions of the domestic and moral courtship novel as the only truly available form. What she does, I want to suggest, is to tap into the deep roots of the Novel as a whole – the Big Novel, not in the sense of the *long* novel but of the larger traditions of prose fiction, going back to antiquity. If a novel is deep enough it can escape the shallowness of contemporary polite and prudential formulas. Austen's depths are very well hidden. She is strikingly unlike her contemporaries, female as well as male, in not overtly alluding to any of the heathen mythology in her novels. Indeed, the allusion to the fact of its existence comes in the form of mockery:

> 'How long ago it is, aunt, since we used to repeat the chronological order of the kings of England ...'
> 'Yes', added the other; 'and of the Roman emperors as low as Severus; besides a great deal of the Heathen Mythology, and all the Metals, Semi-Metals, Planets, and distinguished philosophers.' (*MP* 1:2:21)

Austen is not going to let us catch her making her novels mythical. She customarily shies away even from explicit allegory of names of the type familiar enough in Fielding (with his 'Squire Western' and 'Mr. Allworthy'). We can catch her – just barely – in a name like Mr Knightley. But she uses to a considerable degree and in a very fascinating way what I call the 'tropes of the Novel'.

One of these important tropes is the image of *mud*, the mixture of earth and water, usually combined with a margin, threshold, or no-man's land of in-between. *Mud* is earthy and mobile, the deep primal slime from which things grow, the union of male and female, the party of *hylé*, the celebration of life on earth. Mud is thus exactly what is banned from drawing rooms and has no place in the transcendent. To name mud is to name what is *not* transcendent – it goes with the flesh, the muddy vesture of decay. Mr Knightley has to display his shoes to Mr Woodhouse to reassure him that he has no mud or dirt on them. This dry beginning of *Emma* tells us that relationships are baulked, that this is something of a waste land of sterility – the sterility arising from propriety. When the hero and the heroine at last come together, they are outdoors after a shower. Earth and water have reunited, there is plenty of dirt around, and fertility is possible. To use the image thus is to join in the great Novel-work of celebrating the physical, of resisting the transcendent insofar as that does not honour the world of matter and flesh. Elizabeth Bennet gets mud on her petticoats racing over the fields and leaping over stiles on a rainy day. Her muddy vesture scandalizes the Bingley sisters – but not Mr Darcy or ourselves. The beginning of 'The Watsons' shows the sisters 'As they splashed along the dirty lane' (*LM* 79). Life offers a new beginning.

It is this sense of vitality that offers the deepest pleasure in Austen's work. With this her truest 'religious feeling' (as we sometimes term it) is conjoined. We recognize in her mature novels the places of deception, the arid places where hypocrisy reigns, where the spiritless meets the spiritless. The truly spiritual in Austen is spirited.

In her early fiction, Jane Austen could write with zest and confidence. She had inherited a taste for irony, paradox and 'sparkle' from the eighteenth century. Her early writing is rough, violent, sexy, jokey. It sparkles with knowingness. It attacks whole structures, including cultural structures that had made a regularized and constricted place for the Novel, as well as the very workings (in stylized plot and character) of the English novel itself.

The ordeal of creating her own novel, I would suggest, was an ordeal painful for Jane Austen, a retreat to Kamschatka and a crawling back. The elements that we find in Austen's early short fiction are what kept her later works from dwindling into comfortable prosy little comedies of upper middle-class courtship, with didactic elements carefully inserted. Yet, to a certain extent and not in trifling ways, Austen had to pretend – in order to get published at all – that her mature novels were such innocuous and didactic things. At the beginning of the nineteenth century, Austen had, in effect, been warned that she would have to 'chill out' to match the chillier decorum that constituted the conventions of fiction allowed into public discourse. The original 'Siberia' to which she had been sent was the Siberia of rejection by publishers. She escaped, but at the price of subscribing to conformity, of adapting to the confinements of propriety. Her movements became constricted and she spoke in an altered tone. The early fictions tell us what Austen might have sounded like without such domestication. She had to go a very long way round to get back into fiction – wearing her regency walking dress, which must have been uncomfortable to walk in, and coming from Kamschatka.

NOTES

1. See *Volume the Third* MS, p. 67. I made these observations in preparing my edition of *Catharine and Other Writings*, ed. Margaret Anne Doody and Douglas Murray (Oxford University Press, 1993). See Jenny McAuley's '"A Long Letter Upon a Jacket and Petticoat": Reading Beneath some Deletions in the Manuscript of *Catharine, or the Bower*', a paper that was a product of her work with Kathryn Sutherland on *Jane Austen's Holograph Fiction Manuscripts, Persuasions*, 31 (2009), 191–8.
2. George Holbert Tucker, *Jane Austen: The Woman* (New York: St Martin's Press, 1994), p. 114.
3. Deirdre Le Faye, *Jane Austen: A Family Record* (London: British Library, 1989), p. xxii.
4. See Appendix E in Peter Sabor's edition of the *Juvenilia* in the Cambridge Edition (*J* 365–70).
5. Quoted in Roger Lonsdale, *Eighteenth-Century Women Poets: An Oxford Anthology* (New York: Oxford University Press, 1990), p. 6.
6. Robert Mack, 'Introduction', to Horace Walpole's *Oriental Tales*, ed. Robert Mack (Oxford University Press, 1992).
7. I have explored the 'takers' in the juvenilia in 'Jane Austen, that Disconcerting "Child"', in *The Child Writer from Austen to Woolf*, ed. Christine Alexander and Juliet McMaster (Cambridge University Press, 2005), pp. 101–21.
8. G. K. Chesterton, ed., *Love and Freindship and Other Early Works* (New York: Fredrick A. Stokes, 1922), p. xv.
9. Claudia L. Johnson, *Jane Austen: Women, Politics, and the Novel* (Chicago University Press, 1988), 'Introduction'.
10. Vineta Colby, *The Singular Anomaly: Women Novelists of the Nineteenth Century* (New York University Press, 1970); Sandra M. Gilbert and Susan Gubar, *The Madwoman in the Attic: The Woman Writer and the Nineteenth-Century Literary Imagination* (New Haven, CT: Yale University Press, 1979); Nancy Armstrong, *Desire and Domestic Fiction: A Political History of the Novel* (New York: Oxford University Press, 1987).

6

JANET TODD

'Lady Susan', 'The Watsons' and 'Sanditon'

With the exception of the cancelled chapters of *Persuasion*, nothing remains of the manuscripts of Austen's published novels. Yet she seems to have kept copies of the versions she sent to publishers: when she wrote to Crosby and Co. in April 1809 about 'Susan', an early version of *Northanger Abbey* which Crosby had accepted in 1803 but had not published, she offered to supply another copy of the manuscript.[1] So we can assume that she kept copies and that these were jettisoned once the novels appeared in print. In contrast, Jane Austen and her family were tenacious in preserving those works which existed in manuscript but which were never published: among them, her Juvenilia, neatly copied into three notebooks, the 'Plan of a Novel' and a large number of miscellaneous poems. Most interesting of these manuscripts are three novels (one complete fair copy and two unfinished drafts): 'Lady Susan', 'The Watsons' and 'Sanditon'. These works span Austen's creative years, from the 1790s when she was still a teenager, to a few months before she died at 41, so they cast a unique light on her creative processes from the beginning to the end of her writing career.

'Lady Susan'

Probably composed around 1795, 'Lady Susan' was termed by her young relatives 'an early production' after the 'childish effusions' and before 'the composition of her living works', one of the 'betweenities' 'when the nonsense was passing away, and before her wonderful talent had found it's proper channel'.[2] The fair copy which now survives was made later, probably around 1805, and intended, as far as we know, for readers within the circle of friends and family. Apart from some contributions to the Juvenilia, including the brilliant burlesque 'Love and Freindship', it is the only example of her work in letters: partly because Austen first composed *Sense and Sensibility* and possibly *Pride and Prejudice* in epistolary form, this novella may therefore tell us something distinctive about her creative habits in the major novels. 'The Watsons' and 'Sanditon' are unfinished manuscripts, frustrated attempts at finished works. With their multiple corrections they indicate habits of writing about which the published novels are silent – although they can only hint at the process behind these finished works. They are equally secretive about how they themselves might have looked in their final state, but a comparison between them and the printed novels indicates the kind of changes that Austen's publishers made to her work. They also have significance in their own right: they expand Jane Austen's œuvre and suggest a socially greater range than the finished books alone display.

In 1870 when Jane Austen's initially modest reputation was growing, her nephew James Edward Austen Leigh wrote a memoir to accompany a reprinting of her novels. He noted that the unpublished works were 'not without merit', but that Jane Austen had considered them unworthy of publication.[3] He intended to follow her supposed lead. He was especially concerned about 'Lady Susan', which, with its brisk treatment of an immoral woman, fitted ill with the gentle, refined image of his aunt which he was eager to promote. When the following year he was persuaded to let it into the public domain, he found that many readers agreed with him. The *Athenæum* called the heroine 'simply odious', while New York's *The Nation* considered the work 'thoroughly unpleasant in its characters and its details'.[4] What was most shocking was Lady Susan's avoidance of the sensational fate of usual literary adulteresses or female villains; in Austen's work the protagonist ends up neither dead nor mad, and not even poor. Her schemes do not quite answer her expectations, but she is left unreformed and unabashed.

By using the eighteenth-century form of letters, 'Lady Susan' gives unmediated access to female discourse – and desire. Combining these letters with a final third-person commentary, it has a slight resemblance to the scandalous French masterpiece *Les Liaisons dangereuses* published in France in April 1782, although the French work is far more insidiously immoral and subversive. In any case, the story of a designing society woman or unscrupulous widow has antecedents nearer home, in Restoration drama of the sort the Austens acted in the Steventon barn when Jane was a child, and closer still in English epistolary and first-person fiction by earlier women writers such as Frances Sheridan, Susannah Gunning and Elizabeth Inchbald.[5] But, for all the foreshadowing in such works, there is nothing quite like 'Lady Susan'; and nothing in Austen's own published novels prepares us for its ebulliently amoral effect.

Lady Susan, the heroine or anti-heroine, inhabits a world in which men control property and women must make property of men. A female rake, she is a handsome egotistical widow who enjoys her own energetic duplicity, her sexual allure and above all her manipulative eloquence. She is allowed a remarkably open sexual desire, and a positive relish for adultery. The sexual acts are offstage but they are key to the proceedings throughout. When Lady Susan later becomes the object of honourable love, it bores her and she continues to yearn for her married lover. The enjoyment of the game of sexual mastering even overtops evident self-interest where interest is defined as financial and social security. In the end Lady Susan marries the foolish Sir James for his money, and the epistolary mode gives way to the intrusive narrator: 'Whether Lady Susan was, or was not happy in her second Choice – I do not see how it can ever be ascertained ... The World must judge from Probability. – She had nothing against her, but her Husband & her Conscience' (*LM* 'LS' 77). As can be seen, Austen already has the habit of leaving moral conundrums to 'the World', suggesting a sophisticated audience outside the central self-observing characters. The narrative voice further adds, 'Sir James may seem to have drawn an harder Lot than mere Folly merited' (78) – an urbane comment suggesting that it is naive to fuss too much about sexual impropriety or other moral failings.

Does Lady Susan gain control by assuming male values, by exploiting feminine propriety or through skilful manipulation of language alone? Is she in the end predator or prey? The question remains open. The energy of Lady Susan seems to defeat morality mainly because she is much more entertaining than those around her. This is no surprise: the geisha or courtesan is an entertainer; so too the spirited adulteress. We sympathize or semi-identify with such characters since their creative impulse parallels the author's. If one cannot go so far as to say that the narrative voice of Jane Austen, that which intrudes at the end of 'Lady Susan' and is developed in the mature writing, is the voice of someone like Lady Susan, it is perhaps fair to see it as the voice of a woman who may look sardonically on the absolutes of conventional morality.

'The Watsons'

A decade on from 'Lady Susan', still without any publication and presumably returning at times to the three early novels already drafted, Jane Austen began the work we now know as 'The Watsons' (the manuscript is itself untitled). The fragment thus has huge significance as the only original prose piece extant from the long period between the first completion of what would become *Northanger Abbey* in 1799 and the beginning of *Mansfield Park* in 1811.

The date of composition of 'The Watsons' is not securely known – though the date 1803 is watermarked on its paper – nor the reason for its abandonment. James Edward Austen Leigh maintained that his aunt stopped writing when she realized 'the evil of having placed her heroine too low, in such a position of poverty and obscurity as, though not necessarily connected with vulgarity, has a sad tendency to degenerate into it'; Austen was like a singer who begins on too low a note, then stops because of this false start.[6] Since Austen's fiction had gone on to describe both the refined Fanny Price during her visit to Portsmouth and Anne Elliot during hers to Mrs Smith, in situations also perilously close to vulgarity, this explanation probably reveals less about Jane Austen than about James Edward's mid-Victorian rank-conscious sensibilities.

It is more likely, as many critics have recognized, that Austen's personal circumstances came into conflict with her creative thinking. In 1800 at the age of 70 George Austen retired on a comfortable income to Bath with his wife and two unmarried daughters Cassandra and Jane. On 21 January 1805 he died. The depression and sadness Jane and her family experienced – along with the considerable diminution in their income – must have intersected in a very complex way with Austen's part-written story of dependent women whose circumstances were rendered perilous by the death of a clergyman father.

The manuscript of 'The Watsons' as we have it gives a fascinating insight into the creative processes of Austen the novelist. Evidently a first draft, it shows a wide range of revisions – not in the larger drift of the narrative, but in the more precise areas of sentence structure, and finding the precise word for what Austen wished to convey. Frequently the adjustments refine factual detail: for example Penelope's possible suitor Dr Harding's original ailment of gout was changed to asthma, probably because Mr Watson was later to have a gouty attack; Mr Watson's time at Stanton Parsonage is altered from twelve to fourteen years, making it the same length of time as Emma has been away from home and so giving added point to her unfamiliarity with the neighbourhood; Mrs Robert's child left in Croydon becomes a girl rather than a boy, entailing nine minor adjustments in a short discussion and a change of name from 'John' to 'Augusta'.

Some alterations are made in the cause of accurate impression, changing 'tuning' into the 'scrape' of violins, and some move from the particular to the general, for example the changes to the Edwards' townhouse. Some intensify: in a revision Emma 'longed' for rather than wished for a carriage to take her home. Some modify: Emma's 'wretchedness' becomes 'gloom' then 'Despondence'. Larger changes include names: the town of 'L.' in Sussex becomes the town of 'D.' in 'Surry' and sister Penelope goes husband-hunting in Chichester not Southampton. 'Charles' was the name used not for Musgrave but for the little boy Emma befriends, and Captain Hunter rather than Captain Carr attracts Miss Edwards.

Most of the revisions are local, simply adjusting expression or meaning. But three sections were added later on inserted pieces of paper (neatly cut to meet the required space and attached with a pin). In the first, Austen had second thoughts about an exchange in which Lord Osborne tries to get Emma to provide a lesson in complimenting. The exchange is replaced by a section focusing on Emma herself: instead of 'a cold monosyllable & grave look' (*LM* 'W' 338), Emma now gives a very memorable response to Lord Osborne: 'Female economy may do a great deal my Lord, but it cannot turn a small income into a large one' (116). The second inserted section amplifies the discussion between Robert and his sister Emma, once the darling of a rich aunt and now reduced to a vulnerable dependant. The third piece expands a conversation allowing Mr Howard, the putative hero, to be further presented.

The insertions all come in the later stages of the manuscript when the writing is less confident than at the beginning, and where Austen is clearly struggling to describe Emma's feelings about her family and situation. The manuscript stops at the end of the visit to the parsonage by Robert and his wife, and it is difficult to see how the narrative as a whole could have been concluded, with three unmarried daughters to be disposed of. The trajectory of the heroine however seems secure, and, according to Austen Leigh, Cassandra knew her sister's intentions: 'Mr. Watson was soon to die; and Emma to become dependent for a home on her narrow-minded sister-in-law and brother. She was to decline an offer of marriage from Lord Osborne, and much of the interest of the tale was to arise from Lady Osborne's love for Mr. Howard, and his counter affection for Emma, whom he was finally to marry.'[7]

It may, however, be that 'The Watsons' fulfilled its purposes for Austen in ways other than by its publication, since her published novels seem very thoroughly to mine the ideas and situations created in the fragment. Those who reviewed 'The Watsons' when it was first published in 1871 wrote about it as 'bright with talk, and character, and animation', and 'full of the sparkles of Miss Austen's characteristic playfulness and humour', comments which themselves sound reminiscent of Austen's own playful verdict on *Pride and Prejudice* as 'too light and bright and sparkling' (*L* 203).[8] More recent critics have shown how *Pride and Prejudice*, *Mansfield Park* and *Emma* all in their various ways owe a substantial debt to 'The Watsons', and one went so far as to describe the fragment as 'a pre-text' in the sense of a text that comes before others rather than having its own unique entity.[9]

Later readers have been struck less by sparkle than by bleakness, an uneasiness over the female predicament and an embarrassment and shame about relative and genteel poverty for those travelling down the social scale. Like no other of Austen's works, 'The Watsons' is centrally set in the lower middle class, the rank more famously depicted by Austen's predecessor Frances Burney (whose work Austen admired). More even than Burney, Austen captures the claustrophobia of this group, the struggle for status of those in the shade of the upper ranks but lacking the means to join them, and a genuine concern that failure might mean near-destitution. The fragment well reveals the urgency of women's need to marry, however unappealing the partners presented to them. Desperation about this, revealed momentarily by Jane Fairfax in *Emma* and indeed by Mrs Bennet in *Pride and Prejudice*, is nowhere so acutely presented as here. The bleakness expands from social to psychological when Emma is confronted with her reduced existence: 'from being the life and spirit of a house, where all had been comfort and elegance, and the expected heiress of an easy independence, she was become of importance to no one, a burden on those, whose affection she could not expect, an addition in an house, already overstocked, surrounded by inferior minds with little chance of domestic comfort, and as little hope of future support' (*LM* 'W' 135).

'Sanditon'

Jane Austen's last illness seems to have come on gradually following her care of her sick brother Henry in London late in 1815. Only a month before she began 'Sanditon' on 27 January 1817 (a date inserted at the top of the first manuscript page) she wrote fairly cheerily to her nephew James Edward, noting that, although she could not walk to his sister Anna Lefroy's house a mile or so away, she was 'very well' (*L* 323). This buoyant mood remained for several weeks: she had, she thought, come to understand her condition ('Bile' was at the bottom of it (326–7)) and she hoped for improvement with the better weather. But then she clearly had a relapse: on 23–5 March she admitted that 'about a week ago I was very poorly ... I must not depend upon being ever very blooming again' (235–6). On 6 April she told her brother Charles that she had been very ill for the previous fortnight, 'too unwell ... to write anything that was not absolutely necessary' and later that month she made her will (338). She died on 18 July. In the manuscript of the fragment now known as 'Sanditon' (there was a family tradition that this novel was perhaps to have been called 'The Brothers') the date 'March 18' is written immediately below the final line of the manuscript and records the end of Jane Austen's career as a novelist. She had been writing the work for two months and had achieved 23,500 words.

Although she cannot have known she was dying, Jane Austen was aware that she was ill with varying degrees of seriousness throughout the composing. Her subject – the industry of invalidism – is therefore a startling one. Her vigorous hypochondriac Diana Parker can hardly crawl from her 'bed to the sofa' and is 'bilious' (*LM* 'S' 5:163); Jane Austen believed this her own complaint and added the term 'anti-bilious' to her manuscript where she lists the 'antis' for which the Sanditon sea air is beneficial. She herself was, by the time she stopped writing, living 'chiefly on the sofa' (*L* 335, 343).

Another surprise is the setting of her tale. When writing *Emma* Austen had declared that a country village was 'the very thing to work on' but here she eschews her usual background and puts her story in a nascent seaside resort. Such places had been sighted in Austen's previous works, where they had usually been roundly mocked. In the Juvenilia Brighton is one of Lady Lesley's 'favourite haunts of Dissipation' (*J* 155) and Lydia Bennet in *Pride and Prejudice* dreams of 'the streets of that gay bathing place covered with officers' (*PP* 2:17:258). In *Emma* Mr Knightley regards sea resorts in general as the 'idlest haunts in the kingdom' (*E* 1:18:157). (On the other hand Lyme Regis put the bloom back in Anne Elliot's cheeks.) Other writers too laughed at the fad for resorts, whether by the sea or inland. William Cowper, the poet Jane Austen most admired, mocked the rootlessness displayed by the fashion; 'Flimflamton' in T. S. Surr's *The Magic of Wealth* (1815), despite its library and theatre, fails miserably; while a few years after Austen's death, and long before the existence of the 'Sanditon' manuscript was known, Walter Scott described, in *St Ronan's Well*, a resort existing solely to attract idle painting and poetry-reading tourists and hypochondriacs.

A further shock to many readers is the broad comic element which characterizes 'Sanditon'. Although the last piece of prose fiction Jane Austen wrote, it does not appear as a development of the narrative experiments of her mature novels but rather a reversion to her youthful style of burlesque and caricature. As such the work dismayed James Edward Austen Leigh so much that, when it was first published with 'Lady Susan' and 'The Watsons', he reduced it to a series of short studies of some of the chief characters, Mr Parker, Lady Denham and Diana Parker, a very small proportion of the original manuscript. The full text was only printed for the first time in 1925.

When contemplating *Persuasion* Virginia Woolf considered that, had Jane Austen lived on, 'she would have been the forerunner of Henry James and Proust'.[10] 'Sanditon' would have dashed such hopes since it quite lacks the psychological subtleties of the last three novels. Many early readers thought it of little literary merit; more recently D. A. Miller declared it the 'formal ruination of the Austen Novel as we have come to know it', the style beyond correction and the plot wanting.[11] Mr Parker's speculation seems heading for a crash at odds with the comic marriage plot progressing alongside it, and it is hard to see how the theme of hypochondria, morphing into serious illness, could inhabit a romantic comedy.

And yet 'Sanditon' has much to offer. If it does not continue the nuanced study of character of Austen's most powerful novels, it does develop the light symbolic use of scenes with which she foreshadowed the heavier habits of canonical Victorian writers such as Charles Dickens and George Eliot. The dramatic opening has the Parkers struggling up a sandy lane in completely the wrong part of the country only to be overturned outside some labourers' cottages which they mistake for a genteel *cottage ornée*. They are rescued by an old-fashioned gentleman leading the kind of life Mr Parker turned his back on when he decided to use his hereditary fortune to speculate on his new resort.

Like 'The Watsons', 'Sanditon' reveals much about Jane Austen's composing and drafting, but in this context its most striking feature is clear evidence of an increased authorial confidence – after all, by the time it was written, Austen, as the author of four published novels, was an established professional writer. The narrative is smoother than in 'The Watsons' and unlike the earlier manuscript is neatly divided into chapters. There are no added pieces of text and some pages contain hardly any corrections at all. Austen's spelling of names was always wayward – even in the published version of *Pride and Prejudice* for example Elizabeth Bennet's relatives are variously named as Philips and Phillips – and such spelling variations occur here, as when the owner of the Sanditon library is named randomly as Miss or Mrs Whilby or Whitby (the similarity of Austen's 'l's and 't's merely adds to the confusion). But there is no suggestion of the kind of larger second thoughts about names and places or whole sections of the narrative that are visible in 'The Watsons'. Perhaps Austen had no time to go back for revision as she had with the earlier unfinished work, but perhaps she was happier with what she had written.

The revealed rethinking concerns early accounts of Diana Parker, Lady Denham and Sidney Parker, as well as the houses and buildings of old and new Sanditon. The famous extended paean of praise to Sanditon by Mr Parker in chapter 1 was left as Austen first wrote it, with only one change towards the end: Mr Parker's original 'A measured mile nearer than East Bourne. Only conceive Sir, the advantage of that, in a long Journey' becomes 'One complete, measured mile nearer than East Bourne. Only conceive Sir, the advantage of saving a whole Mile, in a long Journey' ('S' 1:398, 143). Just a few words are adjusted, but the rhythm of the sentence and the comedy of Mr Parker's enthusiasm are both enhanced.

Many critics have followed Jane Austen's niece Anna in believing that the eccentricities of the Parker siblings would (and should) have been toned down, had Austen been well enough to go back to her work to revise. However, the revisions there are on the manuscript show that the author intended rather to intensify them: for example, Diana's declaration that

'I know where to apply' for a medical man to come to Sanditon, becomes 'I could soon put the necessary irons in the fire' (5:446, 163). Diana becomes even more absurd when she claims to have rubbed a sprained ankle 'without Intermission' for six hours rather than the original four. Of the impressionistic phrases that may suggest a new stylistic departure, one concerning Sanditon 'dancing and sparkling in Sunshine and Freshness' (4:161) was a revision (the phrase originally read 'dancing & sparkling under a Sunshiny breeze' (440)), while 'something White & Womanish' (12:207), as a description of the slightly mysterious Clara Brereton, glimpsed through a summer mist, is an original phrase.

All in all there is much to relish in 'Sanditon', a vibrancy and activity in language, a fuller depiction of society than Austen had allowed herself in other novels and an ebullient scepticism about human nature and its bodily desires. The comedy of invalidism is indeed broad, almost Augustan in its mockery of modish practices and fads, but it is creative, lively and wonderfully and paradoxically vital. John Wiltshire notes that the invalids allow their bodies to fill their imaginations and direct their actions. Invalidism becomes the 'pivot of economic activity' and hypochondriacs' bodies 'the grounds of inventiveness and energy, preoccupying their imaginations and becoming the source of sufficient activity to direct the conduct of every hour of the day'.[12] 'Sanditon' is a fascinating evocation of the culture of sickness, a sickness made almost as bracing as the sea air.

Where was it heading? Mary Lascelles remarked on its enigma, noting that none of the other novels, 'if broken off short at the eleventh chapter, [would] have left us in such uncertainty as to the way in which it was going to develop'.[13] Just as some critics have seen the work as a reversion to the burlesque of Austen's young womanhood while others have been struck by the way the narrative style looks forward to the Victorians, so there has been wide disagreement about how the plot would resolve itself. It is quite possible that Sanditon, a village of indigenous fishers and farmers perverted into a place for the rootless and self-indulgent, was designed to come to a bad end. And yet there is something about the sparkling quality of the place and the open spirit of its chief promoter Mr Parker that resists this interpretation. Perhaps there was indeed going to be a financial fall, though not a thorough capitalist collapse; perhaps the newly arrived brother Sidney Parker (evidently designed to be the hero) would save the day with something unexpected from the Isle of Wight. Perhaps the West Indian Miss Lambe, who brings colonialism into the novel as Sir Thomas Bertram brought slavery into *Mansfield Park*, would marry Sir Edward Denham and use her money to create an estate of *cottages ornées* or an elegant crescent. Perhaps the almost Gothic Clara, companion of Lady Denham, would become the kind of villain

Jane Austen had not treated since she created Lady Susan so many years earlier. But all this too is speculation.

NOTES

1. *Jane Austen's Letters*, 3rd edn, coll. and ed. Deirdre Le Faye (Oxford University Press, 1997), p. 174.
2. Copy of a letter from Caroline Austen to James Edward Austen Leigh 1 April [1869?], in National Portrait Gallery correspondence R. W. Chapman / Henry Hake, fo. 5.
3. James Edward Austen Leigh, *Memoir of Jane Austen* (London, 1870), p. 60.
4. E. Quincy, *The Nation*, vol. xiii, 7 September 1871, pp. 164–5.
5. See 'Introduction', in *Later Manuscripts*, ed. Janet Todd and Linda Bree (Cambridge University Press, 2008), pp. liv–lv.
6. Austen Leigh, *Memoir*, 1871, p. 296.
7. Austen Leigh, *Memoir*, 1871, p. 364.
8. Annie Thackeray, *Cornhill Magazine* 24 (1871), pp. 158–74; *The Times*, 22 July 1871.
9. Joseph Wiesenfarth, 'The *Watsons* as Pretext', *Persuasions*, 8 (1986), 109.
10. Virginia Woolf, 'Jane Austen', in *The Common Reader* (London: Hogarth Press, 1925), pp. 180, 183.
11. D. A. Miller, *Jane Austen, or The Secret of Style* (Princeton University Press, 2003), p. 76.
12. John Wiltshire, *Jane Austen and the Body* (Cambridge University Press, 1992), p. 198ff.
13. Mary Lascelles, *Jane Austen and Her Art* (Oxford: Clarendon Press, 1939), p. 39.

7

CAROL HOULIHAN FLYNN

The letters

As she recalls her own memories of Aunt Jane to help brother James Edward Austen Leigh construct his *Memoir of Jane Austen*, Caroline Austen questions the possibility of ever representing a 'life' that already seems too obscure to recover. 'I am sure you will do justice to what there *is* – but I feel that it must be a difficult task to dig up the *materials*, so carefully have they been buried out of our sight by the past generation.'[1] She dismisses the more obvious 'materials' at hand: 'There is nothing in those letters which *I* have seen that would be acceptable to the public – They were very well expressed, and they must have been very interesting to those who received them – but they detailed chiefly home and family events: and she seldom committed herself *even* to an opinion – so that to strangers they could be *no* transcript of her mind – they would not feel that they knew her any the better for having read them –.'[2]

What I find so compelling about Caroline Austen's scepticism is its applicability to Austen studies in every generation. Readers coming to her letters usually find something 'missing' that vexes them. In his introduction to the first edition of the letters, R. W. Chapman recites what will continue to be 'a familiar defence' of the letters. They have been 'robbed of their general interest by Cassandra Austen's pious destruction of all that she supposed might possibly excite general curiosity'.[3] By blaming Cassandra for keeping us from the 'real' Jane Austen, we are able to sustain an idea of the writer regardless of materials, or lack of materials, that occlude the portrait of the artist. We look to the letters for deep feeling, but are kept relegated to the surface of things, rewarded with 'small matters' and 'momentous minutiae'.

Caroline Austen rejects what is *in* Austen's letters, not what is left *out*. Not the mysteriously buried materials, but those mundanely visible above ground, the letters preserved by Cassandra, disappoint her for failing to provide 'a transcript' of the writer's mind. Her concern reveals the investment that readers looking for a transparent relationship between 'mind' and 'art' bring to the letters, an investment her brother seems to share. Like Caroline, he is disappointed by his aunt's epistolary productions, and he warns the reader of his *Memoirs* 'not to expect too much' from his aunt's letters. Their 'materials', he explains, 'may be thought inferior', treating only 'the details of domestic life ... They resemble the nest which some little bird builds of the materials nearest at hand.'[4] It is only recently that the domestic nature of the letters has been freed from such a condescending interpretation. Jo Modert suggests that the very banal domestic surface of the letters offers us a tool for understanding the foundations of Austen's creative production,[5] while Deborah Kaplan and Susan Whealler read Austen's depictions of self-denial and housewifery as subtle productions emerging from a feminine culture which supports the self-expression of women who are conscious of dual allegiances to claims of social class and gender.[6] We are learning to look more carefully at the coded interpretations that Austen and her female correspondents make of their positions of relative powerlessness in their class and gender systems, and to look for their painfully calibrated understanding of the disappointments and adjustments which mark the feminine experience. It is Austen's awareness of the texture of domestic life that generates her densely realized novels.

In the novels, Austen is careful to make certain that her understanding of the 'dual cultures' which claim her allegiance not be made entirely transparent. Her sensitivity to the privileged obligations of class and gender encourages her to disguise her representations of the desire for power and its disappointments, and to frame such situations with ironic pronouncements which undercut desire while they pretend detachment. The very style of her novels, tersely and laconically epigrammatic, insists upon a graceful inevitability of social forms that must triumph over individual acts of rebellion and desire. Nothing is ever so inevitable in Austen's own letters, however, which awkwardly disclose disjointed fragments of everyday social exchange. 'I wonder whether the Ink bottle has been filled', she writes. 'Does Butcher's meat keep up at the same price? & is not Bread lower than 2/6. – Mary's blue gown! – My Mother must be in agonies' (*L* 239). Seldom moderated, extreme positions are more often than not enumerated, blandly, in jarring catalogues of 'little matters' that unsettle a reader looking for coherence.

It is this incoherence that so alarms Caroline Austen, who is looking for a proper 'transcript' of an elegant, composed mind. In her letters, Austen employs a jolting, frustrating style which disallows for subordination. Dashes casually break up endless paragraphs to signal fresh 'matters' inappropriately joined, subjects as momentous as 'a dead Baronet' and as mundane as a dose of rhubarb (*L* 320). Alternately 'ringing the Changes of the Glads & Sorrys' (118), she seems to be exploring the limits of a stream of consciousness located somewhere between Sterne and Samuel Beckett, one that represents her own awareness of the endless nature of her domestic tasks. Since 'correspondence' becomes one of these tasks,[7] she must always be in search of a subject. In fact, it is the search itself which ties her to a constant reading of the vicissitudes of her own mind, the one that Caroline doesn't like to see transcribed.

'There is no reason to suppose that Miss Morgan is dead after all'

In a letter to Fanny Knight, Jane Austen apologizes for the polarities of her state of mind: 'I am feeling differently every moment, & shall not be able to suggest a single thing that can assist your Mind. – I could lament in one sentence & laugh in the next' (*L* 279). Although Austen presents her state as both extreme and unsuitable, it actually underlies much of her more familiar epistolary discourse. Mocking her domestic duties, she produces a typical 'not . . . quite so triumphant . . . account' of daily life:

> We met with no adventures . . . except that our Trunk had once nearly slipt off, & we were obliged to stop at Hartley to have our wheels greazed. – While my Mother & Mr Lyford were together, I went to Mrs Ryders, & bought what I intended to buy, but not in much perfection. – There were no narrow Braces for Children, & scarcely any netting silk; but Miss Wood as usual is going to Town very soon, & will lay in a fresh stock. – I gave 2^s/3^d a yard for my flannel, & I fancy it is not very good; but it is so disgraceful & contemptible an article in itself, that its' being comparatively good or bad is of little importance. I bought some Japan Ink likewise, & next week shall begin my operations on my hat, on which You know my principal hopes of happiness depend. – I am very grand indeed; – I had the dignity of dropping out my mother's Laudanum last night, I carry about the keys of the Wine & Closet; & twice since I began this letter, have had orders to give in the Kitchen: Our dinner was very good yesterday, & the Chicken boiled perfectly tender; therefore I shall not be obliged to dismiss Nanny on that account. (*L* 16–17)

What is characteristic about this excerpt, a small piece from a large letter filled with dashes and memoranda and tidily expressed laments ('I am quite angry with myself for not writing closer; why is my alphabet so much more sprawly than Yours? Dame Tilbury's daughter has lain-in – '), is its low level of affect. Adventures sink into obligatory stops where one's wheels are greased. Purchases are either 'disgraceful & contemptible' or sublime, like Japan Ink elevated ironically into the means to perform an operation upon which 'my principal hopes of happiness depend'.

The grandeur of Jane Austen's 'lesser duties' is undercut by the level of 'obligation' which motivates her actions. 'Twice since I began this letter, I have had orders to give in the Kitchen.' While she is the one giving the orders, she 'has to' give them. Such momentous small matters force writer and reader alike to attend to the domestic duties, even while the writing itself becomes an obligation that she often chafes against ('why is my alphabet so much more sprawly than Yours?'). This particular letter holds within itself the famous, still shocking report that 'Mrs Hall of Sherbourn was brought to bed yesterday of a dead child, some weeks before she expected oweing to a fright. – I suppose she happened unawares to look at her husband' (*L* 17). What is most notable about this statement is not so much its heartless wit, but its context. It becomes in this long and rambling letter just one of many careless-seeming remarks squeezed in between reports about the uncommon largeness of Mary, about to give birth, the lying in of Dame Tilbury's daughter, and the dirtiness of Steventon's lanes.

Austen the novelist addresses the stylistic problem that the oddly juxtaposed detail presents in *Persuasion* when her narrator, quite unexpectedly, exposes the 'large fat sighings' that Mrs Musgrove is guilty of displaying: 'Personal size and mental sorrow have certainly no necessary proportions. A large bulky figure has as good a right to be in deep affliction, as the most graceful set of limbs in the world. But, fair or not fair, there are unbecoming conjunctions, which reason will patronize in vain, – which taste cannot tolerate, – which ridicule will seize' (*P* 1:8:73–4). The narrator's horror of the 'unbecoming conjunction' establishes a canon of taste and decorum that Austen violates frequently and eagerly in her own domestic letters. The Austen that we think we 'know', that writer whose mind could be transcribed, stands as an arbiter of taste, a modest tyrant who insists upon the appropriate forms of discourse. Her letters, however, repeatedly embarrass her own standards in transgressions, which, unlike Mrs Musgrove's, appear to be deliberate and self-conscious.

When she chronicles her 'little matters', Austen exploits with mundane precision the sheer tedium not only of committing oneself to practising 'the civilities, the lesser duties of life, with gentleness and forbearance',[8] but of being obliged to record them in closely written letters for the inspection of others: 'There is no reason to suppose that Miss Morgan is dead after all. Mr Lyford gratified us very much yesterday by his praises of my father's mutton, which they all think the finest that was ever ate' (*L* 24). 'There is no reason to suppose that Miss Morgan is dead after all.' Samuel Beckett could have written such a line. Or Swift. Or closer to home, Austen's own parasyntactic, always obliging Miss Bates, who sees and reports *every thing* with a flat, undistinguished, decidedly unbecoming zeal.

'Fly[ing] off, through half a sentence, to her mother's old petticoat'

Miss Bates is first introduced to the reader as 'great talker on little matters' (*E* 1:3:20). Her aimless, convoluted accounts invest her character with great significance as one who sees and tells the plot of *Emma* as it unfolds. But her conversation also serves as an oddly perverse model for Austen's own epistolary production.[9] Miss Bates' monologues, stuffed with roast pork and baked apples, chimneys that want sweeping, spectacles that need mending, sound suspiciously like her creator's own prosy, rambling letters. Miss Bates is, of course, designed to be exasperating enough to excuse Emma's dread of engaging her in conversation. We are even allowed to laugh at Emma's imitation of Miss Bates, when she imagines the 'evils' of a marriage between Mr Knightley and Jane Fairfax:

> How would he bear to have Miss Bates belonging to him? – To have her haunting the Abbey, and thanking him all day long for his great kindness in marrying Jane? – 'So very kind and obliging! – But he always had been such a very kind neighbour!' And then fly off, through half a sentence, to her mother's old petticoat. 'Not that it was such a very old petticoat either – for still it would last a great while – and, indeed, she must thankfully say that their petticoats were all very strong.' (2:8:243)

But when Emma mimics Miss Bates' 'fly[ing] off, through half a sentence, to her mother's old petticoat', she reproduces Austen's own epistolary use of the trusty dash that she applies in any direction to link together matters great and small:

> I am full of Joy at much of your information; that you should have been to a Ball, & have danced at it, & supped with the Prince, & that you should meditate the purchase of a new muslin Gown are delightful circumstances. – *I* am determined to buy a handsome one whenever I can, & I am so tired & ashamed of half my present stock that I even blush at the sight of the wardrobe which contains them. – But I will not be much longer libelled by the possession of my coarse spot, I shall turn it into a petticoat very soon. – I wish you a merry Christmas, but *no* compliments of the Season. – Poor Edward! It is very hard that he who has everything else in the World that he can wish for, should not have good health too. – But I hope with the assistance of Bowel complaints, Faintnesses & Sicknesses, he will soon be restored to that Blessing like-wise. (L 30)

I chose this particular excerpt because of its conveniently invoked petticoat, but its structure as well as its content connects this very typical mixture of romance, practicality, sentiment and passive aggression to Miss Bates' meditations on rivets, baked apples, civility and the consumption of bread (*E* 2:9:255). Both speakers excel at filling empty space with sentiments, 'I am full of joy ... Poor Edward', that jostle against each other inconsequentially, suggesting the relative meaninglessness of what is being set down. As Miss Bates would say, 'One takes up a notion, and runs away with it' (2:3:189).

When Austen seems to mimic a character that she might have been able to love, but could never admire, her letters reveal a profound consciousness of the artificial and vacant nature of most discourse, which flies off through half sentences because there is nothing substantial to hold it down. 'Do not be angry with me for beginning another Letter to you', she writes to Cassandra from Henrietta Street. 'I have read the Corsair, mended my petticoat, & have nothing else to do. – ' (*L* 257). Employing another petticoat, Austen exploits a comically painful awareness that any discourse will serve to fill up the time and space facing the most adept conversationalists and correspondents, particularly if they are women.

In her letters, the absence of the subject often motivates the writing itself: 'Expect a most agreable Letter; for not being overburdened with subject – (having nothing at all to say) – I shall have no check to my Genius from beginning to end. – Well – & so . . .' (*L* 74–5). Six years later, writing from Southampton, cut off from country life and still unpublished, she sounds less eager to write about 'nothing'.

> My expectation of having nothing to say to you after the conclusion of my last, seems nearer Truth than I thought it would be, for I feel to have but little. I need not therefore be above acknowledging the receipt of yours this morn^g; or of replying to every part of it which is capable of an answer; & you may accordingly prepare for my ringing the Changes of the Glads & Sorrys for the rest of the page. (*L* 118)

'We are all sorry, & now that subject is exhausted', Austen reports, but continues to write doggedly on, vexed over disappointments in getting fish, charmed by a 'little Visitor' who makes her wonder 'What is become of all the Shyness in the World?' With 'nothing to say', Austen uses up all of her writing paper, squeezing in references to sofa covers and carpets below the address panel, and crossing over a rather snide reference to brother James' impending visit. Straining to fit him onto her filled-up page, she complains about the way he takes up too much room, 'walking about the house & banging the Doors, or ringing the Bell for a glass of Water'. She writes here as the recessive, dutiful sister, one who hardly takes up any room at all, observing with careful, painstaking acuity the cost of daily life, as she compares the bumptious excess of her brother's presence to her own relatively empty and tidy surface. The act of writing becomes here a necessary weapon in the domestic war waged against tedium, emptiness and occasional despair.

In closing, Austen reminds Cassandra that she has 'constructed . . . a Smartish Letter, considering my want of Materials. But like my dear Dr Johnson I beleive I have dealt more in Notions than Facts. – ' (*L* 118–21). While she looks to Johnson as her model, she sounds more like Swift and Sterne, writers making their subject the task of writing upon nothing at all. Her choice of materials, however, radically separates her from more self-consciously literary productions – Johnson's Idler, Swift's Hack, Sterne's White Bear – that depend upon the generative power of the literary marketplace. Swift and Sterne and Johnson pretend that they write upon nothing because they are being paid to do so. Austen claims that she is writing upon no subject because she is obliged to do so; epistolary production is one of her domestic duties, what women do for free.

Austen's praise of her brother Frank's epistolary skill ('you write so even, so clear both in style & Penmanship' (L 229)) is complicated by the way that letter-writing is judged in Austen's novels. The greatest admirer of close writing is Miss Bates, who stupefies Emma with her proud reports of Jane Fairfax's literary productions: 'in general she fills the whole paper and crosses half. My mother often wonders that I can make it out so well. She often says, when the letter is first opened, "Well, Hetty, now I think you will be put to it to make out all that chequer-work."' When Emma says 'something very civil about the excellence of Miss Fairfax's handwriting', and is rewarded with 'hearing her own silly compliment repeated twice over' (E 2:1:168) it is clear that Austen has little patience for the fetishizing of the letter. Miss Bingley, fawning over Darcy's talent for writing long letters (PP 1:10:52), Harriet, betraying her 'bad taste' by judging Robert Martin's proposal of marriage to be 'too short' (E 1:7:53), and Lady Bertram, who shines in the epistolary line, all expose their foolish satisfaction with the form of the letter and their dissociation from its substance.[10]

While Austen the novelist can satirize misplaced, self-important dedication to the fine art of letter-writing, Austen the sister, engaged in friendly rivalry, determined to exhibit her social skills, gets 'sick of myself, & my bad pens' (L 131) and 'hates' herself when she writes ill (13). Her doubled consciousness sets her against cultural productions that she herself pursues with great interest. Chafing against the demands of her position, for 'I assure you I am as tired of writing long letters as you can be', she corrects herself, holding tenaciously onto her appreciation of the necessity for the letters that take up so much of her energy: 'What a pity that one should still be so fond of receiving them', she reminds them both (137). The commitment wavers, however, when the writer faces the well-worn *terra cognita* of her epistolary landscape: 'I am not surprised my dear Cassandra, that you did not find my last Letter very full of Matter, & I wish this may not have the same deficiency; – but we are doing nothing ourselves to write about, & I am therefore quite dependant upon the Communications of our friends, or my own Wit' (162). It is, after all, Austen's awareness of such dependency that motivates her most moving characters, unaccommodated women like Miss Bates, *Persuasion*'s Mrs Smith, and perhaps most poignantly, Miss Jane Fairfax, another great letter-writer, 'dependant upon the Communications of [her] friends', quite literally tied to the post.[11]

Determined to hazard nothing

It is in *Emma* that Austen explores the problem of feminine dependence most thoroughly, splitting the source of her anxiety, the unaccommodated woman squeezed by circumstance, into Miss Bates and Miss Jane Fairfax. Miss Bates stands for the exposed, needy, woman 'so very obliged' to the support of *every body*. Her 'simplicity and cheerfulness' might recommend her to her neighbours, but they do not command respect. She deserves rather 'compassion', for sinking 'from the comforts she was born to' (*E* 3:7:408). Austen's more admirable, elegant creation, Miss Fairfax, is never entirely forgiven for her egregious acts of secrecy. Emma might recognize that 'If a woman can ever be excused for thinking only of herself, it is in a situation like Jane Fairfax's. – Of such, one may almost say, that "the world is not their's, nor the world's law"' (3:10:436). But somehow, in spite of the sympathy that her circumstances awaken in the reader, we are always kept on the outside of Jane Fairfax's character, looking in, and irresistibly judging her reserve.

Yet, it is in this oddly faulty Jane Fairfax that we can discover Austen's own elegant, secretive sensibility. To understand Jane Fairfax's clandestine habits of mind is to enter into the hidden world of Jane Austen's own epistolary production. For like her character, Austen, always eschewing both the sentimental response and the angry complaint, aims for, and most often succeeds at, impenetrability. Waiting for the carefully regulated deliveries of clandestine letters from Frank Churchill, Jane Fairfax presents a smooth, invulnerable exterior. But in her necessary reserve, Jane Fairfax, however repulsive she seems to bossy, powerful Emma, resembles most poignantly the Jane Austen, reported by one Miss Hinton to have 'stiffened into the most perpendicular, precise, taciturn piece of "single blessedness"', known for being 'no more regarded in society than a poker or a fire screen, or any other thin, upright piece of wood or iron that fills its corner in peace and quiet', the sort of maiden aunt who at least in her letters 'seldom committed herself *even* to an opinion' for public consumption.[12]

The secret integrity which depends upon silent self-censorship protects Jane Fairfax's and Jane Austen's position of relative powerlessness in a culture which privileges the communications of those rich enough to afford them. Truly marginal characters like Miss Bates are allowed to talk because they don't matter. 'I do not think', Mrs Weston tells Emma, 'Mr. Knightley would be much disturbed by Miss Bates. Little things do not irritate him. She might talk on; and if he wanted to say any thing himself, he would only talk louder, and drown her voice' (*E* 2:8:243–4). The stakes are higher for the less pathetic figures, like Jane Fairfax, looking for more out of life than roast pork and baked apples.

The stakes require silence and cunning, producing a reserve which is often strategic. We can see Austen managing the secrets that are passing between her and her niece Fanny. 'Your sending the Music was an admirable device', she reports; 'it made everything easy, & I do not know how I could have accounted for the parcel otherwise' (*L* 281). In another letter dedicated to the interesting private discussion they are conducting over the merits of Fanny's ultimately unsuccessful suitor, Austen advises her to send her next letter by Saturday, 'as we shall be off on Monday long before the Letters are delivered – and write *something* that may do to be read or told' to the other members of the household (286–7).

Epistolary reserve can also be political, designed to maintain peace in the family commonwealth. It is remarkable how few times Jane Austen complains about her mother in her correspondence, although we sense an implicit criticism in the daughter's veiled references to her hypochondriacal presence. Since explicit remarks made against the mother would unsettle the pretence of harmony, Austen seems to speak most loudly in her silence: 'It began to occur to me before you mentioned it that I had been somewhat silent as to my mother's health for some time, but I thought you could have no difficulty in divining its exact state – you, who have guessed so much stranger things' (*L* 38). Cassandra presides over the letter as its most adroit reader, providing the hidden knowledge that is not allowed into the text.

Reserve and indirection are most valued as weapons against the condescending outside world. It protects the powerless woman from being taken over by the active 'interest' of patrons looking to engage in what Sterne called 'sentimental commerce'.[13] Austen's opposition to sentimentality can be detected in her depiction of Jane Fairfax's struggle to remain free from the power of Emma's sympathy: 'I do pity you', Emma says to herself. 'And the more sensibility you betray of their just horrors, the more I shall like you' (*E* 3:6:394). To be in want is to be open and vulnerable.

Jane Fairfax's struggle to resist Emma's patronizing sympathy makes me wonder just how often Jane Austen herself needed to defend herself against interested, patronizing parties? So many friends and relations must have displayed interest in the trials of poor Cassandra in 1797, the year in which Thomas Fowle died of yellow fever in San Domingo in the West Indies, just weeks before he was to return to his fiancée in England. How did she protect herself from solicitous friends who heard reports of her distress when she learned she would be moving to Bath? Austen knew too well how eagerly the friend, the patron, indeed the reader, looks to dig out evidences of 'sensibility'. Austen herself doesn't want to be 'liked' for sentimental reasons, the sort that motivate Emma to grow fonder of poor, dear Jane. She would rather be taken for a poker or a fire screen, silent, superior, guarded.

In her letters Austen fiercely defends herself against the powers of sympathy. Disgusted by 'fat sighings' seeping from a soft heart, she resists pity, the taking in of it or the giving out of it, in edgy displays of an uncertain, sometimes awkward wit. Her irony contains the most mortal implications, as in the case of Mary Lloyd Austen, ready to deliver her first child, James Edward (who will be his aunt's biographer):

> I am ... to tell you that one of [my Father's] Leicestershire sheep, sold to the butcher last week, weighed 27 lb. and 1/4 per quarter. I went to Deane with my father two days ago to see Mary, who is still plagued with the rheumatism, which she would be very glad to get rid of, and still more glad to get rid of her child, of whom she is heartily tired. Her nurse is come, and has no particular charm either of person or manner; but as all the Hurstbourne world pronounce her to be the best nurse that ever was, Mary expects her attachment to increase. What fine weather this is! Not very becoming perhaps early in the morning, but very pleasant out of doors at noon, and very wholesome – at least everybody fancies so, and imagination is everything. To Edward, however, I really think dry weather of importance. I have not taken to fires yet. I believe I never told you that Mrs Coulthard and Anne, late of Manydown, are both dead, and both died in childbed. We have not regaled Mary with this news ... *Sunday.* – I have just received a note from James to say that Mary was brought to bed last night, at eleven o'clock, of a fine little boy, and that everything is going on very well. My mother had desired to know nothing of it before it should be all over, and we were clever enough to prevent her having any suspicion of it, though Jenny, who had been left here by her mistress, was sent for home. (*L* 20–1)

Leicestershire sheep, a nurse of no particular charm, an irritating sister-in-law plagued with rheumatism and unborn children, fine weather, breeding women, two of them, both dead in childbed. My mother displays some degree of sensibility, not wanting to know anything about 'it' until 'it' should be over. There is no getting into this letter. The imagination revealed here is a particularly fortressed one, expressed laboriously, staving off the enormity of moments of emotional vulnerability. But then, Austen is always uneasy when she writes about childbirth. Her own darling children, her novels, provide her with a more dependable source of reproductive pleasure. Breeding, which turns women into 'animals',[14] too often leads to death.

Policing the paraphernalia

Virginia Woolf imagines the strains of being under Jane Austen's surveillance: 'A sense of meaning withheld, a smile at something unseen, an atmosphere of perfect control and courtesy mixed with something finely satirical, which, were it not directed against things in general rather than against individuals, would be almost malicious, would, so I feel, make it alarming to find her at home.'[15] Is it the natural squalor of domestic life that makes the act of observation so threatening, or the hidden squalor of the observed self? There is a straightness, a 'perpendicular' penchant for order that accompanies strict observation, an intolerance for looseness. When Miss Hinton emphasized this quality of stiff uprightness, she immediately corrected such a representation, adding that once understood to be the author of *Pride and Prejudice*, Austen became regarded as 'a poker of whom every one is afraid. It must be confessed that this silent observation from such an observer is rather formidable ... a wit, a delineator of character, who does not talk, is terrific indeed.'[16]

Letters provide an excellent vehicle for such formidable observation. Silent and reserved, the correspondent can record household faults with impunity. It is, in fact, the letter-writer's duty to describe the 'minute' details of everyday life before her, however offensive they might appear. Thus we find that James' Mary, for one, lying in, 'does not manage matters in such a way as to make me want to lay in myself. She is not tidy enough in her appearance; she has no dressing-gown to sit up in; her curtains are all too thin, and things are not in that comfort and style about her which are necessary to make such a situation an enviable one' (*L* 24).

Offences can also be less personal, shards lodged painfully in the observer's penetrating (and penetrated) eye. In a tartly critical letter, written with a shaking hand ('I beleive I drank too much wine last night'), Austen describes the belle of last night's ball, one Mrs Blount, 'the only one much admired', as having 'the same broad face, diamond bandeau, white shoes, pink husband, & fat neck' that she possessed in September, while the daughter of Sir Thomas Champneys appeared to be 'a queer animal with a white neck'. In a postscript, determined to apprehend that which offends, she adds that she 'had the comfort of finding out the other evening who all the fat girls with short noses were that disturbed me at the 1st H. Ball. They all prove to be Miss Atkinsons of Enham' (*L* 60–3). This surreal account collapses the bland, broad glittering wealth of the Blounts into characteristics that merge together. Which one has the fat neck; and what is it about 'necks' that particular evening that so irked our commentator? By joining a 'white neck', traditionally a body part held in some degree of esteem, to the figure of a 'queer animal', Austen creates a minor monster shocking in her catachrestic singularity. The Miss Atkinsons, more traditionally unappealing, become bizarre in their multitudinous potential to disturb the observer. How many could 'all' be?

The desire to catalogue offences makes Austen a most daunting enforcer of 'straight' conduct. Acting as one long accustomed to repressing her own considerable powers, Austen expected no less from those who looked to her as their monitor. We can see her establishing standards of conduct in a letter to Fanny Knight, reporting on her visit to another niece, Anna Austen Lefroy, newly married.

> Our visit to Hendon will interest you I am sure, but I need not enter into the particulars of it, as your Papa will be able to answer *almost* every question. I certainly could describe her bed-room, & her Drawers & her Closet better than he can, but I do not feel that I can stop to do it ... Her purple Pelisse rather surprised me. – I thought we had known all Paraphernalia of that sort. I do not mean to blame her, it looked very well & I dare say she wanted it. I suspect nothing worse than its' being got in secret, & not owned to anybody. – She is capable of that you know. – (L 285)

John Halperin finds this to be 'perhaps' the 'worst moment' in Austen's correspondence.[17] But it is also rather funny to watch Jane Austen poking into her niece's closet, searching for secrets. This letter supposes a public awareness of the private paraphernalia of married life while it makes particular claims for Austen's expertise in discovery and disclosure. When she takes on the role of monitor to police the pelisse, she is acting out a cultural obligation, one that she has inherited from her novelistic models, and one that she will pass on to her heirs. For if one thing is constant in the domestic novel, it is the exposure of the female, who is always subject to the watchful eyes of others. Richardson might have started this tradition, placing Pamela under Mr B.'s covert gaze, subjecting Clarissa to Lovelace's careful surveillance, but it is in *Sir Charles Grandison*, one of Austen's favourite novels, that we are introduced to the benevolent male monitor, one who will be reproduced in Burney's *Evelina* and *Camilla*, in Austen's own *Emma*, *Mansfield Park* and *Northanger Abbey*, and later in Eliot's *Daniel Deronda*. Austen's talent for surveillance locates her at the centre of a tradition both literary and domestic which requires that the female figure be always ready for inspection.

The familiar letter allowed the powerless to criticize the powerful, but as an instrument serving two cultures, it also served to maintain powerful systems of social control. Austen's position here as critic of Anna's desire, for 'I dare say she wanted it', places her in the service of a larger system of conduct, one that she is in this epistolary moment nurturing. For the codification of manners and the pressures of surveillance will develop into such a carefully policed system that even Jane Austen, however careful she might have been to protect herself from the judgement of others, will be found wanting by her own heirs, by her own Fanny Knight Knatchbull, who will make her infamous remarks about her aunt's lack of refinement. 'Yes my love', she will write to her sister many years later, 'it is very true that Aunt Jane from various circumstances was not so *refined* as she ought to have been from her *talent*, & if she had lived 50 years later she would have been in many respects more suitable to *our* more refined tastes.'[18]

The letters of Jane Austen reveal the difficulties that she faced under a system of checks and repressions that needed to be negotiated. Since Austen keeps reminding us of the challenge of finding 'subject' and 'matter' full enough and proper enough to motivate writing at all, it is particularly appropriate that the last letter we have written by Austen is one heavily edited by her brother Henry. As the original letter is missing, we are left only with his edited version which he published in his 'Biographical Notice'. Austen's brother enters her text to suppress dangerous material:

> She next touches with just and gentle animadversion on a subject of domestic disappointment. Of this the particulars do not concern the public. Yet in justice to her characteristic sweetness and resignation, the concluding observation of our authoress thereon must not be suppressed.

The watchful brother returns us, quite briefly, to Austen herself, who seems herself to regret 'getting too near complaint', but then interrupts her last words once more:

> The following and final extract will prove the facility with which she could correct every impatient thought, and turn from complaint to cheerfulness. (*P* 332)

What follows should not surprise us. By now we should be used to oddly placed domestic and social details – the price of meat, Mary's blue gown, my mother's agonies. Austen appears to be taking up the most mundane social task, recommending one Captain – (the name has been excised by brother Henry), 'a very respectable, well-meaning man, without much manner, his wife and sister all good humour and obligingness, and I hope (since the fashion allows it) with rather longer petticoats than last year' (*L* 343). Petticoats, more petticoats, fly off 'through half a sentence'. If she knew these were to be her last known written words, would Jane Austen, remembering Miss Bates, laugh or lament?

NOTES

1. Deirdre Le Faye, *Jane Austen: A Family Record*, 2nd edn (Cambridge University Press, 2004), p. 276.
2. Le Faye, *Jane Austen*, p. 276.
3. 'Introduction', to the first edition (1932), *Jane Austen's Letters*, ed. Deirdre Le Faye (Oxford and New York: Oxford University Press, 1995), p. ix. Jo Modert argues that Cassandra appears to have taken 'better care of the letters than most of the recipients', and made few incisions in the letters that 'had nothing to do with Jane Austen's emotional expressions or secrets', *Jane Austen's Manuscript Letters in Facsimile* (Carbondale and Edwardsville, IL: Southern Illinois University Press,

1990), pp. xx–xxii. Susan C. Whealler discusses the Cassandra controversy in 'Prose and Power in Two Letters by Jane Austen', *Sent as a Gift: Eight Correspondences from the Eighteenth Century*, ed. Alan T. McKenzie (Athens, GA and London: University of Georgia Press, 1993), pp. 180–4. In *Jane Austen's Textual Lives: From Aeschylus to Bollywood* (Oxford and New York: Oxford University Press, 2005), Kathryn Sutherland suggests, not without irony, that Cassandra Austen 'did biographers a profound service when she censored or destroyed her sister's private papers and correspondence' by licensing 'the imagining of fact, the dream of history' (p. 59).

4. *Memoir of Jane Austen*, ed. R. W. Chapman (Oxford: Clarendon Press, 1926), pp. 59–60.

5. 'Letters/Correspondence', *The Jane Austen Handbook*, ed. J. David Grey (London: Athlone Press, 1986), p. 277.

6. In *Jane Austen among Women* (Baltimore, MD and London: Johns Hopkins Press, 1992), Kaplan argues that Austen worked within a framework of both 'gentry' and 'women's cultures'. Chapter 3, 'The Women's Culture', locates Austen's epistolary habits firmly within a feminine context. Whealler, in 'Prose and Power', argues that it is in the collection and dissemination of 'the minute details of domestic life' that Austen finds the source of 'private power' (p. 195).

7. Kaplan, *Jane Austen among Women*, pp. 47–50.

8. I am citing Marianne Dashwood's resolution, one which Austen certainly shows signs of taking to heart (*SS* 3:10:393).

9. Sutherland is particularly sensitive in chapter 3 to 'Austen's aural/vocal composition and performance of text' (*Jane Austen's Textual Lives*, p. 317).

10. In 'Jane Austen and the Look of Letters', *Romantic Correspondence: Women, Politics and the Fiction of Letters* (Cambridge University Press, 1993), Mary Favret argues for the importance of 'even lines' and 'close writing'. Since the recipients of a letter were usually required to pay postage upon delivery, letters needed to 'look as if they were worth the cost of postage' (pp. 136–7).

11. See Favret, on the importance of the post office for Jane Fairfax (*Romantic Correspondence*, pp. 158–62).

12. Le Faye, *A Family Record*, pp. 221 and 279.

13. 'Preface. In the Desobligeant', *Sentimental Journey* (1768).

14. 'I want to tell you that I have got my own darling Child from London', she reports after receiving her first copy of *Pride and Prejudice* (*L* 201). Real babies do not inspire such rejoicing. Austen complains to Fanny Knight that Anna Austen Lefroy, pregnant again, 'has not a chance of escape … Poor Animal, she will be worn out before she is thirty. – I am very sorry for her. – Mrs Clement too is in that way again. I am quite tired of so many children' (336).

15. Quoted in John Halperin, *The Life of Jane Austen* (Baltimore, MD: Johns Hopkins University Press, 1986), p. 186.

16. Le Faye, *A Family Record*, p. 221.

17. Halperin, *Life of Jane Austen*, p. 265.

18. Quoted in Le Faye, *A Family Record*, p. 279.

8

JULIET McMASTER

Class

We hear of Lady Catherine de Bourgh, one of the most memorable and least likeable characters in Jane Austen's novels, that 'she likes to have the distinction of rank preserved' (*PP* 2:6:182). The obsequious Mr Collins enjoins her guest Elizabeth Bennet to dress simply, and not to emulate the elegant apparel of her high-ranking hostess: the differences in station are not only present, but must be *seen* to be present.

Class difference was of course a fact of life for Austen, and an acute observation of the fine distinctions between one social level and another was a necessary part of her business as a writer of realistic fiction. Nor would she have wished it away, although at the time of writing her novels, she herself – as an unmarried daughter of a deceased country clergyman, like Miss Bates – knew what it was to suffer from the class system. Her favourite niece, Fanny Knight, 'whom she had seen grow up from a period when her notice was an honour' (*E* 3:7:408), was shamelessly patronizing after she married a baronet, and said that her aunt, but for the advantages she gained at Godmersham, would have been 'very much below par as to good Society and its ways'.[1] In certain ways Austen was ideally placed to observe the finely nuanced social distinctions around her. As an unmarried woman she was to some extent outside the game (since women were assumed to take their status from their husbands) and hence could see the more of it. Moreover, she had different vantage points: she could alternate between her relatively humble position of living with her widowed mother and unmarried sister in the Chawton house by the grace and favour of her landlord brother, and visiting that brother's family at his country estate of Godmersham, and drinking French wine (a rare treat) with the opulent (*L* 139).

'There are far finer and more numerous grades of dignity in this country than in any other', claimed Edward Bulwer-Lytton, who was growing up in England while Austen was writing her novels.[2] He and other Victorians like Carlyle and Thackeray became excellent and explicit analysts of class and class difference in England; but Austen had already specialized in the dramatizing of the nuances and intricacies of the subject. My procedure in this chapter will be first to turn snob myself, and erect a social ladder as she represents it, with the personnel of her novels arranged on its rungs in order of precedence; then to try to extract Austen's own attitude to class distinction and the immense importance that some of her characters assign to it.

Although in her own life Austen did have some dealings with royalty, however mediated, when she was graciously invited to dedicate *Emma* to the Prince Regent, she never presents royalty in her fiction, nor any of the great aristocrats who still owned huge tracts of the country and were prominent in its government. So we must start several rungs down the ladder. Among the onstage characters (as opposed to those who are merely mentioned), Lord Osborne in the fragment 'The Watsons' is probably the one with the highest rank in her fiction, and he is not much better than a fool. The indications are that he will be sufficiently educated by the heroine to learn to value her and to propose to her, but that she will turn him down.[3] So much suggests that for Austen there is nothing divine about royalty, and not much that is special about peers. In fact characters with titles – or 'handles to their names', as the Victorians used to say – are seldom admirable in the novels. Sir Thomas Bertram, a baronet, is the best of them, but even he overestimates his own and his family's importance. Sir Walter Elliot's obsession with his status and the *Baronetage* in which it is published is made not only comic but contemptible. (In Sir Walter, Austen anticipates the Victorian social criticism of Carlyle, who characterized the aristocrat as 'The Dandy', obsessed with appearances, and sick with self-love.)[4] Sir John Middleton, who is also presumably a baronet, is well-meaning but vacuous, with a 'total want of talent and taste' (*SS* 1:7:38). A servant's rendering of the title as 'a baronight' suggests that being a baronet can be a somewhat benighted condition (*P* 1:12:114).

A baronetcy is an inherited title, passed down from father to son; a knighthood, also signalled by the title 'Sir' attached to the first name, is awarded for a particular service; since it is not hereditary, it carries less prestige. Even a Mr Lucas, 'formerly in trade in Meryton', can become a 'Sir William Lucas' of Lucas Lodge, and introduce 'St. James's', the palace where he received his knighthood, into every conversation. 'The distinction [of being knighted] had perhaps been felt too strongly', notes the narrator drily (*PP* 1:5:19). A title, it seems, is sometimes almost a guarantee of fatuousness in Austen's fiction. 'The Dowager Viscountess Dalrymple, and her daughter, the Honourable Miss Carteret', merely from the stately parade of their names, are almost bound to be the kind whose status is their only attraction (*P* 1:2:160). So too with the Honourable John Yates, who spends his time in solitary declamation as he rehearses the role of a baron (*MP* 1:18:198). ('Honourable' is a courtesy title given to younger sons and daughters of peers below the rank of marquess.)

Women too sometimes have handles to their names, although they could not inherit a peerage or a baronetcy. Lady Catherine de Bourgh would not want us to miss the fine shades in the title 'Lady'. When it comes attached to the first name – as with Lady Catherine, her sister Lady Anne Darcy, and the unscrupulous Lady Susan Vernon – it signifies that the lady in question has the title 'in her own right', as the daughter of an earl; she is thus 'to the manner born', as the expression goes, and she retains her title irrespective of her husband's status. Lady Bertram of *Mansfield Park*, however, along with Lady Middleton, Lady Russell of *Persuasion* and Lady Denham of 'Sanditon', whose titles are attached only to the last name, hold them only by virtue of being married to a baronet or knight; and the lady would lose it if she were remarried to a plain 'Mr'. In such circles, such things matter.

Lady Anne Darcy is married to plain Mr Darcy, and Lady Catherine makes a point of Darcy's family as being 'untitled'. It is nevertheless 'respectable, honourable, and ancient', and Darcy's fortune, at £10,000 a year, is 'splendid' (*PP* 3:14:394). The long-established but untitled landowning family does seem to gather Austen's deep respect, especially if its income comes from land and a rent-roll; and her two most eligible heroes, Mr Darcy of Pemberley and Mr Knightley of Donwell Abbey, come from this class, the landed gentry. So does Mr Rushworth of Sotherton, however, who despite his long rent-roll is morally and intellectually not worth much more than his name signifies.

Austen is often happy to follow the Cinderella plot, and to make a happy ending out of marrying her heroine to a man notably above her in income and social prestige. The landowning country gentleman is as close to a prince as her heroines approach. As to income, they usually follow, in effect if not in intention, the prudent advice of Tennyson's 'Northern Farmer': 'Doänt thou marry for munny, but goä wheer munny is!' Elizabeth's initial rejection of Darcy usefully assures us that she is not marrying him for his £10,000 a year. But she half-jokingly admits that her love has been influenced by 'his beautiful grounds at Pemberley' (*PP* 3:17:414). Money is only one of a number of factors that count, however.

Elizabeth's marriage to Darcy is the greatest 'match' in the novels, and Mrs Bennet has every right to rejoice in it. But we have different views on the extent of the social disparity between them. In Lady Catherine's eyes Elizabeth is a nobody, with 'upstart pretensions', a woman shrewdly on the make, who will pollute 'the shades of Pemberley' (*PP* 3:14:396). Elizabeth herself, however, is not overwhelmed by the social difference. 'He is a gentleman; I am a gentleman's daughter; so far we are equal', she claims calmly (3:14:395). Austen seems to approve of this relative flattening of the degrees of distinction above the country gentry. But she notes too, with irony, the tendency to be acutely aware of the degrees of distinction in the scale below. Emma Woodhouse is enraged that Mr Elton should 'look down upon her friend, so well understanding the gradations of rank below him, and be so blind to what rose above, as to fancy himself shewing no presumption in addressing her!' (E 1:16:147). Emma too has a vivid sense of the gradations below.

The country gentleman, who leads a leisured existence and who subsists on income from land and inheritance, is at his best the moral and social ideal as a partner for a heroine. But the condition takes some living up to. Like other social commentators, Austen insists that with the privileges go extensive responsibilities. Elizabeth freezes Darcy off when he is proud and pretentious; but she warms to him when she discovers how as master of Pemberley he uses his extensive power for the good of those around him.

> The commendation bestowed on him by Mrs. Reynolds was of no trifling nature. What praise is more valuable than the praise of an intelligent servant? As a brother, a landlord, a master, she considered how many people's happiness were in his guardianship! – ... How much of pleasure or pain it was in his power to bestow! – ... Every idea that had been brought forward by the housekeeper was favourable to his character. (PP 3:1:277)

Emma strikes us as a glowing and optimistic comedy partly because the hero Mr Knightley stands highest in the moral as well as the social scale: he lives, after all, at 'Donwell' Abbey.

The Highbury of Emma is close to presenting a microcosm of Austen's social world. Here, from Mr Knightley (whose knightly moral status is expressed in his name rather than a literal title) to the poor family to which Emma dispenses charity, we have assembled nearly all the levels of society that Austen presents.[5] Moreover, the novel's heroine is one who specializes in social discrimination, and makes prompt though often inaccurate judgements about the social station of the people around her. I will use Emma, therefore, to provide the main example of the levels of the social ladder, while drawing freely on examples from the other novels as well.

Highest in the Highbury circle, then, is Mr Knightley of Donwell Abbey, the first in virtue as in place. Austen insists that part of his virtue is that he refuses to trade on his rank. He walks, when status-conscious people like the Osbornes in 'The Watsons' would make a point of riding in a carriage. When he does get out his carriage, it is to transport Miss Bates and Jane Fairfax, not himself. Though he could leave the management of his estate to an employee, he takes an active interest, is often in conference with his steward William Larkins, and is warmly interested in the domestic affairs of his tenant farmer,

Robert Martin. In *Persuasion*, by contrast, we are invited to consider the derogation of such duties by the bad landlord, Sir Walter Elliot, who is consequently exiled from his estate, and even leaves the farewells to his daughter (*P* 1:5:41). Sir Walter is enraptured by the prestige of his position, but neglects the responsibilities.

Next in status in Highbury is Mr Woodhouse of Hartfield. Hartfield is a gentleman's residence, and it has a farm attached; but Mr Woodhouse clearly has nothing to do with its management, and we hear of no tenants. The fact that Emma has a fortune of £30,000 suggests that much of his income comes from investment rather than from land: hence his status is relatively lower than Knightley's. Mr Bennet of Longbourn in *Pride and Prejudice* and old Mr Dashwood in *Sense and Sensibility* also belong in this category. Though gentlemen of property, and owners of estates, they lack the long-term commitment to the land that makes good stewards and moral aristocrats of Darcy and Knightley.

One might suppose that the siblings in a single family would be almost by definition of the same rank. But even here there are marked differences in status, not only between sons and daughters, but also between one son and another. The aristocracy and the inheritance of land depended heavily on the system of primogeniture. Just as only the eldest son can inherit a peerage, so the bulk of land would normally descend by the same system. The entail, so prominent in *Pride and Prejudice*, legally formalizes this customary practice of inheritance. If an estate were divided equally between all siblings, as our understanding of equitable practice would suggest today, the estate would be dispersed and would ultimately cease to exist. The system of primogeniture, which unfairly privileges one family member by accumulating all property in his hands, was developed as an arrangement for the preservation of the family name and the family estate through the generations. Austen highlights the injustices of this system of inheritance. At the beginning of *Sense and Sensibility* the narrator informs us how a rich old gentleman, Mr Dashwood, so ties up both his money and his estate that it must stay in the male line, and may not be alienated to the girls of the family, even though the son is already amply provided for. 'Wife and daughters' are deprived; and the estate and the money as well must descend 'to his son, and his son's son' (*SS* 1:1:4).

Hence there is a considerable difference in prestige and expectation between elder sons and younger sons, as between sons and daughters. Austen notices this, and dramatizes it; but not without conveying a strong sense of the inequity of such arrangements. The five Bennet girls are to be turned out of Longbourn when their father dies, since the estate is entailed on a distant male cousin, Mr Collins, who shows precious little sign of being morally worthy of it. Even among these five girls, too, there are notable shades of difference in prestige.

Jane, the eldest, is called 'Miss Bennet', while her younger sisters are referred to as 'Miss Eliza', 'Miss Mary', and so on. The elder may be 'out' in society before the younger, and *should* be, according to Lady Catherine; but in this matter, in this family, equity prevails. 'I think it would be very hard upon younger sisters', says Elizabeth, 'that they should not have their share of society and amusement because the elder may not have the means or the inclination to marry early, – the last born has as good a right to the pleasures of youth, as the first' (*PP* 2:6:187). Once married, a sister gains prestige over a sister, whatever the place in the age sequence. 'Lord! how I should like to be married before any of you', Lydia tells her elder sisters ingenuously; 'and then I would chaperon you about to all the balls' (2:16:244). And presently – though not without some moral sacrifice – she gains her wish, and takes pride of place at table at her mother's right hand, saying to her eldest sister, 'Ah! Jane, I take your place now, and you must go lower, because I am a married woman' (3:9:350).

Among the brothers at this level of society the difference is even greater. The eldest, who can expect to inherit the estate and the income that goes with it, if not a title as well, is often bred to idleness; and Austen shows how such expectations can make him spoilt and frivolous, like Frederick Tilney in *Northanger Abbey* and Tom Bertram in *Mansfield Park*. A younger son, like Henry Tilney or Edmund Bertram, who has his living to earn, is sympathetically treated, and becomes a suitable partner for the heroine. Mary Crawford has every intention of marrying an *elder* brother, and is so discontented with herself for falling in love with Edmund by mistake that she wishes his elder brother dead (*MP* 3:14:502). Edward Ferrars, who is an elder son by birth but not by temperament, chafes at the idleness expected of him. 'Instead of having anything to do, instead of having any profession chosen for me, or being allowed to chuse any myself, I returned home to be completely idle' (*SS* 3:1:410). His mother, the rich and powerful Mrs Ferrars, in effect turns him into a younger son (at least economically speaking), by transferring all her money to his younger brother Robert, who relishes idleness. Edward turns to making his living as a country parson.

So much suggests that Austen's best sympathies rest with the professional class – her own, that is. Although her most vivacious heroines (Marianne, Elizabeth and Emma) marry upwards into the landowning gentry, Catherine, Elinor, Fanny and (probably) Emma Watson marry clergymen; clergymen, moreover, who are usually younger brothers. Austen represents the sterling virtues of the profession to which her father and two of her brothers belonged, although she doesn't dwell on their duties or their status within their profession, as Trollope was to do a generation later. In novels where the heroine marries into the gentry, however, Austen permits herself some satire of the ministry. Mr Collins and Mr Elton are parsons on their preferment, servile towards a 'patron' and eager to marry money. Even the highly principled Edmund Bertram, after he has 'been married long enough to begin to want an increase of income', submits to taking a second living, and so becomes a pluralist (*MP* 3:17:547).

A gentleman's son who must earn his living has still rather limited choices in Austen's world: the church, the army, the navy, the law and medicine (and the last was still of dubious gentility). The army was a doubtful proposition as a living, since an officer's commission had to be purchased.[6] Captain Tilney, an eldest son, can expect patronage, as he is following his father's profession. (General Tilney must have inherited his estate, as his army pay would not suffice to buy an abbey.) Colonel Brandon was originally a younger son, but inherits his estate on the early death of his elder brother. Wickham, a lieutenant in the militia, is chronically short of funds. Mr Weston, as a Captain in the militia, was considered beneath the gentry family of the Churchills; and before he can buy himself into Randalls and gentlemanhood he must make his money in trade (*E* 1:2:14–15). The army, that is, though it has prestige, is not a reliable source of income. But Emma, snob as she is, would probably not have taken so kindly to Mr Weston as the husband of her friend if he had not once been 'Captain' Weston.

The navy, of course, is the profession Austen favours next after the clergy. In *Persuasion* she uses it as the model of a system of promotion by merit, to contrast with the old-world system of heredity that Sir Walter Elliot considers sacred.[7] He objects to the navy 'as being the means of bringing persons of obscure birth into undue distinction, and raising men to honours which their fathers and grandfathers never dreamt of' (*P* 1:3:21). Sir Walter's disapproval signals Austen's approval. In her last novel she famously demotes the landed gentry and replaces them by the navy, substituting Admiral Croft for Sir Walter as the proprietor of Kellynch-hall, and allowing her heroine to reject William Elliot, heir to the estate, in favour of a relatively self-made man, the gallant Captain Wentworth. Wentworth, moreover, has made money by his profession. Since England was at war with France and its allies, and moreover dominant at sea, a captain and his crew (whose shares of profits were minutely discriminated) could take 'prizes', capturing enemy ships at sea and realizing huge profits.[8] 'Ah! those were pleasant days when I had the Laconia', muses Captain Wentworth. 'How fast I made money in her' (1:8:72). The woman author's sharp recognition of the economic motive for warfare is implicit in Admiral Croft's bluff hopes for 'the good luck to live to another war' (1:8:75).

Austen shows herself quite knowledgeable not only about prizes and money-making in the navy, but about its internal hierarchy and systems of promotion. It was next to impossible to be genuinely 'self-made': in the absence of money, a man on his promotion would need 'interest', and/or luck. Wentworth's first command, the Asp, is pronounced unfit for overseas service; but Admiral Croft insists, 'Lucky fellow to get any thing so soon, with no more interest than his' (*P* 1:8:70). We see some of this 'interest' at work when Henry Crawford procures William Price's lieutenancy by using his influence with his uncle the Admiral (*MP* 2:13:345–6).

Austen's preference for the navy over the army is signalled by the notice she takes of their uniforms. The susceptibility of young Kitty and Lydia Bennet to 'the regimentals of an ensign' marks them as 'two of the silliest girls in the country', in their father's opinion; and their foolish mother's wistful fondness for 'a red-coat' puts her in the same company (*PP* 1:7:32–3). (There is often a sense of sexual threat attached to army characters, as to the seducers Wickham and Captain Tilney.) On the other hand, we are invited to participate in Fanny Price's association of the naval profession with pride and virtue when she looks on her brother, 'complete in his Lieutenant's uniform, looking and moving all the taller, firmer, and more graceful for it, and with the happiest smile over his face' (*MP* 3:7:444). As usual, however, Austen provides a qualification. Lest she be thought to generalize in her approval of the seagoing professions, she provides us with a negative example in the boozy Mr Price, Fanny's father and a retired officer of the marines, whose 'habits were worse, and his manners coarser, than she had been prepared for' (3:8:450).

For representatives of the other professions we have to turn to relatively minor characters. The law is represented in *Emma* by Mr Knightley's younger brother, John Knightley, who is a respectable attorney in London. Country attorneys, such as Mr Phillips in *Pride and Prejudice*, Robert Watson in 'The Watsons' or the Coxes, father and son, in *Emma*, are seen as verging on the vulgar. When Mary Crawford urges Edmund to 'go into the law', she probably hopes he would become a London barrister, the more distinguished branch of the legal profession, and one that was frequently a route to political office. Austen's sympathies are clearly with Edmund in his defence of his choice to be a clergyman as the more honourable calling (*MP* 1:9:107–9).

Physicians and surgeons, too, are relegated to the sidelines, although Austen notes their rising social status in making a memorable incident out of Mr Perry's changing decision about setting up a carriage in *Emma*. Like an expensive car today, carriages were status symbols. To maintain one's own carriage and horses was a considerable expense, and the decision to do so must be taken with care. For this time Perry postpones the purchase; but we are given reason to believe that in due course he will indeed rise to the carriage-owning class (*E* 3:5:374–5). Perhaps in the heroine's brother Sam, in 'The Watsons', 'only a surgeon, you know' (*LM* 'W' 86), we would have had a sympathetic picture of a medical man; but in the fragment he is in a fair way to being cut out in his courtship of the heire 'military men' (*LM* 'W' 95).

Austen locates few major characters in 'trade', and for many of her ch acters the word has a ring that seems to require apology. It is not surprising that the gentry and professional classes felt somewhat threatened by the large changes that were coming with the Industrial Revolution, and tended to close ranks against the newly powerful and the nouveaux riches. Trade represents new money, and money, like wine, isn't considered quite respectable until it has aged a little. Austen is clearly fascinated by this process: though she doesn't share the snobbish prejudice against trade, she pays close attention to the gradual assimilation of the trading classes into gentility. Emma Woodhouse again can represent the snobbish position, at least in her initial reaction, on the rise of the Cole family in Highbury. But it is important to notice that Emma's attitude evolves and changes. The Coles, as Emma places them, are 'of low origin, in trade, and only moderately genteel'. However, they have prospered financially, and they have 'added to their house, to their number of servants, to their expenses of every sort; and by this time were, in fortune and style of living, second only to the family at Hartfield' (*E* 2:7:223). (Mr Knightley, strictly speaking, is from the nearby parish of Donwell.) Their place and their mobility in society are exactly rendered; Austen pays attention to the assault on gentility of the new mercantile middle class. Emma is stand-offish; she severely disapproves of Mr Elton's 'propensity to dine with Mr. Cole' (2:8:230), and she looks forward to refusing any invitation they may have the presumption to address to her. However, she must learn to swallow her pride. By the time she knows that all the people she likes best are to be assembled at the Coles' dinner party, she is very glad to accept the invitation when it comes. But she is careful not to show any eagerness. 'She owned that, considering every thing, she was not absolutely without inclination for the party' (2:7:225): the sentence, with its careful qualifications and humorous double negative, signals the condescension of the grande dame of Highbury in thus conferring her stamp of approval on the parvenus. Hereafter, apparently, the Coles, for all their tincture of 'trade', will be on visiting terms even with the most exclusive families of Highbury; and perhaps the young Coles of the next generation may aspire to marry the Westons' daughter, or even the offspring of Mr and Mrs Knightley of Donwell Abbey.

Much has to do with manners and tact. However reluctantly, Emma accepts the Coles into the genteel society of Highbury, because they 'expressed themselves so properly', they show 'real attention' (*E* 2:7:225). The new Mrs Elton, however, is another matter. Before meeting her, Emma has ascertained that she is 'the youngest of the two daughters of a Bristol – merchant, of course, he must

tradesman' may not be uttered) (2:4:196). But she
...dgement until she meets the bride in person. When
... confirms Emma's worst prejudices: Emma can't
...sion and under-bred finery' (2:14:301). Moreover,
... a difficult exercise in discrimination to pick apart
... and morals. But Austen enables us to distinguish
...ved social snobbery and her proper moral aversion
...hed self-approval. For instance, like Miss Bingley,
...er newly acquired status to put down others.

A later stage of ... ...similation of one class into another is seen in the
Bingleys of *Pride and Prejudice.* Young Charles Bingley is a gentleman of
leisure, and already associates with such a prestigious member of the country
gentry as Darcy. But his is new money, 'acquired by trade' in the industrial
north of England. We see him in the process of buying his way into the gentry.
His father 'had intended to purchase an estate, but did not live to do it'
(*PP* 1:4:16). Bingley, then, in a leisurely manner, is shopping; by renting
Netherfield manor, he is trying out country gentlemanhood. Once he marries
Jane, he does buy an estate in a county near Derbyshire (3:19:427); so the
'next generation' will be correspondingly a step up in the social hierarchy. In
Bingley we see the best of social mobility. He is good-humoured and charm-
ing, and he never stands on ceremony. Like Elizabeth when she moves into
Pemberley, he will benefit his new social level by not trying to live up to it all
the time. His sisters, however, show the aspect of social mobility that Austen
distrusted. They are status-hungry, 'proud and conceited' (1:4:16), and
Caroline Bingley is overeager to ally herself and her brother with the prestige
of the Darcy family. Conveniently forgetting that her own fortune was made
in trade, she is spitefully scornful of Mr Gardiner, the Bennet sisters' merchant
uncle, 'who lives somewhere near Cheapside', she sneers. 'If they had uncles
enough to fill *all* Cheapside', Bingley bursts out warmly, 'it would not make
them one jot less agreeable' (1:8:40). Generously undiscriminating about
shades of social distinction, he cares more about their manners, the amenable
social conduct that makes them 'agreeable'. His is the approved attitude.

On this issue, however, Darcy realistically argues that the Bennet sisters'
connection with trade 'must very materially lessen their chance of marrying
men of any consideration in the world' (*PP* 1:8:40). His qualification is
presented as a point of fact, and he is not malicious, like Miss Bingley. But
still, Darcy is to go through an evolution in his attitude, at last marrying, like
Bingley, one of the Bennet girls, Cheapside uncle notwithstanding. Indeed, he
comes to value the Gardiners, despite their connection with trade, more
highly than his father-in-law the country gentleman. The quality of humanity
is to be judged by moral and humane standards, Austen suggests, not by social

status; but like her own temporary snobs, Darcy and Emma, she pays full attention to their social status first.

Since the union of the merchant's daughter with the earl's son depicted in Hogarth's *Marriage à la Mode* (1745), England has been famous for its alliances between 'blood' and money, the bargain by which the aristocracy is enriched, and the merchant class can promote its grandchildren into rank and title. 'By this intermixture of the highest aristocracy with the more subaltern ranks of society', Bulwer-Lytton explained, 'there are far finer and more numerous grades of dignity in this country than in any other'. In exploring some of the finely nuanced distinctions that can arise from the subtle intermixture of birth and cash, he notes one marker of consequence that can easily be overlooked.

> You see two gentlemen of the same birth, fortune, and estates – they are not of the same rank, – by no means! – one looks down on the other as confessedly his inferior. Would you know why? His connexions are much higher! (Bulwer-Lytton, *England and the English*, 31)

Austen is alert to this distinction as to others. Emma Woodhouse is indignant that the clergyman, Mr Elton, should dare to propose marriage to her, or to 'suppose himself her equal in connection or mind!' (*E* 1:16:147). 'Connection', like the 'interest' that Wentworth needs in order to get a good command in the navy, is a term fraught with significance. Bingley raises his status (though in his case it is unconsciously done) by being the friend of Darcy, as Harriet begins to be out of Robert Martin's reach when she becomes the friend of Miss Woodhouse.

If those involved in trade hover on the brink of gentility, there are many grades and degrees below them. Mrs and Miss Bates in *Emma* are similarly poised, and a gulf of poverty yawns below them. They are of a class that was later to be called 'shabby-genteel', people who have come down in the world. Once prominent as the wife of the vicar, Mrs Bates as a widow lives on slender means, in cramped quarters in an upstairs apartment, with only one servant, a maid of all work. But though she and her daughter are short of money and can't entertain, they still have connections: they are on visiting terms with the best families of Highbury; and that's more than can be said, as we have seen, for the Coles, with all their money and servants.

Another kind of amphibian, one who can move upwards or sink downwards in society, is the governess. Jane Fairfax, for instance, is well bred and well educated, beautiful and talented. But because her relatives cannot support her, she must earn her living at one of the only professions available to women, as a governess. The novels of Charlotte and Anne Brontë amply dramatize the painful position of well-educated girls from the impoverished upper classes who become virtually the servants of families often much less well bred than themselves. Jane Fairfax speaks in poignant terms of employment agencies for governesses: 'Offices for the sale – not quite of human flesh – but of human intellect' (*E* 2:17:325). The alignment with the slave trade is explicit; there is a passing hint, too, of prostitution. Jane Fairfax, like Jane Eyre, is one of those governesses who survive by marrying into the gentry. But her escape from a life of drudgery, looking after Mrs Smallridge's three children for a pittance, is a narrow one.

The governess in the nineteenth-century novel becomes a culture heroine for the sad army of economically vulnerable single women, who had virtually no means of acquiring independence outside marriage, and little hope of independence within it either. 'You know we must marry', sighs Elizabeth Watson, one of four unmarried daughters of an impecunious clergyman, 'it is very bad to grow old and be poor and laughed at' (*LM* 'W' 82). Charlotte Lucas chooses to marry the pompous and inept Mr Collins, not for love, but because her only alternative is to live as a spinster on the charity of her obnoxious younger brother. Herself a single woman of small means, Austen can represent the bleak existence of such women, as well as the happier fate of the heroine who finds fulfilment in marriage to the right man.

Those who make big money in 'trade' are the merchants and wholesalers. But their great houses are dependent on the small tradesmen, the retailers, who distribute the goods. There is a large social difference between the two. In Thackeray's *Vanity Fair*, a satirical panorama of the nineteenth-century class scene, the hero Dobbin is sneered at and called 'Figs' in school, because his father is a retail grocer, whereas the other boys are wholesalers' sons. 'My father's a gentleman, and keeps his carriage', boasts one young snob (ch. 5). The ladies and gentleman who are Austen's major characters exist in a commodity culture that depends on the retail trade for its luxuries, its status symbols, often its very food and drink. Mrs Allen in *Northanger Abbey* can think of nothing but her clothes; Robert Ferrars in *Sense and Sensibility* brings his whole personality to bear in the choice of a toothpick case; Sir Walter Elliot praises the efficacy of Gowland's lotion in removing freckles: such characters suggest an idle upper class obsessed with material luxuries, and ironically dependent on the very tradesmen they affect to despise. Austen sets some memorable scenes in shops: Harriet and Emma define themselves and their relationship in the matter of buying ribbons, feminine fripperies, in Ford's of Highbury. Anne Elliot has a nervous reunion with Wentworth at Molland's in Bath, where the crowds of the fashionable gather and assert their status: 'altogether there was a delay, and a bustle, and a talking, which must make all the little crowd in the shop understand that Lady Dalrymple was calling to convey Miss Elliot' (*P* 2:7:192). Mary Crawford in *Mansfield Park* humorously notices the elaborate lines of communication in a country community: she gets word of the harp, on its way to the country from London, only when 'it was seen by some farmer, and he told the miller, and the miller told the butcher, and the butcher's son-in-law left word at the shop' (*MP* 1:6:68). These retailers and small tradesmen do not figure prominently as characters, but their presence as part of the busy scene of life is carefully registered. There are many other relatively 'low' and minor characters who help to make society work smoothly in Austen's novels. Mrs Smith's Nurse Rooke, in *Persuasion*, though not in genteel society, knows and transmits more of what goes on there than people who are.

Emma, which provides unobtrusive information on the whole community of Highbury, right down to the poor and the gypsy vagrants, has a number of minor characters who occupy places in the social hierarchy well beyond the gentry and professional classes where Austen's major characters are situated. She writes no explicit analysis, but by passing details she fills in the large social picture and provides indirect commentary. We hear of Wallis the baker, who bakes Mrs Bates' apples; of the village shop, Ford's; of Mr Knightley's steward, William Larkins; his tenant farmer, Robert Martin, a sensitive young man who is bettering himself by reading; of Mrs Goddard's school, an unpretentious establishment 'where girls might be sent to be out of the way and scramble themselves into a little education' (*E* 1:3:21).

The leisured and professional classes of regency England were sustained by a great army of servants, an army which like the actual military had its own internal hierarchy and pecking order. Though Austen doesn't usually give servants speaking parts, she recognizes the unobtrusive influence they have on the lives of their masters.[9] It is a material convenience to Mr Woodhouse of Hartfield, for instance, that his coachman's daughter is placed as the housemaid at Randalls; James therefore never objects to harnessing the horses to the carriage, even though it is a very short drive (*E* 1:3:20). Such little negotiations between one social level and another are the stuff of life.

Beyond the servants comes the great mass of what was yet to be named the working class; but with them Austen's main characters have little to do. Like most 'ladies and gentlemen' of their day, their acquaintance with this huge section of the population would be only through their servants, who are not truly representative. However, we get glimpses. Mary Crawford learns of the 'sturdy independence' of rural labourers at hay harvest time (*MP* 1:6:69). Harriet Smith and a school friend have a disturbing encounter with disreputable gypsies, but the 'whole gang' is swiftly dispersed when Frank Churchill arrives; and we hear that Mr Knightley, as magistrate, is to be informed 'of there being such a set of people in the neighbourhood' (*E* 3:3:362). Dickens might give us scenes of the unleashed fury of the mob in the Gordon riots or olution; but in Austen's novels, by and large, law and order

e seldom mentioned, but they are there, for Lady Catherine to armony and plenty' (*PP* 2:7:190) or for Anne Elliot and Emma ssionately. Although Emma is aware she will probably soon forget the mistress of the poor sick family she visits, she pays them full attention while she is with them, and she is neither arrogant nor sentimental: 'She understood their ways, could allow for their ignorance and their temptations, had no romantic expectations of extraordinary virtue from those, for whom education had done so little . . . and always gave her assistance with as much intelligence as good-will' (*E* 1:10:93). We have the sense of those 'two nations', as Disraeli was later to characterize rich and poor in *Sybil*; but Austen allows for some humane contact between them, however minimal.

Lionel Trilling humorously quotes a reader exasperated by the obsessive attention paid to social class in the English novel: 'Who cares whether Pamela finally exasperates Mr. B. into marriage, whether Mr. Elton is more or less than moderately genteel . . . whether Lady Chatterley ought to be made love to by the game-keeper, even if he was an officer during the war? Who cares?'[10] The novelist (and especially Jane Austen) always cares because it is the business of the novel to represent people – not exclusively, but prominently – in their social roles, and to be precise about the differences between them. It sometimes seems that if class difference did not exist, the novelist would have to invent it, because of the rich potential it provides for definition and fine distinction. Austen, as we have seen, goes in for fine distinctions, whether between the degrees of quality of mind in her characters or the fine shades of difference in their social standing. But to say so much is not to contend that she approved of the bastions of privilege in her very hierarchical society, or resisted the changes towards freer movement between the classes that she saw happening around her.[11] Nor did she subordinate moral and aesthetic judgements to issues of social rank. To use that term of later development that I have applied to Emma, Austen was no snob, though she knew all about snobbery.

According to Lionel Trilling's definition, 'Snobbery is pride in status without pride in function' (203). This applies perfectly to Sir Walter Elliot, who wants all the privilege and prestige belonging to his baronetcy, but none of the responsibilities. Thackeray, the most prominent of the many nineteenth-century commentators on class difference, supplies a definition that emphasizes the vitiated value system of the person who considers social station to be all-important: a snob, he says, is 'he who meanly admires mean things'.[12] To such a person social station is the defining condition that overrides all other categories of judgement – physical, intellectual or moral.

In Jane Austen's world, human worth is to be judged by standards better and more enduring than social status; but social status is always relevant. With amused detachment, she registers exactly the social provenance of each and all of her characters, and judges them for the ways in which they judge each other. The importance assigned to class distinction is the source of much of her comedy and her irony, as of her social satire. In *Emma*, for instance, the snobbish heroine becomes both our guide as to where each character in the novel should be 'placed', and our negative example of one who assigns far too much importance to the matter of status. And the best treatment for her self-importance is laughter. 'Nonsensical girl!' laughs Mr Knightley, when she has indulged in one of her elaborately class-conscious flights of fancy (*E* 2:8:231). But snobbery unchecked raises indignation too. Many of Austen's most contemptible characters are those who place undue emphasis on social station; and they come from all levels of the social ladder: Isabella Thorpe and General Tilney; Mr and Mrs John Dashwood; Lucy Steele and Mrs Ferrars; Miss Bingley; Mrs Norris; Mr Collins and Lady Catherine de Bourgh. Those principal characters with an overdeveloped pride in their position, like Darcy and Emma, must learn the error of their ways.

Before Emma has met Mrs Elton, she reflects that '*what* she was, must be uncertain; but *who* she was, might be found out' (*E* 2:4:196). It is the lady's social identity that can be discovered in advance: whose daughter she is, where she comes from, how much money she has and how it was made. But *what* she is – that is, what sort of person, vivacious or reserved, kind or arrogant, intelligent or silly: all the things that really matter – is another issue altogether, and can be established only by personal contact. Austen brilliantly dramatizes these essential matters of personal identity in the personnel of her novels, and we come to know her people and the individual *feel* of them as intimately as we know any in fiction; but in this chapter I have necessarily concentrated on *who* they are (in Emma's terms), rather than *what* they are.

'Tinker, tailor, soldier, sailor', goes the rhyme, as the child divines possibilities from the cherry stones left on the plate; 'Rich man, poor man, beggar man, thief.' The folk imagination, like the individual's, necessarily busies itself with such matters. Austen's heroines play the cherry-stone game too, and we learn to care whether they will come to reside in 'Big house, little house, pigsty, barn', and dress in 'Silk, satin, cotton, [or] rags.' Her novels are rich in detail of the status symbols and cultural markers of her society: the estates, lands, houses, cottages; the coaches, carriages, barouche-landaus, hatchments, lozenges, liveries; the silks, satins, muslins, pearls, amber crosses, rings and beads. As a sensitive and informed commentator on class, that huge topic of the nineteenth century, Austen shows us amply how such things matter. She also shows us how they should not matter too much.

NOTES

1. Park Honan, *Jane Austen: Her Life* (London: Weidenfeld & Nicolson, 1987), p. 118.
2. Edward Bulwer-Lytton, *England and the English* (1831), ed. Standish Meachum (Chicago and London: University of Chicago Press, 1970), p. 31.
3. See Cassandra Austen's comments on 'The Watsons' as handed down by J. E. Austen Leigh in *A Memoir of Jane Austen*, 3rd edn (London: Richard Bentley, 1872), p. 364.
4. Thomas Carlyle, *Sartor Resartus*, 1st edn 1833–4 (New York: Odyssey Press, 1937), p. 272.
5. See Thomas Keymer: 'It is in *Emma*, where Austen's heroine is not the usual challenger of hierarchy but rather its staunchest upholder, that the fine calibrations of rank are most clearly seen' ('Rank', in *Jane Austen in Context*, ed. Janet Todd (Cambridge University Press, 2005), p. 393).
6. On the prices of commissions, see B. C. Southam, 'Professions', in Todd, *Jane Austen in Context*.
7. See Edward Copeland: '*Persuasion* ... [has] the distinction in Austen's novels of celebrating the professional ranks frankly and openly, of placing them above the aristocracy and gentry as responsible economists' ('The Austens and the Elliots: A Consumer's Guide to *Persuasion*', in *Jane Austen's Business*, ed. Juliet McMaster and Bruce Stovel (London: Macmillan, 1995), p. 150).
8. See Brian Southam, *Jane Austen and the Navy* (London: Hambledon and London, 2000), pp. 121–5.
9. For a study of the servant classes in Austen's novels, see Judith Terry's 'Seen But not Heard: Servants in Jane Austen's England', *Persuasions*, 10 (1988), 104–16.
10. Quoted by Lionel Trilling, in 'Manners, Morals, and the Novel', in *The Liberal Imagination* (New York: Doubleday, 1953), p. 205.
11. Mark Parker believes that in *Emma* Austen argues 'subtly but firmly, for a maintenance of the system' ('The End of *Emma*: Drawing the Boundaries of Class in Austen', *JEGP*, 91(3) (1 July 1992), 34). I read Austen as much more critical of the operation of class ideology than Parker allows, and more open to change.
12. William Makepeace Thackeray, *A Book of Snobs*, by One of Themselves (1846), ch. 2.

9

EDWARD COPELAND

Money

Once upon a time, as the story goes, there lived a beautiful young woman of modest rank and excellent manners, but no significant income to speak of, and a handsome young man of great rank, haughty manners and an estate 'ten miles round'. The beautiful young woman and the handsome young man meet, his haughty manners improve, they fall in love, he proposes marriage, and, in the concluding pages, her very modest means are joined to his very great estate in an event that surpasses even the wildest dreams of her ambitious mother.

It's an irresistible story, so irresistible, in fact, that garbled accounts from the popular press fluttered readers for three years and more with rumours that Jane Austen's text was not only being readied for television, but was going to feature a *nude* Mr Darcy – as if Austen's economic romance were not more complex, shaded and, well, more passionate than mere flesh. If sex were all there were to it, we've seen it before. But when the BBC camera turns its yearning gaze on Britain's historic houses, castles and gardens, their vast acres smiling in the sunshine, their sweeping Capability Brown parks, the splendid house presiding over it all, then the blood begins to pump in earnest.

For the BBC executives, of course, the yearning gaze of the camera and the rising heart of the viewer are little more than tokens in their own game of consumer desire. Industry moguls care nothing for Pemberley and its 10 miles round except as it attracts the consumer eye. Paradoxically, Jane Austen's position as a 'viewer' of Pemberley is a consumer's point of view as well. If desire is most likely to afflict the viewer who is outside the gates, one who does not naturally belong within the charmed circumference of the Pemberley estate, that is to say, a person who could, if *tempted*, become an appreciator of such an estate, and who could, if *convinced*, contemplate becoming a consumer of it, then both Jane Austen and her readers qualify in *Pride and Prejudice*. In short, Pemberley exists as a consumer token in Austen's novels, even as it does for the BBC, but in a much deeper game of desire.

Throughout her career, would-be consumers, over-consumers and wise consumers turn Austen's attention to the economy. From the focus of *Sense and Sensibility*, *Pride and Prejudice* and *Northanger Abbey*, where the single most significant economic problem for women is the lack of a fortune, Austen's works steadily engage women in more and more complex relationships to the economy. *Mansfield Park*, *Emma* and *Persuasion*, each in turn, move through an examination of the economy as measure of social morality, as agent of social disruption, as source of national identity and, in the final fragment 'Sanditon', as 'Activity run mad!'

It may, in fact, still surprise some readers to know that Jane Austen does not write as a member of the landed gentry, or as a representative of the proprietors of such piles as Pemberley, Netherfield, Rosings, Norland, Mansfield Park, Sotherton, Donwell Abbey, Kellynch Hall or any other of the imagined great houses of her novels, but as a member of a somewhat humbler rank that the historian David Spring calls the 'pseudo-gentry': that is, a group of upper professional families living in the country – clergymen or barristers, for example, or officers in the army and navy, retired *rentiers*, great merchants – allied by kinship and social ties, and by social aspirations as well, to their landed-gentry neighbours, but different in an essential economic condition: they do not themselves possess the power and wealth invested in the ownership of land, but depend upon earned incomes. Nevertheless, they *are* gentry of a sort, Spring notes wryly, 'primarily because they sought strenuously to be taken for gentry', through the acquisition of the manners, the education and the same markers of station as their landed-gentry neighbours.[1] The consequence of such aspirations, however, presents this class with a twofold economic burden: first, of course, the need to pay for the necessary markers of their genteel appearance; and, second, the need to soften the inherent weakness of their economic position – with the loss of the breadwinner, there is the loss of his income as well.[2] This essential economic fact attaches itself firmly to Jane Austen's fiction and to her life. Her father, a clergyman living in rural Hampshire, later retired to Bath, with a moderately good income, moderately poor health, and three dependent women (his wife and two spinster daughters), headed a family exposed to exactly the kind of sudden and irreversible fall in fortune implicit to their station in life.

As a consequence, *money*, especially money as spendable income, is the love-tipped arrow aimed at the hearts of Jane Austen's heroines and her readers: first of all, for its power to acquire the material goods that can support the all-important signs of her rank's claims to genteel station; second, as the prod of anxiety that focuses its own potential for loss. In her novels, Austen approaches the subject, money, from three different, but related, points of view. First, as a member of the pseudo-gentry, that is to say, the upper professional ranks of her rural society; second, as a woman in that society, severely handicapped by law and custom from possessing significant power over money; finally, as a novelist who joins other women novelists in a larger conversation about money.[3] And, as Jan Fergus reminds us in this book (see Chapter 1), novel-writing is itself an economic activity, with money the importunate force that moves this conversation along.

The heartbeat of romance lies in a good income. That is the universal truth about which there is no doubt in contemporary women's fiction. The Dashwood women, for example, Elinor and Marianne in *Sense and Sensibility*, name their hearts' desires: 'About eighteen hundred or two thousand a-year; not more than *that*', Marianne confides. '*Two* thousand a-year!' cries Elinor, shocked: '*One* is my wealth!' (*SS* 1:17:106). Marianne defends her two thousand a year as she specifies the consumer expenses appropriate to it: 'I am sure I am not extravagant in my demands. A proper establishment of servants, a carriage, perhaps two, and hunters, cannot be supported on less.' Elinor smiles to hear her younger sister 'describing so accurately', and so transparently, the exact consumer expenses suited to the potential income of her lover, the soon-to-prove-faithless Willoughby. But in her own turn, Elinor's projection of 'one thousand pounds' is the income of the prosperous clergyman family that she longs to be mistress of. There is no room for error in this novel's system of accounting. In the concluding pages, Marianne gets her £2,000 a year, though from a different lover, and Elinor gets her £1,000 a year, or suitably near it.

Incomes are openly discussed in all of Austen's novels, and, when the significant details are not given in the first pages of the novel, and they usually are, they follow when it is most useful for them to appear. *Pride and Prejudice*, for example, commences with the grand announcement of the arrival of Mr Bingley with his fortune of £4,000 or £5,000 a year (*PP* 1:1:4). It is followed by the arrival of Mr Darcy and the invigorating news of his £10,000 a year (1:3:10). Common conversation has it in *Sense and Sensibility* that Willoughby spends beyond his income of £600 or £700 a year (*SS* 1:14:83); that the Dashwood women have only £500 a year for the four of them (1:2:14); and that Colonel Brandon has £2,000 a year and a very nice estate to go with it (1:14:82). When incomes are *not* specifically named by Austen, then the signs of them are: the house, the furnishings, the garden, the park, the number of servants, the presence of a carriage.

Consumer markers of income and rank regularly pace the romances of Jane Austen's novels. In each novel, decisions of domestic economy define the heroine – and the hero – on a scale of expense familiar to contemporary readers. As distant from us as late eighteenth- and early nineteenth-century incomes and spending practices certainly are, there is no difficulty in learning the system.

Except for heiresses, almost all incomes in women's fiction are announced unambiguously as *yearly* incomes: 'two thousand a-year', or 'one thousand a-year', just as the Dashwood sisters refer to them.[4] Heiresses, however, have their fortunes reported in lump sums, like the 'proud and conceited' Miss Bingley in *Pride and Prejudice* who has a fortune of 'twenty thousand pounds' (*PP* 1:4:16), or Miss King, Elizabeth Bennet's richer rival for Wickham's attentions, with her 'ten thousand pounds' (2:3:169). But these heiresses' fortunes are understood immediately by contemporaries as *yearly* incomes through multiplying them by 5 per cent, a procedure that reveals their yearly income from investment in the 5 per cent government funds. Miss Bingley's yearly income from her £20,000 fortune is, thus, £1,000 a year; and Miss King's yearly income from £10,000, figuring it the same way, constitutes a lure of £500 a year for the impecunious Wickham. Elizabeth Bennet's pitifully small fortune of £1,000 is a minor exception, invested at a lower rate of 4 per cent (£40 a year), a fact Mr Collins notes with some minuteness when he proposes to Elizabeth (1:19:119). With this formula for turning inherited money into yearly incomes (as investment at 5 per cent), heiress fortunes quickly come into focus as yearly income – the significant bottom line for romance.

For the present-day reader, however, there remains a problem in how to recognize with Austen's contemporaries the style of life attached to a specific income. Even though Austen herself generally explains each case as it arises, specific incomes also operate as shorthand in her fiction and in the rest of women's fiction – £300 a year, £400 a year, £500 a year, and so on – to express rank, social aspirations and consumer power. The telling range in women's fiction, however, is not large, being made up of those fine gradations of income that mark the aspirations of the middle ranks of society, each income bringing with it a set of specific consumer signs that reveal to the world both the income and the social level attached to its possessor.[5]

Numbers of servants mark incomes at the lower levels; the acquisition of a carriage does it for incomes that are a bit higher; and 'the house in town' certifies the presence of great incomes, usually those belonging to the prosperous landed gentry. Servants, an unfamiliar reckoning device these days, might be considered as the equivalent of modern household conveniences: add a servant, add a convenience – hot water, central heating, a washing machine, and so on.

£100 a year: This is the lowest income that can support the price of a ticket to a circulating library. It embraces poor curates, clerks in government office (both only marginally genteel), and moderately prosperous tradesmen. It could supply a family with a single young maidservant, and that at a very

low wage. When Edward Ferrars and Lucy Steele seem about to marry on an income of £100 a year, Mrs Jennings' immediate reaction is to trim the number of servants she had imagined for them: 'Two maids and two men indeed! – as I talked of t'other day. – No, no, they must get a stout girl of all works. – Betty's sister would never do for them *now*' (*SS* 3:2:314). In *Emma*, the presence of Patty, Miss Bates' only servant, suggests the extreme fragility of the Bates' present claims to genteel station.

£200 a year: Austen's father and mother married in 1764 on a church living of only £100 a year, plus the use of 200 acres of land as a second source of income, but found that even with an increase to £200 a year four years later, then £300 a year, their growing family made it difficult to maintain the appearance of genteel station. Mr Austen was driven to take in students to increase the family's income.[6] Two hundred pounds makes a claim to gentility, but only with the narrowest style of life. The £200 a year income, however, supplies a better servant, 'a Servant-Maid of all Work', at a higher salary.[7]

£300 a year: 'Comfortable as a bachelor', Colonel Brandon says of £300 a year for Edward Ferrars, but 'it cannot enable him to marry' (*SS* 3:3:322).[8] The income brings two servants. Austen's brother James married on this sum, but found it decidedly insufficient to maintain his elevated notions of consumer display: a carriage for his bride and a pack of harriers for himself.[9]

£400 a year: An income that approaches the comforts of genteel life, but not readily. It brings a cook, a house maid and, perhaps, a boy. Isabella Thorpe turns up her nose at James Morland who is granted this income in *Northanger Abbey*. In *Mansfield Park*, Fanny Price's mother has just this amount per year for domestic expense and the requisite number of servants (two), but she manages very badly. Fanny's parsimonious Aunt Norris, Fanny notes, would have done better.

£500 a year: This sum, according to the domestic economists, fills the cup of human happiness. Jane Austen is not so confident. Five hundred pounds a year is the very income that in *Sense and Sensibility* gives rise to such malicious gloating from the Dashwood women's prosperous sister-in-law, Fanny: 'and what on earth can four women want for more than that? – They will live so cheap! Their housekeeping will be nothing at all. They will have no carriage, no horses, and hardly any servants' (*SS* 1:2:14). Fanny is absolutely right on the first two counts (no carriage and no horses), and as for the third, the number of servants, she knows that her mother-in-law, the former mistress of Norland, and her sisters-in-law will now have only the three servants, two women and a man, prescribed by the professional economists for that income. Austen speaks from experience on this one: it is the sum, even a bit more, that she and her mother and her sister had to live on after Mr Austen's death.[10]

£700 to £1,000 a year: This higher range of upper professional incomes marks the most prosperous pseudo-gentry families, though Mary Crawford, the rich

London heiress in *Mansfield Park*, doesn't think much of its potential: 'You would look rather blank, Henry', she tells her brother, 'if your menus plaisirs were to be limited to seven hundred a year' (*MP* 2:5:264). Its most significant consumer marker becomes the ownership of a carriage. Jane Austen's father took a carriage when his income reached £700, though he found it too expensive to maintain on that income.[11] Mr Perry, the local physician in *Emma*, lets his income be known to Highbury when Mrs Perry begins to long for a carriage. The ambitious Mrs Elton in *Emma* rubs everyone's nose in her ownership of a carriage: 'I believe we drive faster than anybody', she boasts (*E* 3:2:348).

£2,000 a year: At £2,000 a year (the landed-gentry income of Mr Bennet in *Pride and Prejudice* and of Colonel Brandon in *Sense and Sensibility*), domestic economy must still hold a tight rein, especially in *Pride and Prejudice* where there are five daughters in need of dowries. Mrs Bennet is noted as a poor economist; Mr Bennet is better, though still inadequate considering his daughters' situation. Mrs Jennings in *Sense and Sensibility* emphasizes the quiet, at-home pleasures of £2,000 a year when she describes Colonel Brandon's Delaford as 'without debt or drawback': 'every thing, in short, that one could wish for ... Oh! 'tis a nice place!' (*SS* 2:8:223).

Above £4,000 a year: Incomes of £4,000 a year and above (Darcy's, Bingley's, Crawford's, Rushworth's) leave behind the cheese-paring cares of middle-class incomes – the problems of £100 to £1,000 a year, and even £2,000 a year – to enter a realm of unlimited genteel comforts. To spend more, according to contemporary wisdom, a man 'must go into horse-racing or illegitimate pleasures'.[12] In terms of consumer show in Austen's novels, any income over £4,000 a year is characterized by its ability to provide a house in London for the social season, the beguiling consumer temptation that brings romantic disaster to both Mary Crawford and Maria Bertram.

The great incomes of this last category comprise those handsome land-based fortunes in Jane Austen's novels that could put to rout all economic anxieties for women, if only they were managed by the prudent economic principles of Austen's own class. But in Austen, this almost never happens – and for good reason. As Gary Kelly notes, and others as well, the larger social picture tends to place Austen, along with other women novelists, in an advance guard of middle-class encroachers on the political and economic turf of the landed interest.[13] Mr Darcy's and Mr Knightley's great estates in *Pride and Prejudice* and in *Emma* are under the safe guidance of heroes who share the author's economic principles, but Northanger Abbey, Rosings, Norland, Mansfield Park, Sotherton and Kellynch are bywords for extravagance and/ or faulty domestic economy. Representatives of this moneyed class show a regular pattern of catastrophe as they stumble without the aid of the economic principles of Austen's own more humble rank: what if Henry Crawford had remained at Everingham to manage his estate properly? What if Mary Crawford had given up her unreasonable demand for a house in town? What if Willoughby had kept out of debt? What if Sir Walter Elliot were not a fool?

In the more intimate, domestic negotiations of the novel, women's fiction turns to the particular relationship that women have with money – that is, no legal title to it for married women, and rights severely curtailed for unmarried women.[14] In a frustrating social irony, the pseudo-gentry woman finds herself responsible for the management of the household, but prevented by law and custom from exercising any significant control over the management of the family's income, a male prerogative. If money affairs go badly, as they certainly will with a feckless, foolish, improvident man such as Willoughby, or with an out-and-out scoundrel such as Wickham, the woman is still responsible for the economic consequences, a victim herself of course, but still responsible. Elinor Dashwood has no illusions about this harsh double bind when she consoles Marianne for the loss of Willoughby:

> Had you married, you must have been always poor ... His demands and your inexperience together on a small, very small income, must have brought on distresses which would not be the *less* grievous to you, from having been entirely unknown and unthought of before. *Your* sense of honour and honesty would have led you, I know, when aware of your situation, to attempt all the economy that would appear to you possible; and perhaps, as long as your frugality retrenched only on your own comfort, you might have been suffered to practise it, but beyond that – and how little could the utmost of your single management do to stop the ruin which had begun before your marriage? (*SS* 3:11:397)

'Just suppose it was your husband!' – a cry that echoes through all women's fiction conceived in the 1790s, including of course *Northanger Abbey*, *Sense and Sensibility* and *Pride and Prejudice*. Sound principles of domestic economy offer at least the protection of a map. Catherine Morland, for example, warmly defends her brother James for not keeping a horse and gig of his own: 'I am sure he could not afford it' (*NA* 1:11:87). Elinor Dashwood prevents her sister Marianne from accepting a horse from Willoughby and thus overburdening the family's £500 a year income. Elinor earlier encourages her mother to sell the carriage as an inappropriate expense. With such an understanding, we can appreciate, along with Austen's contemporaries, why Elinor Dashwood and Edward Ferrars 'were neither of them quite enough in love to think that three hundred and fifty pounds a-year would supply them with the comforts of life' (*SS* 3:13:418), and we can calculate in pounds sterling their later happiness when they do agree to marry on £850 to £900 a year.[15] We also understand how Henry Tilney in *Northanger Abbey* is just the right man for Catherine when the happy couple retire to their cottage at Woodston on his clergyman's income 'of independence and comfort' (*NA* 2:16:259), plus her marriage portion of £3,000, which, invested in the government funds, of course, adds £150 a year to their income. And as for the extraordinary good luck of Elizabeth Bennet who finds £10,000 a year, 'A house in town! Every thing that is charming!' (*PP* 3:17:420), it is a telling triumph of Austen's economic ideology to turn so fabulous a landed-gentry income into the earnest, cash-conscious programme of her own rank.

But money in Jane Austen's first three novels exists for the most part as a set of restrictive anxieties attached to the romance plot by the narrowest definition of domestic economy – fear of debt. In Austen's last three novels, and in the fragmentary final piece, 'Sanditon', far more complex relationships between income and romance are held in centre focus. Debt remains an anxiety of course: Tom Bertram wreaks disaster on the family income in *Mansfield Park*; Miss Bates worries about the cost of medical care for her niece in *Emma*; Sir Walter Elliot loses his estate to renters in *Persuasion*; and Mr Parker seems headed for serious financial difficulties in 'Sanditon'. But the traditional, omnipresent fear of loss no longer holds sway over the narrative. Instead, Austen sets women into an active, working relationship with the economy in a world where economic choice tests the strengths and the limitations of female power.

Income serves as the leading economic trope of *Mansfield Park*. Tom Bertram's debts, of course, are a prominent irritant, but Austen seems little interested in them or in Tom. The novel begins, instead, with the income portfolio of the 'handsome' Ward sisters: Miss Maria has done well, 'at least three thousand pounds short of any equitable claim', by marrying the wealthy Sir Thomas Bertram, Baronet, of Mansfield Park; Miss Ward, less well, being 'obliged to be attached to the Rev. Mr. Norris' and his income of 'very little less than a thousand a year'; and Miss Frances has done very badly indeed, 'fixing on a Lieutenant of Marines, without education, fortune, or connections' (*MP* 1:1:3–4). Marriage, says Mary Crawford, whose assessment of the state never wavers from this focus, 'is a manoeuvring business. I know so many who have married in the full expectation and confidence of some one particular advantage ... who have found themselves entirely deceived, and been obliged to put up with exactly the reverse! What is this', she asks, 'but a take in?' (1:5:53–4). Mary's opinion of Maria Bertram's marriage to the rich, but stupid, Mr Rushworth simply varies the trope: '[S]he will open one of the best houses in Wimpole Street ... and certainly she will then feel – to use a vulgar phrase – that she has got her pennyworth for her penny' (3:9:456).

But, in truth, there is nothing wrong with improving one's income in this novel. Dr Grant and Edmund Bertram engage in an earnest conversation – 'The most interesting in the world', Henry Crawford tells his sister, Mary: 'how to make money – how to turn a good income into a better' (MP 2:5:264). Sir Thomas conscientiously travels to the West Indies to improve the income of his estates in Antigua. But Henry and Mary Crawford's notion of a better income – solely as a higher income, the common understanding of the matter – is challenged by Austen. Mary must decide whether she is willing to marry the man she loves, Edmund Bertram, on their potential married income of £1,700 a year (his moderate-to-good clergyman's income of £700 a year, plus an additional £1,000 a year from the 5 per cent interest on her £20,000 fortune), or to try for better stakes in the London market. In any pseudo-gentry accounting, £1,700 a year is a strikingly good income for a clergyman, *handsome*, but it is not good enough for Mary, who wants a house in town and the income to go with it. In the end, she wants this more than she wants Edmund.

The Crawfords, both Henry and Mary, possess an unyielding and near pathological blindness to any but the most simplistic notion of incomes. In fact, Fanny Price is the only person in the entire novel canny enough to recognize that there is an option of choice and that this complicates the common, unexamined notions of acquisition held by the rest of the characters. Austen, however, gives Fanny no power to make her opinion known. After reading Edmund's letter pledging his undying devotion to Mary Crawford, Fanny cries out in exasperation, to herself alone, of course: 'He is blinded, and nothing will open his eyes, nothing can, after having had truths before him so long in vain. – He will marry her, and be poor and miserable' (MP 3:13:492). But even for Fanny, the dialectic stands in a kind of immiscible suspension in the phrase, 'poor *and* miserable'. She cannot escape the logic herself. Her only revenge is to 'hint' to Edmund, gently of course, of 'what share his brother's state of health' – potentially fatal illness of the heir – 'might be supposed to have in her [Mary's] wish for a complete reconciliation' with Edmund, the younger brother (3:16:531). That gets his attention. But the information is gratuitous, and it only returns choice, marriage, love, to the same corrupt relationship with money that it has been in throughout the novel, of being a 'take in'.

If this is not the opinion shared by Austen, what can we make of Fanny Price's triumph in her marriage to Edmund? Mrs Norris' sanguine promise to Sir Thomas, 'Give a girl an education, and introduce her properly into the world, and ten to one but she has the means of settling well, without farther expense to any body', turns out to be absolutely on the money, though not exactly as she predicts (MP 1:1:7). Fanny's career in the Bertram family is little more, in these terms, than a low-cost–high-yield investment saga, softened happily in the anaesthesia of Sir Thomas' self-serving sentiments, but ledger-like nonetheless: 'Fanny was indeed the daughter that he wanted. His charitable kindness had been rearing a prime comfort for himself. His liberality had a rich repayment' (3:17:546), though in truth, he had tried, unsuccessfully, to unload the girl when the pressure of Tom's debts made it 'not undesirable to himself to be relieved from the expense of her support, and the obligation of her future provision' (1:3:28). The novel concludes with a rousing paean to the industrious Price children, those ideal representatives of their rank, 'all assisting to advance each other' (3:17:547). Henry Crawford with his inherited income is sent packing, and Fanny marries Edmund, happily, on his income from the Thornton Lacey living. But there is no compelling logic to make the happy couple's £700 a year clergyman's income necessarily more virtuous than the £4,000 a year inherited income of Henry Crawford (1:12:139). Henry, if Jane Austen had excused him from the obligatory sexual excess with Maria Rushworth, could have had equal, or better, title to Fanny than Edmund, as Austen admits: 'Would he have persevered, and uprightly, Fanny must have been his reward – and a reward very voluntarily bestowed' (3:17:540). Income, the economic paradigm with which Austen seeks to measure the social and moral dilemmas of *Mansfield Park*, fails to clarify.

In her next novel, Austen chooses consumer signs as her trope, those social markers so important to her own class, to explore society. The action in *Emma* rides forward on a great tide of new consumer display. Mr Weston buys a small estate; the former Miss Taylor, now Mrs Weston, gets a new house, a new husband and a new carriage; Jane Fairfax receives, mysteriously, a Broadwood piano; the Coles have a new dining room and a new pianoforte that none of them can play; Emma has a new round dining table; Frank Churchill buys gloves at Ford's, and Harriet Smith buys ribbons; Mr Elton goes to Bath for a new wife and a new carriage; Mrs Elton boasts lace and pearls and more servants than she can remember; Mrs Perry yearns for a new carriage; and the Martins have 'a very handsome summer-house, large enough to hold a dozen people' (*E* 1:4:27). There are also more homely items on offer: plenty of good wine at Mr Weston's; sweetbreads and asparagus at Mr Woodhouse's; a hind quarter of pork for Miss Bates from Hartfield; apples for Miss Bates from Donwell Abbey; arrowroot for Jane Fairfax from Hartfield; and walnuts for Harriet Smith from Mr Martin, who walks 'three miles around' to get them, though he forgets to enquire for the novels she had mentioned. What can it all mean?

Mr Knightley proves himself the hero of the piece by possessing the sensibility that is the key by which these material goods are to be understood. He keeps warning Emma, over and over, that *things* are not what they seem, or, at least, they are not what *she* thinks they seem. Consumer signs, it is true, provide the system of order that keeps everyday life ticking along in *Emma*.

Servants and carriages, for example, bring the Box Hill episode to a welcome close: 'The appearance of the servants looking out for them to give notice of the carriages was a joyful sight' (E 3:7:407). Tea saves Mr Weston from more unwanted news of Maple Grove: 'They were interrupted. Tea was carrying round, and Mr. Weston, having said all that he wanted, soon took the opportunity of walking way' (2:18:336). 'The saddle of mutton' sets the pace of conversation at Randalls (1:14:128), and tea sets the time for departure. 'Mr. Woodhouse was soon ready for his tea; and when he had drank his tea he was quite ready to go home' (1:15:134). Finally, the length of a carriage ride provides the beginning and the end to Mr Elton's declarations to Emma of 'violent love' (1:15:140).

But consumer goods in *Emma* also trace a society in restless motion. The Coles are on the way up with their new dining room, new pianoforte and an increase in their servants; Mrs and Miss Bates and Jane Fairfax are on their way down with their economies, modest quarters and one maid. Mr Martin is on the way up, as are the Eltons, the Coxes, the Smallridges and the Sucklings. People are passing so rapidly through the gradations of income and the consumer markers associated with them that the old rules of birth and social order are thrown into question.

Mr Woodhouse, who likes everything that is old and settled, marks one end of the scale; Mrs Elton, who likes everything that is new and in motion, marks the other. Emma herself is in a state of confusion, blinded by vanity and social snobbery, but also blinded by the very consumer signs that offer themselves so temptingly to her imagination. Her conclusions about Jane Fairfax's pianoforte are her most embarrassingly public mistake, but her persistent inability to judge behaviour in her society turns, like a scorpion, on the novel itself, the consumer object whose self-proclaimed mandate to interpret social signs most consistently misleads her.

The plot of Jane Austen's *Emma* is, in fact, pre-empted by a tale published in the *Lady's Magazine*, a popular monthly compendium of fiction and fashion, a tale which begins with eerie familiarity:

> Mr. Knightley, a country-gentleman of not very large fortune, but such as was amply sufficient for his mode of living – as he rarely visited the capital, and had an aversion to the expensive pleasures of dissipated life – had married from the purest affection, and an esteem which grew with his knowledge of its object ... a deserted orphan [left] at a boarding-school near the residence of a relation of his whom he sometimes visited. As by this union he made no addition to his property, nor formed any advantageous connexion, he was by some blamed, and by others ridiculed. He however found himself amply compensated, both for the censure and the sneers which he encountered, by the amiable qualities and virtues of his wife; who, like himself, despised

ambition, and sought only the genuine enjoyments of domestic happiness.
(November 1802)

Austen, of course, pointedly rejects the *Lady's Magazine* version of contemporary social life in the conclusion to *Emma*. Her heroine, however, swallows hook, line and sinker the *Lady's Magazine* version of Mr Knightley and the amiable orphan, which, of course, is exactly the admonitory point Austen intends. Cheap fiction is an untrustworthy system for interpreting social signs: Emma's fantasy of Harriet's background, for example, a classic Gothic plot – 'There can be no doubt of your being a gentleman's daughter' (*E* 1:4:30); or another old chestnut, an affair of the heart between Jane Fairfax and her rescuer from the sea, Mr Dixon; or the romance of Frank Churchill and Harriet prompted by the story of Harriet and the gypsies. Finally, when Harriet comes to Emma with her fantasy of Mr Knightley's love, yet another rescue story, Emma falls into the trap again, exactly in the mode of the *Lady's Magazine*: 'It was horrible to Emma to think how it must sink him in the general opinion, to foresee the smiles, the sneers, the merriment it would prompt at his expense . . . Could it be? – No; it was impossible. And yet it was far, very far, from impossible' (3:11:450).

It is, of course, *impossible*. If Emma had only read past the consumer signs of her society (false and misleading) to see and read the 'real' signs of social behaviour before her eyes (true and abiding), then she would not have made such a distressing hash of the situation. But here consumer fiction proves doubly false. The story from the *Lady's Magazine*, flattering fantasy as it is for tradesmen's daughters, is not necessarily wrong. Austen's society *is* experiencing major social change, fuelled in some degree by the very goods – novels among the first – that set themselves up as signs of social truths. The most unexpected people are indeed climbing the social ladder with the aid of money and the social markers it buys. Austen rejects the *Lady's* story for a more acceptable ideological resolution – Harriet Smith gets a farmer and Emma Woodhouse gets Mr Knightley – but a conflicting set of social patterns, also explored in Austen's novel, points the other way. Mr Knightley might just as well have married Harriet as not. After all, Austen's *Emma* is only one novel among many vying to promote its own reading of the 'real' signs of social behaviour.

Persuasion turns to *credit* as the issue that opens the economy, but with a spin that sets the topic apart from the compulsive debtors (Wickham, Willoughby) found in Austen's early works. Austen sends her two old-style debtors in this novel, Sir Walter Elliot and his daughter Elizabeth, to Bath for an early, embalmed retirement. Credit, *good* credit that is, becomes the talisman for future expectations in *Persuasion*. In fact the central romantic dilemma of the novel is, by extension, one of credit: whether Anne Elliot should have waited for Captain Wentworth, as she wanted to do. That is, should she have taken him on credit, or should she have remained with her dreadful father and sister in the conservative, but unhappy position of an unvalued dependant as Lady Russell persuaded her to do? The answer, according to Anne, is a negotiated qualification, but one turned strongly to the side of credit: 'Tell me', Captain Wentworth asks Anne, 'if, when I returned to England in the year eight, with a few thousand pounds, and was posted into the Laconia, if I had then written to you, would you have answered my letter? would you, in short, have renewed the engagement then?' Anne's answer is short, but decisive: 'Would I!' (P 2:11:268).

Anne marries Wentworth and thus joins the active, hard-working and prosperous pseudo-gentry rank she has learned to admire, a class of people who work for their living and know how to live within their means, as opposed to her father, the 'spendthrift baronet', or even as opposed to her gentry brother-in-law, the slack, unfocused Charles Musgrove, future heir to Uppercross, who agrees with his wife in only two things: 'the want of more money, and a strong inclination for a handsome present from his father' (P 1:6:47). The upbeat credit ideology of *Persuasion* rests on two assumptions: first, that the future holds prosperity for the British economy, and second, that a person who works for a living will pay his bills to uphold 'the character', as Lady Russell terms it, 'of an honest man' (1:2:14). 'And *woman*', she might have said, for in *Persuasion* Austen makes women active managers of the family income. 'While Lady Elliot lived', Austen notes, as the first in a string of good women managers in this novel, 'there had been method, moderation, and economy', which had 'just kept' Sir Walter within his income (1:1:9–10). When bill collectors begin to hover around Sir Walter, those two excellent lady economists Lady Russell and his daughter Anne recommend 'vigorous measures' of economy that could have released him from debt in a reasonable amount of time (1:2:13). When Admiral and Mrs Croft negotiate for the lease on Kellynch Hall, the lawyer, Mr Shepherd, notes that Mrs Croft 'asked more questions about the house, and terms, and taxes, than the admiral himself, and seemed more conversant with business' (1:3:25). Mrs Harville in Lyme is another model economist, and on a very small income (1:12:122). Mrs Smith, in Bath, remains cheerful and competent on an even smaller income (2:5:167).

Partnership marriages become the keynote of the new economic arrangement, demonstrated by the Harvilles and the Crofts for the edification of the future Captain and Mrs Wentworth. Wentworth and Anne, 'a sailor's wife', *both* belong 'to that profession which is, if possible, more distinguished in its domestic virtues than in its national importance' (P 2:12:275). The income of the happy couple is reported as well, stamping Austen's seal of economic approval on the marriage at one of the highest reaches of pseudo-gentry prosperity: they will have £1,250 from the interest on Wentworth's £25,000 prize money, plus a small addition from the interest on one-third of the £10,000 of Anne's mother's fortune (when Sir Walter is able to pay it), *and* the promise of more money to come in the navy. It is as if Austen has single-handedly revised the economic priorities of her society: a higher credit line for the pseudo-gentry Wentworths, and a lower one for the baronet Elliots.

In 'Sanditon' the economic future is not so cloudless. Mr Parker, land-owning gentry, has invested heavily in a seaside bathing spa, Sanditon, where it appears likely that he is about to experience some financial rough weather. Investment as 'speculation' seems to be the economic focus of the piece. The failure of Austen's brother Henry's bank in which her uncle, Mr Leigh-Perrot, and her brother Edward lost huge sums of money in March 1816, may well be the inspiration for this new line of economic exploration – 'Sanditon' was roughed out less than a year after the bankruptcy, between January and March 1817, when illness forced her to put the fragment aside unfinished. It seems likely that the fragility of Mr Parker's hold on the economy will be a central issue. Mr Parker's partner in the enterprise is Lady Denham, a parsimonious, tyrannical old woman, and a fearful investor, who will be no support when economic storms arrive. His wife, weak, dependent and ignorant of business, does not promise to be any assistance either, and his two sisters, professional invalids, are equally ineffectual. 'Activity run mad', thinks the heroine, Charlotte Heywood, who is a shocked witness of their fumbling interference in the Sanditon enterprise (*LM* 'S' 9:189).

Austen, as usual, sets out squarely the social and economic corners of her novel's universe. There is the usual cast of economic scavengers: younger relatives of Lady Denham with a hungry eye for an inheritance, and, of course, the overspending Miss Beauforts, pretenders to elegance. There is the figure of conservative economics, Charlotte's father, Mr Heywood – a farmer and landowner with modest investments in the funds – who seems to represent a sound, but old-fashioned and rather out-of-the-fray position. And then there is Mr Parker, the 'enthusiast' for Sanditon, his financial speculation. The investment will probably not be allowed to go under completely: the town is attractive, the sea is beautiful, and there is the competent younger brother of Mr Parker, Sidney, who puts in a brief appearance right before the fragment breaks off – 'well bred', 'very good looking', '7 or 8 & 20', and perhaps a future suitor for the heroine (*LM* 'S' 12:207). Sidney suggests a Jane Austen signature hero for the future: a younger son, rich by 'collateral' inheritance (2:147), not himself landowning gentry, though a pseudo-gentry member of such a family – of 'superior abilities', 'a very clever Young Man', 'always said what he chose of & to us, all' (4:158), and he laughs at the youngest brother, Arthur, for being 'so delicate that he can engage in no profession' (5:162).

From the start of her career, Austen is a shrewd observer of the economic terrain of her class, though always from the chilly and exposed position of an economically marginal female member of it – herself related to the landed gentry through the good fortune of her brother Edward (adopted by wealthy gentry relations), but really no more than a maiden-aunt visitor to his estate and his class.[16] In fact, the shadow of the single woman without money, Charlotte Lucas syndrome, continues to haunt her works to the end. In 'Sanditon', Clara Brereton fits the position, and though she is only vaguely sketched in, her economic position is clear enough: 'more helpless and more pitiable of course than any – and dependant on poverty – an additional burden on an encumbered circle' (*LM* 'S' 4:155).

Joseph Wiesenfarth's useful distinctions between the novel of manners and the Gothic novel in *Gothic Manners and the Classic English Novel* (1988) provide a probe for examining the unresolved presence of this economic shadow.[17] The novel of manners presents a rational 'case', Wiesenfarth argues, whereas the Gothic novel presents a 'riddle'. Obviously, Austen presents a 'case' for the operation of money in each of her novels – in fact, she presents several different cases. On the other hand, the single, unprovided woman carries in her very existence a Gothic 'riddle' that underscores the moral entanglements cast up by her anomalous position in the economy. In the early novels, money comes to her through courtship windfalls – Mr Collins is one – a resolution that Austen rejects in her last three novels to mount the 'case' for more rational relationships to the economy for women. But in each of these later novels, the 'case' regularly falls short before the immovable plight, the riddle of the single woman without money. Fanny Price, Jane Fairfax, even Anne Elliot, are, in the end, left dependent upon purest chance for their entrance into the moneyed world of the 'case'. Moreover, the moral identity of each one of these women must first be asserted *against* the economic 'case' that eventually defines her social identity. Austen acknowledges the moral confusion when she has Emma say feelingly of Jane Fairfax, whose secret engagement to Frank Churchill would never have been condoned by his rich, capricious aunt: 'Of such, one may almost say, that "the world is not their's, nor the world's law"' (*E* 3:10:436). Anne Elliot's situation is equally ambivalent. In Anne's situation, where 'advice is good or bad only as the event decides' (*P* 2:11:268), the clarity of right and wrong, which is the rightful province of romance, edges towards Wiesenfarth's 'Gothic confusion', Austen's tribute to the deepest game of desire, the elusive force that she has pursued all along.

NOTES

1. David Spring, 'Interpreters of Jane Austen's Social World: Literary Critics and Historians', *Jane Austen: New Perspectives*, ed. Janet Todd (New York and London: Holmes and Meier, 1983), pp. 53–72, esp. p. 60.
2. R. S. Neale, in *Bath, 1680–1850: A Social History* (London: Routledge & Kegan Paul, 1981), writes that, 'If . . . a woman through death or desertion should find herself the sole support of a family, the impoverishment of the family was virtually certain' (pp. 279–80).
3. Three essays in *Jane Austen in Context*, ed. Janet Todd (Cambridge University Press, 2005) probe these issues: Jan Fergus, 'Biography', pp. 3–11; David Selwyn, 'Consumer Goods', pp. 215–24; Edward Copeland, 'Money', pp. 317–26. See also Copeland, 'Introduction', in *Women Writing about Money: Women's Fiction in England, 1790–1820* (Cambridge University Press, 1995), pp. 1–14.
4. The major exception for men in Austen's novels occurs in *Persuasion*, where Captain Wentworth's profits from his naval career are reported in lump sum only: a fortune of £25,000.
5. See Copeland, *Women Writing about Money*, pp. 22–33; also Copeland, 'The Austens and the Elliots: A Consumer's Guide to *Persuasion*', in *Jane Austen's Business: Her World and her Profession*, ed. Juliet McMaster and Bruce Stovel (Basingstoke: Macmillan, 1996), pp. 136–53. Contemporary domestic economists include Samuel and Sarah Adams, *The Complete Servant*, first published 1825 (Chichester: Southover Press, 1989); James Luckcock, *Hints for Practical Economy, in the Management of Household Affairs, with Tables, Shewing Different Scales of Expenses, from £50 to £400 Per Annum* (Birmingham: James Drake; London: Longman, *et al.*, 1834); John Trusler, *The Economist* (London: printed for the author, 1774).
6. Deirdre Le Faye, *Jane Austen: A Family Record* (London: British Library, 1989), pp. 14, 19, 13.
7. Samuel and Sarah Adams, *The Complete Servant*, p. 16.
8. Edward's potential income of £300 a year comes from the Delaford living of £200 a year, plus his personal income of £100 a year from an inheritance of £2,000 (*SS* 2:2:168).
9. Le Faye, *A Family Record*, p. 67.
10. *Ibid.*, p. 131.
11. *Ibid.*, p. 102; see also Robin Vick, 'Mr Austen's Carriage', in Jane Austen Society, Chawton, Hampshire, *Collected Reports*, vol. 5 (1996–2000), pp. 226–8.
12. W. Bence Jones, 'Landowning as a Business', *The Nineteenth Century*, vol. II (1882), p. 254. Cited by F. M. L. Thompson, *English Landed Society in the Nineteenth Century* (London: Routledge & Kegan Paul, 1963), pp. 25–6. Sir Thomas Bertram's fortune in *Mansfield Park* is a marked exception, severely shaken by the eldest son Tom's gambling debts and expenses in London and by poor returns from his West Indian estates.

13. Gary Kelly, *English Fiction of the Romantic Period, 1789–1830* (London and New York: Longman, 1989), p. 19. See also Nancy Armstrong, *Desire and Domestic Fiction: A Political History of the Novel* (Oxford University Press, 1987), pp. 8–10.

14. William Chester Jordan, *Women and Credit in Pre-Industrial and Developing Societies* (Philadelphia, PA: University of Pennsylvania Press, 1993), cites studies of rich widows with disposable capital, but concludes that 'risk-taking English women investors' in the early modern period seem 'exceptional' (pp. 67–9). Susan Staves examines the limitations of women's economic independence in *Married Women's Separate Property in England, 1660–1833* (Cambridge, MA: Harvard University Press, 1990); also, Staves, 'Pin Money', *Studies in Eighteenth-Century Culture*, 14, ed. O. M. Brack (Madison: Wisconsin University Press, 1985), pp. 47–77; Ida Beatrice O'Malley presents a general account in *Women in Subjection: A Study of the Lives of Englishwomen before 1832* (London: Duckworth, 1933), pp. 22–6; and Deborah Kaplan, in *Jane Austen among Women* (Baltimore, MD: Johns Hopkins Press, 1992) cites anecdotes from Austen's own neighbourhood (pp. 43–61).

15. Edward and Elinor's joint income comes from the following sources: £100 a year interest from Edward's inheritance of £2,000 (*SS* 2:2:168); £50 a year from the interest on Elinor's £1,000 inheritance (1:1:5) – Mrs Ferrars mistakenly thinks Elinor has '*three*' hundred (3:14:423); £250 a year, 'at the utmost', from the Delaford living (3:14:424), though valued by Colonel Brandon at only £200 a year (3:3:320); finally, £500 a year from Mrs Ferrars' grudging marriage gift of £10,000 (3:14:424).

16. This is how her favourite niece, Fanny Knight, remembered her visits: 'Both the Aunts (Cassandra & Jane) were brought up in the most complete ignorance of the World & its ways (I mean as to fashion &c) & if it had not been for Papa's marriage which brought them into Kent, & the kindness of Mrs. Knight, who used often to have one or the other of the sisters staying with her, they would have been, tho' not less clever & agreeable in themselves, very much below par as to good Society & its ways' (Le Faye, *A Family Record*, p. 253).

17. Joseph Wiesenfarth, 'Introduction', *Gothic Manners and the Classic English Novel* (Madison, WI: University of Wisconsin Press, 1988), pp. 3–22.

10

DAVID SELWYN

Making a living

Jane Austen came from a family who among them followed several of the professions then open to members of the gentry. Her eldest brother, like her father, was a clergyman; another became an army agent and banker before he took holy orders; and her two youngest brothers went into the navy. Only the third brother, Edward, having been adopted as heir to a distant cousin of Mr Austen, inherited landed estates and enjoyed an independent income. So when creating the characters with whom her fiction principally deals – those of the leisured class – Jane Austen would have had plenty of examples in her own family of people who could by no means take an income for granted.

It would be wrong to assume that in the highest levels of the society she portrays nobody actually works. A large estate does not run itself; and the number of people who are dependent on the landowner for their own liveli-hoods brings a degree of social and moral, as well as economic obligation. When Mrs Reynolds describes Mr Darcy as 'the best landlord, and the best master ... that ever lived' and says that there is 'not one of his tenants or servants but what will give him a good name' (PP 3:1:276) she is testifying not only to his personal qualities but also to his diligence in ensuring that Pemberley provides a secure income not just for himself but for everybody who works there. A man who neglects his estate, or fails to balance the income from it with his expenditure, as Sir Walter Elliot does, behaves irresponsibly towards those who are dependent on him; the 'afflicted tenantry and cottagers who might have had a hint to shew themselves' on the day he leaves Kellynch (P 1:5:38) will presumably not feel their loss to be irreparable. Jane Austen was not of course concerned with giving a lesson in the econo-mics of estate government: what she tells us about the way in which wealthy men manage their property is designed to reveal aspects of their character. Thus, though Henry Crawford and Mr Rushworth are not necessarily bad landowners, their essential superficiality is expressed through an interest in 'improvements', those fashionable alterations to houses and grounds designed to emphasize decorative rather than productive functions; even the financially circumspect John Dashwood is intent on replacing the old walnut trees at Norland with a greenhouse which will be 'a very fine object from many parts of the park' (SS 2:11:257). Donwell Abbey, however, is unimproved, and probably little altered since the sixteenth century; and its grounds have not been subjected to the attentions of a landscape gardener such as Repton, as have those of Mr Rushworth's friend Smith, at a price of five guineas a day, but retain their 'abundance of timber in rows and avenues, which neither fashion nor extravagance had rooted up' (E 3:6:389). When Mr Knightley does contemplate change, for example in moving a footpath so that 'it may not cut through the home meadows' (1:12:114), it is to increase the productivity of the estate rather than to respond to an aesthetic whim.

At Donwell we are shown something of the day-to-day business of a working estate. This too of course is to underline the benevolence and solidity of Mr Knightley's character; but by seeing him at work, we understand him to be a vital part of the economic structure of Highbury. The estate is inherited, but his income from it is earned by careful husbandry, under the scrutiny of his loyal bailiff, William Larkins. Thus he is able to give his brother information about 'The plan of a drain, the change of a fence, the felling of a tree, and the destination of every acre for wheat, turnips, or spring corn' (E 1:12:107). A well-run estate is in reality a business. When Mr Knightley sends baking apples to the Bateses, Miss Bates says that William is 'so pleased to think his master had sold so many', since he 'thinks more of his master's profit than any thing' (2:9:257–8). But by making them this extra present (an annual sackful being built into his balance sheet) he has deprived himself of any more for his own use – his housekeeper cannot bear that 'her master should not be able to have another apple-tart this spring'. In the running of the estate Mr Knightley takes his place as one among many people upon whom its success depends: he can spare the apples only because William Larkins lets him keep 'a larger quantity than usual this year'.

Though we know that Emma is the heiress of £30,000 and that Miss Augusta Hawkins has 'so many thousands as would always be called ten' (E 2:4:194), no price is ever attached to Mr Knightley. In most of the novels, the characters' fortune or income is generally made explicit, particularly if they are of marriageable age: in Sense and Sensibility the various amounts are famously gone into in great detail, and elsewhere we are told of Catherine Morland (£3,000), Anne Elliot (£10,000 – at such time as Sir Walter will be able to find it), Mary Crawford (£20,000), Captain Wentworth (£25,000), Bingley (£100,000), Henry Crawford (£4,000 a year), Darcy (£10,000 a year), Mr Rushworth (£12,000 a year), and, in 'Sanditon', Sir Harry Denham ('many thousands a year'). Yet we do not know Mr Knightley's income. One reason for this may be that he is not introduced in the novel as a figure in the marriage market: only gradually do we – and Emma – come to see him as a potential husband. But perhaps too there is the implication that the value of the estate is not a financial one. Mr Knightley, after all, though generous to the Bateses and presumably to other impoverished families, insofar as he can tactfully be so, seems to spend little of his profits on himself; and the real purpose of his land is to be the means by which those dependent on it can make a living, such being the socially beneficial function underlying the 'sweet view' of 'English verdure, English culture, English comfort' that Jane Austen considered the social hierarchy to be bound by.

Though the landowning classes, and to a lesser extent those who like the Woodhouses have inherited wealth, represent the highest level of society that Jane Austen deals with, they were not absolutely at the top of the scale in eighteenth- and nineteenth-century England. Above them in wealth were some of the great aristocratic families, who might expect to enjoy yearly incomes of as much as £60,000; some of these had rents from estates in London or exploited resources on their land that brought them great profits during the Industrial Revolution. On the whole magnates such as these are outside her world, though a tangential character such as the Hon. Miss Morton, daughter of the late Lord Morton, with £30,000, or Miss Grey, with £50,000, are perhaps on the outer edge of it; and Eleanor Tilney becomes a viscountess when she marries a man whose 'unexpected accession to title and fortune' (NA 2:16:260) comes as a surprise equally to themselves, her father and the reader.

The direct management of estates was put in the hands of a steward, or bailiff, with whom a responsible landowner would work closely; even Henry Crawford keeps his eye on his agent at Everingham whom he suspects of trying to get an undeserving cousin into one of his mills instead of the honest man to whom it was promised. Stewards were of crucial importance to the productive maintenance of the land, and had to be carefully chosen. Like that of Mr John Knightley's friend Mr Graham, they often came from Scotland, where the latest farming methods were practised. They did not necessarily depend exclusively on their employment for a living. Bridger Seward, Edward Austen's bailiff at Chawton, was also the tenant of two farms, and in his will styled himself 'gentleman'.[1] On his death, the house that he had lived in was made available to Mrs Austen and her daughters, and Edward seems to have taken on more of his Chawton affairs himself; his niece Caroline recalled: 'He must have been more his own "man of business" than is usual with people of large property, for I think it was his greatest interest to attend to his estates.'[2] Sir Walter Elliot, of whom the same could certainly not be said, employs a lawyer, Mr Shepherd, as his agent, who has also presumably advanced him money, since his 'interest was involved in the reality of Sir Walter's retrenching' (P 1:2:14), and there is an oblique reference to some 'hold' that he may have over him. William Larkins is not of the same order as these, being principally concerned with the farming at Donwell; and indeed Jane Austen probably based him on John Bond, her father's farm bailiff at Steventon. Bond lived in a much more humble way than Bridger Seward, being housed in a fairly small tenement and, it seems, not provided with a horse; on the other hand, he was treated with great consideration by the family, help being hired when he became too old to do much more than look after the sheep, and great trouble taken to find him another situation when Mr Austen retired to Bath.[3]

William Larkins is bailiff of the home farm, the produce of which goes directly to Mr Knightley; similarly, Mr Bennet has the income from his farm at Longbourn and the Hayters from theirs near Taunton. But by 1790 three-quarters of the agricultural land in England was cultivated by tenant farmers like Robert Martin, who rents the Abbey-Mill Farm from the Donwell estate. Emma describes Robert Martin as a member of the yeomanry, but Mr Knightley refers to him as a 'gentleman-farmer', which reflects his growing prosperity; for although he does not own his land, the farm is a large one, and his reading of the *Agricultural Reports*, as well as his frequent visits to the market at Kingston (where Mr Knightley also goes), shows that he takes his business seriously, and that he is well versed in the latest scientific ways of cultivation and determined to get the maximum yield. The average income of a tenant farmer generally amounted to no more than about £300 a year,[4] but with the high food prices of the 1790s and early 1800s, many were able to increase this considerably; such must be the case with the Martins, since the two sisters had been sent to Mrs Goddard's school, and the 'very handsome summer-house in their garden ... large enough to hold a dozen people' is visible proof that they are a family of rising fortunes.

Equally dependent on the land for their living were the various kinds of labourer – shepherds, drovers, milkers, carters, hedgers, ditchers, thatchers, and so on – some of whom lived in, and some who were given cottages; this proportion changed periodically, since when food prices were high farmers found it cheaper to pay them slightly more and let them live out. The regular workforce who lived at the farm, often young men sleeping in a loft or outbuilding, were known as farm servants. Hired by the year, they received wages which, according to a survey carried out in 1770, worked out at an average of £10.8s.6d for 'first men', £6.11s for 'second men' and £3.2s for 'lads'; dairy maids and other female farm servants earned a little over half the wages of second men.[5] Labourers with their own cottages, usually those who had married and had families, were paid twice or three times as much, but in times of inflation (as in the period of the French wars), the rising cost of food meant that their wages were worth less. Day labourers were paid at higher rates, particularly in the seasons of haymaking and harvest, when the working day was longest; but they could be laid off when bad weather or other circumstances meant that there was little to do. We occasionally catch a glimpse of these people in the novels, for example when Robert Martin sends for his shepherd's son to sing for Harriet, or Anne Elliot sees the ploughs at work near Winthrop.

Donwell and Highbury are 'close' parishes, owned by one landlord. Often the agricultural value of the land in such places was reduced by fields or enclosed commons being turned into extensive parks and pleasure grounds, thus depriving the labouring poor of their common rights to grazing, wood gathering or turf cutting. Mr Knightley has not done this; but as we have seen, like many proprietors during the war years of 1793–1815, he has exploited the rising corn prices to make arable fields yield as high an income as possible. Though his farm workers would undoubtedly be well paid and looked after, there are even in Highbury some people who are unable to make any kind of living from the land. The poor cottagers whom Emma and Harriet visit have been made unfit for work by illness, and are dependent on such charity as the village will be able to arrange for them. Like old John Abdy, bedridden and rheumatic, whose son applies to Mr Elton for funds from the parish to help keep him, they are undoubtedly deserving people; but Emma is equally generous to those who are rather less so: 'She understood their ways, could allow for their ignorance and their temptations, had no romantic expectations of extraordinary virtue from those, for whom education had done so little' (E 1:10:93). At the very lowest level of society, the only resources for the desperately poor were the kindness of the rich or relief from the parish.

More visible than the outdoor labourers are the domestic servants whose presence would have been a constant in the lives of all Jane Austen's families, including her own. Throughout the eighteenth century there were on average between 600,000 and 700,000 people engaged in service at any one time – far more than in any other single occupation. From the elaborate hierarchy at Pemberley or Northanger Abbey, to the Bates household with the one girl, Patty, virtually every character that appears in any of the novels would have servants of some description, apart of course from these servants themselves. Wages were on the whole quite low; but they lived in, were provided with their board, often with their clothing or livery, and sometimes had rights to perquisites such as the family's cast-off clothes, which they could wear or even sell. Above all they received vails, or tips, which often added up to more than their pay; when attempts were made to abolish them, there were riots.[6]

On the whole their lives were more secure than those of outdoor labourers, and they were generally well treated. Mr Woodhouse is very considerate of his coachman, Sir Thomas Bertram is on good terms with his butler and even

Mrs Norris busies herself with looking after servants if they are ill. Yet many employers wanted to get the most out of them for as little outlay as possible, and Jane Austen sometimes makes use of a servant to bring out the essential meanness of spirit in one of her characters. Mrs Norris tells Edmund that she turned away the estate carpenter's young son, Dick Jackson, who happened to bring some wood for his father just as the servants' dinner bell was ringing, obviously hoping for a free meal. 'I hate such encroaching people', she says; 'the Jacksons are very encroaching, I have always said so, – just the sort of people to get all they can'. And she unconsciously betrays the difference between Sir Thomas' generosity and her lack of it when she adds 'I hate such greediness – so good as your father is to the family, employing the man all the year round!' (*MP* 1:15:167). Fanny Dashwood appears similarly ungenerous in a discussion about annuities, which were sometimes paid or bequeathed to loyal servants. 'I have known a great deal of the trouble of annuities', she says; 'for my mother was clogged with the payment of three to old superannuated servants by my father's will, and it is amazing how disagreeable she found it. Twice every year these annuities were to be paid; and then there was the trouble of getting it to them; and then one of them was said to have died, and afterwards it turned out to be no such thing. My mother was quite sick of it' (*SS* 1:2:12). But good people valued their servants and interested themselves in their families, looking out for opportunities to recommend them for situations when they needed work, as Mr Woodhouse secures a place for his coachman's daughter as housemaid at Randalls. They might even be willing to help a servant find promotion, like the good-natured Mrs Jennings when she is under the mistaken impression that Colonel Brandon has proposed to Elinor. 'I have just been thinking of Betty's sister, my dear', she says. 'I should be very glad to get her so good a mistress. But whether she would do for a lady's maid, I am sure I can't tell. She is an excellent housemaid, and works very well at her needle' (3:4:325).

Between the people whose incomes were derived from land, or investment in the funds, and the servant or labouring class were those who made their living in the various professions and trades. Younger sons of gentlemen, who could not expect to inherit an estate, had to be found a profession. Of the ones open to them the army was the least likely to provide an adequate income. If a young man wished to join a good regiment, a commission had to be bought, which could cost as much as £1,600 for entry into an elite cavalry regiment such as the Life Guards; even an ensigncy in a regiment of foot such as Darcy purchases for Wickham cost £400. An ensign's pay of 5*s*.3*d* a day was wholly inadequate to meet the deductions for living expenses and maintenance of uniform and equipment for which all officers were liable. Wealthy officers, whether in the regular army or in the militia, are rare in Jane Austen; and such as there are – General Tilney, Colonel Brandon, Colonel Fitzwilliam – owe their wealth to private means.

A career in the navy was, particularly in time of war, far more likely to enable a young man to make his fortune. When Mr Shepherd slyly introduces the idea of some rich admiral who might perhaps be interested in renting Kellynch Hall, Sir Walter observes that Kellynch would indeed be 'a prize' to him: 'rather the greatest prize of all, let him have taken ever so many before' (*P* 1:3:19). Sir Walter's little joke goes to the heart of the origin of riches in the navy. The pay itself was not particularly high: at the time of *Mansfield Park* and *Persuasion*, £101 a year for lieutenants such as William Price, and between £200 and £386 for captains, depending on the size of their ships – and captains, like army officers, had considerable expenses to find. But it was not on their pay that they depended for getting rich, but on what could be gained in prizes when enemy ships were captured. The system was tightly regulated, and rather complex.[7] Ships carrying goods or treasure were valued in prize courts and the resulting money was distributed in differing proportions between the officers and men, the captain and flag officer getting the highest and the ordinary seamen the lowest. Enemy ships of war were bought by the Navy Board and added to the British fleet, their value being similarly distributed among the crew of the ships that had taken them. Ships of the line, particularly if they were blockading, enjoyed fewer opportunities for profitable activity than frigates cruising independently, which could pursue richly laden merchantmen and treasure ships. With the addition of money paid by trading companies or merchants for carrying freight or convoying, very large sums indeed could be made: Edward Pellew, later Lord Exmouth, came out of the war with a fortune of over £300,000.[8] Many captains, Jane Austen's brothers among them, made nothing like this, however; and in periods between ships they had to live quite frugally on half pay, like the Harvilles in their little house at Lyme. Captain Wentworth, of course, has done well, with his fortune of £25,000; on the other hand, as Brian Southam has pointed out, hopeful young William Price is appointed, thanks to the 'interest' used by Admiral Crawford, to a sloop, the poorest of ships, which would have been highly unlikely to offer much opportunity for going after prize money.[9]

The profession most in evidence in Jane Austen's novels is the church; there are clergymen in each of her books, and in three of them the heroine marries one. The value of a country living depended on the agricultural yield of the land in the parish; although some few parsons in the late eighteenth century still collected their tithes in kind, most agreed with the farmers a sum of money in lieu. This income was supplemented by the produce of the glebe, the farmland that belonged to the rectory, which, if it was not large enough to be viable, the parson could extend by renting additional land, as Mr Austen did at Steventon; alternatively, from 1802, when laws prohibiting the leasing of glebe land were rescinded, it could be let to a farmer. Some incumbents held several parishes, employing curates on a fixed stipend to look after ones that they did not visit themselves; this pluralism attracted considerable criticism from the growing evangelical movement, but it did not seem wrong to James Austen, who held three parishes, with an income amounting to £1,100, curate paid. Some clergy had private means, as was the case with James Austen's son, James Edward Austen Leigh, who inherited his great-uncle's estate; others, like Mr Collins, at least had expectations. But the incomes of those who relied entirely on tithes were not always very large.

In about half the parishes in England, the 'great tithes', levied on cereal crops, belonged to the parson, who was the rector of the parish. In the rest, the rights to these tithes had been 'impropriated', that is to say bought at some time in the past by someone else, possibly the patron of the living, who thus became the rector; if he was a layman he had to put in a vicar to read the services and carry out the other duties of a clergyman, for which he would receive only the 'small tithes', on much less valuable produce, in addition to his stipend.[10] Colonel Brandon informs Elinor that Delaford is a rectory, by which she would understand that Edward Ferrars, to whom he is offering the living, will receive the tithes. They will not provide a sufficiently large income, however, for him to marry on: 'the late incumbent', the Colonel tells her, 'did not make more than 200l. per annum, and though it is certainly capable of improvement' – in other words the tithes could be renegotiated – 'not to such an amount as to afford him a very comfortable income' (SS 3:3:320). In Emma, Mr Elton, lacking the connections that were usually necessary for a young man to be presented to a living, is only vicar of Highbury, a fact that Jane Austen clearly decided on to give him a motive for wishing to marry a woman with money. It does however leave open the question of who the rector is. He may be the incumbent of another parish – presumably the one in which Donwell Abbey is situated, and perhaps the Dr Hughes to whom Miss Bates speaks during the ball at the Crown; or he may be a layman, in which case it is probably the patron of both livings, and therefore almost certainly Mr Knightley. In Pride and Prejudice matters are much more clear-cut, since the relations between Mr Collins and his 'patroness' are central to the development of his character (and to the comedy). We are not told what his tithes amount to, but we know that he is assiduous in collecting them, since he names the agreeing of tithes as the first duty of a clergyman. They must be fairly considerable: in his first letter to Mr Bennet he refers to the 'bounty and beneficence' of Lady Catherine which has preferred him to the 'valuable rectory' of the parish (PP 1:13:70); he has 'a good house and very sufficient income' (1:15:78); and in proposing to Elizabeth he is prepared to take as his wife a girl whose dowry extends no further than £1,000 in the 4 per cents, and that only after her mother's death (1:19:119–20).

In some ways Mr Collins has been more fortunate in his career than Mr Elton, since although he was similarly without means or connections, a 'fortunate chance' recommended him to the notice of Lady Catherine when the living of Hunsford fell vacant. Rights of presentation in the Church of England belonged to bishops or cathedral chapters, to the Crown, to Oxford and Cambridge colleges or to private patrons. Many of the latter wished to present relations to them (presumably Lady Catherine had no one suitable, her nephew Colonel Fitzwilliam having chosen a different career); and at that time there was nothing wrong with this kind of provision for needy or deserving members of the family. In fact, it was the offering for sale of advowsons – rights of presentation to a living – about which there were sometimes reservations. Sir Thomas Bertram, who expected to benefit his family with the presentation of Mansfield (the last incumbent was his wife's brother-in-law, Mr Norris), expresses his frustration when his elder son's debts oblige him to sell it instead of putting in someone to hold it until Edmund has taken orders:

> You have robbed Edmund for ten, twenty, thirty years, perhaps for life, of more than half the income which ought to be his. It may hereafter be in my power, or in your's (I hope it will), to procure him better preferment; but it must not be forgotten, that no benefit of that sort would have been beyond his natural claims on us, and that nothing can, in fact, be an equivalent for the certain advantage which he is now obliged to forego through the urgency of your debts. (*MP* 1:3:27)

The smaller living of Thornton Lacey has been held for Edmund, and it is that that he takes up on his ordination, and where he and Fanny live during the early days of their marriage; and eventually the death of Dr Grant enables them to move to Mansfield 'just after they had been married long enough to begin to want an increase of income' (3:17:547) – in other words, when they begin to have children.

A further source of income for the clergy was teaching, either as a private tutor, as 'The Watsons' Mr Howard was to Lord Osborne before becoming the parish priest, or by taking pupils in the rectory. Jane Austen's father, who before his marriage had returned as Usher, or second master, to his old school, Tonbridge, offset the expenses of his growing family by educating boys and preparing them for entrance to the universities. They lived in the rectory and were taught alongside his own children, and were very well looked after by Mrs Austen, who encouraged them and wrote humorous verses to amuse them. In 1779 he had four pupils, contemporaries of James, and his account at Hoare's Bank shows that their fathers paid him some £35 a year each, to cover tuition, board and lodging; twelve years later, when he was teaching boys who were more or less the same age as Jane, the fees had risen to £65, and one rather sickly boy, the son of the Bishop of Exeter, was charged £150, presumably because he needed special attention.[11] For a man, undertaking education of this kind was a perfectly respectable occupation; and even within the confines of a school, to be the headmaster, at least, was certainly compatible with being a gentleman.

For a woman, the position was more ambiguous. Mrs Goddard, mistress and proprietor of a 'real, honest, old-fashioned Boarding-school' standing 'in high repute' is undoubtedly genteel; she probably does little teaching herself, but like Mrs La Tournelle at the Reading Ladies Boarding School which Jane and Cassandra attended, looks after the physical welfare of her pupils and leaves the instruction to her assistants – who are not, it will be noted, included in Emma's social set. At the time when Mr Austen sent his daughters to Reading (1785), the fees were normally 15–16 guineas for ordinary boarders, but he paid Mrs La Tournelle 35 guineas a year each for them to be parlour boarders, that is, to live with the family; the school numbered about forty girls, which means that she enjoyed a fairly high income. Similarly, since Mrs Goddard has 'a train of twenty young couple' walking after her to church (E 1:3:21), of whom we may assume Harriet and Miss Bickerton are unlikely to be the only parlour boarders, she must have an annual turnover of not much less than £700.[12] Mrs La Tournelle (which was not her real name – she started life as Esther Hackett) had been taken on as a teacher of French at the school, which she eventually inherited from the previous proprietors; Mrs Goddard 'had worked hard in her youth' and earned her claim to gentility that way, possibly, it is hinted, with a little assistance from Mr Woodhouse, to whose kindness she 'formerly owed much'. In less favourable circumstances, a woman who tried to make her own way in the world could find things very much harder. If she was from a good family, remained single and had no private means of support, the only course open to her was to become a governess, which is the fate that seems to await Jane Fairfax if she either accepts the post that Mrs Elton has officiously found for her or applies to one of the 'Offices for the sale – not quite of human flesh – but of human intellect' that were set up in London (2:17:325).

The isolation experienced by a governess was often very demoralizing: treated by her employer, to whose class she naturally belonged, as a social inferior, and yet distrusted by the servants, she often found her position in the household to be very lonely. She was of course supplied with her board, and wages varied. While the Edgeworths, in their *Manual of Practical Education*, stated that a governess should receive £300 a year, most were paid far less, usually about 30 guineas; there were exceptions, however, such as Agnes Porter, governess in the Ilchester and Talbot families, whose annual salary was about £100, and who when she retired lived comfortably on £150 in annuities and income from investments in 5 per cent Navy Stock.[13] Miss Taylor's position at Hartfield seems to have been even more fortunate: Mr Woodhouse and his two daughters regard her 'less as a governess than a friend'; her relationship with Emma resembles 'the intimacy of sisters' (*E* 1:1:3); and as a final piece of good fortune, she ends her career not with a pension but in marriage. Jane Fairfax would be unlikely to find such a happy state of affairs in any family with which Mrs Elton is acquainted.

To young men without private resources the law and medicine both offered secure, and to a certain extent respectable, prospects; in each, however, there were marked social distinctions between the different branches of practice. Emma's brother-in-law, Mr John Knightley, is a successful London lawyer, 'rising in his profession' (*E* 1:11:100), living at a very good address and bringing up a family of five on the lucrative proceeds of important legal work that requires him to be in town during the law terms. By contrast, Mr Coxe, the lawyer of Highbury, moves in a circle with which Emma only reluctantly associates herself; she cannot endure to think of his son William ('a pert young lawyer') as a husband for Harriet. Whereas there is no reason for Mr John Knightley not to reach the very peak of his profession, as a judge or even as Lord Chancellor, the Coxes will be confined to their local practice, effecting all sorts of business for their neighbours, and no doubt progressively enriching themselves. Mr John Knightley, as the younger brother, was entered for his profession as a gentleman; though this could also be the case with attorneys, to the Coxes and their sort, the law was a family concern, just as trades were, and like tradesmen they learned by being apprenticed as articled clerks. In *Pride and Prejudice*, Mrs Bennet is the daughter of a local attorney whose clerk, Mr Phillips, married her sister and eventually took on the business.

The same was very often true of the medical profession. Giles-King Lyford, who attended Jane Austen in her final illness, was the son of a Winchester surgeon and nephew of John Lyford, Basingstoke 'surgeon and man-midwife', who treated the Austens at Steventon rectory. The Lyfords were a rising family; Giles-King was appointed Surgeon-in-Ordinary to the County Hospital, John sent his eldest son to Eton and Oxford, and he and a younger son (also a surgeon) both rode with Mr Chute's hounds in the Vine Hunt. Apothecaries were a different matter, however. Jane Austen jokingly corrected Cassandra when she thus referred to the London surgeon Charles Haden, who visited Henry Austen socially; for if surgeons did not have the status conferred on physicians by their being members of a chartered profession, and might even take out newspaper advertisements, like the one that Mr Parker comes across in his search for a medical man for Sanditon, they were very much superior to apothecaries, who were little more than druggists (Mr Jones in Meryton has a shopboy), and who indeed were permitted by law to charge only for the drugs they prescribed, and not for the advice they gave. Yet apothecaries flourished and often grew prosperous; the fact that Mr Perry considers setting up a carriage suggests that he is enjoying a healthy income of between £600 and £700 a year, much of it no doubt derived from his frequent visits to Mr Woodhouse.

At the very bottom of the medical hierarchy, with no prospect of improvement in status or income, were the women who served, untrained, as nurses, either in the hospitals or independently. In *Persuasion* we are given a picture of just such a woman in Nurse Rooke, who attends the incapacitated Mrs Smith. When engaged for childbirths, as she is by Mrs Wallis, or for nursing illnesses, she takes up residence in the family, but when unemployed she has a home with her sister, Mrs Smith's landlady. Not only has she nursed Mrs Smith 'most admirably', she has also taught her to knit and has contrived for her to make 'little thread-cases, pincushions and card-racks', which she then takes round to her patients and encourages them to buy. Mrs Smith, herself so impoverished as to be possibly the only character in any of the novels not to keep a servant, uses the income from these to do 'a little good to one or two very poor families' (2:5:168) in the neighbourhood. Jane Austen here figures a remarkable micro-economic system devoted to serving charitable ends.

As far as commercial trade was concerned, status was dependent upon the size of the fortune it brought. Bingley's inherited property of nearly £100,000, though it derives from trade in the north of England, makes him a perfectly suitable friend for Darcy and will enable him to buy an estate; it is significant, however, that Jane Austen's irony exposes an unmistakable social unease in his sisters, who go out of their way to associate 'with people of rank' and are 'in every respect entitled to think well of themselves, and meanly of others' (*PP* 1:4:16). Sir William Lucas' trade having been in Meryton, it has brought him only a 'tolerable fortune', with which he purchased a house whose comparative modesty is revealed by the palpably disproportionate grandeur of its name, Lucas Lodge. Meanwhile Mr Gardiner, a man presented in the novel without irony and with the wholehearted approval of the author, is 'settled in London in a respectable line of trade' (1:7:31). In *Emma*, it is likewise the heroine, rather than Jane Austen, who makes a distinction between Mr Weston, whose engaging in trade in London brought him enough money 'to secure the purchase of a little estate' (1:2:14) and the Coles, who are 'of low origin, in trade, and only moderately genteel', despite having profited from the economic boom of the period to increase their income so that they are 'in fortune and style of living, second only to the family at Hartfield' (2:7:223).

In an age of huge consumer spending, tradesmen of all kinds proliferated, and their presence is taken for granted in the novels: such are the builders and painters needed to carry out Mrs Dashwood's projected alterations at Barton Cottage, the upholsterers who will fit up the drawing room at Woodston parsonage, the cabinet maker from whom Emma obtains the round table at Hartfield, the coach builder who made John Thorpe's curricle gig, the suppliers of Constantia wine and North Wiltshire cheese, the nurseryman who imposed on Mrs Norris with a Moor park apricot. When Isabella Thorpe asks Catherine how she likes her gown and tells her that the sleeves were entirely her own thought, she has been to a Bath mantua-maker, perhaps the same Mrs Mussell to whom Jane Austen gave detailed instructions for a gown of her own in May 1801. Mantua-makers did not earn a great deal, but Mrs Mussell had the security of being married to a hairdresser; even with the progressive abandoning of wigs, hairdressers, if not their assistants, made a reasonable living: had Frank Churchill had his hair cut when he went to London, he would have been charged between 1s. and 2s. Occasionally we almost have a glimpse of a real shopkeeper: Mr Gray, at whose jeweller's shop in Sackville Street Robert Ferrars deliberates over a toothpick case, Messrs Broadwood, from whom Jane Fairfax's pianoforte is ordered, William Turner, the Portsmouth naval supplier, or Dorothy Molland, proprietor of the famous pastrycook's in Bath.

Highbury is well supplied with honest people making a comfortable living in a way that benefits their customers and contributes to the general well-being of the community: Mrs Ford owns 'the principal woollen-draper, linen-draper, and haberdasher's shop united' (E 2:3:190–1), Mrs Stokes is the landlady of the Crown inn and John Abdy her ostler and head man, and Mrs Wallis is the baker, supplying bread and for a small charge baking people's dinners in her oven (as she does Miss Bates' apples). In Sanditon, however, where commercial enterprise is subjected to direct and penetrating scrutiny, there is an alarming precariousness to the livelihoods of those who have set up in business. The investors, Lady Denham, obsessed with the acquisition of money, and the gullible enthusiast Mr Parker, forever convincing himself that the rows of empty lodgings will soon be let, have replaced the traditional obligations of the landowner with a pursuit of profit detached from the balanced economy of the estate. Rather than supplying the wants and necessities of a genuine society, their tenants attempt to make a living in an idle and unwanted pleasure resort: Mr Stringer the market gardener 'does not do very well' (LM 'S' 4:158); William Heeley puts smart blue shoes and

nankin boots in his window in the hope of attracting the fashionable customers who have yet to appear in Sanditon; and at the circulating library, which
as well as providing books, offers for sale 'all the useless things in the World
that c^d not be done without', Mrs Whitby sits 'in her inner room, reading one
of her own novels, for want of employment' (*LM* 'S' 6:166–7). These, like the
butcher and baker, Jebb the milliner, Mr Woodcock the hotelier and all the
other tradesmen, seem destined to be ruined in the great crash which is surely
about to bring down the entire speculation.

   'Sanditon' is of course a departure for Jane Austen in many ways, and not
least because it places at the centre of the novel the very kind of commercial-
ism which is held at arm's length in her completed works. While it is impossible to know the extent to which the plot would have been concerned with
the collapse of the seaside venture, there can be no doubt that the principal
characters would have been profoundly affected by it; as it is, we see members
of the gentry class involved in the daily process of making money – or hoping
to – in a way that is left decently obscure in, say, the family history of the
Bingleys or the Woodhouses. Sir Thomas Bertram looks into his affairs on the
plantations, but he does so at the safe distance of Antigua, while his family
entertain themselves with theatricals; and though Mr Gardiner is undoubtedly in trade, we do not see him practise it as we accompany him on his
holiday tour to Derbyshire. Mr Parker and Lady Denham, however, in their
rather desperate preoccupation with the letting of lodgings or the provision
of asses' milk, are as much practitioners of commerce as any character in
Dickens or Trollope, whose world 'Sanditon' seems to anticipate. Emma
would be shocked.

NOTES

1. Robin Vick, 'Jane Austen's House at Chawton', Jane Austen Society, *Collected Reports 1986–1995*, vol. IV, pp. 388–91.
2. Caroline Mary Craven Austen, *Reminiscences of Caroline Austen*, Introduction and Notes by Deirdre Le Faye (Chawton: Jane Austen Society, 1986), p. 24.
3. For an account of John Bond, see D. Dean Cantrell, 'John Bond: A Source for William Larkins?', Jane Austen Society, *Collected Reports 1976–1985*, vol. III, pp. 339–44; for a reference to him in a poem by James Austen, see Deirdre Le Faye, 'James Austen's Poetical Biography of John Bond', *Collected Reports 1986–1995*, vol. IV, pp. 243–7; for the whole poem (or as much of it as was written at the author's death), see *The Complete Poems of James Austen*, ed. David Selwyn (Chawton: Jane Austen Society, 2003), pp. 99–116. Jane Austen makes several references to John Bond in the *Letters*.
4. Pamela Horn, *Life and Labour in Rural England 1760–1850* (Basingstoke and London: Macmillan, 1987), p. 34.
5. The survey, by Arthur Young (1741–1820), is discussed in G. E. Mingay, *A Social History of the English Countryside* (London: Routledge, 1990), pp. 93, 100–1.

6. Bridget Hill, *Servants: English Domestics in the Eighteenth Century* (Oxford: Clarendon Press, 1996), pp. 64–92.

7. For a detailed account of the distribution of prize money and other aspects of the honours system in the navy, see Brian Southam, *Jane Austen and the Navy* (London: Hambledon, 2000), pp. 109–32.

8. Southam, *Jane Austen and the Navy*, p. 129.

9. Southam, *Jane Austen and the Navy*, p. 197.

10. Irene Collins gives an invaluable account of the system of tithes in *Jane Austen and the Clergy* (London: Hambledon, 1994), pp. 49–60.

11. Deirdre Le Faye, *Jane Austen: A Family Record*, 2nd edn (Cambridge University Press, 2004), pp. 42, 72–3.

12. T. A. B. Corley, 'Jane Austen's School Days', *Collected Reports 1996–2000*, vol. v, pp. 14–24.

13. *A Governess in the Age of Jane Austen: The Journals and Letters of Agnes Porter*, ed. Joanna Martin (London: Hambledon, 1998), pp. 38–9. A comprehensive view of the governess in the eighteenth and nineteenth centuries is given by Ruth Brandon in *Other People's Daughters: The Life and Times of the Governess* (London: Weidenfeld & Nicolson, 2008).

11

E. J. CLERY

Gender

Introduction

It was inevitable that Austen's irreverent purpose would be directed towards the stifling absurdity surrounding the concept of 'gender', or, to use a critical term introduced at the time of her early adulthood in the 1790s by Mary Wollstonecraft, 'sexual character'.[1] The cultural construction of sexual difference, as distinct from biological sex, had been recognized. Chapter 1 of *Northanger Abbey*, while operating as a satire of novels of sensibility, is also a comic anticipation of Simone de Beauvoir's aphorism: 'One is not born a woman, one becomes one'. Catherine Morland, we are told, was during her infancy 'fond of all boys' plays' and preferred cricket to dolls. Aged 10 she has 'a sallow skin without colour, dark lank hair, and strong features', and although 'seldom stubborn, scarcely ever quarrelsome, and very kind to the little ones' is 'noisy and wild, hated confinement and cleanliness, and loved nothing so well in the world as rolling down the green slope at the back of the house'. But from the age of 15 she begins to curl her hair and for the next two years is 'in training for a heroine'; that is to say, she is not only making preparations to feature as the main protagonist in a fictional adventure, but also equipping herself with the superficial literary education and the techniques of personal grooming that constitute gender identity among the adolescent girls of the propertied classes, and provide the essential passport to the social interactions of the marriage market (*NA* 1:1:5–7).

Austen does not leave the matter of gender constructions and their artificial nature with Catherine's entry into femininity, however. No sooner has her heroine arrived in Bath, visited the Assembly Rooms and been introduced to her first dance partner than the painstakingly achieved fabric of gender distinction begins to unravel again: and this time it is masculinity that seems most fragile. Henry Tilney first appears to Catherine's eyes 'a very gentleman-like young man' but 'there was an archness and pleasantry in his manner which interested, though it was hardly understood by her' (1:3:17). Over tea, after a dance, he launches into a parody of standard polite conversation between new acquaintances of the opposite sex. After questioning Catherine about her impressions of Bath 'with a simpering air' he concludes: 'Now I must give one smirk, and then we may be rational again'. It is in the gap between the smirk and the principle of the self as a 'rational' being that gender practices operate in Austen.

Gender as the basis for comedy continues in this scene. Henry reviews his camp performance by imagining the way it will appear in Catherine's journal: 'was strangely harassed by a queer, half-witted man, who would make me dance with him, and distressed me by his nonsense' (1:3:19). This is swiftly followed by discussion between the two of whether or not women are by nature the better letter-writers, as they are 'generally' held to be – Tilney concludes that the difference is negligible: 'In every power, of which taste is the foundation, excellence is pretty fairly divided between the sexes' (1:3:19–20). He immediately demonstrates his own 'genius' in a realm of taste and judgement conventionally held to be the preserve of women: dress. The dress-obsessed Mrs Allen, Catherine's chaperone, joins the pair and is struck by his exact knowledge of the price and durability of textiles: 'Men commonly take so little notice of those things'. But the younger woman is disturbed even while she is amused by this deviancy: '"How can you," said Catherine, laughing, "Be so –" she had almost said, strange' (1:3:20–1). The comment with the unspoken word hangs in the air, as the discussion of muslin between Tilney and Mrs Allen continues.

Austen's own inclusion of the terms 'queer' and 'strange' in this context may be taken as a prophetic blessing on recent applications of queer theory to her fiction: 'queer' in its current usage describes not only alternative sexual orientations but a general destabilizing of fixed gender identities.[2] In the early nineteenth-century lexicon it carried the sense of an impropriety verging on the antisocial including, explicitly, a resistance to heterosexual norms. The most often-cited instance in Austen is the rakish Henry Crawford's puzzlement at his failure to fascinate Fanny Price in *Mansfield Park*:

'What is her character? – Is she solemn? – Is she queer? – Is she prudish? ... I never was so long in company with a girl in my life – trying to entertain her – and succeed so ill!' (2:6:268–9)

While some among Austen's vast and often socially conservative readership will bridle at the connection, there seems no arguing with the fact that Austen questions the sex–gender system and its categorizing endeavours. The girlification of Catherine Morland and her disconcerting encounter with Henry Tilney are not isolated cases. Instances of 'misdirected' feeling noted by critics include the violation of the codes of heterosocial politeness by Marianne Dashwood's 'masturbatory' absorption in her own pleasures and by Robert

Ferrars' camp intentness on 'style' in *Sense and Sensibility*; the triangulation of desire joining Fanny, Mary Crawford and Edmund Bertram; in *Emma*, the intensities of Miss Woodhouse's association with other women by contrast with her cool dismissal of the prospect of marriage until the final volte-face; the homoerotic overtones found in some of the manuscript writings.[3]

Feminist critical work on Austen has from the start identified the construction of femininity as a topic of debate within her novels. When in *Pride and Prejudice* the ridiculous Revd Mr Collins reads aloud James Fordyce's *Sermons to Young Women* (1766), a work roundly condemned by Mary Wollstonecraft in *Vindication of the Rights of Woman* (1792), for the edification of his young female cousins, Austen's distaste for a still-current ideal of female identity is apparent. The message is underlined by Elizabeth Bennet's rejection of Mr Collins' proposal of marriage, which he chooses to see as the decorous game-playing of 'elegant females': 'Can I speak plainer? Do not consider me now as an elegant female intending to plague you, but as a rational creature speaking the truth from her heart' (*PP* 1:19:122). Gender as social artifice is made visible here, alongside a rival Enlightenment ideal of selfhood distinct from gender, the self as 'rational creature'. More recently, critics have begun considering comparable tensions in the representation of masculinity, most notably in *Emma*'s insistent juxtaposition of the 'tall, firm, upright figure' of Mr Knightley with the vanity and pliant Frenchified gallantry of a Frank Churchill or a Mr Elton (3:2:352).[4] Fordyce, Thomas Gisborne and Vicessimus Knox wrote prescriptive treatises for young men equivalent to their conduct books for young women, and their possible influence on literary representation is yet to be fully explored. It is worth bearing in mind that Jane was raised in what was effectively a small private school for boys, the paying pupils studying alongside her resident brothers, and that the moral and intellectual formation of men was a topic of professional as well as family interest in the Austen household.

Austen's microscopic interest in the performative nature of social roles seems to bear out Judith Butler's influential analysis of gender as intrinsically troubled and unstable; as a '*stylized repetition of acts*' rather than an expression of inner essence or a monolithic construct.[5] Yet Austen's present-day renown is hardly based on her pioneering role as a critical thinker on gender. If anything, the reverse is true; Austen is associated in the present-day imagination with normative ideas of gender difference and heterosexual romance updated for 'postfeminist' times. Gender-theory-driven readings of the fiction collide with the popular stereotype, but the conflict is not without its benefits. The Austen 'industry' of today provides an opening for scholars to intervene in the broader public debate about sexual politics. It is this confrontation that reciprocally fuels an academic interest in screen adaptations, literary spin-offs, and the media commodification and exploitation of the Austen 'label' in general, that may now be as active as critical discussion of the novels themselves.[6]

What we have seen over the last decade or so is an interesting new turn in the long-running Austen 'culture wars', now being fought on multiple fronts, globally, among an ever-increasing array of experts, readers and viewers. In each generation there has been a radical mission to 'rescue' Austen from the common reader or the dominant hermeneutic practices of the day. In the 1970s and 1980s feminist critics endeavoured, with notable success, to wrest Austen free from canonical readings which had largely seen the miniature domestic settings of the novels as an anomaly in a major writer, and to demonstrate the ways in which her engagement with public debate was inflected by categories of gender, and by her experience as a woman. In the early twenty-first century, when Austen has been repackaged as the mother of 'chick lit', the queering of Austen can be understood as the latest manifestation of D. W. Harding's view that Austen was destined to be 'read and enjoyed by precisely the sort of people whom she disliked'.[7] Austen must be 'rescued' from the romance reader and the heritage addict. But they will not relinquish their claims easily. When in 1995, under the headline 'Was Jane Austen gay?' the Stanford academic Terry Castle reviewed the new edition of the *Letters* in the *London Review of Books* and proposed that homosocial intimacy was arguably more important than heterosexual romance in Austen's life and art, it unleashed an extraordinary backlash.[8] The subsequent banal 'romancing' of Austen's biography in the feature film *Becoming Jane* (2007) and television drama *Miss Austen Regrets* (2008) seems to constitute retaliation for the very suggestion. 'Austen' marks the site of an ongoing struggle over valuable 'cultural capital'.[9] There are a variety of issues at stake – contested ideas of class, nation and our relation to history – but the most volatile is surely gender.

It should be asked, what are the consequences of these wider developments for the interpretation of the novels themselves? From the 1970s the field of Austen studies has been dominated by the reconstruction of historical contexts and intertextual relations, attempts to locate Austen within the political and cultural debates of her time. This continues, but it has been joined by a revival of interest in narrative form, as if critics have been driven to re-examine the precise methods by which the famous plots are constructed as a result of their prolific multi-media afterlife.[10] In particular, the afterlife of Austen has served to focus attention even more intensely on those apparently conservative elements in her narrative practice that underpin the popular fantasies attached to the novels: the 'courtship' or 'marriage' plot as instrument of compulsory heterosexuality, and the facets of the narration that give moral weight and a sense of universality to these plots. The queer perspective on Austen shares with much feminist criticism a deep suspicion of the telos of romance, a destination apparently contrary to the abrasive action of irony and satire. There is a sense that the closure in marriage is the point at which Austen concedes to the demands of audiences (then as now), and, for all her brilliance, risks being stupid.[11]

There is plenty of evidence in the novels that Austen herself in fact shared the sense of the risks involved in romance. And yet romance is an undeniable element of her work. Is there a way of avoiding the apparent dichotomy between the Austen who plays with and subverts the certainties of gender difference and Austen the *romancière*? Are the happy endings of the novels always to be understood as a form of false consciousness, obscuring the gender hierarchy so starkly illustrated at other points in the narrative? How can we square the unflinching appraisal of the mercenary underpinnings of marriage among the propertied classes with the use of marriage as the means of narrative closure? It seems to me that these are the key questions in Austen criticism today, and so I have chosen here to link the issue of gender specifically to an investigation of narrative technique in the novels. There are obviously other possible approaches to the topic, including the examination of her works as socio-historical documents, and critical work of this kind will be indicated in Chapter 16, 'Further Reading'. While the following suggestions refer to the historical context of Austen's work – her allegiance to Enlightenment ideals of sexual equality and free social intercourse between the sexes – my main concern is to consider the way gender division is addressed by Austen through literary form, by means of the most technically innovative aspects of her work: her management of point of view and experiments with free indirect discourse.

Austen's resistance to romance

No Austen screen adaptation is complete without a closing kiss, a bodily merging that heals all conflicts and contradictions, although it is well known her heroes and heroines scarcely ever make even the slightest physical contact. This solecism notwithstanding, the voracious desire for a fairy-tale conclusion on the part of consumers of narrative is a phenomenon that Austen anticipates and mocks. She plays with the novel-reader's addiction to the age-old conventions of closure, and punishes it by withholding some of the scenes that would most gratify, or by darkening the auguries of happiness with satire or scepticism. The intrusive, bustling narrator typically sweeps aside opportunities for pathos and lyricism as we hasten 'together to perfect felicity', in the teasing words of *Northanger Abbey* (2:16:259). She refuses to let us listen to Emma's response to Mr Knightley's declaration of love. She won't show us the transformation of Edmund Bertram from brother to lover. It may be objected that these lacunae owe something to conventions of decorum; however they are not passed over in a quiet way, but with a kind of gleeful malice, in order to cause pain to the romantically inclined reader. Close reading reveals that the tendency of the final pages is to undercut, by means of the narrative voice, the appearance of a resolution.

The brusqueness of the mechanisms of closure in the three novels *Northanger Abbey, Sense and Sensibility* and *Mansfield Park* are notorious. In *Northanger Abbey* the promise of 'perfect happiness' for Catherine and Henry is a poor thing, shouldered aside in the final paragraph by the narrator's more vivid interest in the nefarious acts of General Tilney, while the important character Eleanor Tilney is disposed of to an anonymous figure off-stage (2:16:261). The militantly anti-romantic delivery of Marianne to Colonel Brandon in *Sense and Sensibility* is matched in *Mansfield Park* by the similarly pragmatic delivery of Edmund to Fanny (apparently without any conscious will on his part).

Indeed the perversity of *Mansfield Park* in tangling with the reader's expectations is unsurpassed, concluding in its last pages with not one but two 'romantically' wrong flights of desire: of Sir Thomas for Fanny as the embodiment of an abstract ideal ('Fanny was indeed the daughter that he wanted'), and of Fanny herself for Mansfield parsonage (3:17:546). While the pairing with Edmund never evolves beyond lifeless abstraction, the narrator spends the last sentence dwelling on Fanny's developing love for Mansfield parsonage, 'which under each of its two former owners, [she] had never been able to approach but with some painful sensation of restraint or alarm' but which 'soon grew as dear to her heart, and as thoroughly perfect in her eyes, as every thing else, within the view and patronage of Mansfield Park, had long been' (3:17:547–8). And then there is *Sense and Sensibility*, where in the final paragraph the chief concern is good relations between Barton and Delaford, and between the great house at Delaford and the neighbouring parsonage. It's as if constructions of bricks and mortar had replaced lovers as the main protagonists of the narrative. Each of these instances of cathexis, in which libidinal energy is attached to an object or idea rather than a person, lightly recalls to the reader the dynastic and material nature of marriage.

The final lines of *Pride and Prejudice* and *Emma* seem on the face of it more satisfactory in this respect. Both involve the notion of 'union', an important item in Austen's lexicon. Although the word 'union' or variations on it appear in a number of contexts, it is frequently used in place of 'marriage', with an interesting additional set of connotations. It has a distant, slightly formal quality, and also a sense of measured assessment and appraisal. In *Pride and*

Prejudice it appears twice in Elizabeth's reflections about the disaster of Lydia's elopement when she begins to understand the happiness she has conclusively lost with Mr Darcy: 'It was an union that must have been to the advantage of both' and their complementary qualities are reviewed, 'But no such happy marriage could now teach the admiring multitude what connubial felicity really was. An union of a different tendency, and precluding the possibility of the other, was soon to be formed in their family' (3:8:344). Even in Elizabeth's thoughts, then, there is a certain activity of weighing and measuring connected with 'union'. The term appears again in Lady Catherine de Bourgh's outraged speech to Elizabeth insisting on the engagement between Darcy and her own daughter, 'While in their cradles, we planned the union' and she goes on, 'what is to divide them? The upstart pretensions of a young woman without family, connections, or fortune?' (3:14:393). This last example indicates another definitive aspect of the term 'union': it contains the idea of its opposite, division, in a way that neither 'match' nor 'marriage' does. And we see this antinomy played out in the conclusions of both *Pride and Prejudice* and *Emma*.

The final lines of *Pride and Prejudice* run as follows:

> With the Gardiners, they were always on the most intimate terms. Darcy, as well as Elizabeth, really loved them; and they were both ever sensible of the warmest gratitude towards the persons who, by bringing her into Derbyshire, had been the means of uniting them. (3:19:431)

What is that inversion of the first sentence, beginning emphatically 'With the Gardiners', but an attempt to negate what has gone immediately before, a state visit to Pemberley from the divisive Lady Catherine, after a long period of stony disapproval. The Gardiners are the one effective force for cohesion in the world of the novel, to place in opposition to the numerous elements tending to destroy the unity of the Darcy household, all of which have just passed under review in the final chapter.

In *Emma* the threat to unity appears in the very first sentence of the novel with the statement that the heroine 'seemed to unite some of the best blessings of existence' – 'seemed', for without this qualification, and the blow that immediately follows, the loss of Miss Taylor, her surrogate mother and dearest friend (a loss, ironically enough, to marriage), if the 'best blessings of existence' *were* united there would be no matter for the novel (1:1:3). In other words, perfect union is inimical to the playing out of the story.

My point owes something to D. A. Miller's discussion of Austen in *Narrative and Its Discontents*. He claims, to put it baldly, that imperfection – whether of 'character, or situation, or language' – is the very condition of storytelling in Austen, while closure is synonymous with perfection in her work, and the 'non-narratable'.[12] Miller sees Austen the writer as something of a schizophrenic, her narrative forever reaching towards essential principles, truth and closure, while it continues to spin itself out in difficulties and contingencies: 'what it [i.e. the narrative] mocks, criticizes, or even loathes is precisely what it cannot do without'.[13] While everyone would probably acknowledge this dual aspect of her work – satire on the one hand and moral seriousness on the other – it could be questioned whether in these terms her works ever achieve closure; though Miller seems to think they must. The final paragraph of *Emma* is a case in point:

> The wedding was very much like other weddings, where the parties have no taste for finery or parade; and Mrs. Elton, from the particulars detailed by her husband, thought it all extremely shabby, and very inferior to her own. – 'Very little white satin, very few lace veils; a most pitiful business! – Selina would stare when she heard of it.' – But, in spite of these deficiencies, the wishes, the hopes, the confidence, the predictions of the small band of true friends who witnessed the ceremony, were fully answered in the perfect happiness of the union. (3:19:528)

Here again, in an even more vivid way than in *Pride and Prejudice*, we see unity and 'perfect happiness' wrestling with unregenerate elements, and who can say that perfection ultimately wins? There may be a *will* to 'perfect happiness' – wishes, hopes, confidence, predictions – but what we are given here is concrete, visible evidence that it can never be so. Those dashes marking out the speech of Mrs Elton defy full stops; deny even syntactical closure. The dissonant voice will always make itself heard; the wedding ceremony itself is subverted by the traitor in its midst, the Revd Mr Elton, who stands between bride and groom and hears their vows while taking poisonous fashion notes.

The idea that Austen conforms to the template of 'Cinderella' has a long history.[14] But is this really the case? A careful examination of Austen's closing words suggests that however much she might bandy about the *terminology* of a fairy-tale happy ending there is a kind of infantilism about it that Austen the sceptic could never accede to, whether on aesthetic, philosophical or ideological grounds. It is arguable that we never get closure in an Austen novel. A very large number of people do, however, quite obviously get satisfaction from the endings of her novels, or more than that, even derive from them the kind of joy or even rapture associated with the idealism, the anti-realism, of the romance genre.

So where does the romance lie if, as we have seen, Austen in the endings as they were written resolutely denies the perfect closure of the happy ending, hero and heroine glimpsed in a final eternal clinch? This is a complex problem with no simple answer, though I venture a possible solution here. One thing should be established from the start, however: romance in Austen is not easy or 'magical'; it's the hard-won reward of the exertions of the characters on the one hand, and of the author, on the other.[15] Austen's method for generating romantic 'uplift' seems to have been achieved out of a struggle with her own creative sensibility, and represents a radical departure from previous conventions. It is something startling and new in the history of the novel, and it is in part the enduring success of this invention, I will suggest, that helps to maintain her unique place as our contemporary.

Austen's recuperation of romance

In *Persuasion*, the first introduction of the inner life of the heroine also announces a new and more trustful relationship with romance:

> How eloquent could Anne Elliot have been, – how eloquent, at least, were her wishes on the side of early warm attachment, and a cheerful confidence in futurity, against that over-anxious caution which seems to insult exertion and distrust Providence! – She had been forced into prudence in her youth, she learned romance as she grew older – the natural sequel of an unnatural beginning. (1:4:32)

It becomes clear that Anne is not the only one to 'learn romance' in this novel. Austen revisits and rewrites scenes she had treated with lofty irony in previous narratives. We might think of irony as the equivalent of 'over-anxious caution' – at one level it is a prudential kind of writing, which holds back from feeling and empathy. In *Persuasion* Austen goes back to the drawing board.

One of the things she needs to undertake is a review of her own vexed relationship with the word 'union', the ways in which she has previously used it and mercilessly explored its fault lines. She decides to introduce it with apparent inconsequence, shorn of connotation, as if for the first time: reborn. Anne and Captain Wentworth, her lost love, are finally reunited in Union-Street in Bath (2:11:260).

But in fact even this apparently neutralized usage is a form of rewriting, and it would repay us to return for a moment to the start of her career, to *Northanger Abbey*, which in spite of its precedence, was first published in tandem with *Persuasion*. In *Northanger Abbey*, Union-passage, situated parallel to Union-street in Bath, is the scene of another reunion between Isabella and Catherine and their respective brothers. This occurs after Isabella, having noticed 'two odious young men' staring at her, and then found they had left the Pump-room, in order 'to shew … her resolution of humbling the sex' sets off with Catherine 'immediately as fast as they could walk, in pursuit of the two young men' (1:6:36–7). Austen has the two young ladies stop at the archway opposite Union-passage, unable to cross Cheap (meaning 'market')-street, because of its 'impertinent' connection with the London and Oxford roads and consequent volume of traffic. As Isabella and Catherine stand on the other side of Cheap-street and watch their disappearing quarries 'threading the gutters of that interesting alley', it is difficult to ignore the proliferation of innuendo – the fact that 'Union-passage' was before 1789 known as 'Cockes lane' may be strictly fortuitous, but nevertheless seems to support the general drift (1:7:38).[16] The map of Bath proves to be the mirror of Isabella's romance-addled mind – she and Catherine had been discussing 'horrid novels' immediately before.

Hypocrisy, vanity, barter, the battle of the sexes, debased and corrupt versions of 'romance' and 'union', the double-talking that so confuses Catherine – what could be more different than the meeting that takes place between Anne and Wentworth at the climax of *Persuasion* in adjacent Union-street? She has just received a message revealing his feelings for her but does not know if and when there will be an opportunity to speak to him alone and respond in kind. She is being accompanied home by her brother-in-law Charles Musgrove, Captain Wentworth happens upon them, and Anne is handed over to his keeping, Charles having an urgent appointment with a gunsmith. They move to the 'retired gravel-walk, where the power of conversation would make the present hour a blessing indeed' (2:11:261), and at this point there is a striking departure from the smart knowingness of the narrating voice as it describes similar moments in *Sense and Sensibility* or *Emma*. The third-person narrator allows herself to be moved to emotive repetition, describing the 'many, many years of division and estrangement'. The narrator is moreover humbly tentative in her assessment of the characters' own feelings: the couple are 'more exquisitely happy, *perhaps*, in their re-union, than when it had been first projected' (2:11:261, my emphasis).

These lines contain the essence of Austen's romantic method, her formula: the more division, the more exquisite the happiness at reunion not only for the characters but for the reader as well. But division should not be understood simply as deferral, impediments thrown up by the plot; there is suspense that depends on a strict division in our knowledge of the heroine and of the hero. Austen develops a technique, most brilliantly displayed in this novel, of 'estranging' the reader and the heroine from the hero, refusing access to his thoughts and feelings, while bringing the heroine so close to us that we experience her every palpitation, her every flicker of thought. There is the occasional brief, discrete passage allowing a window onto the perspective of the hero or anti-hero. These generally appear at an early stage in the narrative, with the aim of putting in play a set of expectations for the reader which will heighten the tension of future interactions without removing guesswork: Mr Darcy bewitched 'by the beautiful expression' of Elizabeth's 'dark eyes' (*PP* 1:6:36) or Captain Wentworth's accession to free indirect discourse to express his continued fury at Anne, after eight years (*P* 1:7:66). Henry Crawford, at a similarly early stage in his relations with Fanny (*MP* 3:2:376–7), is permitted a page to establish from within the sincerity of his feelings for her. These isolated insights make the general state of unknowing all the more profound.

As a consequence, when the hero and heroine are at last brought together it has an electrical impact – 'the power of conversation', the means of conversing privately and uninhibitedly, should be understood in its fullest sense; a dramatic breaking down of this division of minds, and of the sexes. No previous novelist seems to have recognized this potential in the management of point of view. Austen may have come to it instinctively, taking her first steps in *Sense and Sensibility*, utilizing it flawlessly but perhaps a little heartlessly in *Pride and Prejudice*. It seems clear that by the time she completes *Persuasion* she is fully conscious of its capacity for creating pathos, in the way that she foregrounds the question of communication in the revised version of the ending, the one that was actually published, as well as in the scene of the reunion itself.

In analysing the final sections of *Persuasion* we have the unique benefit of being able to compare it with the rejected version that has survived in manuscript. In this earlier version Anne is tricked into entering the home in Bath of Admiral and Mrs Croft, who suspect and favour the attachment, and then left alone with Captain Wentworth, when the declaration takes place. He edges his chair towards hers 'and a hand taken and pressed; – and "Anne, my own dear Anne!" – bursting forth in the fullness of exquisite feeling, – and all Suspense & Indecision were over. – They were re-united' (*P* Appendix 1:318). A number of commentators have pointed out that the final version is something of an improvement, but Tony Tanner particularly interestingly so: 'The revised and substituted chapters do not merely prolong the suspense and defer narrative gratification through gratuitous complication of plot: they comprise an infinitely richer and more searching examination of the whole problem of communication between men and women.'[17]

'The whole problem of communication between men and women': a problem that involves the overcoming of the gendered division of spheres. Margaret Kirkham has described how in *Persuasion* Austen 'reaches a new point in her treatment of men and women as moral equals, no matter how different their lives and their opportunity of independent action'.[18] The problem is one of social convention, as critics have frequently pointed out. Ashley Tauchert has remarked: 'If Catherine, Elinor, Lizzy, Fanny, Emma, Anne – and even Marianne – could simply have *told* the men they fancied what was troubling them, or *asked* what they needed to know, we would not have Austen's work to worry about.'[19] This supports D. A. Miller's point about the productive potential of difficulty in general: communication problems, with all their accompaniments of deferral and suspense, are a fundamental condition of production for Austen's stories.

But we can go further: the communication problems in Austen are not only a social problem or a psychological problem – as in 'Women are from Venus, Men are from Mars'. They are the result, very specifically, of a decision about narrative structure, and of the radical gender asymmetry in the handling of point of view referred to above. A close enquiry into the role of the hero in Austen leads to the realization that all her narratives, to a greater or lesser extent, operate through a double plot: in the foreground a courtship plot focused on the heroine's consciousness; in the background a plot specific to the hero, of male vocation in the context of war, and the establishment of his independence and proper manliness – a plot which the heroine can only glimpse and speculate about. This feature has not gone unnoticed by the bevy of present-day writers parasitic on Austen; in 2007 not one, but two novels were published under the title *Mr Darcy's Diary*, promising to fill the gaps she considerately left. In the originals, for much of the time, the hero's motives and feelings are opaque and enigmatic for the heroine, and yet her fate depends on the resolution of the hero's plot. In other words, the gulf in communication between hero and heroine *is* the narrative. Here the social conventions dividing men and women are rendered as literary form. The consequence is an unparalleled excitement generated in the build-up to the declaration of love, and catharsis.

It is not surprising that modern romance fiction has taken up Austen's formula with reliable success. What is surprising is that the nature of the debt has been so little considered. Of the many works on the romance novel genre, the most useful in relation to Austen is one of the earliest, Tania Modleski's *Loving with a Vengeance: Mass-Produced Fantasies for Women* (1984). The instructions she cites, provided by the Harlequin press for potential writers, are particularly telling: 'Harlequins are well-plotted, strong romances with a happy ending. They are told from the heroine's point of view and in the third person.'[20] It follows from this formula, with its strictly circumscribed point of view, that the behaviour of the hero will constitute a 'basic enigma' of the story.[21] Modleski suggests that popular romance fictions 'train' women as readers of men through an identification with the heroine, enhanced by their knowledge of the literary conventions:

> In both Harlequins and Gothics, the heroines engage in the continual deciphering of the motives for the hero's behavior. The Harlequin heroine probes for the

secret underlying the masculine enigma, while the reader outwits the heroine in coming up with the 'correct' interpretation for the puzzling actions and attitudes of the man. In Gothics the heroine, in the classic paranoid manner, broods over the slightest fluctuation in the hero's emotional temperature or facial expression, quick to detect in these alterations possible threats to her very life.[22]

In this casting of the heroine as detective and the hero as enigma we can surely recognize Austen's originating handiwork. In both her work and most works of romance fiction, the disclosure of the hero's inner life – his feelings, motives and intentions towards the heroine – could be described as the ultimate goal of the narrative.[23] But there is obviously a world of difference as well – all the elements in Austen that exceed the bare mechanics of romance, including an element that is profoundly philosophical, and even spiritual. I now want to move on to look in some detail at Austen's second and final version of the climax of *Persuasion* in order to think about this transcendental aspect.

Austen and the dream of equality

Richard Simpson, widely regarded as the most perceptive of Austen's nineteenth-century commentators, drew attention to her treatment of 'intelligent love':

> Miss Austen seems to be saturated with the Platonic idea that the giving and receiving of knowledge, the active formation of another's character, or the more passive growth under another's guidance, is the purest and strongest foundation of love. *Pride and Prejudice*, *Emma*, and *Persuasion* all end with the heroes and heroines making comparisons of the intellectual and moral improvement which they have imparted to each other.[24]

There is a long tradition of connection between the claim of sexual equality and neo-platonism, reaching back to the Renaissance and still discoverable in Enlightenment feminism of the eighteenth and nineteenth centuries. In the Platonic model, union with the beloved involves a shedding of the limited perspective, defined by gender among other features, for the broader view, the higher reality, that embraces the perspective of the other. Love is not simply educational but transformative. And although the transformation is spiritual, it is not without its erotic charge.

A more recent commentator, Ashley Tauchert, has persuasively identified a distinctive vocabulary surrounding the conversational rapprochement between hero and heroine in all but one of the novels that borders on the sublime in its elevating mode. For instance, 'Emma's mind was most busy, and, with all the wonderful velocity of thought, had been able – and yet without losing a word – to catch and comprehend the exact truth of the whole' (3:13:469). There is a shift in understanding and in the sense of self which is founded on the revelation of the *whole truth*, and I would add that involves the incorporation of the hero's point of view which *could not previously have been known*, for all the reasons that collectively constitute the plot of the novel.[25] In what is perhaps Austen's first sketch of this trope, in *Northanger Abbey*, the narrator keeps a sceptical distance, referring to 'the extasies of another tête-à-tête' (2:15:253), but as we have seen in *Persuasion*, she gradually comes round to being moved herself, and allowing the reader to be moved.

Ekstasis, a stepping out of oneself into the perspective of another, is most literally enacted in the climactic scene of *Persuasion*. Here, the conversation between Captain Harville and Anne begins with the two of them taking up half-joking stances as combatants in the ancient rivalry between the sexes, the formulaic '*querelle des femmes*', then proceeds to mutual empathy regarding the different types of suffering endured respectively by men and by women, before ending with a touch, Harville 'putting his hand on her arm quite affectionately'. This physical convergence is followed by another, still more striking. Captain Wentworth, overhearing the conversation from a table in the room where friends and family are informally assembled, hurriedly writes a letter explaining his feeling for Anne, leaves the room, then returns leaving the letter on the desk for her. 'The revolution which one instant had made in Anne, was almost beyond expression'; and she moves and sits at the table (Austen is exact), '*sinking into the chair which he had occupied, succeeding to the very spot where he had leaned and written*' (2:11:257, my emphasis).

This climactic meeting point – found in the other novels in less reflective form – is surely the source of those feelings of exhilaration and relief from tension that can be derived from an Austen novel, in a way that the unwarrantable prediction of a happy future can never provide. In *Persuasion*, Austen doesn't even pretend to offer this: Anne must live with 'the dread of a future war', and we are told in the last lines, 'she must pay the tax of quick alarm' belonging to the naval profession (2:12:275). Bharat Tandon in *Jane Austen and the Morality of Conversation* draws attention to the 'sparseness of foretelling' in Austen in contrast to the endings of novelists such as Radcliffe, Burney and Dickens.[26] While these other authors make elaborate bequests for the future maintenance of their characters, there is very little in Austen of what the literary theorist Gérard Genette calls 'external prolepsis' – glimpses of the realm beyond the narrative.[27] The present, singular moment of union is a happiness that is unrepeatable for the characters, though fortunately it is infinitely repeatable for the avid reader.

It may be that Austen scholars too need to 'learn romance', to take the kinship between Austen and romance fiction seriously, and to acknowledge that the popular Austen industry can teach us something genuine about Austen. The final kiss in the screen adaptations may be only a poor metaphor, but it is a reminder of the importance of feeling in her work; or to use Austen's own term, of 'exquisite' happiness, something approaching ecstasy, the dissolution of self, the communion of self and other, the climactic 'power of conversation' and the pleasure of 'those explanations of what had ... preceded the present moment, which were so poignant and so ceaseless in interest', experienced most fully from the written page (2:11:261–2).

Austen is careful to commit to no illusions about the apparatus of marriage or other institutionalized forms of gender difference. The partnership of Admiral and Mrs Croft is the only affirmative portrait of married life, atypical because childless. But the utopian potential of civilized conversation between the sexes is something she can subscribe to, and the novels are the most brilliant realization in literature of this ideal. Recognition of the distinction is one way of understanding the co-existence in her work of critical irony regarding the conventions of gender on the one hand, and romantic transport on the other, without situating her either as a hypocrite or a conservative. Ultimately, I would argue, gender is for Austen a matter of ethics, and her formal innovations and stylistic genius are put to the service of the precious and difficult principle of equality.

NOTES

1. *Vindication of the Rights of Woman* (1792).
2. Clara Tuite, *Romantic Austen: Sexual Politics and the Literary Canon* (Cambridge University Press, 2002), pp. 16–21.
3. E. K. Sedgwick, 'Jane Austen and the Masturbating Girl', *Critical Inquiry*, 17 (1991), 817–37; D. A. Miller, *Narrative and Its Discontents: Problems of Closure in the Traditional Novel* (Princeton University Press, c.1981) and *Jane Austen and the Secret of Style* (Princeton University Press, 2003); Misty C. Anderson, '"The Different Sorts of Friendship": Desire in *Mansfield Park*', in Devoney Looser, ed., *Jane Austen and the Discourses of Feminism* (New York: St Martin's Press, 1995), pp. 167–83; Edmund Wilson, 'Talk about Jane Austen', in Ian Watt, ed., *Jane Austen: A Collection of Critical Essays* (Englewood Cliffs, NJ: Prentice-Hall, 1963), pp. 35–40; Marvin Mudrick, *Jane Austen: Irony as Defence and Discovery* (Princeton University Press, 1952), pp. 181–206; Tuite, *Romantic Austen*, pp. 32–9 and 172–8.
4. Claudia L. Johnson, *Equivocal Beings: Politics, Gender and Sentimentality in the 1790s: Wollstonecraft, Radcliffe, Burney, Austen* (University of Chicago Press, 1995), pp. 191–203; E. J. Clery, 'Austen and Masculinity', in Claudia L. Johnson and Clara Tuite, eds., *A Companion to Jane Austen* (Chichester: Wiley-Blackwell, 2009), pp. 332–42.
5. Judith Butler, *Gender Trouble: Feminism and the Subversion of Identity* (New York and London: Routledge, 1990), p. 140; emphasis original.

6. Claudia L. Johnson, Chapter 15 in this book, 'Austen Cults and Cultures', and 'The Divine Miss Jane: Jane Austen, Janeites, and the Discipline of Novel Studies', *boundary* 2, 23(3) (1996), 143–63; ed. Linda Troost and Sayre Greenfield, *Jane Austen in Hollywood* (Lexington, KT, University Press of Kentucky, 1998); ed. Deidre Lynch, *Janeites: Austen's Disciples and Devotees* (Princeton University Press, 2000); ed. Suzanne R. Pucci and James Thompson, *Jane Austen and Co.: Remaking the Past in Contemporary Culture* (Albany, NY: State University of New York Press, 2003); ed. Gina Macdonald and Andrew Macdonald, *Jane Austen on Screen* (Cambridge University Press, 2003).

7. D. W. Harding, 'Regulated Hatred: An Aspect of the Work of Jane Austen', *Scrutiny*, 8 (March 1940), 346–62.

8. Terry Castle, 'Sister-Sister', *London Review of Books*, 17(15) (3 August 1995), 3–6. Also Clara Tuite, 'Period Rush: Queer Austen, Anachronism and Critical Practice', in Beatrice Battaglia and Diego Saglia, eds., *Re-Drawing Austen: Picturesque Travels in Austenland* (Naples: Liguori Editore, 2004), pp. 305–22.

9. Pierre Bourdieu, 'The Forms of Capital', in John Richardson, ed., *Handbook of Theory and Research for the Sociology of Education* (Westport, CO: Greenwood Press, 1986), pp. 241–55. The works of Austen represent a form of 'objectified' cultural capital to which competing groups lay claim.

10. In addition to Tauchert and Tuite, see for instance Kathy Mezei, '"Who is Speaking Here?": Free Indirect Discourse, Gender and Narrative Authority in *Emma, Howards End*, and *Mrs. Dalloway*', in Kathy Mezei, ed., *Ambiguous Discourse: Feminist Narratology and British Women Writers* (Chapel Hill, NC: University of North Carolina Press, 1996), pp. 66–92; Frances Ferguson, 'Jane Austen, *Emma*, and the Impact of Form', *Modern Language Quarterly*, 61 (2000), 157–80; Daniel P. Gunn, 'Free Indirect Discourse and Narrative Authority in *Emma*', *Narrative* 12(1) (Jan. 2004), 35–54.

11. Tuite, *Romantic Austen*; Miller, *Narrative and Its Discontents*; also *Jane Austen and the Secret of Style* (Princeton University Press, 2003). Vivien Jones has argued that Austen's work displays a postfeminist 'structure of feeling' that underpins its association with present-day 'chick lit', chiefly manifested in its 'conservative' happy endings; 'Feminisms', in Claudia L. Johnson and Clara Tuite, eds., *A Companion to Jane Austen* (Malden, MA and Chichester: Wiley-Blackwell, 2009), pp. 282–91.

12. Miller, *Narrative and Its Discontents*, p. 5.

13. Miller, *Narrative and Its Discontents*, p. 8.

14. Roger Gard, *Jane Austen's Novels: The Art of Clarity* (New Haven, CT and London: Yale University Press, 1992), p. 23.

15. Barbara Everett's 'Jane Austen: Hard Romance', *London Review of Books*, 8 Feb. 1996, would seem to reach the same conclusion, but lacks analysis.

16. Editorial note in *Northanger Abbey, Lady Susan, The Watsons, and Sanditon*, ed. John Davie (1971; Oxford University Press, 1990), p. 382. Jill Heydt-Stevenson makes the case for extensive sexual innuendo in '"Slipping into the Ha-Ha": Bawdy Humor and the Body Politics in Jane Austen's Novels', *Nineteenth-Century Literature*, 55(3) (Dec. 2000), 309–39, but see Brian Southam's reservations in *Jane Austen and the Navy* (London: Hambledon and London Ltd, 2000), pp. 189–92.

17. Tony Tanner, *Jane Austen* (Cambridge, MA: Harvard University Press, 1986), p. 237.

18. Margaret Kirkham, *Jane Austen, Feminism and Fiction* (Brighton and New York: Harvester Press and Barnes and Noble, 1983), p. 146.
19. Ashley Tauchert, *Romancing Jane Austen: Narrative, Realism and the Possibility of a Happy Ending* (Basingstoke: Palgrave Macmillan, 2005), pp. 131–2.
20. Tania Modleski, *Loving with a Vengeance: Mass-Produced Fantasies for Women* (London and New York: Routledge, 1984), pp. 35–6.
21. Modleski, *Loving with a Vengeance*, p. 38.
22. Modleski, *Loving with a Vengeance*, p. 34.
23. Ellen R. Belton, 'Mystery without Murder: The Detective Plot of Jane Austen', *Nineteenth-Century Literature* 43(1) (June 1988), 42–59, discusses the device in terms of authorial reflexivity, rather than as a dramatization of gendered points of view.
24. *North British Review*, 52 (April 1870), 129–52; repr. Brian Southam, ed., *Jane Austen: The Critical Heritage*, vol. 1 (London: Routledge & Kegan Paul, 1968), p. 244.
25. Tauchert, *Romancing Jane Austen*, pp. 16–17. Here I am revising Tauchert's suggestion that 'feminine enlightenment' revolves on 'crisis of judgement'; previous to the act of full communication between hero and heroine, her judgement is necessarily defective because based on incomplete evidence.
26. Bharat Tandon, *Jane Austen and the Morality of Conversation* (London: Anthem Press, 2003), p. 171.
27. Gérard Genette, *Narrative Discourse: An Essay in Method*, trans. Jane E. Lewin (Ithaca, NY: Cornell University Press, 1980), pp. 68–70.

12

GILLIAN RUSSELL

Sociability

The primary definition of sociability in the *Oxford English Dictionary* is 'the character or quality of being sociable, friendly disposition or intercourse'. Jane Austen's fiction represents one of the most sophisticated analyses we have of the elusive 'character or quality' of sociable human interaction – its joys as well as its pains. Yet the importance of this topic in her work, indeed how it is constitutive of her greatest achievement, has rarely been foregrounded in Austen studies. The tendency has been to treat the many references to social activity in the novels, such as balls, visits, walks, shopping, concerts or theatricals, as part of the customs or pastimes of the age which the fiction merely reflects rather than deliberately analyses.

This approach is apparent in R. W. Chapman's seminal edition with appendices on customs such as dancing, a practice of annotation which continues in some editions of the novels today. It is also evident in the numerous book and website guides to Austen's regency world which detail the niceties of Georgian social etiquette. The sense of the sociable rituals of Austen's fiction as reflecting a world which we in the twenty-first century have lost and wistfully hanker for is crucial to explorations of the contemporary cult of Austen in *The Jane Austen Book Club* or the television drama *Lost in Austen*. It manifests itself most strikingly in the current fashion for Austen regency balls, in which, like British and US civil war re-enactments, men and women dance out fantasies of 'becoming Jane' or Mr Darcy. Such occasions, taking place across the world, from Cheltenham to Canberra, register a nostalgic alienation from Jane's world and its irrevocable pastness. By using actual sociability as a mode of Austen appreciation, the twenty-first-century regency ball highlights a key preoccupation of her fiction: the importance of sociability as a performative event, that is, what possibilities or dreams are realized (or, equally, are defeated or fail) by men and women meeting together in a particular place and time.

The 'dream' or ideology of sociability in Austen's fiction had a long-standing history in the cultural and political meanings of association in eighteenth-century Britain – what is referred to as the transformation of the public sphere. Broadly speaking, this transformation describes how, from the late seventeenth century, the emerging upper middle and professional classes created political legitimacy for themselves as the embodiment of universalized public opinion through the development of forums of discussion such as the coffee house and through the medium of print, specifically the newspaper, the periodical press and the novel itself. Considering Austen in the light of this development suggests a new dimension to the importance of sociability in her fiction and to the historical significance of her work as a whole, as well as illuminating how and why Austen is being configured, sociably, in culture today. Focusing on Austen's indebtedness to Frances Burney as a pioneer in the novelization of sociability and on 'The Watsons', a manuscript fragment long considered as minor, this chapter argues that balls and assemblies are not merely settings for the development of plot and character but are historical phenomena subject to artistic exploration in their own right.

Eighteenth-century Britain, as historians have emphasized, is notable for its 'urban renaissance', exemplified by the rise of London to become the pre-eminent city in the western world by 1800 and the development of the provincial town as one of the distinctive achievements of the era.[1] The growth in commerce and industrialization from the late seventeenth-century onwards stimulated the polite leisure economy which in turn galvanized trade by providing a market for goods and services and, most importantly, venues for the circulation of people, thereby sustaining the networks – political, familial and professional – that formed the essential infrastructure of Georgian society. This polite leisure economy took the form of buildings and sites dedicated to cultural enterprise, such as theatres, concert and assembly rooms, circulating libraries and pleasure gardens. Though the activities taking place in these venues might vary, they all shared a commitment to the pursuit of sociability. It was widely believed that social interaction between men and women and to a certain degree between the classes, specifically the elite and the upper-middling orders, was morally and socially beneficial, ameliorating the effects of division and conflict and advancing the ideals of progress. Hence the Scottish philosopher David Hume argued that the meeting of men and women 'in an easy and sociable manner' led inevitably to 'an increase in humanity' from the 'very habit of conversing together, and contributing to each other's pleasure and entertainment'.[2]

Within such valorization of sociability, the role of women was crucial, as exemplars and facilitators of harmony and refinement, who could temper the excesses of men. Polite sociability, as promoted by moral philosophy and practised in the new assemblies, theatres and pleasure gardens across the country, was fundamentally heterosocial, both ideologically and practically: it was promoted as improving or refining the dangers of excessive male conviviality such as drunkenness, sexual immorality and the eruption into incendiary disagreement that could have dangerous political consequences. Polite sociability throughout this period was therefore always shadowed by fear of its other – of social discordance rather than harmony, of revulsion at one's companions, rather than entertainment.

The ideology of sociability offered women a visibility and legitimacy in the public sphere which they exploited to the full. As Amanda Vickery has shown, genteel Georgian women were indefatigable consumers of all kinds of public entertainment in London and the provinces, challenging the long-established feminist historiography which argues for the increasing sequestration of women in the domestic sphere.[3] Austen was born in a decade, the 1770s, which witnessed, according to the historian Paul Langford, a 'full-blown revolution' for women, who were exerting themselves in the spheres of poetry, history, painting, novels and playwriting, music and performance.[4] The prominence of figures such as Catherine Macaulay in history and Angelica Kauffman in painting was accentuated by the development of sites of sociability in London such as the Assembly Rooms of Carlisle House in Soho and the Pantheon in Oxford Street. The latter were temples of fashion in which women literally took centre stage in the form of the elaborate hairstyle, or high head, the towering headdress signifying the enormity or threat of a possible dominance of the public sphere which the new leisure economy and print culture were according to women.[5] (In *Northanger Abbey* the fashion-obsessed Mrs Allen seeks advice from Catherine Morland as to the state of her 'head' as they enter the Assembly Rooms in Bath, a sign of Mrs Allen's affiliation with her sociable sisters of the 1770s.)

The heady days of the 1770s achieve their most sophisticated fictional representation in Frances Burney's highly successful debut, *Evelina* (1778). Subtitled *The History of a Young Lady's Entrance into the World*, Burney's novel represents the transformation of London into the leisure capital of the western world as a prospect of wonder, as well as of apprehension. The sociable occasion was a long-standing narrative device and indeed structuring topos in eighteenth-century fiction, as Terry Castle showed in her magisterial account of the masquerade.[6] Never before, however, had the novel made sociability its subject in such a comprehensive and, moreover, topically realistic way. *Evelina* deals not only with long-established venues of public entertainment such as the Drury Lane and Haymarket theatres but also refers to recently established sites such as the Pantheon and Cox's Museum, an exhibition of automata opened in 1771. The sense of both anticipation and anxiety surrounding these shows of London is dramatized in Burney's detailed descriptions of Evelina getting to and from particular public places.

Her visit to the Italian opera is nearly disastrous for her reputation when her desire to escape from the company of her Branghton relatives leads her to accept the dubious protection of Sir Clement Willoughby, with whom she is seen in the liminal space of the gallery stairs by Evelina's preferred object, Lord Orville. Burney exploits the association of areas such as theatre lobbies with prostitution to suggest the risk entailed for women in seeking to assert their desires. A visit to the pleasure gardens at Vauxhall is similarly fraught with danger when Evelina and the Branghton girls endure a terrifying confrontation with a group of men in one of the gardens' 'dark walks'.

In both episodes and throughout the novel Burney exploits her readers' familiarity with actual venues of sociability in London to enhance the reality effect of her fiction. This innovation has a number of ground-breaking implications. *Evelina* demystifies the ideology of polite sociability with its valorization of women's role in social life as essentially ameliorative. By highlighting the material conditions of class and gender, symbolized by actual places in the novel, Burney sets limits on female participation in the public sphere. The novel suggests that the cultural 'revolution' of the 1770s was only a partial one: commercialized public culture remained profoundly masculinist and in some cases physically dangerous for women. However, by recasting the marvellous elements of traditional romance in terms of the heterosocial modern romance of the ballroom, Burney was able to develop the novel as a vehicle for the transformative potential of sociability. Evelina's initial encounter with Lord Orville at a private assembly fictionalizes as modern romance eighteenth-century culture's investment in sociability as productive of social and personal transformation, thus making the ballroom a paradigmatic site of western fiction, what Mikhail Bakhtin termed a chronotope.[7] Moreover, by representing sociability in such a specific materialized way, *Evelina* established the novel as a kind of sociable space in its own right, a place where readers could imagine themselves participating in a vicarious, virtual sociability through identification with the characters or through a consciousness of their fellows engaged in reading as a collective and companionable activity.

The expansion of the boundaries of the public represented by such imaginative access made the novel potentially the most revolutionary product of the commercialization of culture in the eighteenth century. The novel also enabled women writers such as Burney to negotiate the stigma ascribed to women's active role in the public sphere in the 1770s: imaginative literature was a means of dematerializing themselves from 'the world' while at the same time reconstituting those publics and their own role as authors in a potentially more expansive and far-reaching way.

Jane Austen was profoundly indebted to Burney's innovations in *Evelina*, both in the ways she had made practical sociability a legitimate subject for novelistic romance and for showing how the novel itself could be sociable. If Burney's speciality is the experience of giving oneself over to the metropolitan scene, a thrill which she described as 'to Londonize', then Austen's achievement lies in her exploration of the more 'quiet' sociability of the English provinces, especially the counties in the vicinity of London.[8] Her fiction deals with the intersections between the new cultural opportunities, particularly for women, of the Georgian provincial town, with its theatres, assemblies, shops and circulating libraries, and sociability as practised in the home. The latter, ranging from activities such as dinners, visits, card games, music-making and reading, to more elaborate events such as balls or private theatricals, could be internally focused, as in the cultural activities of the Dashwood women at Barton cottage or the Bingley–Darcy party at Netherfield. More commonly, such sociability involved people outside the immediate family circle and was a means for the Georgian family to sustain and advance its 'place' in the wider society. In connecting the sociability of the home with the polite leisure economy of the provincial town, linked ultimately to the powerhouse of London, Austen explores the new networked culture of late Georgian Britain as lived social experience. She is interested, above all, in sociability as performative, what it creates or destroys, and in that sense her fiction engages directly and deeply with the historical forces that were reshaping her society.

One manifestation of this is the changing meanings of London as a site of sociability in Austen's fiction. The London of *Sense and Sensibility*, for example, is very different to that of Burney's *Evelina*, the visit of Elinor and Marianne Dashwood to the capital being a disappointment to all concerned. Rather than taking in the sights and entertainments as excited initiates, the Dashwoods are compelled to accompany Mrs Jennings on her round of visits to old friends or maintain their Devonshire connections by paying a call on the Middletons while their own 'blood' relatives, in the form of Mr and Mrs John Dashwood, only reluctantly acknowledge them. Their social horizons therefore seem as limited as they were in the country. The one possibility of an *Evelina* experience, the private ball that the sisters attend as guests of Lady Middleton, is the antithesis of the similar kind of event at which Burney's heroine first encounters Lord Orville. Insofar as Willoughby's avoidance of Marianne and the public humiliation which she endures marks the end of love, not its beginning, the ball represents the failure of the romance of sociability, a fact which Austen signals in her description of the sisters' arrival at the party:

> as soon as the string of carriages before them would allow, [they] alighted, ascended the stairs, heard their names announced from one landing-place to

another in an audible voice, and entered the room splendidly lit up, quite full of
company, and insufferably hot. When they had paid their tribute of politeness
by curtseying to the lady of the house, they were permitted to mingle in the
croud, and take their share of the heat and inconvenience, to which their arrival
must necessarily add. (SS 2:6:199–200)

The adventure of eighteenth-century sociability – the liminal act in crossing
a threshold, both real and symbolic, with the prospect of losing or finding
oneself in the company of others – is here rendered as a hollow ritual, which
the Dashwood girls endure as defeated victims of the imperious code of
politeness, to which they must pay necessary 'tribute'. They are supernumer-
aries in an agglomeration of individuals, not proper participants in a vital
social body. What was spontaneous, comedic and inviting about London
sociability in *Evelina*, in spite or because of its erotic danger, becomes dead-
ening or at least unattainable in *Sense and Sensibility*.

In general, no romance in Austen's fiction has its beginnings in a metropolitan social encounter. Rather, the salons of London are places where love
dies. In *Mansfield Park*, for example, it is the temptations of Mrs Fraser's
party which detain Henry Crawford in London, precipitating his affair
with Maria Rushworth and the consequent loss of Fanny Price. Similarly,
Edmund Bertram ascribes the 'spoiling' of Mary Crawford to her return
to the 'fashionable world' of her London woman friends (*MP* 3:13:489).
In nominating women such as Maria Rushworth, Mrs Fraser, Lady
Stornoway, Mary Crawford and the unnamed 'lady of the house' of the
ball in *Sense and Sensibility* as in control of such occasions, Austen is
reflecting the importance of sociability to elite women of this period as one
of the ways they could exert power and influence. The commercialization of
culture in the 1770s and after amplified the significance of the hostess or the
lady patroness as emblematic of fashion's potentially far-reaching feminization of the public sphere. Mary Crawford and the female homosociality
of fashionable London, which seems her natural domain, complicate the
resolution of *Mansfield Park* because, however vitiated, they signify an
alternative to the inevitable destiny for woman as wife and mother. Like
that of another woman of fashion, Lady Susan, in Austen's unpublished
epistolary novel, Mary Crawford's indomitable sociability is therefore a
kind of political act, a reminder of the potential of the 'fashionable world'
as a sphere in which women could realize a form of autonomy. In the
context of regency Britain, however, *Mansfield Park* suggests that the possibility of such autonomy, corrupted by fashion itself, was receding from
British culture much in the same way that Mary Crawford tantalizingly
withdraws from the gaze of Edmund Bertram and the disdain of the antisociable Fanny.

Another version of the 'fashionable world' in Austen's fiction is of course Bath. Insofar as this celebrated resort town pioneered many of the institutions and social practices later adapted by the metropolis – in particular the assembly – Bath suggests that eighteenth-century sociability was fundamentally a product of the provincial town (and vice versa). Bath was the model par excellence of a built environment being dedicated to the concentrated social interaction of a particular community: as an entertainment zone, consisting of the pump and assembly rooms, theatre and concert rooms, bookshops and circulating libraries, even the churches, the city had an economy of scale which was impossible for London to replicate, lending an intimacy as well as an intensity to its significance as a melting pot for the British elite, gentry and middling orders. In that sense Bath, more so than London, was a laboratory of Georgian sociability, the true testing ground of the potential of polite social intercourse to produce, in Hume's terms, 'an increase in humanity'. The significance of Bath sociability was a constant of Austen's career, a topic to which she returned in *Northanger Abbey* and which forms the subject of her last major work, *Persuasion*.

Northanger Abbey's Catherine Morland is a fictional daughter of Evelina, her adventures in Bath having the same topical immediacy and realism as Burney's evocation of 1770s London. As in *Evelina*, Austen places great emphasis on becoming a woman as the corporeal and material experience of socialization – the crossing of an actual threshold into the polite 'world'. Virtually the first thing that Catherine Morland does in Bath is to go to the Assembly Rooms in the company of her chaperone Mrs Allen. Austen describes how the women gingerly navigate the 'throng of men by the door', Catherine linking her arm tightly to Mrs Allen's to avoid being 'torn asunder by any common effort of a struggling assembly' before being impelled to the 'top of the room' where they can see nothing but the nodding high feathers of the ladies in the crowd. Like flotsam, the two women are carried away by the force of a collective socializing humanity, an experience which is dismaying but also exhilarating. On reaching 'the passage behind the highest bench' – the spatial geography of the rooms is precisely delineated – Catherine Morland is able to catch her breath and contemplate the view: 'It was a splendid sight, and she began, for the first time that evening, to *feel herself* at a ball' (*NA* 1:2:13, my emphasis). In contrast to the oppression and exhaustion of the ball in *Sense and Sensibility*, the crush of bodies in the Bath Upper Rooms is invigorating, symbolizing the possibility of Catherine's realizing her identity or 'self' through sociability.

What happens of course is that at another assembly in the Lower Rooms she is introduced 'by the master of ceremonies' to the hero Henry Tilney. The role of the Bath master of ceremonies such as Beau Nash or James King, the historical figure to whom Tilney alludes in the novel (1:3:19), was to regulate the flow of the evening's entertainment and ensure that decorum and social precedence were properly observed: he also acted as a social facilitator and networker by introducing strangers to Bath. The fact that the master of ceremonies had to be invented was a sign that the polite leisure economy was rewriting the ground rules of the Georgian social order. Men such as James King personified the capacity of the commercialization of culture to loosen or dissolve the hierarchies of rank or the hold on individuals of family and connection by bringing together men and women who might otherwise never have met. The circumstance of Henry's taking the hand of Catherine that is offered to him by James King therefore represents the romance of ballroom sociability in its most historically specific and, because 'real', most potent form.

In the second part of the novel the open, commercialized sociability of Bath, in which the parental figures of the Allens and Mrs Thorpe pay a minimal supervisory role, gives way to the constraining regime of General Tilney at Northanger Abbey. There is an implicit contrast between General Tilney's male homosocial networks – the world of the Bath billiard room, the Bedford coffee house or the theatre lobby where John Thorpe gossips with the general – and feminized spaces such as the Pump room where a different mode of surveillance prevails, the disinterested one of the master of ceremonies which allows characters such as Isabella Thorpe to assume their own spectatorial autonomy. 'This is my favourite place', says Isabella to Catherine 'as they sat down on a bench between the doors, which commanded a tolerable view of every body entering at either, "it is so out of the way"' (2:3:145).

The different modes of gendered homosociality represented by the worlds of Bath and Northanger are also reflected in what, how and where the characters read. General Tilney's pamphlets which he pores over alone late into the night and which depend for their circulation on the sociable infrastructure of forums such as the Bedford coffee house, are contrasted with the Gothic novels that are the object of a more open sociable intercourse between Catherine and Isabella in the Pump room. The second half of *Northanger Abbey* can therefore be said to scrutinize the ideals of a commercialized and feminized Enlightenment sociability through the lens of the profound challenge to those ideals in the aftermath of the French Revolution – the political crisis that the General's 'stupid pamphlets' were debating. In the figure of the consumerist General Tilney, who is up to date with styles in crockery and innovations such as the Rumford stove, Austen indicates the capacity of the ruling order to adapt the commercialization of culture in the construction of a veneer of modernity. Such a veneer corrupts a socially responsible paternalism as well as failing to temper power's inherent bias towards self-interest – in other words, its antisociability.

The alternative to General Tilney, the 'hope' of sociability generated by the encounter in the Lower Rooms, is his son Henry. Both men are active in the social worlds of Bath and Northanger but in radically different ways: General Tilney's Bath consists of the shadowy male homosocial spaces and networks that serve his self-aggrandizement, whereas Henry makes himself visible in the mixed-sex domains of the theatre box or under the benign light of the chandeliers of the Assembly Room. He allows Mr King to introduce him to a stranger, Catherine Morland, which is in line with his later expression of confidence in the capacity of 'social and literary intercourse' to 'lay every thing open', sustained by the innovations in transport and print culture – 'roads and newspapers' – that had made the polite leisure economy possible in the first place (NA 2:9:203). The openness to which Henry is committed has its locus in the Bath ballroom, making him exemplary of the capacity of sociability to 'increase humanity'. This is affirmed by the eventual marriage of Henry to Catherine Morland, but the counter-example of the General is a reminder of the capacity of the commercialization of culture to effect a superficial make-over of power, to close doors, rather than open them.

The kind of sociability practised in Bath was replicated, if often on a much more modest scale, throughout the British Isles and its empire. A largely unnoticed aspect of Jane Austen's fiction is how it marks the importance of the country assembly in provincial life, and indeed, commemorates its passing. 'The supreme arena of polite leisure', according to Amanda Vickery, the assembly room ranged in scale and opulence from the imposing neo-classical rooms at York, designed by the aristocrat and architect Richard Boyle, Third Earl of Burlington, to more modest accommodation, often connected with inns, such as the Angel at Basingstoke, at which Austen attended balls on a number of occasions.[9] Organized on a subscription basis and regulated by masters of ceremonies and ladies designated as 'queens' of the occasion, the assembly was comparatively open insofar as it offered an opportunity for the emerging elites of towns to mix with each other and with the neighbouring gentry and aristocracy, if the latter condescended to patronize these occasions. Assemblies were important in the entertaining, and presumably vetting, of genteel 'strangers', such as attendees of local assizes or races. As venues in which locally based militia officers, often from other parts of the country, could circulate with the civilian elite, assemblies were also vital to the sociability that sustained Georgian military culture and hence the nation's war effort. Most important, however, was the provincial assembly's character as primarily a venue for mixed-sex sociability, distinct from local clubs or societies which were exclusively male, or from private sociability within the home determined by the roles of men and women within the family. The provincial assembly therefore offered an opportunity for women in particular to perform a different kind of social identity. As Helen Berry notes in her account of the Assembly Rooms in Newcastle, for this and other reasons there was a certain 'bravado' to such enterprises: they were acts of faith in the enduring value of polite sociability in the face of fluctuating economic fortunes or, as Austen suggests, the tenuousness of communal solidarity in the face of the realities of gender, class and human nature.[10]

The idea of the provincial assembly as epitomizing something brave is apparent in the manuscript fragment 'The Watsons', which was probably written between 1803–5, after Austen left Steventon. The fragment consists largely of an account of an assembly at the White Hart Inn in the town of D., probably Dorking in Surrey, and begins with the journey of two genteelly 'poor' sisters, Emma and Elizabeth Watson, from their small village to the town where Emma is to make preparations for the evening. Emma Watson has been forced to return to her family after the death of her uncle who has brought her up, and the assembly represents her 'first public appearance' in the neighbourhood. When Miss Osborne, the sister of the local magnate Lord Osborne, fails to fulfil her promise to dance with a 10-year-old boy, Emma steps into the breach and dances with him instead, a gesture which gains the attention of all the gentlemen in the room. Emma later overhears Lord Osborne, who is attending the ball for political expediency, 'to please the Borough', commenting favourably to another man on her appearance. The narrative then deals with the private sociability that follows in the wake of the assembly in the form of visits to the Watson household, before it breaks off with Emma refusing to accompany her brother and sister-in-law to their home in Croydon, in spite of their assurances of its being a place with numerous balls and parties where 'there is always something lively going on'.

The last comment highlights the focus of 'The Watsons' on the viability of polite sociability in the world beyond London or provincial centres such as Bath. Croydon is a kind of Mecca for D., which is a small town with only one notable family, the Edwardses, and a banker, Mr Tomlinson, who has a newly erected house with a shrubbery on the outskirts. The journey of the Watson sisters is a literal as well as symbolic crossing of gradations of civility, as they rock along the unpaved 'dirty' lanes, through the turnpike gate, that epitome of Georgian modernity, before they enter the 'pitching of the town'. The latter refers to the cobblestones of D.'s streets but also suggests an idea of the women pitching or cresting the wave of urban social energy, however small-scale and insignificant D. might actually be. Austen gives a detailed account of the para-sociability of an assembly, the 'happy occupation, the first bliss' of the preparation for the ball, and the exhilaration of being 'transported from the quiet warmth of a snug parlour, to the bustle, noise and draughts of air in the broad entrance-passage' (*LM* 'W' 93) that leads ultimately to the ballroom. The participants are sucked into a sociability that while lacking the glamour of Bath and London – only 'the first scrape of one violin' can be heard as the ladies mount the staircase to the assembly room – nonetheless does not fail to live up to 'blissful' expectation: Emma's 'feelings perfectly coincided with the re-iterated observations of others, that it was excellent ball' (*LM* 'W' 96).

'The Watsons' is significant in Austen's œuvre in two main ways. First, it reconfigures the idea of the ball as a romance of sociability by its emphasis on woman meets boy rather than on girl meets man. By assuming the male prerogative in asking the 10-year-old Charles Blake to dance, Emma uses the comparative openness of the assembly to act outside the conventions that determine male and female social behaviour, much in the same way as the event gives her access to 'private' conversation between men that would normally be excluded from her. The dance with Charles Blake signals Emma's marginal status in the marriage market, to which Miss Osborne gives precedence by rejecting the child in favour of Colonel Beresford. Paradoxically it is this very declaration of her ineligibility for what is supposed to be the preferred destiny for women which makes Emma interesting to the gentlemen in the room. The 'public appearance' which the assembly represents for Emma Watson is therefore an entry into a different kind of public from that of Catherine Morland's Bath. The 'bliss' of the event relates to the possibility of a viable social identity for women outside the categories of marriage or family, or the deforming influence of metropolitan fashion (though Cassandra Austen was convinced that Jane in her unrealized plans for 'The Watsons' had intended Emma to find a suitable marital partner). Emma Watson's dance with Charles is, as his mother acknowledges, an act of pure 'kindness': it represents Austen's exploration of the possibility of that Enlightenment ideal, a disinterested sociability that might 'increase humanity'.

'The Watsons' is also significant formally in that it shows Austen trying to capture the liveness of sociability in its material and temporal specificity, as in the following description of the arrival of Emma and her friends at the assembly:

> The party passed on – Mrs. Edwards's satin gown swept along the clean floor of the ball-room, to the fireplace at the upper end, where one party only were formally seated, while three or four officers were lounging together, passing in and out from the adjoining card-room. (*LM* 'W' 94)

The floor across which Mrs Edwards' gown regally passes is 'clean' in readiness for the dancing feet which will later raise the dust that Austen claimed had injured her eyes at a ball she had attended, an example of her own familiarity with the assembly as an intensely corporeal/material experience.[11] Like the nonchalance of the officers reluctant to commit themselves to formality, the implied swish of moving satin over a clean wooden floor conveys the full emptiness or static of an event just before it happens.

Writing about sociability was therefore instrumental, I would argue, in Austen's development of what Kathryn Sutherland calls the 'accomplished minimalism' that characterizes her mature style; it was the bridge between the 'untransformed banalities' of the letters and the 'precious trivia' of the novels.[12] But in a sense writing about sociability took Austen too far in that the details of the D. assembly become more important than the marriage plot, more important than following Emma Watson through to the inevitable destinies of marriage and motherhood. The pure 'kindness' of the dance with Charles Blake, and Austen's sensitive evocation of the fragile bravery of the sociality of the provincial nobodies, had eclipsed such necessities. 'The Watsons' could only 'be' the occasion of the assembly on a dark October night in a small town in rural England – no other story was possible.

As Joseph Wiesenfarth has noted, 'The Watsons' is the 'pretext' of much of Austen's later fiction.[13] The D. assembly is reconfigured as the ball at Meryton which opens *Pride and Prejudice* and which also features the heroine overhearing a conversation between men concerning her. On this occasion, however, the view of the gentleman is uncomplimentary, Darcy pointedly catching Elizabeth Bennet's eye as he makes his famous put-down of 'She is tolerable; but not handsome enough to tempt *me*' (*PP* 1:3:12). Lord Osborne's reluctant attendance at the D. assembly is reworked in *Pride and Prejudice*, with less political specificity, in the form of Darcy's aloofness at the Meryton ball. As a visitor with no stake in property in the area, Darcy is emphatically a stranger to the town, making his behaviour more profoundly antisociable in that he does not even have the excuse of local status. The onus is on him as a gentleman outsider to exhibit the highest standards of politeness in such a context and he fails to perform the required role. In *Pride and Prejudice* the idea of the assembly as representing the possibility of social connectedness – a contact zone between the elite and the middling orders, or between the dominance of men and the dependency of women – seems less realizable than is the case in 'The Watsons' or *Northanger Abbey*. The stranger Darcy resists assimilation, while the Meryton community, as represented by its collective pronouncements on his and Bingley's behaviour, seems incapable of a proper understanding or appreciation of outsiders. It is noteworthy that in *Pride and Prejudice* there is no return to the kind of public space represented by the Meryton assembly in the rest of the novel: Elizabeth and Darcy get to know each other through the private and more exclusive sociability of house parties and the ball at Netherfield and later the visit to Pemberley.

This development reflects on the one hand an emphasis on Darcy's anti-sociability as a more trustworthy sign of gentlemanly virtue than the specious sociability of a Wickham. On the other, it signals an increasing scepticism about the viability of open, commercialized sociability as a means of promoting meaningful social intercourse and cohesion. This is apparent in Darcy's curt response to Sir William Lucas' commendation of dancing as 'one of the first refinements of polished societies': 'Every savage can dance' (*PP* 1:6:28). The comment is a repudiation of Sir William himself as someone whose social advancement has been based on the cultivation of politeness. It also asserts the impossibility of transcending or disguising the 'natural' fact of difference through social performance, a 'truth' which Darcy's ultimate acknowledgement of his incivility to Elizabeth at the Meryton assembly does not fundamentally alter.

The 'DNA' of 'The Watsons' is also discernible in *Emma*. Emma Watson's act of kindness in dancing with Charles Blake is echoed in the way that Knightley comes to the rescue of Harriet Smith at the Crown Inn ball, after Mr Elton pointedly refuses to partner her. As in 'The Watsons', Knightley's gesture is an act of benevolence, transcending the conventional meanings of dancing as a form of courtship, although Harriet is unable to recognize this. The fact that this incident takes place at a ball in the more public venue of the Crown Inn, as opposed to Randalls or Hartfield, is also significant. Like D. in 'The Watsons', the Highbury of *Emma* is a small-scale, quietly prosperous county town on the margins between London – only 16 miles away – and the rural hinterland beyond, the kind of place in which the polite assembly had thrived in the previous century. Unlike the White Hart Inn of 'The Watsons', however, the ballroom of the Crown Inn is no longer dedicated to dancing: 'its brilliant days had long passed away', and the large room which had been added to the 'inconsiderable' original inn is now occupied by a gentleman's whist club, a return to the male homosociality which the assembly had temporarily supplanted. So small is this gathering that there is no risk of the candles of the whist club exposing the 'dreadfully dirty' wallpaper and 'forlorn' wainscoting which dismay Mrs Weston. Significantly Mr Woodhouse, the head of one of the two leading families of Highbury, 'had never been in the room at the Crown in his life', nor is he personally familiar with the landlord, a sign of his detachment from the wider community and the obligations of his social position. The revival of dancing in the assembly room at the Crown, instigated by the restless Frank Churchill, is therefore an attempt to recover something that has been lost from Highbury and which is perhaps irrecoverable.

William Galperin interprets Frank's scheme as 'nostalgia' for a time when 'people are perhaps not as separated on the basis of either class or wealth or even gender'.[14] The context of Austen's exploration of a similar assembly in 'The Watsons' suggests a specific historical dimension to that nostalgia: what was possible in the early 1800s was becoming tenuous a decade later. *Emma* therefore marks the beginning of the end of the assembly, 'one of the most striking features in our social life', according to one Victorian commentator who dated its 'rapid decline' to precisely this period.[15] If a distinctive feature of modern culture is an awareness of the ephemerality of its institutions, then Austen's fiction represents a formative example of this awareness in its focus on the assembly. The vacant room in the Crown Inn into which Frank Churchill peers wistfully – he 'stopt for several minutes at the two superior sashed windows which were open, to look in and contemplate its capabilities, and lament that its original purpose should have ceased' (*E* 2:6:213) – is a precursor of other material traces of sociable entertainment, such as the cinema, which have left their mark on the urban landscape and in the modern imaginary.

The alternative to the assembly in the form of the private sociability of a more narrowly constituted social world is also shown to be deficient in *Emma*. Even before Emma makes her unkind remarks to Miss Bates the Box Hill outing is a failure of sociability: there is 'a want of union, which could not be got over. They separated too much into parties' (*E* 3:7:399). The sense of an increased stratification and fragmentation in the regency social order, of a fundamental 'want of union' also informs Austen's return to the subject of Bath in *Persuasion*. In this last completed fiction the centrality of the assembly room to the idea of Bath as a social laboratory or melting pot is diminished. The fashionable elite, in the form of Sir Walter Elliot and his daughter Elizabeth, has withdrawn from such intercourse into the 'elegant stupidity' of private parties. When given the choice to go to the theatre with the Musgroves or accompany her father and sister to the Dalrymples, Anne Elliot expresses a desire for the former, a declaration, designed for Wentworth's benefit, which is an implicit rejection of the narcissistic society of rank in favour of the more inclusive public of the playhouse. Significantly too, Anne makes this declaration in the hotel where the Musgroves are staying, i.e. in a place of commercialized social traffic. *Persuasion* suggests that the withdrawal from active social responsibility by the class represented by the Elliots meant that spaces such as the assembly room or the theatre could no longer function in the way they had in *Northanger Abbey* or indeed in Burney's *Evelina*. Instead the romance of the ballroom is relocated in *Persuasion* to more explicitly commercial spaces such as Molland's confectioner's shop where Anne Elliot is able to use the comparative autonomy and anonymity of the sociability of consumption to stage an encounter with Wentworth. Her movement between the seat in the shop and the outer door, enacting an impulse to see if Wentworth is visible that she pleasurably half acknowledges, is as much a dance as any cotillion or minuet performed between Catherine Morland and Henry Tilney. This exteriorized and more socially expansive sociability is also apparent in Lady Russell's immersion in the 'winter pleasures' of Bath as she enters the town 'amidst the dash of other carriages, the heavy rumble of carts and drays, the bawling of newsmen, muffin-men and milkmen' (*P* 2:2:146).

The romance of a unified public sphere signified by the innovations in public culture in the 1770s and 1780s and exemplified hitherto by Austen's fascination with the assembly room is superseded in *Persuasion* by recognition of the necessity, and inescapability of, multiple, diverse publics. This is highlighted by Austen's account of the conversation marking Anne and Wentworth's 're-union' which takes place in the gravel-walk in Bath: they walk and talk heedless of the company of 'sauntering politicians, bustling house-keepers, flirting girls ... nursery-maids and children' (*P* 2:11:261–2). The public of the gravel-walk, like that of the muffin-men that pass by Lady Russell's carriage, is heedless of Anne and Wentworth too. 'Society' is configured here as an unconscious sense of communality in which the different classes and men and women can saunter together in blissful ignorance of each other's demands, needs or precedence. The crest of the gravel-walk is the high point of Austen's exploration of sociability as the most far-reaching achievement of the commercialization of culture in the Georgian period. Her fiction is enduring testimony to our own investments in the companionability of culture, our need to say, as Admiral Croft responds to Anne Elliot when she takes his arm outside the print shop in Bath, 'This is treating me like a friend' (2:6:183).

NOTES

1. Peter Borsay, *The English Urban Renaissance: Culture and Society in the Provincial Town 1660–1770* (Oxford: Clarendon Press, 1989).
2. David Hume, 'Of Refinement in the Arts', in *Essays Moral Political and Literary* (Oxford University Press, 1963), p. 278.
3. Amanda Vickery, *The Gentleman's Daughter: Women's Lives in Georgian England* (New Haven, CT: Yale University Press, 1998).
4. Paul Langford, *A Polite and Commercial People, England 1727–1783* (Oxford University Press, 1992), p. 603.
5. Gillian Russell, *Women, Sociability and Theatre in Georgian London* (Cambridge University Press, 2007).
6. Terry Castle, *Masquerade and Civilisation: The Carnivalesque in Eighteenth-Century English Culture and Fiction* (London: Methuen, 1986).

7. Mikhail Bakhtin, *The Dialogic Imagination: Four Essays*, ed. Michael Holquist, trans. Michael Holquist and Caryl Emerson (Austin, TX: University of Texas Press, 1981).

8. Fanny Burney, *Evelina*, ed. Edward A. Bloom and Lillian D. Bloom (Oxford University Press, 1982), p. 25.

9. Vickery, *Gentleman's Daughter*, p. 239.

10. Helen Berry, 'Creating Polite Space: The Organisation and Social Function of the Newcastle Assembly Rooms', in Helen Berry and Jeremy Gregory (eds.), *Creating and Consuming Culture in North-East England, 1660–1830* (Aldershot: Ashgate, 2004), pp. 120–40, p. 140.

11. *Jane Austen's Letters*, ed. Deirdre Le Faye, 3rd edn (Oxford University Press, 1995), p. 36.

12. Kathryn Sutherland, 'Jane Austen's Life and Letters', in Claudia L. Johnson and Clara Tuite (eds.), *A Companion to Jane Austen* (Oxford: Blackwell-Wiley, 2009), pp. 13–30, pp. 18, 19.

13. Joseph Wiesenfarth, 'The Watsons as Pretext', *Persuasions*, 8 (1986), 101–11, 109.

14. William H. Galperin, *The Historical Austen* (Philadelphia: University of Pennsylvania Press, 2003), p. 205.

15. John Harland, *Collectanea Relating to Manchester and its Neighbourhood, at Various Periods* (Chetham Society, 1867), p. 41.

13

ISOBEL GRUNDY

Jane Austen and literary traditions

Jane Austen inherited no obvious, no precisely defined tradition: not the classical canon which her brothers studied at school; not (like so many of her literary great-granddaughters and beyond) the canon as studied for a BA in English literature; not the full sweep of her predecessors in English fiction, many of whom remained unknown to her; not the intellectual framework offered by any regular course of study. 'Her reading was very extensive in history and belles letters.'[1] It was steady and purposeful, yet in selection it was desultory. She was never in a position, even had she wished it, to work through the kind of subject-bibliography which Emma is always drawing up; instead, she was dependent on titles which happened to come her way.

What came her way was by no means negligible. She was luckier than some of her heroines: than Marianne Dashwood, who thinks her family library 'too well known to me' to provide 'anything beyond mere amusement' (SS 3:10:388–9), or Catherine Morland, who says, 'new books do not fall in our way' (NA 1:6:35). Austen's first library, her father's, ran to more than 500 books.[2] Though her school experience was brief and insignificant, most of the usual school books were accessible at home. Most importantly, the whole family were avid book borrowers and book exchangers. Chawton, the scene of her most sustained and productive period of writing, had a better reading group than she had found at Steventon or Manydown, as she was at pains to point out.[3] Her letters teem with every possible kind of reference to books: simple reports of what she or the family is reading; opinions; quotations applied sometimes straightforwardly but more often with multiple layers of irony; affectionately joking reference to details from novels in which she treats them just like actual life. Only a highly literary sister would write to a brother about to visit Sweden: 'Gustavus-Vasa, & Charles 12th, & Christiana, & Linneus – do their Ghosts rise up before You?' (L 214). This remark alone would place Austen squarely in the centre of the Enlightenment tradition of European learning of the long eighteenth century.

We have, therefore, a paradox of real knowledge and expertise combined with real intellectual deprivation (of which she probably became more conscious as her literary career gathered momentum). She picked her reading matter for herself from a wide range of rich and multiple traditions; but she knew no tradition systematically or comprehensively. One result of this situation is that she never assumes the role of disciple or student, let alone that of pedagogue. She recognizes no canonical status, acknowledges no literary authority. She assumes the sufficiency of her own taste as guide to literary value, admiring authors because she likes them and not because of their currency value as great or respected names; when she admires a Great Name she expresses that admiration in terms of personal friendship, not literary appreciation.[4] Her novels are full of particular responses to particular moments in other novels, but no other novelist exerted a deeply entrenched or widely distributed influence on her work. She never engages in specific dialogue with a particular forerunner, as so many other women novelists engaged in dialogue with Richardson.

Nor did she apparently think in terms of a Great Tradition. She does not, like many of her contemporaries, seek to raise the status of the novel and confer authority on her own fictions by heading chapters with literary quotations. Nor does she seek to endow fictional characters with status and value by making them familiar with great writers. Henry Fielding gives this kind of familiarity to both Parson Adams and Will Booth;[5] but both techniques are popular among contemporaries of Austen whose literary quality is more questionable. Eleanor Sleath, for instance, in *The Orphan of the Rhine* (one of Isabella Thorpe's choices) is unreliable as to grammar but uses Shakespeare, Milton, Pope, Burns and other canonical authors to head her chapters, and makes her heroine at 13 an enthusiast for Ariosto and Petrarch. Sleath's next novel, *The Nocturnal Minstrel*, quotes Ariosto in Italian and Horace in Latin;[6] clearly she felt the need to attach herself to a tradition of literary value.

Austen's way of using the tradition is not Sleath's. Books are of service to her novels because of the daily uses that people make of their reading, in conversation, argument and the shaping of imaginative experience. She presents them through the minds of her characters, coloured and differentiated by the imagined reader.[7] When she mentions Shakespeare or Pope it is not to boast of knowing them herself, but to delineate a fictitious character through her or his response to them. Books are a vital part of the flow of life surrounding her; knowledge of books and feelings about books are, for her, continuous with other forms of knowledge and feeling.

I hope to establish here the broad outlines of Jane Austen's reading, and some slight sketch of the uses to which she puts it in her fiction. From an early age she read like a potential author. She looked for what she could use – on her own terms, that is, not by quietly absorbing and reflecting, but by actively engaging, rewriting, often mocking. Evidence of her reading comes largely from her letters; it is, therefore, always fragmentary. Most of the time the Austen family group would be reading some book together; Jane would be reading another book on her own. Her letters mention only a very small proportion of all these books; and what they mention is designed to convey meaning not to a twentieth-century reader, but only to the letter's original recipient, who shared all kinds of private knowledge with which to make sense of what the letter says.

Almost every item of evidence, therefore, requires analysis and explanation, and this must necessarily be speculative. Austen's references to authors do not flatly deliver approval or disapproval: she has less direct, but perhaps more interesting, impressions to convey. This is not to say that her approval or disapproval is unimportant. As with characters, so with books: judgement, both moral and intellectual, is an important part of the response she solicits. But judgement is invited (against Mrs Norris and Mr Elton, for Miss Bates and Mrs Smith) under the cloak of amusement and pleasure in the quirks of individuality. In the same way Austen does not, like a reviewer, attach quality rankings to books. She leaves it to her readers (the beloved recipients of her letters, the anonymous public of her novels) to discover her judgements for themselves. She does not praise or analyse George Crabbe: instead she launches a long-running joke about her hopes of seeing him in London and her efforts to detect his marital status from his writings, culminating in a resolve, elaborated with curlicues of fantasy, to marry him now he is a widower. She disguises her admiration for Thomas Clarkson, historian of the slave trade, and for Charles Pasley, writer on British governance in India, under the same metaphor of a woman assessing a man as husband material.[8]

A reader who mocks literary admiration under the guise of husband-hunting is not one to signpost her favourites or her influences, if any. In fact in her own work she is chary of influence, taking pains always to avoid anybody else's manner of doing anything. She is as little given to direct imitation as she is to self-congratulatory allusion, or the scoring of points through canonical epigraphs.

In the teeth of her reticence and non-cooperation, I shall endeavour to reconstruct an outline of her extremely catholic reading, with some comments on its contribution to her work, although such contributions are often buried. I shall comment on her relationship with books as it appears in her letters (where the issues of revelation and concealment are different from what they are in her published work) and on the reading of her fictional characters (not only what they read, but how they in turn use their reading).

We no longer find it easy to believe Austen's claim to be 'the most unlearned, & uninformed Female who ever dared to be an Authoress' (*L* 306). When she wrote this she was, after all, crafting a graceful but absolute refusal of James Stanier Clarke's invitation to build a novel around a clergyman 'entirely engaged in Literature', who, as she herself noted, would discourse 'on subjects of Science & Philosophy' and 'be occasionally abundant in quotations & allusions' (*L* 296–7, 306). The meaning of 'occasionally' here is not 'from time to time' but 'to match the occasion'. Clarke means the kind of clergyman whose response to the daily events of life draws *habitually* on the tags and phrases provided by his reading. Such a man is moulded by his 'Classical Education' and his 'very extensive acquaintance with English Literature, Ancient & Modern'. We may suppose that Austen, as she made, 'with all possible Vanity', her boast of ignorance, felt profoundly grateful to be disqualified from writing about this imaginary clergyman; occasional abundance in quotation is not something that appeals to her.

Most of her own quotations and allusions are deliberately mismatched to their occasion. She takes a rhapsodic description of natural beauty and yokes it by violence with news of an unsatisfactory social occasion: '"T'is Night & the Landscape is lovely no more", but to make amends for that, our visit to the Tyldens is over' (*L* 226). She echoes Falstaff's (disingenuous) appeal to time measured by Shrewsbury clock, on no better excuse than the fact that someone involved in her story 'once lived at Shrewsbury, or at least at Tewksbury' (*L* 64). Here she makes mock both of the seizing of occasions for quotation, and the vapidity of the tags quoted.

Austen's letters, that is, consistently debunk some uses of literary tradition, but of course such debunking is a tradition in itself. The Augustan writers loved to make fun of reference to canonical authors: mocking not the authors themselves, but pedantic dependence on them. Pope's 'I cough like Horace', Henry Fielding's mock-epic descriptions of vulgar brawls, innumerable half-submerged references in Johnson's letters, indulge themselves in this kind of fun. Austen herself, in mocking avid Shakespearians, is nonetheless also indicating familiarity with *Henry IV*, Part I.

Some early commentators on Austen accepted her claim to 'ignorance' at face value, but recent years have seen a steady growth in critical attention to her reading and her influences. A century ago, just as the university syllabus for English literature was beginning to emerge, the American literary journalist William Branford Shubrick Clymer began the 'placing' of Austen in literary history. Together with her contemporary Sir Walter Scott, he said, she marked the half-way point between Richardson's day and Clymer's own.

Richardson, Fielding, and Smollett, the first novelists in England (for Defoe's stories of adventure are not precisely novels as the term is now understood), had been followed by a romantic and by a sentimental school, the former growing from Horace Walpole, through Clara Reeve and Mrs Radcliffe, to Scott; and the latter including men so dissimilar as Sterne, Mackenzie, and Goldsmith. The sentimentalists were virtually a thing of the past, and the romanticists were in full career when Jane Austen, cutting loose from both influences, set again on a firm basis the realistic study of manners taught her by Richardson and Fielding ... She belongs to a small group of women who excelled in what has been well called 'fictitious biography'; of that group – comprising Miss Edgeworth, Miss Ferrier, and herself ... she is incontestably the finest artist.

Her work, says Clymer, is the slender thread which carried the strain of realism safely through the Romantic age from the hands of Fielding and Richardson to those of Thackeray and Trollope.[9] This account, now itself a part of literary history, has a simpler outline than anything that might be proposed today. Clymer's early act of canon construction is open-minded and non-rigid in its judgements. It names women as well as men as members of fictional schools which did not retain their place in a central canon, and it names Edgeworth and Ferrier (though not Frances Burney) as sharing in Austen's connective function.

Canon construction also involves pigeon-holing. Since Austen is a novelist, it is among works of fiction that Clymer seeks her tradition. In fact she cares nothing for generic boundaries, but a great deal for the way the tradition of fiction interwove with those of history, and essays, and drama, and poetry. The English novel was seen in her day as a legitimate heir of Shakespeare, working as it did with dialogue and character and passion and interaction. Defoe did not yet enjoy the paternal status which historians of the novel later accorded him, and the works of Defoe's female predecessors and contemporaries (Behn, Davys, Barker, Aubin, Haywood) had already been forgotten. For Austen as for Clymer the great age of the novel had dawned with Samuel Richardson and Henry Fielding. Fiction moved between the poles represented by these two, and Austen, alert to their unlikenesses, learns from and disputes with each.

More recent critics have charted the broad range of influences on Austen's art. Detailed and sensitive attention has been paid to the ties that link her with the Augustan tradition of Addison and Johnson, to the landscape writing of Gilpin, and to a broad range of fiction with special attention to texts by women, by Richardson[10] and by her immediate contemporaries. She has been discussed as a novelist of ideas, with views on political, philosophical and legal issues of her day.

This new willingness to take her seriously as a thinker does not involve forgetting her own statements about disliking to be taken *too* seriously. Now that we know she never turned her back or closed her ears to the intellectual debates raging around her, we should also remember her necessarily tenuous and deliberately oblique relation to such debates. She says that 'a Woman … like me' *cannot* abound in quotation and allusion; none of her writings suggests for an instant that she wanted to. Quoting many writers, she almost without exception quotes them 'slant'. Whether to read this as female outsidership or as traditional Augustan irony is a matter of taste. While maintaining the superiority of the Chawton to the Steventon reading club, she inveighs against 'enormous great stupid thick Quarto Volumes'. For herself, she 'detest[s] a Quarto', does not want to learn 'everything in the World' and prefers 'a Man who condenses his Thoughts into an Octavo' (L 206). Such anti-pedantry is not anti-intellectualism, but it keeps a deliberate toehold in irresponsibility.

Both in letters and fiction, Austen mock-curtseys to or answers back at books which have caught her interest, without regard to their canonical or non-canonical status. Her reprocessing often makes strange bedfellows. For instance, Oliver Goldsmith's *History of England*, a text regularly fed to passive pupil consumers, is pressed into service in her 'History of England' (1791); but so is the essence of the innumerable novels treating the opposition between Queen Elizabeth and Mary Queen of Scots – which, for devotees of the novel, was a more compelling pair of alternatives than Roundhead and Cavalier.[11] Goldsmith on the one hand, historical novelists on the other: the 16-year-old Austen takes the classic ruling that literature should combine instruction and pleasure, and divides it between two parties, neither of which, therefore, conforms fully to the rule.

It is safe to assume that even at this age Austen knew this classical rule, knew that it was propounded by the Roman poet Horace, and knew the much-quoted tags (*utile dulci*, useful and sweet, and the slightly less hackneyed *jucunda et idonea*, merry and proper) in which it was embodied. Above all, however, she would know, more deeply and feelingly with advancing years, every shade of pedantry, or superiority, or self-importance, with which such tags were trotted out in mixed conversation. Her enquiring mind and retentive memory could not fail to pick up a good smattering of classical learning: what she did not pick up was any faith that these fragments carried the stamp of exceptional value. Like George Eliot later, she connected the idea of classical authors with the idea of little boys studying them.[12] For her the ancients remained subject to the same kind of critical scepticism (whether feminist or Augustan scepticism) as other sources. She calls a woman in childbed a 'sister in Lucina'; but she detects 'pedantry & affectation' in the title of Hannah More's *Cœlebs* (that is, celibate or bachelor) *in Search of a Wife*, 1808, and demands rhetorically: 'Is it written only to Classical Scholars?'[13]

Austen does not relate to the classics as does a devotee of a Great Tradition; she does not turn to the Latin language for authority or authorization. Yet, though she dislikes pedantry, I would not accept that she dislikes scholarship.[14] She went to some trouble to ensure factual accuracy in works by herself and her nieces. She likes to let foolish characters expose their foolishness by garbling texts. John Thorpe categorically misstates what is and is not contained in Burney's *Camilla, A Picture of Youth*, 1796: he has got only as far as chapter 4 of a voluminous novel, as readers of it will recognize. In the first chapter of 'Sanditon' Mr Parker garbles the context of a quotation from Cowper: what Cowper praises as a virtue in an old woman is confusingly converted into a deficiency in a seaside resort. The reader feels licensed to despise these inadequate readers – but no more than we feel free to despise Mrs Elton for garbling a traditional saying or cliché by making Surrey, instead of Kent, 'the garden of England'. Mrs Elton is an inadequate listener in just the way that Thorpe and Mr Parker are inadequate readers.

While she approached the classics through the filters supplied by those with a classical education, Austen had direct, almost continuous contact with another body of texts whose roots lie far back in antiquity. The texts of the Christian religion, and of the Anglican branch of it, were variously written by nomadic desert chiefs and priests, by poorly educated rural folk in a province of the Roman Empire, by a Roman ex-civil servant (St Paul) – and by English Renaissance churchmen. They were either written or translated nearly two hundred years before Austen as a child first became familiar with them; their language was obsolete, and their morality (in the Old Testament) often alien or unacceptable. Yet in their basically Renaissance English form they helped to shape Jane Austen's style as well as her habit of thought, and constitute a living influence on her in a way that the classics do not.

The Bible (Authorized Version or King James Bible) and the Book of Common Prayer, as Austen used them, dated from 1611 and 1662 respectively; but they were closely based on work done by Tyndale and Cranmer during the sixteenth century. Linguistically, therefore, they were a door opening backwards into 'English Literature, Ancient'; and they were familiar to her in a way that only a few texts become familiar to anyone: familiar from daily or weekly or yearly repetition, aloud, marked with the different speech habits of the different voices that pronounced them.[15] Even if she had never read the Bible herself (as she did) she would have heard the passages appointed to be read at the services of the church (read, no doubt, with varying degrees of expertise). The passages appointed for Sundays and for the great festivals would be heard every year. The book of Psalms would be worked through during the church's year; in addition, certain psalms, as well as canticles and prayers, occurred every week as part of the service.[16] The prayers which Austen wrote herself reflect her familiarity with prayer-book rhythms: her words compose themselves into an order which is perfectly in tune with Elizabethan liturgical discourse, foreign to her usual practice but none the less securely hers.[17]

Austen's fictional style or styles may seem remote indeed from anything in the Bible or prayer book: not only from ancient annals or martial poetry, but from St Paul's letter-sermons and St John's apocalyptic visions. Careful scrutiny, however, reveals the traces left by some of these familiar cadences. The almost prehistorical authors of the Old Testament have bequeathed her their rapidity and spareness of narrative, the New Testament writers their remarkable ability to enter the common mind and to conjure an illusion of verisimilitude by means of a single detail – the qualities that Erich Auerbach notices when he writes about St Mark's gospel in *Mimesis*.[18] The Bible, Austen's daily bread, must have helped her to plot the moral consequences (momentous for them) of such humdrum errors as Elizabeth's feeding her vanity with Wickham, or Emma's feeding hers with Harriet, while most novelists needed at least the *idea* of some momentous causes for whatever was deeply to affect their heroines. The Bible also helped to keep Austen's rhythms free from the verbosity which afflicts so many of her contemporaries. In narrative passages (a comparatively small part, but an important one, of her novels) her taste for brief declarative sentences is something she shares with the gospels. 'Henry and Catherine were married, the bells rang, and every body smiled' (*NA* 2:16:261.). That is in its way a very New Testament sentence.

These original Anglican texts had their later descendants. As well as listening regularly to sermons, Austen read them in printed form, subscribed to one collection, and transcribed her father's sermons (*L* 388 n. 12; xvii–xviii). Jacobean churchmen and later preachers contributed their copia and orotundity, their preference for using two words where one would do, if not directly to Austen then certainly to Mr Collins.[19]

After the Bible, Shakespeare is 'part of an Englishman's constitution' (*MP* 3:3:390–1). The implications of Henry Crawford's remark reach beyond his intention, particularly in view of the exclusion of women from public life, and of Austen's generally mocking attitude to the institutional or property-owning approach to texts. It is, perhaps, an English birthright to know Shakespeare, as Edmund Bertram replies, 'in bits and scraps' (to refer parrot-fashion, for instance, to Shrewsbury clock without recalling anything about Falstaff's deplorable conduct on the battlefield and without being able to tell

Shrewsbury from Tewkesbury). But it is a birthright which Austen subjects to
scrutiny. Birthright in general is a male prerogative, and quoting in bits and
scraps, with frequent, minute inaccuracies (which modern scholarship would
stigmatize as misquotation) was generally accepted by the eighteenth century
as gentlemanly 'ease': a sign that quotations come from knowing an author
'pretty thoroughly', not from thumbing through texts. The birthright relation
of reader to author, a relaxed and unpedantic relationship, assumes a right to
be inaccurate. But changing Shrewsbury into Tewkesbury implies that inac-
curacy invites mockery.

Austen takes familiarity with Shakespeare for granted; what she validates is
not familiarity so much as appreciation. She makes a good deal hang on
Fanny Price's delight in Crawford's reading; and at least once I believe she
makes a good deal hang on a quotation from Shakespeare. Ronald Blythe,
who believes that Highbury society is essentially philistine, omits from his
sparse enumeration of its literary references a Shakespearian quotation from
Emma. 'The world is not theirs, nor the world's law', she says of governesses,
echoing (approximately) what Romeo says of the starving apothecary who
sells him poison.[20] This is an interesting case. Some might argue that it proves
that Emma, in the style of Catherine Morland, has been reading Shakespeare
selectively, on the lookout for pathos to grace the speech of a heroine. But,
quite apart from the fact that Emma leans less towards the role of heroine
than that of producer or director, quite apart from the fact that her reading
and her memory of *Romeo and Juliet* got all the way to the last act, the fact
that she picks her example of pathos from this speech about need and
oppression, contempt and beggary, rather than from the emotional pathos
of the lovers, indicates a strong mind reading against the grain, ignoring
hackneyed phrases but taking sustenance from a canonical text for her own
independent thinking. Her Shakespeare allusion is one of several straws in the
wind to suggest that marriage to the tirelessly, practically benevolent
Mr Knightley will suit her down to the ground.

Those critics are surely right who see Austen's natural place in the course of
English literature as being among the Augustans. She knows the established
canon: Addison, Pope, Gay, the Swift of *Gulliver's Travels*,[21] Thomson,
Gray, Goldsmith and Charlotte Lennox, whose *Female Quixote; or, The
Adventures of Arabella* (1752), renews her admiration on rereading (*L* 116).
She loves these writers and uses them, though she does not enlist herself under
their banner. When Elinor Dashwood expects Marianne to delight in
Willoughby's admiring Pope 'no more than is proper' (*SS* 1:10:57), she
implies more than can be rapidly unpacked about the consequences of
using literary preference like this as a touchstone of personal worth or
sensitivity. Marianne, who prides herself above all on spontaneity, is revealed

as having pre-decided what view of Pope can pass muster. She denies Pope a fuller admiration, perhaps because he is a satirist, perhaps because he writes in the outmoded couplet form. But Austen, and Elinor, surely know that two early, emotional works by Pope are perfectly formed to give pleasure to Marianne: *Eloisa to Abelard* and *Elegy to the Memory of an Unfortunate Lady*.[22] Austen herself apparently relished both Pope's insight and his later *ex cathedra* manner: in a letter she writes, '"Whatever is, is best." – There has been one infallible Pope in the World' (L 245). But she allows Marianne, or Willoughby, to be demeaned through their literary opinion: not through what they like or dislike, but through their eagerness to exact conformity of taste – especially while overlooking some highly relevant texts.

Austen's best-loved authors are those with Augustan affinities, those like Richardson, Johnson, Cowper, Burney and Crabbe. To all these she pays the compliment of frequent and familiar reference. Not only does she quote them from memory, as she quotes Shakespeare or Pope; she also takes liberties with them, using them freely as part of the background of her life. She 'could not do without a Syringa' for the garden because of the way Cowper described it; she writes that 'like my dear Dr Johnson ... I have dealt more in Notions than Facts' (L 119, 121). This is what Johnson says he does in his *Journey to the Western Islands of Scotland*, with which Austen thus demurely ranks her own letter.[23] At one point she owned a set of the standard poetry anthology, Dodsley's *Collection of Poems*, originally published in 1748. Her Augustan texts are not limited to books. She is able to project on Cassandra's mind's eye the whole trajectory of the series of paintings or prints by Hogarth entitled the 'Harlot's Progress', by observing that if she travelled to London with nowhere to stay, 'I should inevitably fall a Sacrifice to the arts of some fat Woman who would make me drunk with Small Beer' (L 88, 12).

Cowper threads through Austen's novels, loved passionately by Marianne and soberly by Fanny Price, and quoted by Mr Knightley. Edward Ferrars, having been judged deficient in spirit and animation by Marianne on the basis of his reading of Cowper aloud, demonstrates both these qualities in imagining how Marianne, if she had money, would buy up every extant copy of Cowper and other favourites, 'to prevent their falling into unworthy hands' (SS 1:17:107). Edward's combination of shyness, secret anguish and whimsical humour in private might even suggest a hint of Cowper in character.

Richardson's *Sir Charles Grandison* (1753–4) and Burney's *Camilla* (1796) probably share the palm for frequency of mention in Austen's surviving letters, though *Evelina, or, A Young Lady's Entrance into the World* (1778) runs them close. (*Camilla*, so far as we know, is the only novel which Austen honoured by continuing its story beyond the ending, as she sometimes did for her own books.) She indulges in comic self-identification with their heroines: 'I shall be just like Camilla in Mr Dubster's summer-house'; 'Like Harriet Byron I ask, what am I to do with my Gratitude?' (The parallel is comic in each case because Austen's situation, though perhaps reminiscent of Camilla's or Harriet's, is infinitely less grave and less extreme.)[24] But minor characters, minor situations in these novels are reckoned to be equally memorable. Austen writes of the thirst for travelling 'which in poor James Selby was so much reprobated' or of 'Our own particular little brother', confident that her correspondent will pick up her allusions.[25] John Thorpe cannot get through *Grandison*, but thinks *Tom Jones* the best novel written until Matthew Lewis' charnel gothic *The Monk* (1796). From Thorpe's admiration we might surmise that Austen prefers Richardson to Fielding. Yet what could be more Fieldingesque than the technique she uses to comment on *Grandison* here, the technique of praising with loud damns from a bad judge? Thorpe praising Fielding, dispraising Richardson, owes something to the famous scene in *Tom Jones* where Partridge praises the loud voice and stiff action of the actor playing Claudius, and dispraises Garrick's performance as too natural to be good acting. To attribute favourites to Austen is not to suppose she failed to appreciate, or to learn from, the rest of the Augustan tradition.[26]

Johnson is a special case in Austen's letters and novels. Opinions shared with him pervade her fiction at a deep level vital to meaning and structure. She knew his correspondence with Hester Thrale, which the latter published in 1788, as well as letters printed in Boswell's *Life* (1791). Her letters resemble Johnson's in their minute detail and in their guessing games of half-submerged, shorthand reference. She might have modelled all her letters to Cassandra on his injunction about the need for 'petty talk upon slight occurrences', for letters to prevent the 'great inconvenience of absence, that of returning home a stranger and an enquirer'. The letter containing Johnson's phrase about notions and facts is explicitly presented as an exercise in the art of writing a letter with nothing to say: what he calls the 'great epistolick art'.[27]

Besides his minute particulars, Austen relished Johnson's habits of playful intertextuality and hidden meanings. Thus he implies an equation of himself with Lovelace's rakish friends when he writes, 'So I *comforted and advised him*.' When she writes 'Now this, says my Master will be mighty dull', she is assuming the language and therefore the mantle of the Johnson–Thrale correspondence, in which Henry Thrale is regularly 'my Master'.

Austen makes Cowper stand generically for rural, domestic life and Johnson for urban, social life when she writes (of a manservant who prefers the country) 'He has more of Cowper than of Johnson in him, fonder of Tame Hares & Blank verse than of the full tide of human Existence at Charing Cross' (L 250). In calling this preference 'a venial fault', she implies that she herself might side with Johnson, in spite of Cowper's remarkable power to unite in his support Marianne Dashwood, Edward Ferrars, Fanny Price and George Knightley. Another kind of opposition between Johnson and Cowper implicitly underlies *Sense and Sensibility*: between Elinor's Johnsonian attempts to combat grief and depression through mental activity, and Marianne's Cowperesque savouring of melancholy. Fanny Price unites Johnson and Cowper, sense and sensibility.

While so many of Austen's characters thus admire Cowper, their narrator is consistently Johnsonian. The spoof aphorism which opens *Pride and Prejudice* is not mockery of Johnson, but Johnsonian mockery: he too loves to burlesque the aphoristic manner with unreliable matter, as he does when he passes off as a 'great truth' what he surely regards as a modish error: 'In a Man's Letters you know, Madam, his soul lies naked.' Marianne in her penitence and self-knowledge acquires Johnsonian sentiments and Johnsonian cadences: 'His remembrance can be overcome by no change of circumstances or opinions. But it shall be regulated, it shall be checked by religion, by reason, by constant employment' (*SS* 3:10:393). When Elinor smiles to see her sister 'introducing excess' into her scheme for rationality and self-control (*SS* 3:10:389), she might have practised exactly the same smiles in response to a reading of *Rasselas*. While Henry Tilney uses Johnson's dictionary to overpower ladies in debate (as if he is copying Johnson in 'talking for victory' as well as in his linguistic views), the novelist draws on Johnson's ideas about history to allocate them to both Eleanor Tilney and Catherine. The latter's perception of history as a dark record of wars and pestilences, the former's philosophical speculations as to the reliability of sources, can both be found in more than one passage of Johnson, who is various enough to animate all these three very different contributors to the discussion (*NA* 1:14:109–10).

Critics have noted that Fanny Price and Anne Elliot are both reliant on Johnson for their moral thinking. (It is with Johnson that Anne seeks to counter the influence of Scott and Byron on Captain Benwick.) Johnson's effect on Emma is perhaps more surprising, but equally important. In her Box Hill experience of causing pain through overeagerness to display her wit, she follows in the footsteps of a number of *Rambler* examples (e.g. nos. 16, 101, 141, 174) of the potential of intellectual excellence to lead its possessor astray. In her struggles for self-knowledge, when presented with detachment and irony, she recalls young female characters who take up their pens in the *Rambler* (e.g. nos. 51, 55, 62, 84, 191); but in her thoughts in the final chapters, in her steady aspiration after self-knowledge, rationality and candour, she recalls the persona of Mr Rambler himself.

Austen's tradition did not exclude the modern; it did not end with Johnson's death or with Boswell's *Life* – which, along with his *Journal of a*

Tour to the Hebrides, the Austen family sought out to buy (*L* 22). The family continued to read and digest fiction and non-fiction, the most notable titles of every year. Throwaway reference to the plays of Hannah Cowley suggests that these recent and popular texts had an established status in Austen's mind.[28] She also read pedagogical works, books of travel, history, and political and medical pamphlets. At dates close to their publication, the Austens read Francis Lathom's *The Midnight Bell* (1798), Samuel Egerton Brydges' *Arthur Fitz-Albini* (1798) (which receives perhaps Austen's worst review ever), Genlis' *Alphonsine* (which displeased by being indelicate),[29] Southey's *Letters from England* (1807), Anne Grant's *Memoirs of an American Lady* (1808) and Henrietta Sykes' *Margiana, or Widdrington Tower, A Tale of the Fifteenth Century* (1808).[30]

Austen's judgements of those publishing contemporaneously with herself are complicated by an extra element of irony and indirection: that of feigned or exaggerated envy and rivalry. In another reminiscence of Johnson, she repeatedly asserts her refusal to admire any work that might compete with her own. Hannah More, Jane West, Sir Walter Scott, all fall under this ban. She first implies prejudice against Scott while his reputation is solely that of a poet, feeling not 'very much pleased' with *Marmion*, while acknowledging that perhaps she ought to be. She then promotes him to the honour of affectionately inappropriate citing and quoting. Then, when he switches from poetry to fiction, she reverts to rivalry, and does not 'mean to like Waverley if I can help it – but fear I must'.[31]

In this context, her judgements on contemporaries are particularly slippery to assess. The accolade for Edgeworth (whom she calls the only novelist outside the family she is willing to like) is exceptional. Some other opinions – her delight in Barrett's satirical *The Heroine*, her disappointment at Sarah Harriet Burney's debut in *Clarentine* (1796) – are directly expressed and can be trusted. So can her recommendation of Germaine de Staël's *Corinne* (1807).[32] One of her relations, Cassandra Cooke, author of *Battleridge* (1799), is apparently exempt from professional envy. But when Austen salutes Elizabeth Hamilton as 'such a respectable Writer', the compliment *may* be as backhanded as 'good Mrs West' or the expectation that *Ida of Athens* by Sydney Owenson (later Morgan) must be 'very clever' because written in only three months.[33] In making these comments she assumes, not the authority of a reviewer, but the kind of passions and prejudices that animate a member of Grub Street.

There has been debate over the question whether Austen's literary judgements reflect any partiality towards her own sex (who, by this date, dominated the field of fiction). Such partisanship, like concern for her own fame, she would express only by indirection, with playful hyperbole or understatement. One can hardly mistake her treatment of the 'very Young Man, just entered of Oxford, wears Spectacles', who 'has heard that Evelina was written by Dr Johnson'. His so easily believing (and so authoritatively communicating?) what he has heard invites the reader to convict him of having a prejudice against women writers and no ear for style (*L* 43). When Austen disliked Sir Jenison Gordon for uttering 'once or twice a sort of sneer at Mrs Anne Finch', it seems possible that the sneers were directed at Anne Finch, Lady Winchilsea, an important poet of a century earlier. The eventual Lady Winchilsea remained well known by the name she bore before her husband inherited the title; she lived at, and loved, and wrote about, the Finch family seat at Eastwell (where, during a visit, the sneers were uttered), and lay buried in the church there.[34] If Austen was indeed referring to the historical Anne Finch, not to a modern one whom she knew, then this sentence is probably her strongest expression of solidarity with another woman writer; but as so often she is impossible to pin down.

In her eloquent defence of the novel as a genre, Austen is implicitly defending the writing of women. But novelists of her own sex are exempt neither from her serious literary judgement nor from her outrageous teasing. Mary Brunton's *Self-Control* (1811) is 'excellently-meant, elegantly-written', but its failures in nature and probability invite, and receive, severe ribbing. *Rosanne; or, A Father's Labour Lost* (1814), by Laetitia Matilda Hawkins, is judged 'very good and clever, but tedious'. Delightful on religion and other serious subjects (the heroine has a father influenced by Voltaire and a governess who believes in human perfectibility), it becomes, 'on lighter topics', improbable and absurd. The flamboyant *Wild Irish Girl*, by Sydney Owenson, later Morgan, would be worth reading in cold weather if only 'the warmth of her Language could affect the Body'. Hester Piozzi's colloquialisms are taken off in a sentence which is repeatedly, ramblingly prolonged by further second or third thoughts tacked on the end.[35] Mme de Genlis' *Olimpe et Theophile* is energetically repudiated for tormenting its characters; even at Austen's 'sedate time of Life', she tells her niece Caroline, she could not reread it 'without being in a rage. It really is too bad! ... Don't talk of it, pray' (*L* 310). Here Piozzi and Genlis, though they are targets of mockery, are also offered a slightly dubious compliment: one feels that Austen has enjoyed the former's self-indulgence in the slapdash and slipshod, and been moved, albeit against her better judgement, by the latter's sentiment.

For failure of original thought, for rehashing of stereotypes (by writers of either sex), she has no mercy. In fiction she reprobates 'thorough novel slang', 'the common Novel style': diction like 'vortex of Dissipation', characters like the handsome, amiable young man who loves desperately and in vain (*L* 277). The cant of critics fares no better. Early in her career, in *Northanger*

Abbey, and at its end, in 'Sanditon', she holds up in disgust the well-worn phrases of anti-novel cant: 'threadbare strains of the trash with which the press now groans', the 'mere trash of the common circulating library' (*NA* 1:5:30, *LM* 'S' 8:181). The pedagogical tradition (which dealt largely in stereotypes) gets equally short shrift. Catherine Morland is right to hate the lamentable 'Beggar's Petition' by the Revd Thomas Moss.[36] Lydia Bennet is never more sympathetic than when she meets James Fordyce's *Sermons to Young Women* (1766) with yawning and interruption, in contrast to her sister Mary's eternal copying of extracts.[37]

Austen treats the exaggerated conventions of the novel of terror rather differently from other stereotypes. Her father borrowed from the library at least one novel admired by Isabella Thorpe: Francis Lathom's *The Midnight Bell*.[38] Austen's delight in Henrietta Sykes' fifteenth-century *Margiana* equals Henry Tilney's in Radcliffe's *Udolpho;* as usual she signifies pleasure by pretending the action is real, and pretending she can participate. The family, she says, 'like it very well indeed. We are just going to set off for Northumberland to be shut up in Widdrington Tower, where there must be two or three sets of Victims already immured under a very fine Villain' (*L* 164).

She responded rather similarly to Mrs Rachel Hunter of Norwich, using her twice (in collaboration with two of her nieces) for the favourite game of taking fiction to be true stories about actual people. Twelve-year-old Fanny Austen (later Knight) used the opening story from Hunter's *Letters from Mrs. Palmerstone* to convey a private message about her own behaviour;[39] Anna Austen (later Lefroy) received a letter ostensibly addressed in the third person to Mrs Hunter herself, chatting about the most pathetic characters in her *Lady Maclairn, the Victim of Villainy* (1806). Since Austen also alluded to another episode in *Lady Maclairn* in the elopement of Lydia Bennet,[40] she surely felt some affection for Hunter.[41]

It would take too much space to set about tracing the ways in which Austen learned from the writers who made up her tradition: how she developed her mastery of balance from Pope, wisdom and playfulness from Johnson, gendered power struggle and immediacy of representation from Richardson, relation of books to life from Lennox, pathos and domesticity from Cowper, grotesquerie from Burney, etc. She tends to stand a little outside the beaten paths of discipleship. She could not have written as she did without the work of Richardson, Henry Fielding or Frances Burney, and her works enter into dialogue repeatedly and in important ways with these fellow novelists. But she reflects a consciousness of limitations in each one. Fielding attracts the admiration of John Thorpe, and Richardson that of the equally obtuse Sir Edward Denham. Fielding's manner is remote from her own, and she avoids most of the characteristics of later Richardsonians: models of unmixed virtue or vice, the infliction of extremes of distress (which she also indirectly criticizes in Burney), and heavy-handed poetic justice. The mind of Cowper perhaps interests her more than that of any of the novelists, and the mind of Johnson is closest of all to her own, though she never calls on his authority or imitates his style.

Each of Austen's works occupies a particular position in relation to the community of literary texts. She commonly defines her characters in part through their reading habits; and the text itself inevitably engages in dialogue with texts by others. The juvenile volumes First, Second and Third make explicit reference to sixteen works or writers; they are twice as funny for readers with some idea of contemporary fashions in fiction as for those with none.[42] Their parodic spirit gives way to the self-sufficient imaginative world of 'Lady Susan', where books are never mentioned, but where the epistolary novel's traditional inclusion of some callously self-seeking, cynical character is transformed by the simple device of switching this person's gender. Emma Watson turns thankfully to a book in time of trouble, for 'the employment of mind, the dissipation of unpleasant ideas which only reading could produce' (LM 'W' 135). But 'The Watsons', even in its fragmentary condition, challenges several conventions of the contemporary novel, as if Austen were giving notice that she did not plan to abide by the rules. One such convention was the usual level of social and financial status enjoyed by fictional characters. If it is a novel that Emma Watson reads for solace, it probably depicts a level of society closer to the one she has just lost than to the one she has just found. It was conventional to give a heroine's financial affairs more dignity than those of the Watsons. (Eliza Parsons created fictional problems for her heroine involving £4,000, in Murray House, 1804, at a time not long after she had herself faced debtors' prison for the sum of £12.)[43] Elizabeth Watson, too, is a most unorthodoxly mixed character: a woman who is vulgar and obsessively concerned with getting married, yet who has none of the associated negative qualities of an Anne Steele or a Mrs Bennet, but only a warm heart and strong sense of duty.

Sense and Sensibility and Northanger Abbey each makes fun of a particular literary ideology, yet literature is validated in each. The Dashwoods are probably Austen's most studious family, and Catherine is far better educated than many readers notice. Elinor's pity for Lucy Steele's lack of education, her 'illiterate' state, is genuinely felt. Marianne's 'knack of finding her way in every house to the library, however it might be avoided by the family in general' is not an aspect of her behaviour that needs modification (SS 1:22:146, 3:6:344). Mrs Dashwood can allude to a little-known novel by Richard Graves (Columella, the Distressed Anchoret, 1776) and expect to be understood by her daughters and Edward Ferrars.[44] Plans of study

(Marianne's after her heart is broken, and their mother's for young Margaret) are subjected to some teasing from the narrator. Still, the atmosphere overall is far more favourable to reading and study than is usual in either of *Sense and Sensibility*'s two prototype genres: the novel of misguided reading, like Lennox's *Female Quixote*, or the novel contrasting good and bad sisters, as written by Elizabeth Helme, Jane West and others. If books and ideas have led Marianne astray, encouraging her to seek intensity of emotion as the greatest good, then books and ideas, and especially meditation and self-examining, are to play some part in her redemption. This makes a highly original resolution of a familiar fictional dilemma.

Catherine Morland is educated squarely within the Augustan tradition. She resists the 'trembling limbs' and emotional blackmail of Moss's aged beggar; but she has no trouble learning a poem from fifty years earlier, 'The Hare and Many Friends' by the underrated John Gay (a little gem of irony and black humour). The hunted hare evidently wrings her heart as the beggar does not. At 14 her dislike of 'books of information' is matched by delight in those which are 'all story and no reflection'. At 17 she has read Shakespeare, Pope, Thomson and Gray, even if only in order to comb them for aphorisms and sentiment.[45]

Austen's supposed dislike of scholarship is hard to square with Henry Tilney. He has scholarly tastes; he delights in the cut and thrust of argument; on linguistic niceties he overpowers ladies with Johnson's dictionary and Hugh Blair's *Lectures on Rhetoric*. His sister (herself a reader of the historians David Hume and William Robertson) thinks the scholar in him liable to prevail over the gentleman. Where Burney's Edgar Mandlebert as Camilla's mentor acts repressively, issuing no instructions but letting the uninstructed heroine go wrong and incur rebuke, Henry behaves like a skilled tutor, eliciting Catherine's ideas, consistently questioning received opinion, playing down his pleasure in conscious intellectual superiority (*NA* 1:14:107–13).

Northanger Abbey famously defends novels by setting them, too, squarely at the centre of the literary tradition. Novels exhibit 'genius, wit, and taste'. They display, in 'the best chosen language', 'the greatest powers of the mind … the most thorough knowledge of human nature … the liveliest effusions of wit and humour'. This praise would be as apt for Pope or Johnson as for Burney and Edgeworth. But while novelists shine so brightly, says Austen, modern men of letters (reviewers, editors, anthologizers) do not; the revered *Spectator* is really guilty of the 'improbable circumstances, unnatural characters' of which the novel stands accused.[46]

While she defends her own 'literary corporation', Austen engages it in debate. Having introduced Henry challenging received opinion (the cliché that women write better letters than men) she quickly issues her own challenge to Samuel Richardson's opinion 'that no young lady can be justified in falling in love before the gentleman's love is declared' (*NA* 1:3:22). This was also, famously, the view of Camilla's father;[47] so *Camilla*, explicitly lauded by the narrator, is also criticized, implicitly but radically, in the action.

Catherine must learn to throw off her gothic illusion and cease to expect in life the trappings of villainy: concealment of suspected horrors, as in Ann Radcliffe's *Mysteries of Udolpho* (1794), or ancient texts testifying to female suffering, as in Parsons' *Castle of Wolfenbach* (1793) (one of Isabella's favourites), Eliza Kirkham Matthews' *What Has Been* (1801), and many, many more. But first and more importantly she must learn to throw off the social timidity which makes her vulnerable to the Thorpes' social tyranny, as Evelina was vulnerable to that of the Branghtons. Catherine trapped in John Thorpe's carriage, breaking her word to the Tilneys against her will, strongly recalls Evelina trapped in Lord Orville's carriage which has been borrowed in her name against her will. If Radcliffe is reproved through Catherine's gothic fantasies, Burney is endorsed through the way that Catherine's experiences recall Evelina's. Johnson, who made one woman advise another to consider herself 'a being born to know, to reason, and to act',[48] is endorsed, too, through Catherine's learning to assume these roles.

Literary reference is less central to *Pride and Prejudice*. Burney contributes the novel's title;[49] but *Cecilia*'s pride and prejudice belong to the older generation, while Elizabeth's and Darcy's are their own. Elizabeth may be less of a reader than Elinor, Marianne or Catherine, but her impromptu comment on picturesque grouping shows she knows her Gilpin (*PP* 1:10:58). Free spirit that she is, she is hedged around with ineffectually repressive texts: her father's library, Mary's improving books,[50] the gender-obsessed Fordyce, with whom Mr Collins replaces more solid Christian thinkers.

Mansfield Park is another battleground of texts. It has been shown that Austen was familiar with contemporary pro- and anti-slave-trade debates. (Johnson's letters on the Mansfield case would have brought the matter to her attention, even if she had not read and fallen 'in love with' Thomas Clarkson.)[51] Issues of governance at Mansfield therefore (like Mrs Norris' meanness to servants, which is worthy of a caricature by Pope) are related to issues of governance in the West Indies, whence Sir Thomas returns as more of a domestic oppressor than he was before. But behind the heavyweight 'books of information', used for this novel only, stand the familiar books of imagination which feed all of Austen's work. Sir Charles Grandison and his loving extended family provide a silent commentary on that of the Bertrams. The caged starling in Sterne's *Sentimental Journey* (which is agonized over but never let out) provides a sudden, shocking parallel to Maria's prospects in marriage. Kotzebue's *Lovers' Vows* (a play of passion, translated by the radical Elizabeth Inchbald, 1798) offers the delusory escape of fiction. Fanny keeps both her heart and mind alive with books. Cowper (well known as an opponent of the slave trade) is her alter ego, Lord Macartney on China her serious reading, Crabbe and (especially) Johnson her relaxations. Against her heartfelt reading of, for instance, Scott, is set the uncommitted facility with which the Crawfords can draw on the phrases of Milton or of seduction poems, or can imitate an imitator of Pope (*MP* 1:4:49, 1:17:189, 2:12:339).

The literary situation in *Emma* resembles that in *Pride and Prejudice*. Emma is a woman of action who knows the world of ideas through bibliographies, but never actually reads the books; still, her use of Shakespeare is significant. Mr Knightley is an outdoors man, a glutton for practical work, yet he is familiar with Cowper. Books are not forgotten. Robert Martin's knowledge of Goldsmith's *Vicar of Wakefield* (1762), and the *Elegant Extracts* edited by Vicesimus Knox in 1789, his ignorance of Radcliffe or Regina Maria Roche, mark him squarely as an unmodish, middlebrow reader; nobody but Harriet or Emma finds this dismaying. Mrs Elton, raised like Catherine Morland on Gay's 'Hare and Many Friends', shows it by shatteringly inappropriate quotation.[52]

Austen's last completed novel brings two of her traditions, the writers of feeling and the writers of thinking, into direct confrontation over the soul of the bereaved Captain Benwick. As Anne urges him to read moralists, letter-writers and 'memoirs of characters of worth and suffering', Johnson makes another masked appearance in the text at two levels. Along with sermon-writers like Austen's favourite Thomas Sherlock (*L* 278), he is the most obvious moralist for Benwick to read; he is also an important source of Anne's own creed of activity and benevolence and self-control. Anne shows that knowledge of fiction can be illuminating, not misleading: she does not model herself on any fictional character, but in monitoring her own behaviour she compares herself both to an exaggeratedly self-abnegating romantic heroine of Matthew Prior and to the awful Miss Larolles in Burney's *Cecilia* (1782).[53]

Austen's final novel, the fragment 'Sanditon', would have been her most literary. Charlotte Heywood's reading habits recall Anne's: she is 'a very sober-minded young Lady, sufficiently well-read in novels to supply her imagination with amusements, but not at all unreasonably influenced by them' (*LM* 'S' 6:169). Comparing herself with Camilla leads her to deliver a mental *coup de grâce* to that tale of outrageous female suffering which had haunted Austen's imagination for years: 'She had not Camilla's youth, and had no intention of having her distress' (6:167). The misreaders in this story are male: Mr Parker and Sir Edward Denham. Sir Edward can quote without conveying meaning of any kind (by repeating, for instance, 'Oh! Woman in our Hours of Ease – ' without a verb, without a statement) (7:175). He hops from Scott to Burns to Montgomery[54] to Wordsworth to Thomas Campbell and back; but none of these writers is to blame for his incoherence. As always in Austen, what matters is what you make of your reading. Sir Edward's intellectual digestion malfunctions: he draws 'only false principles from lessons of morality, and incentives to vice from the history of its overthrow ... only hard words and involved sentences from the style of our most approved writers' (8:183).

Austen returns at last to Lennox's *Female Quixote*, to reverse the gender of its protagonist and to present, so far as I know unprecedentedly in English fiction, a man misreading the world in the light of his misreading of fiction. In a typically daring reversal, the female protagonist is a reader in calm control of her texts.

Her literary traditions give depth to Austen's fiction. That fiction depicts a society whose overall level of interest in ideas and books is very high, in which novels rank with poetry, drama and 'essays, letters, tours and criticisms' (8:183). For her and for her central characters books and life are not divided; books are a vital part of life. In this as in other matters, her manner of proceeding sets her squarely in the steps of Richardson and Burney, Johnson and Cowper, and closely in touch with neglected fields and forgotten chambers, with John Gay and Richard Graves, Rachel Hunter and Henrietta Sykes. She is perhaps too strong a mind, too original a writer, to be the most apt for influence studies, but her work incorporates ideas from and offers responses to a wide range of texts, and her allusions are commonly so nuanced as to be worth carefully teasing out.

NOTES

1. Henry Austen, 'Biographical Notice of the Author' in *Northanger Abbey*, ed. R. W. Chapman (Oxford University Press, 1969), p. 7.
2. D. J. Gilson, 'Jane Austen's Books', *The Book Collector*, 2(3) (1974), 27.
3. *Jane Austen's Letters*, 3rd edn, coll. and ed. by Deirdre Le Faye (Oxford and New York: Oxford University Press, 1995), pp. 198–9. Twelve years after visiting Dawlish she remembered its 'particularly pitiful & wretched' library (*L* 267).
4. Sometimes her stance is jokingly appropriative: Dr Edward Percival wrote 'Moral Tales for Edward to give to me' (*L* 145).
5. *Joseph Andrews* (1742), I, ch. 17; *Amelia* (1751), VIII, ch. 5.
6. *The Orphan of the Rhine*, ed. Devendra P. Varma (London: Folio Press, 1968), p. 31; *The Nocturnal Minstrel*, ed. Varma (New York: Arno Press, 1972), pp. 1, 64, 209. Austen owned Ariosto's *Orlando furioso* in John Hoole's translation, 1783: a copy later bought by Virginia Woolf (Gilson, 'Jane Austen's Books', 30–1).
7. Lascelles says this of her presentation of the natural world (*Jane Austen and Her Art*, p. 1).

8. *L* 218, 220–1, 243,198.

9. 'A Note on Jane Austen', *Scribner's Magazine*, Feb. 1891, repr. in B. C. Southam, ed., *Jane Austen: The Critical Heritage: Volume 2, 1870–1940* (London and New York: Routledge & Kegan Paul, 1987), pp. 199–200.

10. See, among several valuable studies, Jocelyn Harris, *Jane Austen's Art of Memory* (Cambridge University Press, 1989).

11. The popularity of this opposition was fostered though not begun by Sophia Lee, *The Recess* (1783–5).

12. She wrote for Frank some verses which 'seemed to me purely classical – just like Homer & Virgil, Ovid & Propria que Maribus' (*L* 170). After three names of great ancient poets comes a heading from a Latin grammar: a sly suggestion that classical allusion often rests on shallow foundations.

13. *L* 224, 172. She had another reason to dislike More, whose *Strictures on the Modern System of Female Education* (1799) called novels a principal source of moral corruption: 'The glutted imagination soon overflows with the redundance of cheap sentiment and plentiful incident' (pp. 422–3).

14. In his edition of *Emma*, Ronald Blythe says she disliked scholarship 'very much' (Harmondsworth: Penguin, 1966), p. 467.

15. Perhaps the nearest parallel for Austen would be the motley collection of plays her family performed at home, from Susanna Centlivre and (probably) Fielding to Richard Brinsley Sheridan. Deirdre Le Faye, *Jane Austen: A Family Record* (London: British Library, 1989), pp. xvi–xvii.

16. Said rather than sung. See Irene Collins, *Jane Austen and the Clergy* (London: Hambledon, 1994), p. 181.

17. See Bruce Stovel, '"The Sentient Target of Death": Jane Austen's Prayers', in Juliet McMaster and Bruce Stovel (eds.), *Jane Austen's Business* (London: Macmillan, 1995), pp. 192–205.

18. Erich Auerbach, *Mimesis: The Representation of Reality in Western Literature*, 1946, trans. Willard R. Trask (Princeton University Press, 1953), pp. 40–9. Auerbach does not, regrettably, mention Austen.

19. *PP* 1:19:118–22. Note his repetitions and self-elucidations, his *first* and *secondly*.

20. *E* 3:10:436. 'The world is not thy friend, nor the world's law' (*Romeo and Juliet*, v.i; *Emma*, ed. Blythe (Harmondsworth: Penguin, 1966), pp. 467–8).

21. *L* 47.

22. Catherine Morland finds a line to remember in the *Elegy* (*NA* 1:1:8).

23. Samuel Johnson, *Journey to the Western Islands of Scotland*, ed. Mary Lascelles (New Haven, CT: Yale University Press, 1971); to Boswell, 7 July 1774. Lascelles borrowed the phrase *Notions and Facts* from Johnson *and* Austen, as the title of a book, 1973.

24. *L* 357, 6, 234; also 9, 220.

25. *L* 93, 38. It is unfortunate that this edition of the letters does not index authors or titles of books, so that these allusions remain untraceable in the volume. *Evelina* is referred to on pp. 120, 302.

26. *Tom Jones*, XVI, ch. 5. This novel enters her letters in connection with the dashing Tom Lefroy's white coat, *Tristram Shandy* in connection with a praiseworthy servant, *Robinson Crusoe* only as a servant's reading (*L* 93, 95).

27. To Hester Thrale, *The Letters of Samuel Johnson*, ed. Bruce Redford (Princeton University Press, 1992–4), III: 50, 89.

28. Cowley's *Which is the Man?* was also acted by request of Eliza de Feuillide at Tunbridge Wells in 1786 (*L* 74; *J* 83; Le Faye, *A Family Record*, 57).
29. *L* 15, 22, 115.
30. *L* 141, 164. Susan Brown, Patricia Clements and Isobel Grundy (eds.), Henrietta Sykes' entry, Writing Screen, *Orlando: Women's Writing in the British Isles from the Beginnings to the Present* (Cambridge University Press On-line, 2006–), at: http://orlando.cambridge.org, accessed 21 January 2009.
31. *L* 131 (1808), 194 and 202 (1811, 1813), 277 (1814).
32. *L* 278, 255, 120, 161.
33. *L* 252, 311, 166.
34. Austen, who was particular about modes of address, normally uses 'Miss Finch' for the present-day Anne Finch, and 'Mrs Finches' for her and her sister (*L* 106; e.g. 8, 38, 107, 108).
35. 'He is more comfortable here than I thought he would be, & so is Eliz: tho' they will both I believe be very glad to get away, the latter especially – Which one can't wonder at *somehow*' (*L* 44). Footnoted as referring to Piozzi's edition of Johnson's letters, this is far more likely aimed at her *Observations in the Course of a Journey through Italy . . . 1789*, whose style was widely reprobated as too like gossipy speech.
36. *NA* 1:1:6. Written when its author was an undergraduate and frequently anthologized or reprinted in periodicals, it voices a flatly pathetic appeal to 'Pity the sorrows of a poor old man!' Moss, *Poems on Several Occasions* (1827), pp. 18–21.
37. *PP* 1:12:67. Against her expectations, however, Austen enjoyed Thomas Gisborne's *Enquiry into the Duties of the Female Sex* (1797) (*L* 112).
38. *L* 15; *NA* 1:6:33.
39. *L* 107; *Letters from Mrs. Palmerstone to her Daughter, Inculcating Morality by Entertaining Narratives* (1803), first story.
40. Hunter's eloping Lydia resembles Austen's in character; her family resembles Austen's in reaction. *Lady Maclairn*, III: 223; IV: 144–8.
41. *L* 195, 407 n. 3, 408 n. 6, 269. Cf. Deirdre Le Faye, 'Jane Austen and Mrs Hunter's Novel', *N&Q*, 230 (1985), 335–6; Isobel Grundy, 'Rachel Hunter and the Victims of Slavery', *Women's Writing: The Early Modern Period*, 1 (1994), 25–34.
42. Jan Fergus, *Jane Austen: A Literary Life* (London: Macmillan; New York: St Martin's Press, 1991), p. 39.
43. Brown, Clements and Grundy (eds.), Eliza Parsons' entry, Life and Writing Screens, *Orlando* (2006–), at: http://orlando.cambridge.org, accessed 21 January 2009.
44. There is something highly instructive in the way she uses, casually and unexplained, the name of Graves' protagonist, and the way that Austen scholars (versed in the classical tradition but not in that of eighteenth-century fiction) at first supposed she meant an obscure Latin writer who shares that name (*SS* 1:19:119 and Chapman's note: *Sense and Sensibility* ed. Chapman, p. 384).
45. *NA* 1:1:8. Her mother later selects for her improvement a periodical, *The Mirror*, which, although written by Henry Mackenzie, belongs not in the sentimental but in the social–Addisonian category. Mrs Morland is mistaken in thinking that pedagogy can help in this crisis; but her choice of pedagogue is traditional and sound. (Alyson Bardsley and Jeff Ewing pointed this out on the Eighteenth-Century List.)

46. *NA* 1:5:30–1. Some surprise has been expressed at Austen's finding the *Spectator*'s language coarse; but a word-count of a few terms like 'whore' and 'cuckold' would explain her reasons.

47. 'A Sermon', *Camilla*, v, ch. 5.

48. *NA* 1:11:82–9; *Evelina*, vol. 11, letter 23; *Rambler* 133.

49. Burney, *Cecilia*, final chapter. The words 'pride and prejudice' also occur in Robert Bage's *Hermsprong; or, Man As He Is Not* (1796), which Austen owned (Gilson, 'Jane Austen's Books', 31).

50. Mary even parodies Evelina's Mr Villars in the aftermath of Lydia's loss, with parroted comment on female reputation: 'no less brittle than it is beautiful' (*PP* 3:5:319; *Evelina*, vol. 11, letter 8).

51. *L* 198. R. W. Chapman once supposed this referred to Clarkson's *Memoirs of William Penn*, 1813; but his *History of the Abolition of the African Slave Trade*, 1808, is immeasurably more likely.

52. She embarrasses Jane Fairfax and no doubt amuses Emma with 'For when a lady's in the case, / You know all other things give place' (lines 41–2) – originally said by a bull intent on sex (*E* 3:16:495).

53. *P* 1:12:125, 2:8:206. Lady Mary Wortley Montagu thought the 'monstrous folly' of Prior's heroine in 'Henry and Emma' (1709) likely to lead young readers astray. *Complete Letters*, ed. Robert Halsband (Oxford: Clarendon Press, 1965–7), III: 68.

54. Presumably James Montgomery (1771–1854), another poet who wrote against the slave trade.

14

KATHRYN SUTHERLAND

Jane Austen on screen

film = visual
novel = imagined

Film, like the novel, is intrinsically temporal and good at telling stories. Both succeed by absorbing us into an illusion of comprehensive life – worlds, societies, relationships in which we live intensely for the duration of the telling. Both succeed insofar as they persuasively select what we need to know, and jettison what we do not, and in such a way that we never miss what is not there. That said, these completely absorbing worlds are built from different elements: the one from motionless words; the other from moving pictures. Unlike the novel, film reality is visual; unlike film, novel reality is imagined: that is, the pictures we make as we read are unconstrained by the mechanics of seeing. In *Mansfield Park* the narrator tells us that, with Mary Crawford's help, Fanny's dress to be worn at the ball held in her honour was 'settled in all its grander parts' (*MP* 2:8:299). Two chapters later, she writes of the dress's 'neatness and propriety', of Sir Thomas Bertram's approval of its effect when he speaks 'of [Fanny's] beauty with very decided praise' (2:10:316), and the rest is left to our imagination – to our mental picture-making. Not so on screen, where the film-maker must decide whether the dress is white or cream, plain or spotted, muslin or silk, with what particular neckline and bodice; and the viewer, no longer free to imagine, takes what she sees into what she knows about Fanny, the eye determining interpretation. While this is a general distinction in the narrative systems of the two media, telling us something about the relationship of content to form in each, it is compounded in the case of Jane Austen's novels by a strong distrust of visual understanding. Within the sensory and cognitive means available to the novel form, Austen confirms the activity of the eye, of imaginary seeing, less readily than most.

By contrast, Austen appears to resist a marked tendency of the nineteenth-century novel to represent reality (and the triumph of realism) as the enforcement of the eye's higher rhetorical power. This is not Austen's brand of realism. More precisely, she renders the visual encounter with knowledge problematic for two particular reasons. First, she wishes to make us

✱

Visual encounter:
1. Wants to make us suspicious of what we see
2. Emphasis on hearing as understanding

KATHRYN SUTHERLAND

suspicious of trusting what we see. Accordingly, she selects and restricts visual details with unusual tact, in the process exposing objects, things, sights as rarely purely descriptive and rarely simply attributive – she makes us doubt our eyes. Second, she wishes to throw the emphasis of understanding upon hearing, the faculty that in eighteenth-century aesthetics was associated with the social passions of sympathy, shared values and custom, as opposed to the more individuated, speculative and unbounded range of the visual. The distinction is between the holistic knowledge of the eye and the partial truths of the ear, the truths that Samuel Johnson called 'living information',[1] because they are found in speech, listening and the interplay of voices. In Austen's novels, time and again, the imagination's ear rather than its eye proves the better guide. In the later novels, in particular, vision is liable to illusion. Vision promises to link us directly with a world of objects – with real solid things – but those solid things can and do refuse to connect; they especially refuse to endorse the heroine's way of seeing. By contrast, conversation and gossip talk down the confident truths of the synthesizing eye. Through conversation, Austen's heroines reach self and social understanding – their faulty vision is corrected – and her village communities reach consensus and assert control.[2]

ear better than eye

through hearing, heroines reach understanding

As critics have regularly noted, in an Austen novel even the everyday objects of ordinary existence take on a complicating 'pathology' when they are drawn into the reader's view.[3] From the spareness of its deployment, visual detail can assume a peculiar intensity, on occasion a repulsive fascination ('the cups and saucers wiped in streaks, the milk a mixture of motes floating in thin blue, and the bread and butter growing every minute more greasy' (*MP* 3:15:508)), similar to the camera effects of *cinéma-vérité*. Dead sister Mary's silver penknife shockingly severs Fanny's illusions of a happy homecoming to Portsmouth (*MP* 3:7:446–7); Harriet Smith's mementos of Mr Elton's mistaken regard – a pencil stub minus its lead and 'a small piece of court plaister' (*E* 3:4:366) – are pitiless tokens to both her suffering and her moral triviality. Claudia Johnson perceptively remarks that, 'when objects are made to stand out with specificity in Austen's novels, something is wrong'.[4] By this way of thinking, there will always be something wrong when film adapts an Austen novel, because film is necessarily intensely preoccupied with the surface, the contours and the space that objects occupy. Technologies for reproduction (print or film) and modes of reading (words or images) are complexly related. When film adapts the novel – any novel – it must redeploy narrative features for immediate effect and in terms of its own higher informational requirements. Film is necessarily more intrusive in its description of reality: if the camera does not record it, it is not there. When film warns you not to trust your eyes, it invites you to contemplate a paradox. An equivalent

film = concerned with emphasizing objects

in the novel would be to cast doubt on the veracity of what is written – a tactic Austen occasionally employs in her use of letters to unsettle our interpretation of character or events. Where the novel casts vision in doubt, how might film rehabilitate it as a means of understanding?

Film is not novel but a translation of a story and a mode of narration into another medium. In thinking about how a film is like or unlike a novel we should primarily be concerned with the capacity (or incapacity) of a form of expression to authenticate its materials. The challenge of adaptation is to persuade us that words can become images and that content can survive its form.[5] As a topic for study, and as the activity engaging the writer of screenplay and shooting script, director and actors, film adaptation requires a series of complex distinctions: we must first agree that content can be stripped of form and that something essentially true remains; we must then agree that this essential truth can be 'reformed' and that this new form will be true to its content. Only under these terms can we find material and technical equivalences or analogies between novel and film and appreciate film as an artful object in its own right. Many studies of adaptation never get this far, tending towards defensiveness rather than assertiveness and speculation about the valid contribution of the shift in medium.

According to this way of thinking, adaptation is neither good film nor honest dealing with its source. Discussions of literary film adaptation, in particular, can ignore what is fruitfully different in the two media to focus on issues of fidelity rather than translation or medium-specific authentication. The concept of translation at least allows us to speculate over what it is that gets translated: meaning, spirit or some emotional charge. Walter Benjamin wrote of the translator's task as being to find 'that intended effect upon the language into which he is translating which produces in it the echo of the original'.[6] We can speculate, too, on why a translation is made: ranging from crudely commercial reasons to more complex issues of wider cultural presence. Translation is part of a work's fame and its afterlife. It gestures to a reciprocity between languages and it is always a transformation: what the bibliographer Randall McLeod, pointing to the part played by difference or transformation in all methods of transmission, has labelled transformission.[7] Stories change as they are transmitted, even when, in our print-based culture, they appear to stay exactly the same: print transmitted as print. Over time, they acquire new meanings; words do not retain the same significance. What modern reader hears the words 'she found ... Mr. Elton making violent love to her' (E 1:15:140) as a reader did in 1816?

Austen's visual transformation began at the end of the nineteenth century. Lavish illustrated editions of the novels were in vogue in the 1890s in the same years that saw the first public film screenings. The earliest literary adaptations for film – from Dickens, Shakespeare and Conan Doyle's Sherlock Holmes stories – date from this time and show film developing its modes of narration in terms of the proto-cinematic features of older genres and media: combining frozen frames with moving scenes in ways that replicate contemporary techniques in dramatic tableaux and book illustration; exploiting montage and the kind of parallel cross-cutting between simultaneous and contrasting centres of action that Dickens had taken into the structure and pace of the novel from stage melodrama. As early as 1897, *The Death of Nancy Sykes* was shot in America as a stand-alone scene from *Oliver Twist*; a pre-cinematic slide version (using two magic lanterns and images mounted side by side) of *Gabriel Grub*, a story from *Pickwick Papers*, dates from 1880–1910; the 1901 *Scrooge; or, Marley's Ghost* had a running time of around 11 minutes. There were almost one hundred film versions of Dickens before sound. Rather than relegating literary adaptation as a secondary cinematic form, it is possible to argue from early evidence that cinema discovered its identity by consciously deploying the expressive devices of stage and novel, and long before Sergei Eisenstein traced an origin in Dickens.[8]

By contrast, adaptations of Austen's novels for stage and then radio did not produce a screen version until Helen Jerome's stage dramatization of *Pride and Prejudice*, after successful runs in New York (1935) and London (1936), became the basis of Aldous Huxley and Jane Murfin's screenplay for Metro-Goldwyn-Mayer's 1940 film, starring Laurence Olivier as Mr Darcy and Greer Garson as Elizabeth Bennet. MGM's *Pride and Prejudice* notoriously dressed the Bennet girls in American Victorian (ante-bellum) crinolines, petticoats and huge bonnets, and enclosed the production within a series of artificial, claustrophobic sets – stuffed drawing rooms and gardens festooned with paper flowers. If Darcy (Olivier) recites Byron ('She walks in beauty like the night'), the risky, regency implications are drowned by the film's obvious appeal to mid-twentieth-century middle-class America's expectations of feminine domesticity and morality, while its representation of an idealized Merry England served a particular purpose in 1940, before America entered the Second World War.[9] Greer Garson subsequently played the title role in MGM's *Mrs Miniver* (1942), a propaganda film aimed at finally ending America's isolation from the war, and Olivier made the 1945 morale-boosting *Henry V*. Both performances reinforce the link between Austen's classic status and urgent cultural and political imperatives.

There were no further big-screen versions of Austen before the mid-1990s. Adaptations from the late 1940s onwards, overwhelmingly of *Pride and Prejudice* and *Emma*, were made as television plays or serials. The BBC classic serials for television began as live broadcasts in the early 1950s and were inspired by radio dramatizations, obeying the same principles of fidelity to the

[handwritten margin note: Classic novel adaptations = moving cameras, quick cuts openess of outdoor location and musical score]

original and reliance on dialogue.[10] Like the 1940 Hollywood *Pride and Prejudice*, they carried over techniques from the stage: artificial indoor sets, little or no outdoor action or naturalistic setting. Cameras were fixed, shots dominated by close-ups of talking heads, no tracking or long shots, and all other sensory effects were subordinated to a consciously theatrical dialogue and period-style aesthetic distance. What now appears most obviously missing is the energy we associate with moving cameras, quick cuts, the openness of outdoor location filming and the intensity of a strong musical score – all features that currently identify classic novel adaptations for large and small screen. The 1980 BBC mini-series *Pride and Prejudice*, directed by Cyril Coke and with a screenplay by Fay Weldon, marked the emergence of this newer mode. All productions down to the 1970s also perpetuated the style of visualization associated with the 1890s illustration or 'Cranfordization', as it became called, of the novels by Hugh Thomson. Thomson's skilful packaging, through regency details of costume and setting, created our easy familiarity with the manners of what we long took to be Jane Austen's world. In his case, it was a whimsical, chocolate-box idyll, reflecting nostalgia for an idealized pre-industrial England just out of reach. Thomson had a particular gift for capturing the quirks of facial expression and the intimate exchanges of social intercourse. It is easy to dismiss his mixture of whimsy and wit; but his illustrations were visually influential far into the twentieth century, until the brasher images of smouldering heroes, the wet-look Mr Darcy and material girls on the make of the 1990s Austen film industry radically adjusted our expectations.[11]

[handwritten margin note: first film version was 1940s – next was 1990s]

Currently Jane Austen catches the public imagination and captures the kind of media attention that any living author would envy. Where for much of the twentieth century, during which time her elite critical reputation was decisively made, her esteem was essentially literary and book-bound, now it is more accurately described as an intermedial phenomenon: what Martin Wroe, writing in the *Observer* in March 1996, dubbed our Austen 'heroine addiction'.[12] Wroe was commenting on the seemingly insatiable appetite for all things Austenian in the wake of three iconic screen translations of the novels, all from 1995: the BBC mini-series *Pride and Prejudice*, Columbia's *Sense and Sensibility* and the BBC telefilm of *Persuasion*. Over a decade later, after more film versions of all the novels and two major biopics of Austen's own life, our dependency shows no prospect of a cure. Film is not novel; yet its promotional energy and interpretative agency are now impossible to disentangle from an understanding of Austen's novels: film versions circulate in their orbit; their impact on readers' expectations of the novels themselves can neither be precisely gauged nor firmly and confidently denied. Current adaptations are part of the rebranding of Jane Austen as the godmother of

[handwritten margin note: film = interpretative agent of novels; impacts expectations of novels]

Austen = godmother of 21st century romance [handwritten margin note]

twenty-first-century romance. This Jane Austen is not what she once was: a writer of impeccable Johnsonian credentials, barbed wit and complex morality; now she is savvy, sexy and very modern.

In his *Observer* article, Wroe drew unlikely links between two films released within weeks of each other: the film of Irvine Welsh's novel *Trainspotting* and Columbia's *Sense and Sensibility*, directed by Ang Lee with screenplay by Emma Thompson; or as he provocatively put it, between those elements in late twentieth-century society who were either 'Trainspotters or Janespotters', 'smackheads or bonnetheads'. Both films, he argued, played on a turn-of-the-century fascination with heritage, and both exposed aspects of 1990s Thatcherite society: one from the bleak perspective of post-industrial, unemployed northern Britain; the other from the perspective of the southern Home Counties, and the different cultural impoverishment of Laura Ashley consumerist kitsch – what another film critic summed up as costume drama's 'Quality Street–National Trust village–Empire line' values.[13] One hundred years earlier, at the turn of the nineteenth to twentieth centuries, kitsch was already on the agenda; Austen's novels appeared to deliver a world her readers recognized as undistorted by art yet unbetrayed by the brutality of real life. It is tempting to see the nostalgia that shaped Austen's 1890s appeal and her revived post-1980s filmic reinvention as strengthened in each case by larger issues of heritage: notably, the establishment of the National Trust in 1895 and the English Heritage Acts of 1980 and 1983 which had such powerful impact on the British film industry in the later 1980s and 1990s. It is also worth remembering that it was out of this same 1890s nostalgia for the values of a lost age, captured so effectively by Thomson and his contemporary illustrators, that Jane Austen's early academic and popular reputations both grew – that, instructively, her high-brow and low-brow circulations have regularly been intimately linked. We need to recover our understanding of the validity of this link if we hope to do justice to the current screen lives of her novels, and to the way in which our appreciation of classic literature is always bound up with its retelling or transformation into something different from what it was.[14]

According to A. C. Bradley, first occupant of the Chair of English at Liverpool (1882), in a Cambridge lecture of 1911, the strength of Jane Austen's novels, like Shakespeare's plays, is to be found in characters who exhibit a habit of life beyond the function of the plot. Hence his conviction that there is more to Elizabeth Bennet, that her textual life is only a part of what is knowable about her. He wrote: 'In reading about Elizabeth Bennet ... it is impossible for me to doubt either the author's intentions or my own feelings. I was meant to fall in love with her, and I do.'[15] Though now unfashionable as a professional protocol for reading, 'caring for' or identifying with fictional characters remains highly important when it comes to

[Margin note: National Trust and English Heritage Acts – impact on British film industry]

[Margin note: Strength of Austen's novels found in characters who exhibit a habit of life beyond the function of the plot.]

explaining why we read novels for pleasure. For the generation of readers and critics after Bradley, it was through their capacity to efface all signs of their production – to seem real – that Austen's characters and texts functioned as the highest art – the art that convinces of its power for stating essential human truths.

This identification appeared to be revived in ITV's *Lost in Austen* (2008), a four-part transposition or 'reinvention' of *Pride and Prejudice*, written by Guy Andrews, that plays intelligently with our contemporary intermedial Austen fascination. As Amanda Price, modern-day time-traveller, confides in its opening scenes, 'I patch myself up with Jane Austen'. To be precise, Amanda, a twenty-something Londoner, disenchanted with life and love in a dingy bedsit, has discovered a turnstile through which she passes into Georgian Austen land trading places with Elizabeth Bennet who fetches up in modern day Hammersmith. (We are reminded of Edmund Bentley's 1905 clerihew that 'The novels of Jane Austen | Are the ones to get lost in'.) The idea that a book absorbs us as we read is familiar enough. But the opportunity literally to enter its pages and eject the heroine in the process offers unusual scope – both for our understanding of how fiction works and for developing a more critical relationship to adaptation. Amanda walks into the opening scenes of *Pride and Prejudice* a proficient Janeite having read the novel many times. 'I'm not hung up on Darcy', she confides, 'I love the manners and the language and the courtesy.' The accessibility of Austen's stories to our reimagining is nothing new: we have been adapting them for more than a century, finding in their decorous and muted incidents some essential solace. Their suppression of specific knowledge stimulates her readers to supply what is not there; her economy feeds our fantasies about how her characters' lives intersect with our own.

It is this intimate and direct compact between reader and character that recent repackagings of the novels as film tie-ins aim to reignite; for they ambitiously resist and revise a powerful trend in our reading of classic litera-ture. In 2006, under the logo 'It's time to fall in love again', the Headline imprint of Hodder & Stoughton set a new standard with annotation-free texts in bright pink wrappers designed to entice reluctant teenage girls to discover in Austen a contemporary agony aunt. Headline offers helpful hints on how to set up reading-group discussions and a website, featuring 'What Readers Today Think'. *Persuasion*, we are reassured by the Headline blurb, is 'a Cinderella story for anyone who's ever felt overlooked – or anyone who's ever had their heart broken'. Not to be out-marketed, Penguin Books followed swiftly with Red Classics, also footnote-free, 'stories that speak for themselves'. In Britain, over several weeks in March 2007, the *Daily Telegraph* and *Daily Express* teamed up with Everyman and Penguin, Costa Coffee shops and the nation-wide bookseller W. H. Smith to distribute price-free (and annotation-free) rival copies of Austen's novels in exchange for newspaper tokens. Each novel, in the Penguin–*Daily Express*–W. H. Smith series sported on its covers a portrait of the author, aka Anne Hathaway, after Miramax's *Becoming Jane* (2007), an extremely loose adaptation of elements from *Pride and Prejudice* masquerading as a biopic of Austen's early life. Where the trend in the preparation of classic novels for the student market is currently towards denser and denser annotation – to the point where the latest edited Austen volumes now drag behind them their own bodyweight in 'elucidatory' information – the audacious suggestion that her novels are accessibly modern – a pleasure to read rather than a struggle to study – is refreshing; moreover, it is directly linked to the assumption that reading follows seeing.

Strictly speaking, such editions of the Austen novels function as novelizations – the novels of the film.[16] It is a powerful genre. Like textual annotation, film is a form of interpretation, a gloss on text. For the last ten or fifteen years it is the form of annotation and interpretation that has shaped most effectively Austen's reception. For the majority of her younger readers film is either the primary textual encounter or its interpretative filter; under the aegis of film she is again accessible. The heritage movie genre, in particular, into which classic novels tend to be transposed for film, is weighed down with its own version of annotation, in the form of sumptuous props drenched with material significance: not just glamorous costumes, but grand indoor sets crammed with priceless art objects and antique furniture, and luxurious out-of-doors period-styled tableaux. Such heightened visual packaging signals film's entry into the cultural space of literary annotation. The high production values of 1990s adaptations directed our attention to Austen's classic status through a predictable visual inventory. Heritage-inflation loaded films like Columbia's *Sense and Sensibility* and Miramax's *Emma* (1996) with a hypertrophic supply of eye-popping spectacle: grander and grander balls in ever more sumptuous stately piles, groaning dinner tables, the sensual excess of the apple-strewn orchards through which Gwyneth Paltrow (Emma Woodhouse) and Toni Collette (Harriet Smith) wander. We cannot simply put this down to the Hollywood fantasy machine, because British television productions (the 1995 *Pride and Prejudice* and *Persuasion*) were thick with the same visible tokens of high cultural value. Like textual annotation, film's visual specificity prioritizes some elements over others and similarly directs us towards the meanings we see in the work as a whole. Like annotation, heritage luxury risks eclipsing Austen's physical and moral thrift, burying it beneath a pile of objects of complicating significance – what Henry James called the 'empire of "things"'. Or, as Andrew Higson observes, '[t]he effect is to transform narrative space into

[margin note: film = interpretation*]*

[margin note: heritage luxury = buries physical and moral meanings*]*

Jane Austen on screen

heritage space: that is, a space for the display of heritage properties rather than for the enactment of dramas.'[17]

More recently, such rich signification has given place to an equally resonant minimalism. By the conventions of classic adaptation, Austen's novels have always posed a bit of a problem: they are pre-Victorian; but the production values that signal classic status inevitably Victorianize and clutter (like the illustration frenzy of the 1890s editions). By contrast, more recent adaptations show us big houses, but they are emptier and draughtier, their rooms less opulent, their furnishings competing less for our attention. The new minimalism also encompasses a new shabbiness or filmic equivalent of realism – crumbs on tables, pigs in the parlour and the muddy-hem facts of life in the country, as seen in Working Title's 2005 *Pride & Prejudice*. Where high production values in general pay tribute to Austen's national-treasure or classic status, a greater subtlety over the last decade in the deployment of locations, costumes, objects suggests a new discrimination in how the past is represented. Film images always have a semi-independent life because our awareness of them always exceeds narrative function.[18] Such expressiveness is central to our pleasure as viewers; recent Austen adaptations appear to tease out imagery's lyric potential. In place of the choreographed scenes which suspended characters at a formal distance from us, a persistent feature of recent screen productions is the hand-held camera that wobbles and noses its way into fresh intimacies with the mundane details of our fantasy: rain on a window pane, a dirty glass, a smear of mud on a face (all visual gestures in the 2005 *Pride & Prejudice*).

Film is not novel – it is interpretation, an act as valid in the medium of film as it is in the medium of words. If we find it acceptable that an Austen novel should carry around with it – literally held inside its covers and legitimized via its title-page – a seemingly indispensable dense interpretative gloss in the form of annotation and commentary – then we have already conceded the power of someone else's interpretation as essential to shape our own. Different kinds of annotation produce different texts because they make the same text available in different ways to different readings. Film too might be thought of as a valid interpretative context that produces from its different medium different understandings. For example, since Edward Said's attention to *Mansfield Park* in his influential 1993 study *Culture and Imperialism*, a whole generation of annotators and, in turn, readers has felt compelled to comment on the novel's references to Antigua and the slave trade, where previous generations remained as silent as the Bertrams. We are always reading new novels even when they are the same old novels. Patricia Rozema's Said-influenced postmodern interpretation of *Mansfield Park* (Miramax, 1999) was an ambitiously overloaded account of much more than the novel, and a box-office

Film emphasizes features of the novel, providing an opinion regarding content

failure.[19] Other hybrid films, like Amy Heckerling's *Clueless* (Paramount, 1995) and Gurinder Chadha's *Bride and Prejudice* (Miramax, 2004), are not adaptations so much as transcultural commentary and critical levers upon the novels they daringly transpose. Any interpretative act involves choice of features to emphasize and in so doing becomes an opinionated statement on the constitution of the text from which it begins – we are rarely dealing in facts. Where annotation parades what the annotator believes to be the raw ingredients of Austen's cooked art, there is an equivalent sense in which film also works by disassembling and reconstituting everything. Both are critical interventions that appear to challenge the authority implied in a concept of authorship: the annotator traces the author's complex indebtedness to a range of sources; film is a network of production that exposes the very concept of authorship as problematic, with screenplay writer, director, actors all contestants for the title.[20] Both annotation and film authenticate their own activity by drawing out what is subject to adaptation in the original and by questioning and reconfiguring ideas of property in the text. So what does the interpretative power of film contribute to the Austen we now find so accessible?

Insofar as it delivers spectacle where Austen is more apt to explore sound, film turns her narratives inside out, making her stories visually comprehensible by lingering on settings, details of dress and appearance – all those things she leaves to our imaginations. To repeat: sight, unlike hearing, is the sense Austen engages remarkably little in her readers in the normal course of things, though in the abnormal (or unreliable) course, sight is of great moment. Usually, where she mentions the colour of eyes or hair or dress such details function as a brisk shorthand to lead us as swiftly as possible to a more profound (non-visual) kind of assessment: '[Harriet Smith] was short, plump and fair, with a fine bloom, blue eyes, light hair, regular features, and a look of great sweetness' (*E* 1:3:22); '[Robert Martin's] appearance was very neat, and he looked like a sensible young man' (1:4:31); Mr John Knightley is 'tall and gentlemanlike' (1:11:100); Mr Elton, dressed for dinner at Randalls, is 'spruce, black, and smiling' (1:13:122). By contrast, visual imagery dominates screen pleasure; its illusion of authenticity is one of the main criteria by which we judge novel adaptation. In Austen's case, unlike Dickens', whose written art is from the start twinned with illustration, this represents a profound shift in register. The effect is to throw the stress upon context in much the way that textual annotation does: in both cases, we are offered a form of commentary on the materials out of which she worked with equal meticulousness. In the case of annotation, we are given exact sources for literary allusions, definitions or explanations for obsolete phrases, historical elucidation; in film, it is hairstyles, costumes, fabrics, foods, domestic interiors, carriages. Both risk

Film provides visual information regarding what Austen leaves to our imagination

Sight = not important

hearing more so

Vision dominates film

[handwritten margin note: Two examples of screen intervention that impacts how we read Austen: male leads and sub-plots]

something parodic as well as pleasurable: the excess that broods dangerously over our attempts to imagine and come to terms with so exquisitely slight and thrifty an artist.

There is of course far more to this excessive visualization of a supremely non-physical novelist; for it represents a shift in our mode of comprehension as profound as that signalled by Austen's entry around 1975 into the arena of history, of her contemporary 'war of ideas', from which we can date the need for heavyweight annotation.[21] Let me give two examples of screen intervention which have had momentous impact on the way we read Jane Austen: one concerns her male leads and the other her sub-plots. It was not until we saw him on screen that we gave much thought to Austen's hero as anything more than a yardstick, an educator or a moral ideal. But now he has a body, physical and emotional expressiveness, and of course breeches. He fences, swims, boxes, strips off, and he smoulders. Whole scenes were added to the 1995 BBC *Pride and Prejudice* enhancing Darcy's (Colin Firth's) barely restrained eroticism and making him an object of obvious visual pleasure. Our recognition of Jane Austen as romantic novelist lies in such powerful imagery. What is rendered ambivalent in the novels (the hero's ultimate importance in the heroine's maturing and her wider relations with society) is shorn of almost all complexity in film, where the male protagonist's attractions are inevitably overspecified.

One effect of the tunnelled vision of adaptation is to jettison the sophisticated system of manipulative social relations, encompassing both the subtle imbalances of power between men and women and between women and women, in which the novels trade. One consequence of this difference (as much a matter of medium as anything else) is the intense concentration on the marriage or rather the sex plot in the screen contract with the viewer. In particular, its happy conclusion – something Austen can question, delay and then hurry through with embarrassing haste – is anticipated from the outset by film's visual codes. We can believe in reading *Emma* that the youthful, high-spirited Emma does not recognize the older, staid Mr Knightley as lover until the substitute match-making plot to find Harriet a husband is almost played out; on screen, by contrast, their compatibility cannot be suppressed beyond the opening frames because it is invisible neither to Emma nor the viewer. More precisely, part of the pleasure of rereading *Emma* lies in tracing the gradual correction of Emma's faulty vision and discovering, through her eyes, how this is bound up with seeing Mr Knightley. It is not until Volume 3, chapter 2, that Emma describes his 'tall, firm, upright figure', and not until Volume 3, chapter 11, that '[i]t darted through her, with the speed of an arrow, that Mr. Knightley must marry no one but herself!'. In the 1996 film this late revelation of Cupid's true aim is transposed to an early scene in which

Emma and Mr Knightley practice archery on a splendid lawn by a lake, a screen moment that contains a further visual allusion to the archery scene in the 1940 MGM *Pride and Prejudice*. On screen, it is all about heroes and heroines and sex appeal – not simply how they look together, but how they look: how they engage in looking. At key moments in all Austen's novels the eye refuses to see.[22] Debate over the exchange of looks that takes place in film, as well as the late entry of the female spectator into such argument, is of great importance in understanding the form's appeal.[23] With rare exceptions, the subtler insights from this exchange have still to be brought to bear on both the practice of Austenian adaptation and its critique.

Summing up the 'new approach to Jane Austen' as evidenced by screen adaptations of the 1990s, Sue Birtwistle, producer of the 1995 *Pride and Prejudice*, argued: 'When Darcy emerges from his swim in his wet shirt the fantasy is complete: sex and money made easy and wrapped in the respectable cloak of a classic. This was a new phenomenon.' During the same years television was awash with make-over shows. In this context, Mr Darcy's now iconic screen moment, absent from the novel's text, may yet represent, within its own proper medium and for its largely female audience, an equivalent to A. C. Bradley's 1911 response to Elizabeth Bennet – 'I was meant to fall in love with her, and I do'. Both Andrew Davies' screenplay and Bradley's criticism offer spirited illumination and defence of Elizabeth's original mercenary impulse in her reply to her sister Jane's question of how long she has loved Mr Darcy: 'It has been coming on so gradually ... But I believe I must date it from my first seeing his beautiful grounds at Pemberley' (*PP* 3:17:414). Davies found a way to explain to a 1990s audience the utter relevance to their own intensely material preoccupations and fantasies, stimulated by other television offerings, of what Barbara Everett has insightfully described as Austen's hard romance.[24]

My second example concerns the Austenian sub-plot. As we know, the major action of all Austen's novels offers the private lives of characters where action converts relatively straightforwardly into conversations around the tea table, social visits, dinner parties, games of speculation and dances. As an early fan, Kipling's Humberstall, noted as long ago as 1924, "Twasn't as if there was anythin' *to* 'em ... They weren't adventurous, nor smutty, nor what you'd call even interestin'.'[25] Austen rarely deals in extremes of human behaviour. But lurking in the background of such a probable range of experience is always the sensational incident, the staple ingredient of what her contemporary Wordsworth called the 'frantic novel'.[26] Think of Maria Rushworth's elopement with Henry Crawford and her subsequent savage banishment; of Frank Churchill's selfish manipulation of both Emma and Jane Fairfax; of Wickham's seduction of Georgiana Darcy. Inside the naturalist machine of Austen's intensely critical novels there is always the ghost of a gothic plot. Austen wrote her novels as a form of critical engagement with the novel itself. And as Virginia Woolf noted, through adaptation film inhabits and reanimates novels:[27] what Austen, with her appeal to reflection and rereading, turned outside in, film, with its antithetical emphasis on analysis and perception, turns inside out again.[28]

Sometimes, the appeal to sensation is more powerful than the inward-driven work of the novelist. In the 2008 BBC mini-series *Sense and Sensibility*, Andrew Davies was faced with the question of how to deal with Willoughby's seduction and abandonment of Colonel Brandon's 15-year-old ward Eliza, an event occurring beyond the narrative and only related by Brandon to Elinor as late as Volume 2, chapter 9. Davies could not omit it because it provides a vital element in both Willoughby's eventual condemnation and Brandon's characterization. What he does is bring it out from the shadows to become the repeated opening scene of each episode, where it is teasingly dramatized – a confusion of firelight, roving hands, throbbing female flesh and Willoughby's unmistakable profile. What for Austen nails Willoughby as false only *after* his betrayal of Marianne, serves in Davies' emotional chronology as the interpretative, 'frantic' frame for Marianne's rash love and a device for clarifying from the start Willoughby's worthlessness. By this neat inversion, a heavily contrived sub-plot that risks real redundancy in Austen's narrative, becomes for Davies the crime that drives the whole. Though at a stroke this dissolves some of the novel's moral ambiguities, it is also an intelligent resolution of the problem of Colonel Brandon as hero.

Andrew Davies has dominated television adaptation of classic novels for more than a decade, injecting energy with his quick cuts and instantly recognizable rakish visual style. Above all, Davies is proud of his ability to inhabit Austen's language. He reads her texts closely, culling them for choice sentences and emphasizing through his direction her dramatic talent for building up to the big scene and for well-paced dialogue. But we should not be fooled: there is incautious infidelity at the heart of this homage. Davies' skill lies in writing lines that either sound like Austen's or that the context persuades us she might have written. Marianne's 2008 screen observation – 'What strange creatures men are . . . What do they want from us? Perhaps they see us not as people but as playthings, Elinor' – is later disturbingly recalled when Elinor comments on Colonel Brandon's gentle treatment of her sister as like that of the 'great tamers of horses' and again, in the closing scenes, when we see Marianne and the free-flying hawk return together to his hand when bidden. We might search Austen's text in vain for any of these moments. The effect is to trouble the marriage ending that Davies has worked so hard to make

[handwritten annotation: Film: good at delivering secrets and silences, intercepting stolen glances]

plausible and to cast doubt, after all, on the compatibility of Brandon and Marianne, of 'thirty-five and seventeen' (*SS* 1:8:45). As he further secures his position as adaptor-in-chief, Davies takes daring liberties to make Austen ventriloquize his words, a further sign, perhaps, of screen's confidence to re-form what we read.

Austen's tales of two sisters, two cousins, two friends, or in Anne Elliot's case two selves, and their parallel emotional journeys of falling in love transfer well to screen. The playing out of her double plots full of internal echo and variation provides satisfying moral conundrums and compelling emotional, visual dramas. Film is also good at delivering secrets and silences; at intercepting stolen glances and moments of inner struggle as recorded on the face, a form of dumb eloquence that serves Austen's indirect narration particularly well. The sequence of mainly silent images suggestive of the turmoil of Anne Elliot's inner life in the opening scenes of the 1995 *Persuasion* work so well because we are seduced into sympathy by Amanda Root's reticent performance. There is no intrusive voice-over, no coy Hollywood-style diary-writing or mirror-gazing to bring the viewer up to speed, and when she looks camera-wards her gaze is inward. More recently, Gwyneth Hughes, an acclaimed crime dramatist, crafted a taut and compelling script from the few details we have of Austen's later life. *Miss Austen Regrets* is a made-for-television film that aired on the BBC in April 2008. It was compiled from the slightest of evidence, though of course no slighter than the many, heavy print biographies that thudded onto the market throughout the twentieth century. How might Austen's life appear if we view it from her decision to renege on a promise to marry? What are we to make of the inclusion in her two late novels, *Emma* and *Persuasion*, of one woman (Mrs Weston) who marries in middle age and another whose broken engagement eight years before has left her in an emotional wasteland? By drawing skilfully on Jane Austen's letters to her sister Cassandra and niece Fanny Knight, stitching in and reapportioning to these later years social and personal observations and insights from much earlier correspondence, Hughes used film with tact and penetration, breathing new life into old biographical speculation. Austen's letters have received far less critical attention than the novels, yet they fizz with wit and malice, alternately obliging and bitter on the demands of relationships, unflinchingly self-aware on the subject of her own ageing and delighted or oppressed by domestic trivia. Fragments of social and psychic drama, they translate effectively to screen, finding in Hughes' script a voice whose authenticity and modernity may take many by surprise.

Austen's relationship with her niece Fanny prompts the film's emotional journey. Played with great assurance by Olivia Williams this is a complicated, controversially adult Austen: tart and barbed, amusing, desperately flirtatious, lonely, by turns intolerant, dependent and afraid, a complicated biographical portrait that works because film, unlike words, can trade effectively in silence. Less constrained by the anxieties of adaptation, *Miss Austen Regrets* reaches a new level in exploiting the differences between the media of print and film, making an innovative contribution to both Austen biography and the Austen screen industry. There is a tactful understanding that gaps in the evidence need not be filled with anything more foreclosing than the observing eye – of camera or subject; still interpretation, of course, but less determining than the wordy speculations of biography. The result is a bleak and beautiful film. Its representation of Williams/Austen as another camera eye is startling and disturbing, a visual equivalent to the nice discriminations of Austen's critical writing style. There is a noticeably European feel to the camera's close focus on Williams' eye or its sudden shift to another's ear or shoulder as the angle creates the effect of our appraising characters and even dissecting them as if from Austen's point of view. We are constrained within the orbit of her observation – literally at times within her body; in consequence we share a sensory and a critical kinship with her, reaching a disturbing climax in the triangulation of Austen, Fanny and the young physician Charles Haden towards the end of the film.

Miss Austen Regrets has found a new style, more observational (more truly filmic) and less encumbered than either the heritage-heavy sets of the 1990s or the muddy-hem sprightliness of recent adaptations. Detail is alternately drab, like the frugally recycled wardrobe given to Austen/Williams, or luminous. This extends to the domestic particulars of the Austen women's lives at Chawton, where objects, bathed in light and seen through doorways or framed in windows, are discovered in shape, colour and texture as simply themselves, the 'little matters' of Jane Austen's life and letters. At last, it seems, Austen adaptation has found roots in film rather than novel, and in consequence we begin to discriminate between ways of seeing rather than confronting the problematic differences between word and image.

NOTES

1. Samuel Johnson, 'Preface' to *A Dictionary of the English Language* (1755), in *Samuel Johnson: A Critical Edition of the Major Works*, ed. Donald Greene (Oxford University Press, 1984), p. 323.
2. See Casey Finch and Peter Bowen, '"The Tittle-Tattle of Highbury": Gossip and the Free Indirect Style in *Emma*', *Representations*, 31 (1990), 1–18; and Kathryn Sutherland, 'Conversable Fictions', in Paula R. Backscheider and Catherine Ingrassia, eds., *A Companion to the Eighteenth-Century English Novel and Culture* (Oxford: Blackwell, 2005), pp. 399–418.
3. Bharat Tandon, *Jane Austen and the Morality of Conversation* (London: Anthem Press, 2003), p. 191: 'Like James after her, Austen was a poet of domestic pathology'.

4. Claudia Johnson, 'Jane Austen's Relics and the Treasures of the East Room', *Persuasions*, 28 (2006), 222, 217–30.
5. There is a vast literature on literary film adaptation. Among the best, see George Bluestone, *Novels into Film* (1957; Baltimore, MD and London: Johns Hopkins University Press, 2003); Brian McFarlane, *Novel to Film: An Introduction to the Theory of Adaptation* (Oxford: Clarendon Press, 1996); *Film Adaptation*, ed. James Naremore (New Brunswick, NJ: Rutgers University Press, 2000); Kamilla Elliott, *Rethinking the Novel/Film Debate* (Cambridge University Press, 2003); Robert Stam, *Literature through Film: Realism, Magic and the Art of Adaptation* (Oxford: Blackwell, 2005); and *The Literature/Film Reader*, ed. James M. Welsh and Peter Lev (Plymouth: Scarecrow Press, 2007).
6. Walter Benjamin, 'The Task of the Translator', in *Illuminations*, trans. Harry Zohn (London: Fontana, 1973), p. 77.
7. Randall McLeod (Random Clod), 'Information Upon Information', *TEXT*, 5 (1991), 246, 241–81
8. Sergei Eisenstein, *Film Form: Essays in Film Theory* (1949), ed. and trans. Jay Leyda (London: Dennis Dobson Ltd, 1977), p. 213; and see Grahame Smith, *Dickens and the Dream of Cinema* (Manchester University Press, 2003).
9. Ellen Belton, 'Reimagining Jane Austen: The 1940 and 1995 Film Versions of *Pride and Prejudice*', in Gina and Andrew Macdonald, eds., *Jane Austen on Screen* (Cambridge University Press, 2003), p. 182.
10. Robert Giddings and Keith Selby, *The Classic Serial on Television and Radio* (Basingstoke and New York: Palgrave Macmillan, 2001).
11. For Hugh Thomson and other 1890s illustrators, see Kathryn Sutherland, *Jane Austen's Textual Lives: From Aeschylus to Bollywood* (Oxford University Press, 2005), pp. 1–10. For adaptations of Austen's novels (mainly to this point non-filmic), see Andrew Wright, 'Jane Austen Adapted', *Nineteenth-Century Fiction*, 30 (1975–6), 421–53; supplemented by David Gilson, *A Bibliography of Jane Austen* (1982; corrected edn, Winchester: St Paul's Bibliographies, 1997), pp. 405–17 ('dramatizations' only). For film adaptations, see Sue Parrill, *Jane Austen on Film and Television: A Critical Study of the Adaptations* (Jefferson, NC: McFarland, 2002); and 'Jane Austen Adaptations Filmography', www.pemberley.com/filmography.
12. Martin Wroe, 'Hard Drugs and Heroine Addiction', *Observer*, 10 March 1996, p. 13.
13. Wroe, 'Hard Drugs'; and Giddings and Selby, *The Classic Serial*, p. 102.
14. Cf. Erica Sheen, 'the study of adaptation is, at its broadest level of significance, a study of authorship in a state of historical transformation', in 'Introduction', in Robert Giddings and Erica Sheen, eds., *The Classic Novel: From Page to Screen* (Manchester University Press, 2000), p. 4.
15. A. C. Bradley, 'Jane Austen', *Essays and Studies*, 2 (1911), 29.
16. Jan Baetens, 'Novelization, A Contaminated Genre', *Critical Inquiry*, 32 (2005), 43–60.
17. Henry James, *The Ambassadors* (1902), Book 3, ch. 2; Andrew Higson, *English Cinema, English Heritage: Costume Drama Since 1980* (Oxford University Press, 2003), p. 39.
18. André Bazin, 'The Ontology of the Photographic Image' in *What is Cinema?* Vol. 1, trans. Hugh Gray (Berkeley, CA: University of California Press, 1974), p. 15.

19. Sutherland, *Jane Austen's Textual Lives*, pp. 349–51.

20. There is a wide literature of varying complexity on the vexed issue of film authorship. See, for example, Peter Wollen, *Signs and Meaning in the Cinema* (London: Secker & Warburg, 1972); Robert Lapsley and Michael Westlake, *Film Theory: An Introduction* (Manchester University Press, 1988); Robert Stam, *Film Theory: An Introduction* (Oxford: Blackwell, 2000); Bernard F. Dick, *Anatomy of Film*, 5th edn (Boston, MA: Bedford/St Martin's Press, 2005), pp. 223–53. For a challenging early critique, see V. F. Perkins, *Film as Film: Understanding and Judging Movies* (1972; Cambridge, MA: Da Capo Press, 1993).

21. Marilyn Butler, *Jane Austen and the War of Ideas* (1975; rev. edn, Oxford: Clarendon Press, 1987) represents this sea change in Austen studies.

22. Compare with the mutual acknowledgement in *Emma*, the final declaration of love in *Pride and Prejudice*, where 'Had Elizabeth been able to encounter his eye, she might have seen . . .' (3:16:407).

23. Laura Mulvey, 'Visual Pleasure and Narrative Cinema' (1975), repr. in *Visual and Other Pleasures* (Basingstoke: Macmillan, 1989); and E. Ann Kaplan, *Looking for the Other: Feminism, Film, and the Imperial Gaze* (London and New York: Routledge, 1997).

24. Barbara Everett, 'Hard Romance', *London Review of Books*, 8 February 1996, pp. 12–14.

25. Rudyard Kipling, 'The Janeites', collected in *Debits and Credits* (London: Macmillan, 1926), pp. 156–7.

26. William Wordsworth, 'Preface' to *Lyrical Ballads* (1800), in *The Prose Works of William Wordsworth*, ed. W. J. B. Owen and Jane Worthington Smyser, 3 vols. (Oxford: Clarendon Press, 1974), vol. I, p. 128.

27. Virginia Woolf, 'The Cinema' (1926), in *The Essays of Virginia Woolf*, ed. Andrew McNeillie, 4 vols. (London: Hogarth Press, 1986–94), vol. IV, pp. 349–50.

28. For the difference between the novel and film in these respects, see Karl Kroeber, *Make Believe in Film and Fiction: Visual vs. Verbal Storytelling* (New York and Basingstoke: Palgrave Macmillan, 2006), pp. 69–79.

15

CLAUDIA L. JOHNSON

Austen cults and cultures

Ever since Henry James, early in the twentieth century, observed that a 'body of publishers, editors, illustrators, [and] producers of the pleasant twaddle of magazines' found 'their "dear", our dear, everybody's dear, Jane so infinitely to their material purpose', two things have been abundantly clear: first, that Austen has been not a mere novelist about whom one might talk dispassionately, but a commercial phenomenon and a cultural figure, at once formidable and non-threatening; second, that many of Austen's most acute admirers have been unhappy with this extravagant popularity. An Austenian descendant himself, James aims his criticism not so much at Austen but at her faddish commodification by publishers and marketers. He had a point. Since 1832, Austen's six novels were available separately in the Standard Novels series published by Richard Bentley. But even though Bentley reprinted the novels at various times in the coming decades, joined by other printers once his copyrights expired, Austen's novels were hardly bestsellers. Indeed, she remained an artist admired intensely by a few, such as George Lewes and Thomas Macaulay. 'Janeitism' – the self-consciously idolatrous enthusiasm for 'Jane' and every detail relative to her which James is alluding to – did not burgeon until the last two decades of the nineteenth century. It was spurred on by J. E. Austen-Leigh's *A Memoir of Jane Austen* in 1870, which provided biographical information about the quaint and saintly obscure spinster aunt who lived in a quieter time, and by Bentley's deluxe *Steventon Edition of Jane Austen's Work* in 1882 (the first collected edition of Austen's novels), which included 'Lady Susan', the *Memoir*, a frontispiece portrait of Austen and woodcuts of Chawton Church and Steventon Parsonage, and which thus put most of Austen's famous little 'world' into a tidy bundle.[1] Janeitism boomed with the wider publication of Austen's novels singly and in sets, ranging from Routledge's cheap issues of 1883, and the Sixpenny Novel series starting in 1886; to Macmillan's 1890 issues, lavishly if inanely illustrated by Hugh Thomson; to the quasi-scholarly ten-volume set of R. Brimley Johnson for Dent in 1892, reissued five times in as many years.[2]

Aggravated by such commercial promotion, James denounces the 'special bookselling spirit' which, with all its 'eager, active interfering force' (rather like a nautical Mrs Norris), whips up a 'stiff breeze', driving the waters of reputation above their natural levels, and flooding the literary marketplace to promote the sales of its own titles. Though inclined to disparage Austen as an unconscious artist, James acknowledges that she would not be so 'saleable if we had not more or less . . . lost our hearts to her' in the first place.[3] But the truth is that James cannot stand the fact that Austen is loved in the wrong ways by the wrong sorts of people, people evidently incapable of assessing her just value, or discriminating her real merits.

If James, revolted by middlebrow culture and its purveyors, lambastes the ubiquity of Austeniana in 'pretty reproduction in every variety of what is called tasteful . . . form', how would he recoil today, when Austen comes to us in dazzling movies from Hollywood and the British film industry featuring our favourite stars, in more ponderous BBC adaptations, in published sequels, imitations and homages, on radio broadcasts and editorial pages, on bumper stickers announcing 'I'd rather be reading Jane Austen', on book bags and T-shirts sporting Cassandra's portrait of her sister, on coffee mugs averring, via Kipling, that there is no one to beat Jane when you're in a tight place? Clearly, once her reputation thrived beyond a small circle of enthusiasts, Austen's appeal has been wide enough to be a worry, for it reaches beyond the authority of those who consider themselves entitled to adjudicate not only who but how it is proper to enjoy 'great' literature.

Other chapters in this book treat Austen and her novels as an object of study. This chapter addresses not Austen's works per se, but our reception of them, the ideas about culture Austen has been thought to represent, and the uses to which we have put her and her achievement. Needless to say, the extent to which any writer can be pondered independently from her or his reception remains a vexed question. But Austen is a cultural fetish: loving – or hating – her has typically implied meanings well beyond any encoded in her works. Because she has proved essential to the self-definition of so many contending interests – people who see themselves as delicate escapists or as hard-nosed realists, as staunch defenders of morality or as exponents of ludically amoral theatricality, as elitists or democrats, as iconoclasts or conventionalists, as connoisseurs or as common readers – it is conspicuously difficult to disentangle the 'real' Austen from the acknowledged or unacknowledged agendas of those discussing her.

One vociferous segment of Austen's reading public missing from the above assortment are professional academics, and I omitted us solely for the purpose of more exclusive emphasis here. The claim to unbiased enquiry is foundational to our enterprise as teachers and students, but we too have been an interested and decidedly high-handed party contending for access to the real Jane Austen, and thus stand to learn a great deal from recognizing how some of our most basic assumptions about how to read her novels were calculated to consolidate the authority of a new professorate, with its distinctive programme and concomitant visions of class, gender and national identity, and at a time when the novel was still entering the curriculum at Oxbridge (having been included decades earlier in the curricula of US colleges and universities, where classical models held less sway). What follows is not an exhaustive analysis of Austenian criticism among diverse readerships for the past two centuries, but a more modest attempt to historicize our notions about her, in the hopes of demonstrating the numerous ways in which she has been a cultural presence.

Modern Austenian criticism begins not with a literary critic or a novel scholar, but with psychologist D. W. Harding. The fundamental principle of his path breaking 1940 essay is that Austen's 'books are . . . read and enjoyed by precisely the sort of people whom she disliked'. To be sure, this was not the first time anyone had argued that Austen's relation to her subject matter was satirical rather than reverential – one thinks, for example, of Mrs Oliphant's remarks on the 'feminine cynicism' and '[quiet] jeering' in Austen's works.[4] Nor, as James' remarks above indicate, was this the first time anyone asserted the superiority of his own powers of discrimination by trashing others' love of Austen as mindless, excessive or otherwise undisciplined. But it was, I think, the first time anyone claimed that Austen herself was above her admirers, and attempted to place criticism on a proper footing by rescuing her from them.

But who were these admirers, and what is it precisely that Harding is trying to get away from? Not the hoi polloi, the philistine Janeites James had castigated, for whom an admiration of Austen stood as an example of high culture in its least challenging form, and for whom an admiration of her works served as a badge of gentility. The social and political horizon had radically changed, and when Harding thinks of Janeites, men of the upper classes come to his mind, the 'exponents of urbanity', the 'sensitive' and 'cultured', the 'Gentlemen of an older generation than mine' who disseminate Austeniana 'through histories of literature, university courses, literary journalism, and polite allusions'. Because we now live in a cultural environment when it can be assumed that literature written by women is literature written for women, it may at first seem counter-intuitive that, in its most influential forms, the Janeitism of the early twentieth century was, with the prominent exception of Shakespearian scholar Caroline Spurgeon, principally a male enthusiasm shared among publishers, professors and literati such as Montague Summers, A. C. Bradley, Lord David Cecil, Walter Raleigh, R. W. Chapman and E. M. Forster. At the Royal Society of Literature (RSL) in particular Austen's genius was celebrated with an enthusiasm that would be regarded as dotty in the conferences or classrooms of today. Far from regarding their interest in Austen as level-headed 'work' necessitated by the complexity of her novels, Janeites flaunt it as ecstatic revelation: she was not merely their *dear* Jane, but their *divine* Jane, their *matchless* Jane, and they were her *cult*, her *sect*, her *little company* (*fit though few*), her *tribe* of ardent adorers who celebrate the *miracle* of her work in flamboyantly hyperbolic terms, archly suggesting – to my ear at least – the incommensurateness of their fervour to the primness of its object. Although their zeal is genuine, the self-parody implicit in these pronouncements tells us that we are in an insider's society of scholar gentlemen at play.[5]

Janeites constituted a reading community whose practices transgress the dogmas later instituted by professional academics presiding over the emergent field of novel studies – dogmas holding, for example, that it is inappropriate to talk about characters as if they were real people or in any way to speculate upon their lives before, after or outside the text itself; that biographical information about an author is irrelevant at best and heretical (i.e. a 'fallacy') at worst; that the business of studying is serious indeed, requiring analytic skills and specialist knowledges available through courses of study at colleges and universities; that Austen's novels are essentially about marriage, and that the courtship plot – rather than, say, the category *character* – is the major event in her fiction. To exemplify and to account for ways in which Janeite reading practices resist these truths *not* universally acknowledged, I will turn briefly to Rudyard Kipling's 'The Janeites', a story often alluded to in Austen criticism, but quite obviously not very often or very carefully read.

A story within a frame story, 'The Janeites' is set in a London Masonic Lodge during 1920, where shell-shocked veteran Humberstall talks about a secret society into which he was inducted while serving under the supervision of Sergeant Macklin as an officers' mess-waiter with his First World War artillery battery in France.[6] One day as the officers discuss whether or not 'Jane' died without leaving 'direct an' lawful prog'ny', Macklin (who is very drunk) loudly interrupts the officers' conversation with the claim 'She did leave lawful issue in the shape o' one son; an' 'is name was 'Enery James' (124). Puzzled that the superior officers, far from punishing such insubordinate intrusiveness, actually order him to be taken off to bed and cared for, Humberstall finds out more about the secret club whose membership brings such extraordinary privileges. After selling him the password (*'Tilniz an' trap-doors'*, a phrase from *Northanger Abbey*), Macklin imparts to him the mysteries of Jane, which make the horrors of the front companionable: 'It was a 'appy little Group' (132), Humberstall later murmurs nostalgically. When half the battery is killed in a German artillery attack, Humberstall is the only Janeite to survive. As he struggles to board a hospital train, only to be put off by a chattering nurse insisting the train is too crowded, Humberstall implores the head nurse to 'make Miss Bates, there, stop talkin' or I'll die', and the head nurse – evidently an initiate herself – recognizes a fellow's password and eagerly obliges, even filching a spare blanket for his comfort (136).

As a story both about readings and readers of Austen's novels, 'The Janeites' is highly suggestive. Unlike virtually all academic readers of Austen since the 1950s, Janeites in foxholes do not think Austen's novels are about courtship and marriage. The love story plot is less than inevitable for them. In their civilian lives, they are chilly towards women (Jane 'was the only woman I ever 'eard 'em say a good word for' (123) Humberstall remembers), and chary of domesticity (the senior Janeites are a Divorce Court Lawyer and a Private Detective specializing in adultery cases). Even Humberstall himself, having been discharged from an earlier stint of service, can so little tolerate the company of his mother, sister and aunts that he actually re-enlists. Of course, the Janeites recognize that novels are 'all about young girls o' seventeen ... not certain 'oom they'd like to marry', but for them (unlike non-Janeites in the story) this narrative fact is levelled with other narrative facts that also constitute part of what the novels are 'all about' – including 'their dances an' card parties an' picnics, and their young blokes goin' off to London on 'orseback for 'aircuts an' shaves', a detail which, like the wearing of wigs, is especially engaging to a hairdresser like Humberstall. As far as Austenian plots are concerned, 'there was nothin' *to* 'em nor *in* 'em. Nothin' at all' (128).

Defended by mere school lads, equipped with superannuated cannon, and mobilized by a dilapidated train rather than modern transport caterpillars, the Janeites' battery is pitifully doomed. As readers they cathect onto Austen's novels precisely because they appear to have no plots. Again, unlike current students and scholars of narrative, for whom plot bears virtually all significance in narrative, Janeite readers resist plot with all its forward-moving momentums, its inevitabilities and its closure, and they dwell instead on atemporal aspects of narration, such as descriptive details, catchy phrases and especially characterization. As in the bulk of belletristic Janeite commentary from the mid-nineteenth century on, Janeites in the foxholes rhapsodize over the verisimilitude of Austenian characters. By identifying characters and things in their own experience and renaming them according to Austenian prototypes the soon-to-be-slaughtered Janeites piece out their brutally shattered world.

Because Janeites outside Kipling's story would be decried as escapists taking solace in the supposedly rehabilitative placidity of Austen's world, it is worth stressing that Kipling's Janeites do not quite fit this model, and indeed are drawn to Austen precisely because she is like the world of the foxholes. Their Jane Austen – as distinct from the Austen celebrated in the prefatory poem as 'England's Jane' (120) – is never described by them as a repository of ethical wisdom, nor is she linked with a feminine elegiac ideal of England whose very vulnerability is what knightly menfolk are fighting to protect. At the end of the story, Humberstall avidly reads Austen's novels not because they enable him to recapture the safe world which war has not shaken, but because they remind him of the trenches: 'it brings it all back – down to the smell of the glue-paint on the screens. You take it from me, Brethren, there's no one to touch Jane when you're in a tight place' (137).

Since many within the academy and outside of it as well often assume that Austen and her admirers are hyper-conventional, it is also worth emphasizing that Janeite confederacies had rather little truck with bourgeois domestic morality. Kipling's story mentions two exclusive societies – the Masons and the Janeites – but several details suggest that Austen's fiction promoted a secret brotherhood of specifically homoerotic fellowship too. When Humberstall chalks the names of Austenian characters onto the casements of the guns, he rouses the ire of the Battery Sergeant Major, who reads Humberstall's cockney spelling of 'De Bugg' for De Bourgh as a reference to sodomy. Determined to punish him and Macklin for 'writin' obese words on His Majesty's property', the BSM takes the case to the officers on the grounds that "e couldn't hope to preserve discipline unless examples was made' (131). What he does not foresee is that the officers will not discipline one of their own: they dismiss the charges after perfunctory admonitions, send the BSM away, and proceed to entertain themselves by quizzing Humberstall on Jane. The narrator, not a Janeite, closes the story by observing that Austen was 'a match-maker' and her novels 'full of match-making' (138), and by hinting at a secondary character's marriage to Humberstall's sister. And as if this were not going far enough, Kipling attaches a sequel-poem entitled 'Jane's Marriage', in which Jane enters the gates of Heaven and is rewarded by matrimony to Captain Wentworth. But these efforts to instate the marriage plot are not only risible (after all, Wentworth is both fictional and already married!) but are also at odds with the spirit of Janeitism narrated within the story, and thus the frame itself appears to be a sop thrown to 'a pious post-war world' which requires what the narrator has already called 'revision[s]' and deletions (129). Janeites are committed to club rather than domestic society. The reproduction in which they are interested pertains not to spouses and children – in fact, they are as barren of 'direct an' lawful prog'ny' as Austen herself, leaving no issue we know of, the surviving Humberstall being a stranger to women. The reproduction they engage in is the dissemination of Janeite culture itself. Just as Austen brought forth Henry James, Janeites bring forth other Janeites by recruitment, peopling the world with Austenian characters, thus continually enlarging her world beyond the confines non-initiates are wont to dismiss as narrow. Macklin is highly satisfied when Humberstall renames the guns after Austenian characters – 'He reached up an' patted me on the shoulder. "You done nobly", he says. "You're bringin' forth abundant fruit, like a good Janeite"' (130).

As Kipling's story suggests, early twentieth-century Janeitism is a construction that emerges from specific historical needs. Before the First World War, Frederic Harrison described Austen as a 'heartless little cynic ... penning satirettes against her neighbours whilst the Dynasts were tearing the world to pieces, and consigning millions to their graves'.[7] Harrison of course deplored Austen's supposed isolation from the real world, but once the dynasts of our own century went at it, many Janeites loved precisely this ahistoricity, indulging in a fantasy about the elegiac Austen which Kipling's story both conjures and also, in my view, undermines. To Janeites outside Kipling's story, her novels evoke a world *before* history blew up, *before* rules and codes lost their efficacy, particularly in defining masculinity in relation to other men. Christopher Kent has shown that Austen's novels were actually recommended to British veterans suffering post-traumatic shock syndrome in the years following the war.[8] For soldiers whose minds were shattered by dynastic history, the (in)famously limited dimensions of Austen's fictional world could feel rehabilitative; her placid interiors could feel manageable; her scepticism about the turbulence of sexual passion could feel a relief; her triviality could feel redemptive. Assumptions about *feminine* propriety embedded within this fantasy about Austen – about transparency, restraint and poise – helped to shore up masculine lucidity and self-definition when these, along with English national identity itself, were under threat. The notion, then, that Austen could be therapy for people whom history has made sick has an origin in global crisis and in a profound yearning for a world still sufficient to its own forms and rituals.[9]

Harding and the tradition of academic criticism he inaugurated ridiculed the idyllic figure of 'England's Jane' whose work 'provide[s] a refuge for the sensitive when the contemporary world grew too much for them', and he refers with contempt to those who place her beyond the ugly world of politics, crisis and machine-guns.[10] But the Janeitism of this period was more productive than he admits. For one thing, it gave us Chapman's *The Novels of Jane Austen*, published by Clarendon Press in 1923, and ever since (at least until the emergence of the new Cambridge Edition used in this book) acknowledged to be the authoritative edition of her works. Because novel studies have since moved to the centre of university curricula, while Greek and Latin departments are struggling to survive, it is easy to forget that Chapman's was the first scholarly edition of any English novelist – male or female – ever to appear. His title page touted that 'The [Texts are] based on a Collation of the Early Editions', and, as reviewers were quick to note, he treated Austen's novels with a scrupulousness customarily reserved for classical authors. What prompted such anomalous magisteriality at such a moment? The answer can be found in the collection of short essays Chapman wrote during his own wartime duty in Macedonia, where he recurs to his birthright as a classically educated English gentleman as if to bolster his morale in an alien world: he recites Horace's odes from memory on long marches or on quiet nights at observation posts; he animadverts on the decline of English syntax, on proposals for British spelling reform which would 'involve us in dangers and inconveniences of unsuspected magnitude'; he muses on his passion for collecting silver spoons, closing on a note of imperial melancholy: 'There are no spoons in Macedonia.'

Given Chapman's sense of his stewardship to English culture, felt acutely during his isolation from it, it is no wonder that he declared 'To restore, and maintain in its integrity, the text of our great writers is a pious duty.' Having fondly remembered not only Horace's odes, as it turns out, but also 'a series of summer evenings in Perthshire, when a lady read *Persuasion* to admiration', Chapman places Austen alongside Samuel Johnson as a monument to the redemptive glory of England's bygone days.[11] To be sure, Victorian publishers preserved Austen too, and with hype loud enough to offend James' ears. But while their volumes, replete with Victorian-styled illustrations and typography, perforce made Austen one of their own, the edition Chapman prepared to preserve this treasure in its 'integrity' includes chronologies of plot events based on early nineteenth-century almanacs, reproductions of regency fashion plates and dancing manuals, and not least of all facsimiles of the original title pages, thus placing Austen safely within the national past the better to secure her there as a refuge from the present. Most of Chapman's reviewers recognized and gratefully approved of this enterprise: the reviewer for the *New Statesman* specifically praises the illustrations and historical apparatus for helping to make Austen's novels 'a *refuge* from present realities'; while the *Edinburgh Review*, likewise bemoaning its modernity, maintains that 'It is something to have escaped, if only for a moment, from this "world" that is "too much with us" to that other world, the leisured, "country-featured" and homely world of Jane Austen.'[12] Pressing Austen into the service of this national nostalgia, Chapman not only piously preserves the past, of course, but decides exactly *which* past to preserve, tracking down allusions to Shakespeare, Johnson and Cowper with indefatigable energy, but passing over references to slavery in Antigua or riots in London as if they and the unrest to which they allude did not exist. *That* past – which so compels our generation, with its very different premiums on ideological rupture and political conflict – was not to the purpose of Chapman and his fellows.

Although some of the methods, if not the motives, of Janeitism would surface in later academic criticism under the banner of historicism, it was foundational to the practice of Austenian criticism in the academy to discredit the Janeites such as existed in Kipling's story, in the Royal Society of Literature, and of course in later Jane Austen Societies in England and North America. Deploying an invidious distinction between the 'attentive' and 'urbane', Harding accomplished this by asserting that Austen's admirers are her worst readers: '[S]he is a literary classic of the society which attitudes like hers, held widely enough, would undermine.' Harding's own qualifications as a good reader, it is implied, derive from his own rigorously tough-minded alienation from upper-class mores, an alienation Austen herself is said to have shared. Claiming Austen would never 'have helped to make her society what it was, or ours what it is', Harding trumps the Janeite 'posterity of urbane gentlemen' by disaffiliating Austen from them and the doddering, weak-minded complacency they are said to represent.[13]

Harding's depiction of Austen as a subversive opponent of dominant values proved helpful to the next generation of academics, especially feminists, who also considered Austen at odds with dominant values, and to all readers who took candidly non-moralistic and non-moralizing pleasure in her sarcasm. But Harding's intentions were anything but open-minded, and his immediate heirs were not slow to elaborate the nasty class- and gender-inflected attacks implicit in his essay. Defining Janeite escapists as effete gentlemen, Harding hinted that Austen was in some ways more of a real man, astringent and unblinking, than they were. F. R. Leavis is more direct in *The Great Tradition* (1948), which is among other things a running diatribe against Janeite extraordinaire, Lord David Cecil. Leavis dignifies Austen as well as the great tradition of English fiction she originated by insisting on her moral seriousness, and accordingly, the leisured amateurism of Janeites – with their fondness for entertainment, performance and comedy – is noxious to him. His class-based attack upon Lord David, which includes charges of decadence, aestheticism, over-sophistication and evil, contains a homophobically charged gender component as well, for when Leavis casts aspersions on Lytton Strachey and the culture of Bloomsbury, he is aiming to taint Lord David by association.[14]

Citing the 'feral' animosity of writers like Twain, Lionel Trilling opined that Austen aroused 'man's panic fear at a fictional world in which the masculine principle, although represented as admirable and necessary, is prescribed and controlled by a female mind', but Trilling's explanation misrepresents the problem as a conflict between the two sexes rather than as a conflict about sexuality per se, regardless of the sex of the offender in question.[15] The history of Austenian criticism has often been darkened by the umbrage Austen-haters have taken against her representations of men as idle creatures absorbed in village tittle-tattle, and male Janeites have had much to endure at the hands of a world that frowns upon their passion. H. W. Garrod's 'Depreciation', a virulent attack upon Austen and her admirers both, was written 'for a pleasant occasion, and in lightness of heart' as a lecture to fellow members of the RSL. But its misogyny is still toxic, and it spatters onto men as well. Garrod opens by questioning the virility of Janeites in his audience: 'There is a time to be born and a time to die, and a time to be middle-aged and read Miss Austen. Some men are born middle-aged, some achieve middle age of their preference, others have it thrust upon them.' A man content to read novels by 'a mere slip of a girl', Garrod suggests, must somehow be womanish as well. Having feminized themselves not simply by idolizing a woman writer – which is bad enough – but even worse by then idolizing a sharp-tongued woman who fails to honour the virility of men, Janeites by Garrod's account are doubly queer.[16]

What makes Harding's and Leavis' attacks on the unmanfulness of Janeites different from Garrod's and others' is that they like Austen, and seek to clear themselves from the charge of gender deviance by wresting Austen from gentlemen scholars and literati and making Austen safe for real men engaged in real study. C. S. Lewis' 1954 essay 'A Note on Jane Austen' continues this process: '[Austen] is described by someone in Kipling's worst story as the mother of Henry James', he taunts, referring to 'The Janeites', '[but] I feel much more sure that she is the daughter of Dr. Johnson'. Engaging in a frontal assault on the playful, ironized Austen – which might make her fiction in his eyes a sort of regency *The Importance of Being Earnest* – Lewis insists that Austen's comedy is inspired by 'hard core morality' and a vein 'of religion'.

Post-Second World War Austenian reception participates in that demand to consolidate and reinvigorate masculinity elsewhere visible in the larger context of British and American culture. Academic literary criticism of the 1940s and early 1950s saves Austen from her admirers and for a middle-class professorate by celebrating her acerbity and seriousness, championing her fiction as a legitimate object of study in the as yet young field of novel studies over and against the ostensibly frivolous appreciation of Janeites. But while this criticism – to which in varying degrees that of Lascelles, Watt and Edmund Wilson could be added – conduced to the rise of Austen as an academic field, it did not as yet foster any particular method of reading narrative, nor did it privilege the marriage plot as the most important structural and thematic principle.[17] Indeed, Austen's very scepticism about romantic love is in part what qualifies her as a tough-minded fellow traveller. True,

Marvin Mudrick's profoundly influential *Jane Austen: Irony as Defense and Discovery* (1952) moved in this direction, but this was by omission. For Mudrick, Austen's artistic brilliance – i.e., her formidable irony and control – results from her pathology as a woman – i.e., her formidable irony and control. Mudrick looks to Austen's novels for tender marriage plots, and is scandalized by their absence. He takes as his epigraph Harding's allusion to Austen being loved by people she hates; but while Harding likes Austen's steely lucidity, Mudrick deplores it as deviance – cast, as in Emma Woodhouse's case, sometimes as frigidity and sometimes as lesbianism.[18]

It was not until the 1960s that the marriage plot gained the prestige it still enjoys inside the academy, and this happened in a direct attempt to recuperate Austen's normality. Wayne Booth's widely reprinted 'Control of Distance in Jane Austen's *Emma*' (1961) passionately defends Emma Woodhouse's heterosexuality, which Wilson and Mudrick had doubted. Chafing at the contention that Emma has infatuations with women even at the conclusion, he links the proper reading of Austen's novels with a proper respect for the self-evidence of marital felicity in novels and outside them:

> Marriage to an intelligent, amiable, good, and attractive man is the best thing that can happen to this heroine, and the readers who do not experience it as such are, I am convinced, far from knowing what Jane Austen is about – whatever they may say about the 'bitter spinster's' attitude toward marriage.

When novels themselves lacked the cultural prestige of poetry and drama, people who studied them could be considered lightweight as well, for so long as novels were believed to be about characters, novel studies could seem to be a species of gossip of precisely the sort in which Janeites delight. But according to Booth's influential brand of Chicago-school formalism, marriage in Austen's novels is not a matter of who marries whom, as it is, say, in G. B. Stern and Sheila Kaye-Smith's book *Speaking of Jane Austen* (1944), a Janeite repository of chit-chat, which Booth ridicules for treating characters like real people. Instead, the marriage plot becomes the novel's fundamental meaning, the telos towards which the narrative has moved since the first page. Booth endorses Mudrick's judgement that Emma's 'chief fault' is her 'lack of ... tenderness', but to him plot itself brings about 'the reform in [Emma's] character' – a reform defined solely in terms of the destiny of heterosexual love: only when she 'learns' this is she 'ready for marriage with the man she loves, the man who throughout the book has stood ... for what she lacks'; only then is the novel ready to end. Evidence is not necessary to sustain this view. Countless readers have claimed that the absence of 'love scenes' in Austen's novels must mean *something*. But for Booth, norms about gender and sexuality are encoded onto the plot, thus making the representation of the kisses or palpitations famously lacking in Austen's œuvre superfluous to begin with.[19] Compare this view of the courtship plot to that of self-confessed Janeite, E. M. Forster, whose *Aspects of the Novel* (1927) was still taught in fiction courses as late as the 1970s, alongside Booth's *Rhetoric of Fiction*: 'a man and woman ... want to be united and perhaps succeed'. The compulsory nature of the love story is acknowledged here, and that compulsion has obvious ideological import. But the marriage plot as Forster sceptically presents it falls not under the headings *Plot* or *Story*, but under the heading *People*. Considering the love plot as conventional rather than structural, Forster sees it as one among many 'facts of human life' – with people, birth, food, sleep and death – that interest people and novelists who write about them.[20]

Rescuing Austen from Mudrick, who held that she 'convert[ed] her own personal limitations into the very form of her novel', Booth succeeded in celebrating Austen's mastery over point of view and plot as a positive thing, and contributed immeasurably to the development of novel study as an analytic discipline. But discipline obviously has repressive as well as productive elements. Booth's reading is as bullying as Harding's, equating the perversity of women who indulge same-sex 'infatuations' with the perversity of novel-critics who refuse to accept a happy ending when they see one. Eve Sedgwick has remarked that Austenian criticism belongs to the knuckle-rapping (or more pruriently spanking) 'Girl Being Taught a Lesson' model of narrative analysis, where that lesson is invariably accomplished through the 'discipline' of the marriage plot.[21] As a description of academic criticism since the late 1950s, she is right. Critics as diverse as Mark Schorer, Lionel Trilling, Ian Watt, Arnold Kettle, Marilyn Butler, Tony Tanner, Patricia P. Brown and Mary Poovey, among many others, tend to follow Booth in judging character development, formal control and resistance or compliance with norms as mediated through marriage, as an institution and plot device.

Indeed, so entrenched is this respect and so short our institutional memory about the history of novel criticism itself that we have forgotten that there are other ways to read, and the very different reading traditions of the Janeites can accordingly now enrich our own. Many of the Janeite reading practices discussed earlier with respect to Kipling's story flourish today under less trying circumstances in the largely amateur Jane Austen societies throughout English-speaking countries. When Mudrick wrote that Austen 'was interested in a person, an object, an event, only as she might observe and recreate them free of consequences, as performance, as tableau', he was complaining about Austen's detachment, but he might just as well have been describing the ludic enthusiasm of these amateur reading clubs, whose 'performances' include teas, costume balls, games, readings and dramatic representations, staged with a campy anglophilia in North America, and a brisker antiquarian meticulousness in England, and whose interests range from Austenian dramatizations to fabrics, to genealogies and to weekend study trips, in no particular order and without any agenda-driven priority. Even though lectures by academic Austenian scholars are featured at Jane Austen Society and Jane Austen Society of North America conferences, and even though JAS's *Collected Reports* and JASNA's *Persuasions* often publish a tremendous amount in the way of sheer information, most academics I know take a rather dim view of these galas, where enjoyment rather than hermeneutic mastery is assumed to be the reward of reading, where reading is sociable rather than solitary, and where the stuff of erudition itself seems so different. On quizzes – a staple of JASNA meetings – academics fare quite poorly: having been taught to regard only certain relationships, scenes and (typically, closural) structures as significant, we rarely recollect the colour of this character's dress or that servant's name. We sometimes suffer the additional mortification of discovering our own papers becoming yet another relatively undifferentiated, unhierarchicalized item in the great repository of Austeniana assiduously collected by Janeites and compiled in newsletters and reports, printed somewhere between recipes for white soup and the latest word jumble.

Clearly more than a mood of reading is at stake here, but a method as well, one that strikes to the heart of our disciplinary self-identity. Trained to regard the text itself as a sacred boundary which must never be violated, we are confounded by the common Janeite game of imagining how a character in one novel might behave towards a character in another, or of speculating how the novels might continue *after* the wedding (a practice Austen herself authorized by gratifying the curiosity of her nephews and nieces). If for academics meaning is generally foreclosed by the comic ending of marriage, Janeites from Kipling on treat her novels instead as one capacious middle: balls, blunders, picnics, incomes, hunting dogs and marriages vie equally for our attention, none taking determinative priority over another, and where, moreover, all manner of 'extra-textual' material on sailors, Addison's disease and petty theft is welcome so long as it somehow qualifies as a Janean artefact.

The process by which academic critics deprecate Austenian admirers outside the academy is very similar to the way, as Henry Jenkins has shown, Trekkies, fans and mass media enthusiasts are derided and marginalized by dominant cultural institutions bent on legitimizing their own objects and protocols of expertise.[22] But there is an important difference: unlike *Star Trek*, Austen's novels hold a secure place in the canon of high as well as popular culture. Claiming the legitimacy of her novels as a subject for professional study has meant not assailing the *object* of amateur or belletristic study, but instead the triviality of its (non-)knowledge. But at a time when so many scholars and theorists worry that the grip of ideology upon representation is so withering that novels themselves are a form of the police, what Janeite readers supposedly do not know may help us all. By contextualizing Austenian commentary, examining the contrast between earlier reading practices and those that prevailed once novel study was professionalized, and by insisting that reading Austen is a social practice contingent upon our desires, needs and historical circumstances, I would like to suggest that it may not be the novel that polices us, but novel criticism as a discourse that has done so. If Dr Johnson, one of Austen's favourite writers, was correct in opining that the purpose of literature was to help us better to enjoy or endure life, then we must be glad, *pace* James, that 'Jane' is 'theirs', 'yours' and 'ours' after all.

NOTES

1. According to the *Supplement* to the *OED*, the word 'Janeite' entered the language in 1896, but the self-consciously hyperbolic zeal for her works surely pre-dates this. Although I cannot concur in his tendency to minimize the cultural importance of Janeites and anti-Janeites as an amusing controversy, I am much indebted to B. C. Southam for having uncovered so much fascinating material in his *Critical Heritage* volumes and in 'Janeite/Anti-Janeites', in J. David Grey, ed., *A Jane Austen Handbook* (London: Athlone Press, 1986), pp. 237–43. For a brief but informative sketch of the term 'Janeite', see Lorraine Hanaway, '"Janeite" at 100', *Persuasions*, 16 (1994), 2, 8–9.
2. For the publication history of Austen's novels, I am vastly indebted to B. C. Southam's invaluable 'Introduction' to *Jane Austen: The Critical Heritage*, vol. II: 1870–1940 (London and New York: Routledge & Kegan Paul, 1987), esp. pp. 58–70; David Gilson, *A Bibliography of Jane Austen* (Oxford: Clarendon Press, 1982), pp. 211–34; Geoffrey Keynes, *Jane Austen: A Bibliography* (London: Nonesuch Press, 1929); and Jan Fergus' invaluable *Jane Austen: A Literary Life* (Houndmills and London: Macmillan, 1991).
3. James, 'The Lesson of Balzac' (1905), in *Jane Austen: The Critical Heritage*, vol. II, p. 230.
4. From 'Miss Austen and Miss Mitford', *Blackwood's Edinburgh Magazine* (March 1870), reprinted in B. C. Southam, *Jane Austen: The Critical Heritage*, vol. I (London: Routledge & Kegan Paul, 1968), p. 217.
5. Quoted from Montague Summers, 'Jane Austen: An Appreciation', *Transactions of the Royal Society of Literature*, 36 (1918), 1–33. Summers' language of divine election is typical of all Janeites.
6. 'The Janeites' is included in *Debits and Credits* (1926). It was begun in 1922, finished in 1923, and was first published in 1924, in a slightly different version than that published in 1926. All quotations are from *Debits and Credits*, ed. Sandra Kemp (Harmondsworth and New York: Penguin, 1987), pp. 119–40. I supply page references in the text.
7. Letter to Thomas Hardy. Quoted in F. B. Pinion, *A Jane Austen Companion* (London: Macmillan, 1973), p. 24.

8. According to Kent, H. F. Brett Smith, an Oxford tutor, served in the First World War as an adviser in British hospitals, and his special responsibility was the prescription of salubrious reading for the wounded; and he recommended Austen's novels to 'severely shell-shocked' soldiers. I am much indebted to Kent's fine essay. Christopher Kent, 'Learning History with, and from, Jane Austen', in J. David Grey, ed., *Jane Austen's Beginnings* (Ann Arbor, MI and London: UMI Research Press, 1989), p. 59.

9. D. A. Miller admits to some Janeism when he says that he once – back in the days before the AIDS crisis – believed that Austen's novels could make him well. See 'The Late Jane Austen', *Raritan*, 10 (1990), 55–79.

10. 'Regulated Hatred: An Aspect of the Work of Jane Austen', in Ian Watt, ed., *Jane Austen: A Collection of Critical Essays* (Englewood Cliffs, NJ: Prentice-Hall, 1963), p. 167. Harding singles out Eric Linklater's Janeite Prime Minister in *The Impregnable Women* and Beatrice Kean Seymour's *Jane Austen*, where she wrote: 'In a society which has enthroned the machine-gun and carried it aloft even into the quiet heavens, there will always be men and women – Escapist or not, as you please – who will turn to her novels with an unending sense of relief and thankfulness.'

11. Chapman, 'Reading Aloud', in *The Portrait of a Scholar and Other Essays Written in Macedonia, 1916–1918* (Oxford University Press, 1920), p. 46.

12. *New Statesman*, 22 (1923), 145; *Edinburgh Review*, 239 (1924), 32.

13. Harding, 'Regulated Hatred', p. 170.

14. See *The Great Tradition* (Garden City, NY: Doubleday and Co., 1954), pp. 19, 25.

15. Lionel Trilling, *The Opposing Self* (New York: Viking Press, 1955), p. 209.

16. H. W. Garrod's 'Jane Austen: A Depreciation' was originally delivered at the Royal Society for Literature in May 1928, and published in *Essays by Divers Hands: Transactions of the Royal Society of Literature*, VIII (1928): 21–40; and reprinted in numerous other places. I quote it as printed in William Heath, ed., *Discussion of Jane Austen* (Boston, MA: Heath and Company, 1961), pp. 32–40. If Garrod launched his attack because he suspected that Janeites liked women too much, B. C. Southam would hint that Garrod himself did not like women enough: 'a clue' to Garrod's dislike of Austen lies in the fact that he was 'a distinguished classical scholar who moved to English studies in the 1920s. He spent much of his life at Oxford, unmarried, where he had rooms in Merton College for over fifty years'; in *Jane Austen: The Critical Heritage*, vol. II, p. 154. Since many passionate Janeites, past and present, answer to this description, the 'clue' explains nothing. I examine the role Austen plays in the policing of gender as well as genre in 'The Divine Miss Jane: Jane Austen, Janeites, and the Discipline of Novel Studies', in *boundary* 2, 23 (autumn 1996).

17. The brilliance of Mary Lascelles' *Jane Austen and her Art* (Oxford University Press, 1939) I regard as exceptional to the argument I am making.

18. In *Jane Austen: Irony as Defense and Discovery* (Princeton University Press, 1952), Mudrick holds that 'The fact is that Emma prefers the company of women' (p. 192); 'for a time at least … Emma is in love with [Harriet]' (p. 203). On the lesbianism question specifically, Mudrick acknowledges his debt to Edmund Wilson's 'A Long Talk on Jane Austen', which first appeared in the *New Yorker*, 20 (24 June 1944).

19. Booth's essay first appeared in *Rhetoric of Fiction* (University of Chicago Press, 1961), pp. 243–66. I quote from pp. 260, 263, 244.
20. *Aspects of the Novel* (New York and London: Harcourt Brace Jovanovich, 1927), pp. 67–82. I quote from p. 54. In an excellent discussion of Forster's *Aspects*, Paul Morrison argues that Forster's remarks on narrative are much less emancipatory than what I suggest here. See 'End Pleasure', *GLQ*, 1 (1993), 53–78.
21. 'Jane Austen and the Masturbating Heroine', in *Tendencies* (Durham, NC: Duke University Press, 1993), p. 125.
22. *Textual Poachers: Television Fans and Participatory Culture* (London: Routledge & Kegan Paul, 1992). Jenkins draws from Michel de Certeau's *The Practice of Everyday Life* (Berkeley and Los Angeles: University of California Press, 1984) and Pierre Bourdieu's *Distinction* (Cambridge, MA: Harvard University Press, 1979) to show how high culturalists feel tainted by the adoption of high-culture protocols for use with respect to low culture objects, and to suggest that fans transgress against bourgeois structures of cultural valuation.

16

BRUCE STOVEL AND MARY M. CHAN

Further reading

Biography

The dominant force in Jane Austen's life was her family, and her family has also been the dominant force in the study of her life. For more than one hundred years after Austen's death in 1817, the major biographies of her were written by family members, and the biographies since then have relied largely on unpublished or obscurely published family manuscripts. Furthermore, the Austen family has been determined from the start to present its most famous member to the world as a figure of exemplary gentility and piety. Some five months after her death, Jane Austen was introduced to her readers as the author of her six novels, in the 'Biographical Notice' at the front of the volume containing her two posthumously published novels, *Northanger Abbey* and *Persuasion*, but this seven-page account by her favourite brother, Henry Austen, is in tone an obituary. Her life is depicted as faultless – 'She never uttered either a hasty, a silly, or a severe expression' – and the emphasis is upon the pious manner of her death.

Thus Jane Austen the person remained unknown to her growing readership for the first half-century after her death. The public's curiosity was satisfied, and yet the author's dignity was preserved, in the first biography, *A Memoir of Jane Austen* (1870), by James Edward Austen Leigh, Jane Austen's nephew, a clergyman and the son of her eldest brother, James. He was 16 when his aunt died and had known her well. His book is a tribute from someone who feels great affection for both his aunt and her novels: it is filled with nostalgic reminiscences and celebrates its subject's wit and high spirits as well as her domestic virtues. The book is concise (fewer than 150 pages), elegantly written and cites abundantly from Austen's letters. It has been republished (2002), ably edited by Kathryn Sutherland, whose introduction

On 12 January 2007, the community of Austen readers and scholars lost Bruce Stovel, who died suddenly. Stovel's chapter in this collection has been expanded by Mary M. Chan, one of his former students.

provides information about the creation and reception of the 1870 *Memoir*, and who includes 'other family recollections', such as Henry's 'Memoir of Miss Austen' from an 1833 edition of *Sense and Sensibility* and Anna Lefroy's 'Recollections of Aunt Jane'.

The main outlines of Jane Austen's life and personality are all there in the *Memoir*: the happy family life at Steventon, the precocious childhood writing as the family madcap, the attachment to Cassandra, the depression and sterility of the Bath and Southampton years, the renewed happiness and creative surge of the Chawton years, increasing admiration and her corresponding determination to maintain her privacy as the novels are published from 1811 onwards, the tragic final illness and death at 41. Even Austen's three brushes with love and marriage – the youthful flirtation with Tom Lefroy, the relationship with a mysterious admirer met on the Devonshire coast in 1801, the acceptance and rejection the next morning of a marriage proposal by a wealthy neighbour, Harris Bigg-Wither – are described, if in general and muffled terms. Jane Austen was a name and nothing more to her readers before 1870; as Claudia L. Johnson shows elsewhere in this book, the *Memoir* produces the engaging, if idealized, figure generally associated with that name.

The Austen family divulged more information in the next few decades. The first (and incomplete) edition of her letters, with a rambling 110-page introduction on Austen family life, was published by Lord Brabourne, son of Jane Austen's favourite niece, Fanny Knight, in 1884. Constance Hill's *Jane Austen: Her Homes and her Friends* (1902) cites from family manuscripts. In 1906 J. H. Hubback and his daughter Edith Hubback (the grandson and great-granddaughter of Jane Austen's brother Frank) published *Jane Austen's Sailor Brothers*, printing for the first time Jane's letters to Frank and tracing the exciting wartime careers of Frank and Charles Austen, who both became admirals.

The 'official' biography, *Jane Austen: Her Life and Letters. A Family Record*, by William Arthur Austen-Leigh (son of James Edward) and Richard Arthur Austen-Leigh (William's nephew), appeared in 1913. It is indeed a family record, bringing together material from the different branches of the family. In the Victorian life-and-letters manner, it cites virtually every one of the surviving letters and is, in fact, largely a running commentary on the letters. Much more readable is Elizabeth Jenkins' *Jane Austen*, first published in 1938. Unencumbered by footnotes, its tale of Jane Austen's maturation as an artist and growing public success has the narrative drive of a novel – not surprisingly, since Jenkins was herself a popular novelist. Like the *Memoir*, this forms an ideal place to begin reading about Jane Austen's life.

Several other biographies have appeared since then. Jane Aiken Hodge's *The Double Life of Jane Austen* (1972) takes up an idea implicit in Jenkins and makes it a thesis: that Jane Austen in private life was much more rebellious, much less conventional, than Jane Austen the dutiful family member. John Halperin's *The Life of Jane Austen* (1984) takes the image of an angry Austen to iconoclastic extremes: his Jane Austen is consumed by smouldering resentment at her lot, incapable of love and cynical about personal relationships, and her novels are for him correspondingly acrid. Like David Nokes in *Jane Austen: A Life* (1997), Halperin's attempt at correction goes too far. By contrast, Lord David Cecil's *A Portrait of Jane Austen* (1978) is an affectionate tribute; a picture-book in form (with 101 illustrations), elegantly written, it presents the old-fashioned Jane Austen, cultivated, genteel, sensible, principled.

Meanwhile, the Austen family has gone on publishing biographical information. Mary Augusta Austen-Leigh produced *James Edward Austen-Leigh*, a memoir of her father, in 1911, and in 1920, at the age of 82, published *Personal Aspects of Jane Austen*. Both books fill in details of the Chawton years. R. A. Austen-Leigh, co-author of the *Life and Letters*, produced a series of pamphlets and articles, as well as editing *Austen Papers, 1704–1856* (1942), which contains a wealth of fascinating material: letters by both of Jane Austen's parents, for instance, and the correspondence from Steventon of Jane Austen's dazzling cousin Eliza de Feuillide. (Deirdre Le Faye has edited de Feuillide's letters in *Jane Austen's 'Outlandish Cousin': The Life and Letters of Eliza de Feuillide* (2002).) The reminiscences of Caroline Austen, the sister of James Edward Austen-Leigh and his collaborator in the 1870 *Memoir*, have been published in two slim volumes, *My Aunt Jane Austen: A Memoir* (1952) and *Reminiscences of Caroline Austen* (1986).

Two books by George Holbert Tucker are carefully researched and very readable: *A Goodly Heritage: A History of Jane Austen's Family* (1983) and *Jane Austen the Woman* (1994). Forthrightly feminist, Deborah Kaplan's *Jane Austen among Women* (1994) uses fresh research to define Austen's life by examining those of other women in her family circle and neighbourhood. Jon Spence's *Becoming Jane Austen* (2003) presents a psychological portrait of Austen gleaned from the novels and supplements existing biographical materials with the wills and legacies of the Austen family.

Five excellent biographies have appeared in recent years. Park Honan's *Jane Austen* (1987) is a sympathetic and thoroughly researched account, making use throughout of unpublished family papers. Honan's main thesis is that Jane Austen was much more implicated in events of her revolutionary times than has been realized. Throughout, Honan narrates his story as if he were a novelist, providing, for instance, a ten-page account of the vacillations within Jane Austen's mind as she first accepts and then rejects Harris Bigg-Wither's proposal (189–98). Thus, despite its length (450 pages) and thoroughness, this book is highly readable.

Deirdre Le Faye's *Jane Austen: A Family Record* (1989, 2004) also makes use of family papers; her book is authoritatively factual, from the 10-page 'Chronology' of Jane Austen's life with which it begins – reprinted in this book – to the thirteen pages of family pedigrees with which it ends. Le Faye also draws on research of her own into parish records, county archives, wills, cemeteries, and other sources. The resulting account is meticulously accurate – except for the title page, which identifies this book as a revised and enlarged version of the 1913 *Life and Letters*, when it is in fact a wholly new account which owes little more to the original than its chronological framework. The person who reads this book, even more than the reader of Honan's, experiences Jane Austen as an actual person – sharp-edged, various, untransparent – and not as the neat hypothesis (either delightfully good or secretly rebellious) of previous biographies. Le Faye also edited Austen's letters (1995), providing a wealth of information in the notes, 'Biographical Index' and 'Topographical Index', and her meticulous research has culminated in *A Chronology of Jane Austen and Her Family* (2006), an expansive, thorough and indispensable reference. The *Chronology* focuses mainly on events during Austen's lifetime but covers 400 years in roughly 15,000 entries detailing events important or relevant to Austen's family.

Claire Tomalin's *Jane Austen: A Life* (1997) also uses new research (about Austen's neighbours in Hampshire) to present a biography as a story. Tomalin's care in distinguishing between facts and surmises never detracts from her ability to draw the reader into Jane Austen's life, and she reaches fresh conclusions about Austen's relationship with her sister and the effects of growing up in a house full of rambunctious boys (the *Juvenilia* no longer seem out of place in Austen's œuvre). Her tone is intimate rather than authoritative; the Austen who emerges is a complex woman and artist.

Two other biographies are shorter than those of Honan, Le Faye and Tomalin, but are the more searching for being compact. Jan Fergus' *Jane Austen* (1991) is one in Macmillan's Literary Lives series, which aim at tracing writers' professional careers and their contexts. As in her chapter in this book (Chapter 1), Fergus provides fascinating information on the literary marketplace – the going price for a first novel, the kinds of contracts offered to authors, publication runs, readership – and Austen's place in it. The book's focus is on Jane Austen the professional woman: Fergus offers a carefully stated, and convincing, feminist interpretation of Jane Austen's personal situation and of her novels. In *Jane Austen* (2001), Pulitzer Prize-winning novelist Carol Shields also deals with Jane Austen the writer, though from a personal rather than professional perspective. Shields' book is a part of the Penguin Lives series, monographs in which famous writers pen short biographies of famous subjects. The result is a sensitive, insightful biography that focuses on the often complicated influences of home and family in Austen's writing.

Criticism to 1970

The history of Austen criticism can be divided into four phases, with the help of the boundaries used in B. C. Southam's two anthologies of earlier criticism, *Jane Austen: The Critical Heritage* (1968), which covers 1811 to 1870, and *Jane Austen: The Critical Heritage, Volume II: 1870–1940* (1987). The first phase of Austen criticism thus runs from the novels' publication to 1870, the date of the *Memoir*; a second phase continues up to 1939, the date of the first valuable full-length study, Mary Lascelles' *Jane Austen and her Art* (1939); a third phase extends from 1940 until about 1970; from that date onwards, new conceptions of Austen's achievement and rigorous new critical methods predominate. The summary of Austen criticism below outlines the high points up to 1970, and after that point, as books became more frequent and hindsight more scarce, offers a quick survey of the critical books published on Austen's novels.

Until the publication of the *Memoir* in 1870, Jane Austen's novels had a small, if growing and appreciative, audience. No books on Austen were published during this period, and of the few essays that appeared, three are particularly interesting. Sir Walter Scott's review-essay on *Emma* in 1816 argues that *Emma* represented a major new kind of unromantic fiction. Richard Whately, reviewing *Northanger Abbey* and *Persuasion* in 1821 but displaying a shrewd grasp of all six novels, shows that Austen is like Shakespeare in her vivid, carefully differentiated characterization, that her plots follow Aristotelian principles, and that her novels present, if indirectly, 'moral lessons'. Richard Simpson's 25-page 'review' of the *Memoir* in 1870 outlines an original and searching conception of Jane Austen's novels. Drawing on the *Memoir*'s account of the juvenilia, he argues that Jane Austen began as an ironic debunker of romantic love and developed her own ideal of 'intelligent love'.

After the *Memoir*'s appearance in 1870, there was a flood of new editions of the novels, many illustrated, and a host of new biographical and critical studies. There is a cosy, self-congratulatory quality to almost all of this new enthusiasm: as early as 1852, an anonymous author claims, 'readers of more refined taste and critical acumen feel something like dissatisfaction with almost every other domestic novelist after they have once appreciated Miss Austen' ('Female Novelists', 136). One suspects that it is this 'refined' adulation, rather than the novels themselves, that accounts for the violent distaste for Austen's novels expressed in this period by Charlotte Brontë, Emerson, Mark Twain and D. H. Lawrence (as well as Henry James' condescending praise).

Surprisingly little in the seven decades between 1870 and Mary Lascelles' book in 1939 is of critical interest (as opposed to curiosity value) today. Two novelists, Virginia Woolf and E. M. Forster, offer shrewd and illuminating comments in essays that, because of their authors' stature, received wide circulation in, respectively, Woolf's *The Common Reader* (1925) and Forster's *Abinger Harvest* (1936). A. C. Bradley, Professor of Poetry at Oxford and the author of *Shakespearean Tragedy* (1904), published an essay on Austen in 1911 that gave her work an academic imprimatur. Beginning with the view, 'There are two distinct strains in Jane Austen. She is a moralist and a humorist' (7), he comments on the interrelationship of these two strains and suggests that stage comedy influenced her fictional comedies; he also explores for the first time her debt to eighteenth-century writers such as Johnson and Cowper. In 1917 Reginald Farrer published a centenary tribute that was much more original, penetrating and provocative than anything since Simpson's essay. Writing for the general reader, he argues that the Jane Austen most readers know is largely a fiction produced by sentimental biography and the book trade – and that, instead, she is a conscious artist and a dispassionate critic of her own society.

Mary Lascelles' *Jane Austen and her Art* (1939) forms a watershed: it was the first full-length, thorough and searching study of the novels. Jane Austen's use of language, of narrative technique, of timing and many other artistic issues were explored with precision and sensitivity. The following year, 1940, saw the publication of an influential revisionist essay, D. W. Harding's 'Regulated Hatred'. Harding took Farrer's conception of Austen several steps further, presenting her as a distinctively twentieth-century figure: isolated and misunderstood, protecting her integrity as a person and an artist by subversive ironies. The view of Austen as an isolated ironist, critical of her society, received full-length exposition in Marvin Mudrick's *Jane Austen: Irony as Defense and Discovery* (1952). Mudrick's schematic, closely argued reading of the novels is one that few readers can accept entirely, but that all will find thought-provoking. If criticism of the novels could no longer be innocent after Lascelles, after Mudrick it would usually be strenuous and combative.

Since then, critical books and essays – most by academics – have proliferated. Several studies from the 1950s and 1960s remain virtually required reading, such as Lionel Trilling's essays championing *Mansfield Park* (1954) and *Emma* (1957). B. C. Southam's *Jane Austen's Literary Manuscripts* (1964, new edition 2001) is the standard study on its subject – and is especially useful as a guide to the juvenilia, 'Lady Susan', the two incomplete novels ('The Watsons', 'Sanditon') and Austen's dramatic adaptation of Samuel Richardson's *Sir Charles Grandison*. Howard Babb's *Jane Austen's Novels: The Fabric of Dialogue* (1962) argues that characters define themselves by the way they use (and misuse) general concepts in conversation.

Joseph Wiesenfarth's *The Errand of Form* (1967) provides a vigorous close reading of the novels, reinstating Jane Austen the moralist. Kenneth Moler's *Jane Austen's Art of Allusion* (1968) is a pioneering detailed study of Austen's debt to Burney, Edgeworth and other novelists of her time. Perhaps the most useful book of criticism in this period is A. Walton Litz's *Jane Austen* (1965); concise, lucid, bringing into focus a great deal of previous scholarship and criticism, this book is, like Lascelles' book, a one-volume critical compendium. Another useful compendium is *Jane Austen: A Collection of Critical Essays*, ed. Ian Watt (1963), which contains essays on Austen by Woolf, Harding, C. S. Lewis and Edmund Wilson, and critical essays on each novel.

Criticism since 1970

Beginning in about 1970, and running parallel to the general re-theorizing of literary study in the last four decades, Austen's novels were increasingly analysed as products of a specific culture. Alistair Duckworth's *The Improvement of the Estate* (1971) and Marilyn Butler's *Jane Austen and the War of Ideas* (1975), watersheds in Austen criticism, regard her novels as ultimately conservative statements in the social, moral and political controversies of Austen's time. The historical analysis is taken up in Warren Roberts' study of Austen's politics, *Jane Austen and the French Revolution* (1979) and *The Politics of Jane Austen* (1999) by Edward Neill, who opposes Butler's claims. Explorations of Austen's engagement with the Enlightenment and the Romantic period include Susan Morgan's *In the Meantime: Character and Perception in Jane Austen's Fiction* (1980), Peter Knox-Shaw's *Jane Austen and the Enlightenment* (2004), William Deresiewicz's *Jane Austen and the Romantic Poets* (2004), Clara Tuite's *Romantic Austen: Sexual Politics and the Literary Canon* (2002) and Colin Winborn's *The Literary Economy of Jane Austen and George Crabbe* (2004). Education is the focus in D. D. Devlin's *Jane Austen and Education* (1975), Laura Mooneyham's *Romance, Language, and Education in Jane Austen's Novels* (1988) and Barbara Horwitz's *Jane Austen and the Question of Women's Education* (1991). Jan Fergus in *Jane Austen and the Didactic Novel* (1983) relates Austen's first three novels to educational thinking. Austen's connection to the literature of her era is examined in Mary Waldron's *Jane Austen and the Fiction of Her Time* (1999) and Anthony Mandal's *Jane Austen and the Popular Novel: The Determined Author* (2007). Jocelyn Harris explores Austen's creative reading of earlier authors such as Shakespeare, Chaucer, Milton and Richardson in *Jane Austen's Art of Memory* (1989).

In addition to political and literary contexts, Austen's novels have benefited from multiple studies that place her novels in socio-historical contexts. Julia

Prewitt Brown's *Jane Austen's Novels: Social Change and Literary Form* (1979) focuses on society's changing conception of marriage. The historian Oliver MacDonagh, in *Jane Austen: Real and Imagined Worlds* (1991), links the novels and social history, as do Maija Stewart's *Domestic Realities and Imperial Fictions: Jane Austen's Novels in Eighteenth-Century Contexts* (1993) and Roger Sales' *Jane Austen and Representations of Regency England* (1994). Two books that consider social rituals in the novels are David Monaghan's *Jane Austen: Structure and Social Vision* (1980) and John Dussinger's *In the Pride of the Moment: Encounters in Jane Austen's World* (1990), and aspects of Austen's social world are explained in David Selwyn's *Jane Austen and Leisure* (1999) and Brian Southam's *Jane Austen and the Navy* (2000). Studies that approach the novels from specific social contexts include Glenda Hudson's *Sibling Love and Incest in Jane Austen's Fiction* (1992) and Barbara Britton Wenner's *Prospect and Refuge in the Landscape of Jane Austen* (2006). Two books by Penny Gay and Paula Byrne, both entitled *Jane Austen and the Theatre* and both published in 2002, examine Austen's view of theatre and the importance of drama to her novels. Edward Said's provocative chapter on *Mansfield Park* in *Culture and Imperialism* (1993) galvanized post-colonial approaches to Austen, including the collection *The Postcolonial Jane Austen*, ed. You-me Park and Rajeswari Sunder Rajan (2000) and Gabrielle D. V. White's *Jane Austen in the Context of Abolition* (2006). James Thompson sees the novels as dramatizing the conflict between landed and exchange values in *Between Self and the World: The Novels of Jane Austen* (1988) and Edward Copeland has a chapter on Austen's relation to economic realities in his *Women Writing about Money: Women's Fiction in England, 1790–1820* (1995). The religious context is the subject of Gene Koppel's *The Religious Dimension in Jane Austen's Novels* (1988), *Jane Austen and the Clergy* (1994) by historian Irene Collins and *Jane Austen and Religion: Salvation and Society in Georgian England* by Anglican priest Michael Giffin (2002). Austen's relationship to classical and biblical virtues is examined in Anne Crippen Ruderman's *The Pleasures of Virtue: Political Thought in the Novels of Jane Austen* (1995) and Sarah Emsley's *Jane Austen's Philosophy of the Virtues* (2005). John Wiltshire, in *Jane Austen and the Body* (1992), analyses the novels in the light of medical thinking about illness and the body.

Alongside contextual considerations, analyses of Austen's style and form also thrive. K. C. Phillipps in *Jane Austen's English* (1970), Karl Kroeber in *Styles in Fictional Structure: The Art of Jane Austen, Charlotte Brontë, and George Eliot* (1971) and Norman Page in *The Language of Jane Austen* (1972) concentrate on language conventions. J. F. Burrows' *Computation into Criticism* (1987) uses computer-based statistics to study Austen. The best study of Austen's style is D. A. Miller's slim and sparkling *Jane Austen, or the Secret of Style* (2003). Narrative strategies are examined in Tara Ghoshal Wallace's *Jane Austen and Narrative Authority* (1995) and Barbara K. Seeber uses the theories of Mikhail Bakhtin to challenge conventional readings of Austen's novels in *General Consent in Jane Austen: A Study of Dialogism* (2000). Kathryn Sutherland's *Jane Austen's Textual Lives: From Aeschylus to Bollywood* (2005) examines the cultural commodification of Austen from the various editions of the novels to the film adaptations. Michael Williams' *Jane Austen* (1986) applies reader-response theory to the novels. Reception studies include Annika Bautz's *The Reception of Jane Austen and Walter Scott: A Comparative Longitudinal Study* (2007) and *The Reception of Jane Austen in Europe*, ed. Anthony Mandal and Brian Southam (2007).

Many of these specialized studies are written for the academic, rather than the general, reader. Paying rigorous attention to cultural context, many are gracefully written and provide eloquent close readings of the novels. On the other hand, many excellent studies of Austen appeared that owed little to the changed critical climate. Stuart Tave's *Some Words of Jane Austen* (1973) is a showcase for sensitive close reading, as is Barbara Hardy's *A Reading of Jane Austen* (1976). Several other notable books in this category are Jane Nardin's *Those Elegant Decorums: The Concept of Propriety in Jane Austen's Novels* (1973), Lloyd Brown's *Bits of Ivory: Narrative Techniques in Jane Austen's Fiction* (1973), Darrel Mansell's *The Novels of Jane Austen* (1973), John Hardy's *Jane Austen's Heroines* (1984), Roger Gard's significantly-titled *Jane Austen's Novels: The Art of Clarity* (1992) and Juliet McMaster's *Jane Austen the Novelist* (1995), which reprints three of the four essays in her earlier *Jane Austen on Love* (1978). Several helpful guides for the general reader appeared: Christopher Gillie's *A Preface to Jane Austen* (1974), Douglas Bush's *Jane Austen* (1975), John Lauber's *Jane Austen* (1993), and in this category might be placed Tony Tanner's popularizing *Jane Austen* (1986). Also of note are Christopher Brooke's *Jane Austen: Illusion and Reality* (1999), Richard Jenkyns' *A Fine Brush on Ivory: An Appreciation of Jane Austen* (2004) and Darryl Jones' *Jane Austen* (2004).

The most invigorating new approach has been feminism. Brief discussions of Austen's novels figure in several of the books that established feminism as a distinct form of literary analysis, notably Patricia Meyer Spacks' *The Female Imagination* (1975), Ellen Moers' *Literary Women* (1976), Elaine Showalter's *A Literature of their Own* (1977), Nina Auerbach's *Communities of Women* (1978) and Rachel Brownstein's *Becoming a Heroine* (1982). Two influential books contain extended discussions of Austen as a victim of the society she depicts: Sandra Gilbert and Susan Gubar, *The Madwoman in the Attic* (1979) and Mary Poovey, *The Proper Lady and the Woman Writer* (1984). A similar view of Austen's novels as enacting a constricting ideology is presented in

Nancy Armstrong's chapters on *Pride and Prejudice* and *Emma* in her *Desire and Domestic Fiction* (1987). Jane Spencer discusses Austen's novels as the culmination of a tradition of women's fiction in *The Rise of the Woman Novelist* (1986). The first book devoted to Austen as a feminist was Margaret Kirkham's *Jane Austen, Feminism, and Fiction* (1983), which argues that Austen dramatizes the concerns of Enlightenment feminists of her day like Mary Wollstonecraft. Other feminist readings include Leroy W. Smith's *Jane Austen and the Drama of Woman* (1983), Mary Evans' *Jane Austen and the State* (1987), Alison Sulloway's *Jane Austen and the Province of Womanhood* (1989), Gabriela Castellanos' *Laughter, War, and Feminism: Elements of Carnival in Three of Jane Austen's Novels* (1994) and the critical collection *Jane Austen and the Discourses of Feminism* (1995), edited by Devoney Looser. More sophisticated and provocative than any of these is Claudia L. Johnson's *Jane Austen: Women, Politics, and the Novel* (1988), which postulates that, in an England threatened by revolutionary France, the domestic novel became politicized, a forum in which Edmund Burke's favourite analogy of the ordered family to the conservative state could be tested. One essay shows how much a feminist reading opens up to view: Margaret Anne Doody's 40-page introduction to the Oxford World's Classics *Sense and Sensibility* (1990). Jillian Heydt-Stevenson takes a feminist and cultural studies approach in *Austen's Unbecoming Conjunctions: Subversive Laughter, Embodied History* (2005), which examines the subversive potential of minor characters, events and even words in Austen's work.

The spate of film and television adaptations of Austen's novels in the 1990s saw a critical response in two collections of essays: *Jane Austen in Hollywood*, 2nd edn, ed. Linda Troost and Sayre Greenfield (2001) and *Jane Austen on Screen*, ed. Gina Macdonald and Andrew F. Macdonald (2003). Three collections that contain multiple contributions about Austen include: *Janespotting and Beyond: British Heritage Retrovisions since the Mid-1990s*, ed. Eckart Voigts-Virchow (2004); *Re-Drawing Austen: Picturesque Travels in Austenland*, ed. Beatrice Battalia and Diego Saglia (2004); and, as mentioned before, *The Postcolonial Jane Austen*, ed. Park and Rajan (2000). Two Special Issues of *Persuasions On-Line*, the web edition of the journal of the Jane Austen Society of North America, have been devoted to movies: adaptations of *Emma* (1999) and the 2005 feature film *Pride & Prejudice*. Criticism of Austen screen adaptations also appears in books that locate the adaptations within the larger phenomenon of Austen's popularity. Such collections include *Janeites: Austen's Disciples and Devotees*, ed. Deidre Lynch (2000) and *Jane Austen and Co.: Remaking the Past in Contemporary Culture*, ed. Suzanne R. Pucci and James Thompson (2003). The most cogent exploration of the Austen phenomenon is

John Wiltshire's *Recreating Jane Austen* (2001), which argues that screen adaptations are not bastardizations, but rather readings and interpretations of the novels, creations in their own right.

Of course, many studies fit into none of the above categories. John Odmark applies phenomenology in *An Understanding of Jane Austen's Novels* (1981), Richard Handler and Daniel Segal bring to bear anthropological ideas about ritual and class in *Jane Austen and the Fiction of Culture* (1990) and Maggie Lane examines *Jane Austen and Food* (1995). Two books relate Austen's knowledge of music to the novels: Patrick Piggott's *The Innocent Diversion: Music in the Life and Writings of Jane Austen* (1979) and R. K. Wallace's *Jane Austen and Mozart* (1983). Two studies that draw eclectically from a range of theories are Bharat Tandon, *Jane Austen and the Morality of Conversation* (2003) and Ashley Tauchert's *Romancing Jane Austen* (2005). The latter examines the significance of Austen's shifting from a realist narration to a romance-inflected 'happy ending' in her novels.

Many helpful collections of critical essays have appeared since Watt's book. The most notable of these are: *Critical Essays on Jane Austen*, ed. B. C. Southam (1968); *Jane Austen Today*, ed. Joel Weinsheimer (1975); *Jane Austen: Bicentenary Essays*, ed. John Halperin (1975); *Jane Austen's Achievement*, ed. Juliet McMaster (1976); *Jane Austen in a Social Context*, ed. David Monaghan (1981); *Jane Austen: New Perspectives*, ed. Janet Todd (1983); *Jane Austen's Business*, ed. Juliet McMaster and Bruce Stovel (1996); *Critical Essays on Jane Austen*, ed. Laura Mooneyham White (1998); *The Talk in Jane Austen*, ed. Bruce Stovel and Lynn Weinlos Gregg (2002); and *Jane Austen: Introductions and Interventions* by John Wiltshire (2003, 2006). The three books from the 1970s are bicentennial tributes (Austen was born in 1775); special issues of two scholarly journals, *Nineteenth-Century Fiction* and *Studies in the Novel*, were devoted to essays on Austen in 1975. *Women's Writing* devoted an issue to Austen in 1998. There are several casebooks gathering critical essays on individual novels, critical editions of the novels from Norton and cultural editions from Longman and Broadview, a dozen or so monographs devoted to a single novel, and scores of valuable introductions to paperback editions; R. W. Chapman's scholarly editions of the novels (1923) and the minor works (1954) contain valuable textual and background information, as do the new Cambridge editions (2005–9), under the general editorship of Janet Todd. And then there are chapters in books on larger topics, such as Dorothy Van Ghent's much-reprinted essay on *Pride and Prejudice* in *The English Novel* (1953) or Wayne Booth's chapter on *Emma* in *The Rhetoric of Fiction* (1961) or Raymond Williams' pages on Austen in *The Country and the City* (1973) or Claudia L. Johnson's essay on masculinity in *Emma* in *Equivocal Beings:*

Politics, Gender and Sentimentality in the 1790s (1995). The *Annual Reports* of the Jane Austen Society in England have been published since 1949, and *Persuasions*, the annual journal of the Jane Austen Society of North America, has appeared each year since 1979, with an exclusive web journal, *Persuasions On-Line*, publishing since 1999. Handbooks that offer orientation include: F. B. Pinion's *A Jane Austen Companion* (1973), which provides a running commentary on the novels and their background, as well as items such as a glossary of Austen's usage and an index of characters and places in the novels; *The Jane Austen Companion* (1986), ed. J. David Grey, with sixty-five essays by forty contributors on a vast range of topics; and most recently *Jane Austen in Context*, ed. Janet Todd (2005). David Gilson's *A Bibliography of Jane Austen* (1982) contains a list of all biography and criticism published up to 1978. Two books that contain detailed summaries of books and articles are *An Annotated Bibliography of Jane Austen Studies*, 1952–1972, by Barry Roth and Joel Weinsheimer (1973) and *An Annotated Bibliography of Jane Austen Studies*, 1973–1982, by Barry Roth (1985). A valuable critical tool is the three-volume *Concordance to the Works of Jane Austen*, by Peter De Rose and S. W. McGuire (1983).

Today readers who have enjoyed Austen's novels and begin reading criticism are almost too lucky: they may be blinded by too much light. It is a testament to Jane Austen's talent that her œuvre of six novels and a handful of minor works has produced a legacy of so much knowledge.

Works cited

Biography

Austen, Caroline, *My Aunt Jane Austen: A Memoir* (London: Spottiswoode, Ballantyne, 1952).

Reminiscences of Caroline Austen (Winchester: Jane Austen Society, 1986).

[Austen, Henry,] 'Biographical Notice of the Author', in *Northanger Abbey and Persuasion*, ed. R. W. Chapman (Oxford University Press, 1969).

Austen, Jane, *Jane Austen's Letters*, ed. Deirdre Le Faye (Oxford and New York: Oxford University Press, 1995).

Austen Leigh, James Edward, *A Memoir of Jane Austen*, ed. R. W. Chapman (Oxford University Press, 1926).

A Memoir of Jane Austen; and Other Family Recollections, ed. and intr. Kathryn Sutherland, Oxford World's Classics (Oxford University Press, 2002).

Austen-Leigh, Mary Augusta, *James Edward Austen-Leigh: A Memoir by His Daughter* (privately printed, 1911).

Personal Aspects of Jane Austen (London: Murray, 1920).

Austen-Leigh, Richard A., ed., *Austen Papers, 1704–1856* (London: Spottiswoode, Ballantyne, 1942).

Austen-Leigh, William, and Richard A. Austen-Leigh, *Jane Austen: Her Life and Letters. A Family Record* (London: Smith, Elder, 1913).

Brabourne, Edward, 1st Lord, 'Introduction', *Letters of Jane Austen*, 2 vols. (London: Bentley, 1884).

Cecil, Lord David, *A Portrait of Jane Austen* (London: Constable, 1978).

Fergus, Jan, *Jane Austen: A Literary Life* (London: Macmillan; New York: St Martin's Press, 1991).

Halperin, John, *The Life of Jane Austen* (Baltimore, MD: Johns Hopkins University Press, 1984).

Hill, Constance, *Jane Austen: Her Homes and Her Friends* (London and New York: Lane, 1902).

Hodge, Jane Aiken, *The Double Life of Jane Austen* (London: Hodder and Stoughton, 1972); issued as *Only a Novel: The Double Life of Jane Austen* (New York: Coward, McCan, and Geohegan, 1972).

Honan, Park, *Jane Austen: Her Life* (London: Weidenfeld & Nicolson, 1987).

Hubback, J.H., and Edith Hubback, *Jane Austen's Sailor Brothers* (London and New York: Lane, 1906).

Jenkins, Elizabeth, *Jane Austen: A Biography* (London: Gollancz, 1938).

Kaplan, Deborah, *Jane Austen among Women* (Baltimore, MD: Johns Hopkins University Press, 1994).

Le Faye, Deirdre, *Jane Austen's 'Outlandish Cousin': The Life and Letters of Eliza de Feuillide* (London: British Library, 2002).

Jane Austen: A Family Record (2nd edn, Cambridge University Press, 2004).

A Chronology of Jane Austen and Her Family (Cambridge University Press, 2006).

Nokes, David, *Jane Austen: A Life* (New York: Farrer, Straus and Giroux, 1997).

Shields, Carol, *Jane Austen* (New York: Viking Penguin, 2001).

Spence, Jon, *Becoming Jane Austen* (London and New York: Hambledon and London, 2003).

Tomalin, Claire, *Jane Austen: A Life* (London: Viking, 1997).

Tucker, George Holbert, *A Goodly Heritage: A History of Jane Austen's Family* (Manchester: Carcanet, 1983).

Jane Austen the Woman: Some Biographical Insights (New York: St Martin's Press, 1994).

Criticism to 1970

Austen, Jane, *The Novels of Jane Austen*, ed. R.W. Chapman, 5 vols. (Oxford: Clarendon Press, 1923; rev. edn, 1965–6).

Minor Works, ed. R.W. Chapman, vol. 6 of *The Works of Jane Austen* (Oxford University Press, 1954; rev. edn, 1969).

Babb, Howard S., *Jane Austen's Novels: The Fabric of Dialogue* (Columbus, OH: Ohio State University Press, 1962).

Booth, Wayne C., *The Rhetoric of Fiction* (University of Chicago Press, 1961).

Bradley, A. C., 'Jane Austen: A Lecture', *Essays and Studies by Members of the English Association*, 2 (1911), 7–36.

Shakespearean Tragedy (London: Macmillan & Co. Ltd, 1904).

Farrer, Reginald, 'Jane Austen, ob. July 18 1817', *Quarterly Review*, 228 (October 1917), 1–30.

'Female Novelists', *New Monthly Magazine*, 95 (May 1852), 17–23; cited from Southam, *Jane Austen: The Critical Heritage*, pp. 131–9.

Forster, E. M., 'Jane Austen', in *Abinger Harvest* (London: Arnold, 1936), pp. 3–14.

Harding, D. W., 'Regulated Hatred: An Aspect of the Work of Jane Austen', *Scrutiny*, 8 (1939–40), 346–62; repr. in Watt, *Jane Austen: A Collection of Critical Essays*, pp. 166–79.

Lascelles, Mary, *Jane Austen and Her Art* (Oxford: Clarendon Press, 1939).

Litz, A. Walton, *Jane Austen: A Study of Her Artistic Development* (London: Chatto & Windus; New York: Oxford University Press, 1965).

Moler, Kenneth L., *Jane Austen's Art of Allusion* (Lincoln, NE: University of Nebraska Press, 1968).

Mudrick, Marvin, *Jane Austen: Irony as Defense and Discovery* (Princeton University Press; Oxford University Press, 1952).

[Scott, Sir Walter,] review of *Emma*, *Quarterly Review*, 14 (October 1815), 188–201; cited from Southam, *Jane Austen: The Critical Heritage*, pp. 58–69.

[Simpson, Richard,] review of J. E. Austen-Leigh, *A Memoir of Jane Austen*, *North British Review*, 52 (April 1870), 129–52; cited from Southam, *Jane Austen: The Critical Heritage*, pp. 241–65.

Southam, B. C., *Jane Austen's Literary Manuscripts: A Study of the Novelist's Development through the Surviving Papers* (Oxford University Press, 1964).

Southam, B. C., ed., *Critical Essays on Jane Austen* (London: Routledge & Kegan Paul; New York: Barnes and Noble, 1968).

Jane Austen: The Critical Heritage (London: Routledge & Kegan Paul; New York: Barnes and Noble, 1968).

Jane Austen: The Critical Heritage, Volume II: 1870–1940 (London: Routledge & Kegan Paul; Totowa, NJ: Barnes and Noble, 1987).

Tanner, Tony, 'Introduction', *Mansfield Park* (Harmondsworth: Penguin, 1966).

'Introduction', *Sense and Sensibility* (Harmondsworth: Penguin, 1969).

Trilling, Lionel, '*Mansfield Park*', *Encounter*, 3(3) (September 1954), 9–19, and *Partisan Review*, 21 (1954), 492–511; repr. in his *The Opposing Self: Nine Essays in Criticism* (London: Secker & Warburg; New York: Viking, 1955), pp. 206–30.

'*Emma*', *Encounter*, 8(6) (June 1957), 49–59; repr. in his *Beyond Culture: Essays on Literature and Learning* (New York: Viking, 1965; London: Secker & Warburg, 1966), pp. 31–55.

Van Ghent, Dorothy, *The English Novel: Form and Function* (New York: Holt, Rinehart, and Winston, 1953).

Watt, Ian, ed., *Jane Austen: A Collection of Critical Essays* (Englewood Cliffs, NJ: Prentice-Hall, 1963).

[Whateley, Richard,] review of *Northanger Abbey and Persuasion*, *Quarterly Review*, 24 (Jan. 1821), 352–76; cited from Southam, *Jane Austen: The Critical Heritage*, pp. 87–105.

Wiesenfarth, Joseph, *The Errand of Form: An Assay of Jane Austen's Art* (New York: Fordham University Press, 1967).

Woolf, Virginia, 'Jane Austen', in *The Common Reader* (London: Hogarth Press, 1925), pp. 168–83; cited from Watt, *Jane Austen: A Collection of Critical Essays*, pp. 15–24.

Criticism since 1970

Armstrong, Nancy, *Desire and Domestic Fiction: A Political History of the Novel* (New York: Oxford University Press, 1987).

Auerbach, Emily, *Searching for Jane Austen* (Madison, WI: University of Wisconsin Press, 2004).

Auerbach, Nina, *Communities of Women: An Idea in Fiction* (Cambridge, MA and London: Harvard University Press, 1978).

Battaglia, Beatrice, and Diego Saglia, eds., *Re-Drawing Austen: Picturesque Travels in Austenland* (Naples: Liguori, 2004).

Bautz, Annika, *The Reception of Jane Austen and Walter Scott: A Comparative Longitudinal Study* (London and New York: Continuum, 2007).

Brooke, Christopher, *Jane Austen: Illusion and Reality* (Cambridge: D.S. Brewer, 1999).

Brown, Julia Prewitt, *Jane Austen's Novels: Social Change and Literary Form* (Cambridge, MA: Harvard University Press, 1979).

Brown, Lloyd W., *Bits of Ivory: Narrative Techniques in Jane Austen's Fiction* (Baton Rouge, LA: Louisiana State University Press, 1973).

Brownstein, Rachel, *Becoming a Heroine: Reading about Women in Novels* (New York and London: Viking, 1982).

Burrows, J. F., *Computation into Criticism: A Study of Jane Austen's Novels and an Experiment in Method* (Oxford: Clarendon Press, 1987).

Bush, Douglas, *Jane Austen* (London and New York: Macmillan, 1975).

Butler, Marilyn, *Jane Austen and the War of Ideas* (Oxford: Clarendon Press, 1975).

Byrne, Paula, *Jane Austen and the Theatre* (London and New York: Hambledon, 2002).

Castellanos, Gabriela, *Laughter, War, and Feminism: Elements of Carnival in Three of Jane Austen's Novels* (New York: Peter Lang, 1994).

Collins, Irene, *Jane Austen and the Clergy* (London: Hambledon, 1994).

Copeland, Edward, *Women Writing about Money: Women's Fiction in England, 1790–1820* (Cambridge University Press, 1995).

De Rose, Peter L., and S. W. McGuire, *A Concordance to the Works of Jane Austen*, 3 vols. (New York: Garland, 1983).

Deresiewicz, William, *Jane Austen and the Romantic Poets* (New York: Columbia University Press, 2004).

Devlin, D. D., *Jane Austen and Education* (London: Macmillan, 1975).

Doody, Margaret Anne, 'Introduction', *Sense and Sensibility* (Oxford and New York: Oxford University Press, 1990).

Duckworth, Alistair M., *The Improvement of the Estate: A Study of Jane Austen's Novels* (Baltimore, MD and London: Johns Hopkins University Press, 1971).

Dussinger, John, *In the Pride of the Moment: Encounters in Jane Austen's World* (Columbus, OH: Ohio State University Press, 1990).

Emsley, Sarah, *Jane Austen's Philosophy of the Virtues* (Basingstoke: Palgrave Macmillan, 2005).

Evans, Mary, *Jane Austen and the State* (London and New York: Tavistock, 1987).

Fergus, Jan, *Jane Austen and the Didactic Novel: 'Northanger Abbey', 'Sense and Sensibility', and 'Pride and Prejudice'* (London: Macmillan; Totowa, NJ: Barnes and Noble, 1983).

Gard, Roger, *Jane Austen's Novels: The Art of Clarity* (New Haven, CT: Yale University Press, 1992).

Gay, Penny, *Jane Austen and the Theatre* (Cambridge University Press, 2002).

Giffin, Michael, *Jane Austen and Religion: Salvation and Society in Georgian England* (Basingstoke: Palgrave Macmillan, 2002).

Gilbert, Sandra M., and Susan Gubar, *The Madwoman in the Attic: The Woman Writer and the Nineteenth-Century Literary Imagination* (New Haven, CT: Yale University Press, 1979).

Gillie, Christopher, *A Preface to Jane Austen* (London: Longman, 1974).

Gilson, David, *A Bibliography of Jane Austen* (Oxford: Clarendon Press, 1982).

Grey, J. David, *The Jane Austen Companion* (New York: Macmillan, 1986); issued as the *Jane Austen Handbook* (London: Macmillan, 1986).

Jane Austen's Beginnings: The Juvenilia and 'Lady Susan' (Ann Arbor, MI: UMI Research Press, 1989).

Halperin, John, ed., *Jane Austen: Bicentenary Essays* (Cambridge University Press, 1975).

Handler, Richard, and Daniel Segal, *Jane Austen and the Fiction of Culture: An Essay on the Narration of Social Realities* (Tucson, AZ: University of Arizona Press, 1990).

Hardy, Barbara, *A Reading of Jane Austen* (London: Owen; New York University Press, 1976).

Hardy, John, *Jane Austen's Heroines: Intimacy in Human Relationships* (London: Routledge & Kegan Paul, 1984).

Harris, Jocelyn, *Jane Austen's Art of Memory* (Cambridge University Press, 1989).

Heydt-Stevenson, Jillian, *Austen's Unbecoming Conjunctions: Subversive Laughter, Embodied History* (New York: Palgrave Macmillan, 2005).

Horwitz, Barbara, *Jane Austen and the Question of Women's Education* (New York: Lang, 1991).

Hudson, Glenda, *Sibling Love and Incest in Jane Austen's Fiction* (Basingstoke: Macmillan, 1992).

Jenkyns, Richard, *A Fine Brush on Ivory: An Appreciation of Jane Austen* (Oxford University Press, 2004).

Johnson, Claudia L., *Jane Austen: Women, Politics, and the Novel* (University of Chicago Press, 1988).

Equivocal Beings: Politics, Gender, and Sentimentality in the 1790s: Wollstonecraft, Radcliffe, Burney, Austen (Chicago and London: University of Chicago Press, 1995).

Jones, Darryl, *Jane Austen* (Basingstoke: Palgrave Macmillan, 2004).

Kirkham, Margaret, *Jane Austen: Feminism and Fiction* (Brighton: Harvester; Totowa, NJ: Barnes and Noble, 1983).

Knox-Shaw, Peter, *Jane Austen and the Enlightenment* (Cambridge University Press, 2004).

Koppel, Gene, *The Religious Dimension in Jane Austen's Novels* (Ann Arbor, MI: UMI Research Press, 1988).

Kramp, Michael, *Disciplining Love: Austen and the Modern Man* (Columbus, OH: Ohio State University Press, 2007).

Kroeber, Karl, *Styles in Fictional Structures: The Art of Jane Austen, Charlotte Bronte, and George Eliot* (Princeton University Press, 1971).

Lane, Maggie, *Jane Austen and Food* (London: Hambledon, 1995).

Lauber, John, *Jane Austen* (New York: Twayne, 1993).

Looser, Devoney, *Jane Austen and the Discourses of Feminism* (New York: St Martin's Press, 1995).

Lynch, Deidre, ed., *Janeites: Austen's Disciples and Devotees* (Princeton and Oxford: Princeton University Press, 2000).

MacDonagh, Oliver, *Jane Austen: Real and Imagined Worlds* (New Haven, CT: Yale University Press, 1991).

Macdonald, Gina, and Andrew F. Macdonald, eds., *Jane Austen on Screen* (Cambridge University Press, 2003).

McMaster, Juliet, ed., *Jane Austen's Achievement: Papers Delivered at the Jane Austen Bicentennial Conference at the University of Alberta* (London: Macmillan, 1976).

Jane Austen on Love (Victoria, BC: University of Victoria Press, 1978).

Jane Austen the Novelist: Essays Past and Present (London: Macmillan, 1995).

McMaster, Juliet, and Bruce Stovel, eds., *Jane Austen's Business: Her World and Her Profession* (London: Macmillan, 1996).

Mandal, Anthony, *Jane Austen and the Popular Novel: The Determined Author* (Basingstoke: Palgrave Macmillan, 2007).

Mandal, Anthony, and Brian Southam, eds., *The Reception of Jane Austen in Europe* (London: Thoemmes Continuum, 2007).

Mansell, Darrel, *The Novels of Jane Austen: An Interpretation* (London: Macmillan, 1973).

Miller, D. A., *Jane Austen, or The Secret of Style* (Princeton and Oxford: Princeton University Press, 2003).

Moers, Ellen, *Literary Women* (New York: Doubleday, 1976).

Monaghan, David, *Jane Austen: Structure and Social Vision* (London: Macmillan, 1980).

ed., *Jane Austen in a Social Context* (London: Macmillan; Totowa, NJ: Barnes and Noble, 1981).

Mooneyham, Laura G., *Romance, Language, and Education in Jane Austen's Novels* (London: Macmillan; New York: St Martin's Press, 1988).

Morgan, Susan, *In the Meantime: Character and Perception in Jane Austen's Fiction* (Chicago and London: University of Chicago Press, 1980).

Nardin, Jane, *Those Elegant Decorums: The Concept of Propriety in Jane Austen's Novels* (Albany, NY: State University of New York Press, 1973).

Neill, Edward, *The Politics of Jane Austen* (New York: St Martin's Press, 1999).

Park, You-me, and Rajeswari Sunder Rajan, eds., *The Postcolonial Jane Austen* (London: Routledge, 2000).

Pucci, Suzanne R., and James Thompson, eds., *Jane Austen and Co.: Remaking the Past in Contemporary Culture* (Albany, NY: State University of New York Press, 2003).

Odmark, John, *An Understanding of Jane Austen's Novels: Character, Value, and Ironic Perspective* (Oxford: Blackwell, 1981).

Page, Norman, *The Language of Jane Austen* (Oxford: Blackwell, 1972).

Phillipps, K. C., *Jane Austen's English* (London: André Deutsch, 1970).

Piggott, Patrick, *The Innocent Diversion: Music in the Life and Writings of Jane Austen* (London: Cleverdon, 1979).

Pinion, F. B., *A Jane Austen Companion: A Critical Survey and Reference Book* (London: Macmillan, 1973).

Poovey, Mary, *The Proper Lady and the Woman Writer: Ideology as Style in the Works of Mary Wollstonecraft, Mary Shelley, and Jane Austen* (University of Chicago Press, 1984).

Roberts, Warren, *Jane Austen and the French Revolution* (New York: St Martin's Press, 1979).

Roth, Barry, *An Annotated Bibliography of Jane Austen Studies, 1973–1983* (Charlottesville, VA : University of Virginia Press, 1984).

Roth, Barry, and Joel Weinsheimer, *An Annotated Bibliography of Jane Austen Studies, 1952–1972* (Charlottesville, VA: University of Virginia Press, 1973).

Ruderman, Anne Crippen, *The Pleasures of Virtue: Political Thought in the Novels of Jane Austen* (Lanham, MD: Rowman & Littlefield, 1995).

Said, Edward, *Culture and Imperialism* (New York: Knopf, 1993).

Sales, Roger, *Jane Austen and Representations of Regency England* (London and New York: Routledge, 1994).

Seeber, Barbara K., *General Consent in Jane Austen: A Study of Dialogism* (Montreal: McGill-Queen's University Press, 2000).

Selwyn, David, *Jane Austen and Leisure* (London: Hambledon, 1999).

Showalter, Elaine, *A Literature of their Own: British Women Novelists from Brontë to Lessing* (Princeton University Press, 1977).

Smith, Leroy W., *Jane Austen and the Drama of Woman* (New York: St Martin's Press, 1983).

Spacks, Patricia Meyer, *The Female Imagination: A Literary and Psychological Investigation of Women's Writing* (New York: Knopf, 1975).

Spencer, Jane, *The Rise of the Woman Novelist: From Aphra Behn to Jane Austen* (Oxford: Blackwell, 1986).

Stewart, Maija, *Domestic Realities and Imperial Fictions: Jane Austen's Novels in Eighteenth-Century Contexts* (Athens, GA: University of Georgia Press, 1993).

Stovel, Bruce, and Lynn Weinlos Gregg, *The Talk in Jane Austen* (Edmonton, AB: University of Alberta Press, 2002).

Southam, Brian, *Jane Austen and the Navy* (London and New York: Hambledon, 2000).

Jane Austen's Literary Manuscripts: A Study of the Novelist's Development through the Surviving Papers, new edn (London and New York: Athlone Press, 2001; orig.1964; corrected edn 1966).

Sulloway, Alison G., *Jane Austen and the Province of Womanhood* (Philadelphia, PA: University of Pennsylvania Press, 1989).

Sutherland, Kathryn, *Jane Austen's Textual Lives: From Aeschylus to Bollywood* (Oxford University Press, 2005).

Tandon, Bharat, *Jane Austen and the Morality of Conversation* (London: Anthem, 2003).

Tanner, Tony, 'Introduction', *Mansfield Park* (Harmondsworth: Penguin, 1966).

'Introduction', *Sense and Sensibility* (Harmondsworth: Penguin, 1969).

'Introduction', *Pride and Prejudice* (Harmondsworth: Penguin, 1972).

Jane Austen (Cambridge, MA: Harvard University Press, 1986).

Tauchert, Ashley, *Romancing Jane Austen* (Basingstoke: Palgrave Macmillan, 2005).

Tave, Stuart M., *Some Words of Jane Austen* (Chicago and London: University of Chicago Press, 1973).

Thompson, James, *Between Self and World: The Novels of Jane Austen* (University Park, PA: Pennsylvania State University Press, 1988).

Todd, Janet, ed., *Jane Austen: New Perspectives* (New York: Homes and Meier, 1983).

   ed., *Jane Austen in Context* (Cambridge University Press, 2005).

   ed., *Cambridge Edition of the Works of Jane Austen*, 9 vols. (Cambridge University Press, 2009).

Troost, Linda, and Sayre Greenfield, eds. *Jane Austen in Hollywood*, 2nd edn (Lexington, KY: University Press of Kentucky, 2001).

Tuite, Clara, *Romantic Austen: Sexual Politics and the Literary Canon* (Cambridge University Press, 2002).

Voigts-Virchow, Eckart, ed., *Janespotting and Beyond: British Heritage Retrovisions since the Mid-1990s* (Tubingen: Gunter Narr Verlag, 2004).

Waldron, Mary, *Jane Austen and the Fiction of Her Time* (Cambridge University Press, 1999).

Wallace, Robert K., *Jane Austen and Mozart: Classical Equilibrium in Fiction and Music* (Athens, GA: University of Georgia Press, 1983).

Wallace, Tara Ghoshal, *Jane Austen and Narrative Authority* (New York: St Martin's Press, 1995).

Weinsheimer, Joel, ed., *Jane Austen Today* (Athens, GA: University of Georgia Press, 1975).

Wenner, Barbara Britton, *Prospect and Refuge in the Landscape of Jane Austen* (Aldershot: Ashgate, 2006).

White, Gabrielle D. V., *Jane Austen in the Context of Abolition: 'A Fling at the Slave Trade'* (Basingstoke: Palgrave Macmillan, 2006).

White, Laura Mooneyham, ed. *Critical Essays on Jane Austen* (New York: G. K. Hall, 1998).

Williams, Michael, *Jane Austen: Six Novels and their Methods* (London: Macmillan, 1986).

Williams, Raymond, *The Country and the City* (London and New York: Oxford University Press, 1973).

Wiltshire, John, *Jane Austen and the Body: 'The Picture of Health'* (Cambridge University Press, 1992).

   Recreating Jane Austen (Cambridge University Press, 2001).

   Jane Austen: Introductions and Interventions (Basingstoke: Palgrave Macmillan, 2003, 2006).

Winborn, Colin, *The Literary Economy of Jane Austen and George Crabbe* (Aldershot; Burlington, VT: Ashgate, 2004).

INDEX

Entries for Austen's works appear separately by title.

Almack's club 59
Aristotle 40
Arnold, Matthew 81
Auden, W. H. 36
Auerbach, Erich 199
Austen, Anna 4
Austen, Caroline 97–9, 146
Austen, Cassandra 11, 22, 91, 97
  as JA's heir 16, 20
  death of fiancé 105
Austen, Edward 15, 140
Austen family
  financial losses 15
  professions 144
Austen, Francis 1, 103
Austen, George 3, 8, 128
Austen, Henry 2, 6, 8, 12, 13
  bank failure 15, 140
  'Biographical Notice' 1, 9
  The Loiterer 4
Austen, James
  The Loiterer 4
Austen, Jane
  attitudes to money 11, 128
  breadth of reading **192–211**
    (*see also Letters*)
  circumstances in 1805 90
  early short fiction (*see* juvenilia)
  health 15, 16, 92, 154
  as professional writer 1–7
  reviews of novels 7–8
  schooling 153
  social status 111
Austen, Mary Lloyd 106, 107
Austen Leigh, James Edward 88, 90, 91, 92,
  93, 151
  Memoir of Jane Austen 97, 106, 232

Bakhtin, Mikhail 179
Barbauld, Anna Laetitia 49

Barker, Mary 6, 7
Barrett, Eaton Stannard 28, 204
'Beautifull Cassandra, The' 79
Beckett, Samuel 100
Behn, Aphra 77
Benedict, Barbara 24, 31
Benjamin, Walter 217
Benson, Maria 9, 11
Bentley, Richard 1, 232
Berry, Mary 78
Bible 198–9
Birtwistle, Sue 226
Blair, Hugh 208
Blythe, Ronald 200
Boccaccio, Giovanni 82
Boileau-Despréaux, Nicolas 82
Bond, John 147
Booth, Wayne 242, 243
Borges, Jorge Luis 80
Bradley, A. C. 220, 226
Bradshaigh, Lady 23
Brontë, Anne 121
Brontë, Charlotte 121
Brown, Capability 127
Brunton, Mary 205
Brydges, Samuel Egerton 204
Buckingham, George Villiers, Duke of 51
Bulwer-Lytton, Edward 111, 121
Buonaparte, Napoleon 63, 76
Burney, Charles 78
Burney, Frances 2, 3, 16, 29, 172, 206
  Camilla 4, 28, 108, 198, 201,
    209, 210
  Cecilia 210
  Evelina 178–9, 201, 209
  JA's debt to 177, 179
  The Wanderer 51–2, 76, 84
Burney, Sarah Harriet 204
Butler, Judith 161
Butler, Marilyn 33

Byrne, Paula 45, 46
Byron, George Gordon, Lord 10, 13, 65,
    81, 203

Cadell and Davis, publishers 8
Carlyle, Thomas 111, 112
Castle, Terry 24, 162
Catharine, or the Bower 72–6
Cecil, Lord David 240
Cervantes, Miguel de 79
Chapman, R. W. 12, 97, 176, 238–40
Chapone, Hester 72
Chesterton, G. K. 80
Cibber, Colley 52
Cinderella plot 113, 166
Clarke, James Stanier 14–15, 76–7, 195
Clarkson, Thomas 194, 209
class in JA's novels 111–25
    country gentry 114–16
    hierarchy of characters 112–24
    professions 149–55
    'snobbery' 124
    trade 119–21
    working class 123, 147–9
Clutterbuck, Mrs 5
Clymer, William 195
Colby, Vineta 83
Collier, Jane 28
Colman, George 45
Cooke, Cassandra 4, 204
Copeland, Edward 6, 16
Cowley, Hannah 45, 204
Cowper, William 32, 93, 198, 201, 202–3,
    207, 210
Crabbe, George 194
Crawford, Anne 45
Crosby, Benjamin, publisher
    and *NA* 8, 15, 22, 26, 80, 87
Cumberland, Richard 49

Davies, Andrew 226, 227–8
Dickens, Charles 94, 172, 224
Diderot, Denis 78, 80
Disraeli, Benjamin 124

Edgeworth, Maria 16, 28, 29, 33, 76, 84, 204
    Patronage 51–2
Egerton, Thomas 13
    as publisher of *MP*, 1, 12
    as publisher of *PP* 10–11
    as publisher of *SS* 8–10
Eisenstein, Sergei 218
Eliot, George 94, 108, 197

Emma 55–63
    Crown Inn ball 188
    compared with *Persuasion* 69
    English–French contrast 59–61
    flawed heroine 55–6
    money in 136–8
    publication of 7
    as social microcosm 114
'Evelyn' 73

Fenwick, Eliza 73
Fergus, Jan 129
Fielding, Henry 41, 51, 85, 193, 195, 196,
    202, 206
Fielding, Sarah 2, 28, 78
film versions of JA's novels: *see* screen
    adaptations
Finch, Anne 76, 205
First Impressions 3, 8, 22
    (*see also* Pride and Prejudice)
Firth, Colin 225
Fordyce, James 161, 206
Forster, E. M. 243
Fowle, Thomas 105

Galperin, William 189
Garrick, David 45, 47, 49, 51
Garrod, H. W. 241
Garson, Greer 218
Gay, John 210
Gay, Penny 41, 45, 50
gender identity
    enigma hero 170
    feminist criticism 161
    in *NA* 159–61
    and narrative technique 163–7
    queer perspectives 163
    recuperation of romance 167
    resistance to romance 163
Genette, Gérard 172
Genlis, Mme Stephanie de 204, 205
George III 73, 75
George IV (as Prince Regent) 14, 75, 76,
    81, 112
Gifford, William 13
Gilbert, Sandra 83
Gilpin, William 196
Gisborne, Thomas 161
Goethe, Johann Wolfgang von 82
Goldsmith, Oliver 197, 210
Gore, Catherine 84
Grant, Anne 204
Graves, Richard 207

Gubar, Susan 83
Gunning, Elizabeth 35, 88

Halperin, John 108
Hamilton, Elizabeth 204
Harding, D. W. 162, 234, 238, 240
Harris, Jocelyn 63
Harrison, Frederic 238
Hawke, Cassandra, Lady 4
Hawkins, Laetitia Matilda 6
Haywood, Eliza 77
Heliodorus 82
'Henry and Eliza' 79
Heyer, Georgette 75
'History of England' 197
Horace 197
Hogarth, William 121, 201
Hookham and Carpenter, publishers 5, 6, 18
Hughes, Gwyneth 228
Hume, David 177, 208
Hunter, Rachel 206
Huxley, Aldous 218

illustrated versions of JA's novels 217,
    219, 232
Inchbald, Elizabeth 2, 88, 210

James, Henry 2, 93, 232–3, 237
Jane Austen Book Club 176
Jerome, Helen 218
Johnson, Claudia 81, 216
Johnson, Samuel 48, 102, 195, 201, 202–3,
    205, 245
Joyce, James 36
juvenilia 72–4, 212–13
    physicality in 78–80 (see also individual
        titles, Catharine, etc.)
    as short fiction 77
    updating to current fashion 74

Kaplan, Deborah 98
Kauffman, Angelica 178
Kean, Edmund 45, 51
Kelly, Gary 132
Kelly, Isabella 35
Kent, Christopher 238
Kernan, Alvin 2–3
Kipling, Rudyard
    'Janeites, The' 226, 235–8
King, James 182
Kirkham, Margaret 169
Knight, Fanny 17, 99, 105, 108, 111, 206
Knox, Vicessimus 161, 210

Laclos, Pierre Choderlos de 88
Lascelles, Mary 95
'Lady Susan' 40, 87–9, 207
    precedents for 88
    sexual impropriety in 88, 89
Lady's Magazine 137
landed gentry 114–16, 144–9
    servants 148
    stewards 146
Lanford, Paul 178
Lathom, Francis 204
La Tournelle, Mrs 153
Le Faye, Deirdre 24, 73
Leavis, F. R. 240
Lee, Ang 220
Lefroy, Anna Austen 92, 94, 108, 206
Lefroy, Anne 4
Leigh, James Henry 4
Leigh-Perrot, James 15, 140
Lennox, Charlotte 28, 83, 200, 208, 211
'Lesley Castle' 81, 93
Letters of JA 97–109, 228
    domestic content 98
    letters in the novels 103
    Miss Bates as model in 100–3
    paraphernalia in 106–7
    petticoat motif in 101, 102, 109
    references to books in 192
Lewis, C. S. 241
Lloyd, Martha 10
Locke, John 41, 42
Loiterer, The 4, 8
Longman, publisher 9, 11, 18
'Love and Freindship' 80, 87
Lyford, Giles-King 154
Lynch, Deirdre 31

Macaulay, Catherine 178
Mack, Robert 78
McLeod, Randall 217
McMaster, Juliet 47
Mansfield case 209
Mansfield Park
    Lovers' Vows in 39, 47–8, 51
    money in 134–6
    publication of 12, 19
    reading in 209–10
    theatricality in 45–53
Marie Antoinette, Queen 59
Marmontel, Jean-François 78
Milbanke, Anne Isabella 10
Miller, D. A. 93, 165, 170
Milton, John 25

Mitford, Mary Russell 8
Modert, Jo 98
Modleski, Tania 170
money 127–41
  incomes and buying power 129–32 (see also
    individual works)
  in NA, SS, PP 128–9, 134
  women and money 128
More, Hannah 33, 198
Mudrick, Marvin 241
Murfin, Jane 218
Murray, John 7, 12
  as publisher of E 13–14
  as publisher of P and NA 16
Mussell, Mrs 156

Nash, Beau 182
Northanger Abbey 23–31
  Bath in 182
  Blaise Castle in 29–30
  General Tilney in 30–1
  girlification of Catherine 160
  Gothic novel in 21, 24–6
  publication of 15–16
  reading in 208–9
  revision of 22–3
  title 23–4

Olivier, Laurence 218
Opie, Amelia 2, 17
Owenson, Sydney 205

Parsons, Eliza 207
Pasley, Charles 194
Peacock, Thomas Love 24, 84
Pellew, Edward 150
Persuasion 63–70
  cancelled chapter 67–9, 169
  Cinderella motif in 64, 67
  compared with Emma 69
  feminism in 68
  money in 138–40
  navy in 63
  poetic imagination in 65–7
  publication of 15–16
  social spaces in 189–90
Piozzi, Hester (see Thrale, Hester)
'Plan of a Novel' 77, 87
Pope, Alexander 193, 195, 200
Pride and Prejudice 40–4
  assembly in 187–8
  dramatic devices in 40–4
  publication of 10–11

reviews of 10
'sparkling' 76
Prior, Matthew 210
professions 116–19, 149–55
  army 117, 149
  clergy 116, 150–3
  governess 121, 153
  law 118, 154
  medicine 154
  navy 117, 150
Proust, Marcel 93
publication, forms of 4–6

queer theory 160, 163

Rabelais, François 80
Radcliffe, Ann 2, 3, 5, 24, 172, 209
  Mysteries of Udolpho 26
Radcliffe, William 3
rank in JA's novels ('class')
Regency romance 75
Repton, Humphry 145
Richardson, Samuel 23, 78, 196
  Clarissa 40, 47, 49, 73, 108
  Sir Charles Grandison 26–7, 40, 108, 201,
    202, 206, 209,
Robertson, William 208
Robinson, Mary Darby 17
Roche, Regina Maria 25
Root, Amanda 228
Rousseau, Jean-Jacques 82
Rowe, Nicholas 49
Roworth, Charles 9
Rozema, Patricia 223

Said, Edward 223
'Sanditon' 16, 117, 64, 92–6
  invalidism in 92, 95
  money in 140–1, 156
  reading in 210
  revisions 94–5
Scott, Sir Walter 7, 13, 65, 76, 84, 93, 204
  review of Emma 7, 21
screen adaptations
  Becoming Jane (2007) 162, 222
  Bride and Prejudice 224
  Clueless (1995) 224
  Emma (1996) 222, 225
  Lost in Austen (2008) 176, 221
  Mansfield Park (1999) 223
  Miss Austen Regrets (2009) 162, 228–9
  Persuasion (1995) 219, 228
  Pride and Prejudice (1940) 218, 226

Pride and Prejudice (1980) 219
Pride and Prejudice (1995) 219, 225
Pride & Prejudice (2005) 223
Sense and Sensibility (1995) 219,
    220, 222
Sense and Sensibility (2008) 227
visual vs. verbal 215–18
Scudéry, Madeleine de 83
Sedgwick, Eve 243
Sense and Sensibility 31–6, 207
    as didactic contrast novel 33–4, 208
    and novel of sensibility 21, **32–3**
    publication of **8–10**, 11
    revision of 22
    sales 1
Seward, Bridger 146
Shakespeare, William 51, 193
    JA's references to 199–200
Shelley, Mary 25
Sheridan, Frances 88
Sheridan, Richard Brinsley 51
Sherlock, Thomas 210
Siddons, Sarah 45
Simpson, Richard 171
slave trade 30, 62, 122, 209, 223, 239
Sleath, Eleanor 193
Smith, Benjamin 3
Smith, Charlotte 2, 3, 27, 74
social spaces **177–90**
    assembly room 177
    in Bath 182–5
    in London 178–81
    in 'The Watsons' 185–9
    women and sociability 177
Southam, B. C. 2, 63, 150
Spence, Elizabeth Isabella 32
Spring, David 128
Staël, Germaine de 1
Stanton, Judith Phillips 2
Sterne, Laurence 98, 102, 105, 209
Surr, T. S. 93
'Susan' 8, 74
    (*see also Northanger Abbey*)
Sutherland, Kathryn 187
Swift, Jonathan 100
Sykes, Henrietta 204, 206

Tandon, Bharat 172
Tanner, Tony 23, 169
Tauchert, Ashley 169, 171
Tennyson, Alfred 113
Thackeray, William Makepeace 111,
    122, 196
Thompson, Emma 220
Thomson, Hugh 219, 232
Thrale, Hester 202, 205
'Tour through Wales, A' 78
Trilling, Lionel 124, 240
Trollope, Anthony 116, 196
'Three Sisters, The' 79
trade 119–21
Tucker, George Holbert 73
Tylney, Richard 25

Vanburgh, John 52
Vickery, Amanda 178
Victoria, Queen 84
Voltaire 78

Walpole, Horace 24, 78
Warner, Richard 26
Waterloo 76
'Watsons, The' **22, 89–92**, 122
    assembly in 185–9
    creative process 90
Watt, James 24
West, Jane 33
Wiesenfarth, Joseph 141, 187
Williams, Helen Maria 14
Williams, Olivia 228
Wiltshire, John 95
Weldon, Fay 219
Whealler, Susan 98
Wollstonecraft, Mary 33, 161
women and marriage 92, 141
women and money 133
women publishing 2–3, 205
Woolf, Virginia 93, 106
Wordsworth, William 21,
    76, 226
Wroe, Martin 219, 220

Yates, Mary Anne 45

Cambridge Companions to ...

AUTHORS

Edward Albee edited by Stephen J. Bottoms

Margaret Atwood edited by Coral Ann Howells

W. H. Auden edited by Stan Smith

Jane Austen edited by Edward Copeland
and Juliet McMaster (second edition)

Beckett edited by John Pilling

Bede edited by Scott DeGregorio

Aphra Behn edited by Derek Hughes
and Janet Todd

Walter Benjamin edited by David S. Ferris

William Blake edited by Morris Eaves

Brecht edited by Peter Thomson and
Glendyr Sacks (second edition)

The Brontës edited by Heather Glen

Frances Burney edited by Peter Sabor

Byron edited by Drummond Bone

Albert Camus edited by Edward J. Hughes

Willa Cather edited by Marilee Lindemann

Cervantes edited by Anthony J. Cascardi

Chaucer edited by Piero Boitani and Jill Mann
(second edition)

Chekhov edited by Vera Gottlieb and Paul Allain

Kate Chopin edited by Janet Beer

Caryl Churchill edited by Elaine Aston and
Elin Diamond

Coleridge edited by Lucy Newlyn

Wilkie Collins edited by Jenny Bourne Taylor

Joseph Conrad edited by J. H. Stape

Dante edited by Rachel Jacoff (second edition)

Daniel Defoe edited by John Richetti

Don DeLillo edited by John N. Duvall

Charles Dickens edited by John O. Jordan

Emily Dickinson edited by Wendy Martin

John Donne edited by Achsah Guibbory

Dostoevskii edited by W. J. Leatherbarrow

Theodore Dreiser edited by Leonard Cassuto
and Claire Virginia Eby

John Dryden edited by Steven N. Zwicker

W. E. B. Du Bois edited by Shamoon Zamir

George Eliot edited by George Levine

T. S. Eliot edited by A. David Moody

Ralph Ellison edited by Ross Posnock

Ralph Waldo Emerson edited by Joel Porte
and Saundra Morris

William Faulkner edited by Philip M. Weinstein

Henry Fielding edited by Claude Rawson

F. Scott Fitzgerald edited by Ruth Prigozy

Flaubert edited by Timothy Unwin

E. M. Forster edited by David Bradshaw

Benjamin Franklin edited by Carla Mulford

Brian Friel edited by Anthony Roche

Robert Frost edited by Robert Faggen

Gabriel García Márquez edited by
Philip Swanson

Elizabeth Gaskell edited by Jill L. Matus

Goethe edited by Lesley Sharpe

Günter Grass edited by Stuart Taberner

Thomas Hardy edited by Dale Kramer

David Hare edited by Richard Boon

Nathaniel Hawthorne edited by
Richard Millington

Seamus Heaney edited by Bernard O'Donoghue

Ernest Hemingway edited by Scott Donaldson

Homer edited by Robert Fowler

Horace edited by Stephen Harrison

Ibsen edited by James McFarlane

Henry James edited by Jonathan Freedman

Samuel Johnson edited by Greg Clingham

Ben Jonson edited by Richard Harp
and Stanley Stewart

James Joyce edited by Derek Attridge
(second edition)

Kafka edited by Julian Preece

Keats edited by Susan J. Wolfson

Lacan edited by Jean-Michel Rabaté

D. H. Lawrence edited by Anne Fernihough

Primo Levi edited by Robert Gordon

Lucretius edited by Stuart Gillespie
and Philip Hardie

Machiavelli edited by John M. Najemy

David Mamet edited by Christopher Bigsby

Thomas Mann edited by Ritchie Robertson

Christopher Marlowe edited by Patrick Cheney

Andrew Marvell edited by Derek Hirst
and Steven N. Zwicker

Herman Melville edited by Robert S. Levine

Arthur Miller edited by Christopher Bigsby
(second edition)

Milton edited by Dennis Danielson
(second edition)

Molière edited by David Bradby and
Andrew Calder

Toni Morrison edited by Justine Tally

Nabokov edited by Julian W. Connolly

Eugene O'Neill edited by Michael Manheim

George Orwell edited by John Rodden

Ovid edited by Philip Hardie

Harold Pinter edited by Peter Raby
(second edition)

Sylvia Plath edited by Jo Gill

Edgar Allan Poe edited by Kevin J. Hayes

Alexander Pope edited by Pat Rogers

Ezra Pound edited by Ira B. Nadel

Proust edited by Richard Bales

Pushkin edited by Andrew Kahn

Rabelais edited by John O'Brien

Rilke edited by Karen Leeder and Robert Vilain

Philip Roth edited by Timothy Parrish

Salman Rushdie edited by Abdulrazak Gurnah

Shakespeare edited by Margareta de Grazia and
Stanley Wells (second edition)

Shakespearean Comedy edited by
Alexander Leggatt

Shakespeare on Film edited by Russell Jackson
(second edition)

Shakespeare's History Plays edited by
Michael Hattaway

Shakespeare's Last Plays edited by Catherine
M. S. Alexander

Shakespeare's Poetry edited by Patrick Cheney

Shakespeare and Popular Culture edited by
Robert Shaughnessy

Shakespeare on Stage edited by Stanley Wells
and Sarah Stanton

Shakespearean Tragedy edited by
Claire McEachern

George Bernard Shaw edited by
Christopher Innes

Shelley edited by Timothy Morton

Mary Shelley edited by Esther Schor

Sam Shepard edited by Matthew
C. Roudané

Spenser edited by Andrew Hadfield

Laurence Sterne edited by Thomas Keymer

Wallace Stevens edited by John N. Serio

Tom Stoppard edited by Katherine E. Kelly

Harriet Beecher Stowe edited by Cindy
Weinstein

August Strindberg edited by Michael Robinson

Jonathan Swift edited by Christopher Fox

J. M. Synge edited by P. J. Mathews

Tacitus edited by A. J. Woodman

Henry David Thoreau edited by Joel Myerson

Tolstoy edited by Donna Tussing Orwin

Anthony Trollope edited by Carolyn Dever
and Lisa Niles

Mark Twain edited by Forrest G. Robinson

Virgil edited by Charles Martindale

Voltaire edited by Nicholas Cronk

Edith Wharton edited by Millicent Bell

Walt Whitman edited by Ezra Greenspan

Oscar Wilde edited by Peter Raby

Tennessee Williams edited by Matthew
C. Roudané

August Wilson edited by Christopher Bigsby

Mary Wollstonecraft edited by Claudia
L. Johnson

Virginia Woolf edited by Susan Sellers
(second edition)

Wordsworth edited by Stephen Gill

W. B. Yeats edited by Marjorie Howes and
John Kelly

Zola edited by Brian Nelson

TOPICS

The Actress edited by Maggie B. Gale
and John Stokes

The African American Novel
edited by Maryemma Graham

The African American Slave Narrative edited by
Audrey A. Fisch

Allegory edited by Rita Copeland
and Peter Struck

American Modernism edited by
Walter Kalaidjian

American Realism and Naturalism
edited by Donald Pizer

American Travel Writing edited by
Alfred Bendixen and Judith Hamera

American Women Playwrights edited by
Brenda Murphy

Ancient Rhetoric edited by Erik Gunderson

Arthurian Legend edited by Elizabeth Archibald and Ad Putter

Australian Literature edited by Elizabeth Webby

British Romantic Poetry edited by James Chandler and Maureen N. McLane

British Romanticism edited by Stuart Curran (second edition)

British Theatre, 1730–1830 edited by Jane Moody and Daniel O'Quinn

Canadian Literature edited by Eva-Marie Kröller

Children's Literature edited by M. O. Grenby and Andrea Immel

The Classic Russian Novel edited by Malcolm V. Jones and Robin Feuer Miller

Contemporary Irish Poetry edited by Matthew Campbell

Crime Fiction edited by Martin Priestman

Early Modern Women's Writing edited by Laura Lunger Knoppers

The Eighteenth-Century Novel edited by John Richetti

Eighteenth-Century Poetry edited by John Sitter

English Literature, 1500–1600 edited by Arthur F. Kinney

English Literature, 1650–1740 edited by Steven N. Zwicker

English Literature, 1740–1830 edited by Thomas Keymer and Jon Mee

English Literature, 1830–1914 edited by Joanne Shattock

English Novelists edited by Adrian Poole

English Poetry, Donne to Marvell edited by Thomas N. Corns

English Poets edited by Claude Rawson

English Renaissance Drama, second edition edited by A. R. Braunmuller and Michael Hattaway

English Renaissance Tragedy edited by Emma Smith and Garrett A. Sullivan Jr.

English Restoration Theatre edited by Deborah C. Payne Fisk

The Epic edited by Catherine Bates

Feminist Literary Theory edited by Ellen Rooney

Fiction in the Romantic Period edited by Richard Maxwell and Katie Trumpener

The Fin de Siècle edited by Gail Marshall

The French Novel: From 1800 to the Present edited by Timothy Unwin

German Romanticism edited by Nicholas Saul

Gothic Fiction edited by Jerrold E. Hogle

The Greek and Roman Novel edited by Tim Whitmarsh

Greek and Roman Theatre edited by Marianne McDonald and J. Michael Walton

Greek Lyric edited by Felix Budelmann

Greek Mythology edited by Roger D. Woodard

Greek Tragedy edited by P. E. Easterling

The Harlem Renaissance edited by George Hutchinson

The Irish Novel edited by John Wilson Foster

The Italian Novel edited by Peter Bondanella and Andrea Ciccarelli

Jewish American Literature edited by Hana Wirth-Nesher and Michael P. Kramer

The Latin American Novel edited by Efraín Kristal

The Literature of Los Angeles edited by Kevin R. McNamara

The Literature of New York edited by Cyrus Patell and Bryan Waterman

The Literature of the First World War edited by Vincent Sherry

The Literature of World War II edited by Marina MacKay

Literature on Screen edited by Deborah Cartmell and Imelda Whelehan

Medieval English Literature edited by Larry Scanlon

Medieval English Theatre edited by Richard Beadle and Alan J. Fletcher (second edition)

Medieval French Literature edited by Simon Gaunt and Sarah Kay

Medieval Romance edited by Roberta L. Krueger

Medieval Women's Writing edited by Carolyn Dinshaw and David Wallace

Modern American Culture edited by Christopher Bigsby

Modern British Women Playwrights edited by Elaine Aston and Janelle Reinelt

Modern French Culture edited by Nicholas Hewitt

Modern German Culture edited by Eva Kolinsky and Wilfried van der Will

The Modern German Novel edited by Graham Bartram

Modern Irish Culture edited by Joe Cleary and Claire Connolly

Modern Italian Culture edited by Zygmunt G. Baranski and Rebecca J. West

Modern Latin American Culture edited by John King

Modern Russian Culture edited by
Nicholas Rzhevsky

Modern Spanish Culture edited by
David T. Gies

Modernism edited by Michael Levenson

The Modernist Novel edited by Morag Shiach

Modernist Poetry edited by Alex Davis
and Lee M. Jenkins

Narrative edited by David Herman

Native American Literature edited by Joy Porter
and Kenneth M. Roemer

*Nineteenth-Century American Women's
Writing* edited by Dale M. Bauer and
Philip Gould

Old English Literature edited by
Malcolm Godden and Michael Lapidge

Performance Studies edited by Tracy C. Davis

Postcolonial Literary Studies edited by
Neil Lazarus

Postmodernism edited by Steven Connor

Renaissance Humanism edited by
Jill Kraye

Roman Satire edited by Kirk Freudenburg

The Roman Historians edited by
Andrew Feldherr

Science Fiction edited by Edward James and
Farah Mendlesohn

The Spanish Novel: From 1600 to the Present
edited by Harriet Turner and Adelaida López de
Martínez

Travel Writing edited by Peter Hulme and
Tim Youngs

Twentieth-Century Irish Drama edited by
Shaun Richards

The Twentieth-Century English Novel edited by
Robert L. Caserio

Twentieth-Century English Poetry edited by
Neil Corcoran

Utopian Literature edited by Gregory Claeys

Victorian and Edwardian Theatre edited by
Kerry Powell

The Victorian Novel edited by Deirdre David

Victorian Poetry edited by Joseph Bristow

War Writing edited by Kate McLoughlin

Writing of the English Revolution edited by
N. H. Keeble